A Tender Lion

A Tender Lion

The Life, Ministry, and Message
of J. C. Ryle

Bennett W. Rogers

Reformation Heritage Books
Grand Rapids, Michigan

A Tender Lion
© 2019 by Bennett W. Rogers

Reformation Heritage Books
2965 Leonard St. NE
Grand Rapids, MI 49525
616-977-0889
orders@heritagebooks.org
www.heritagebooks.org

Printed in the United States of America
19 20 21 22 23 24/10 9 8 7 6 5 4 3 2 1

Library of Congress Cataloging-in-Publication Data

Names: Rogers, Bennett W., author.
Title: A tender lion : the life, ministry, and message of J.C. Ryle / Bennett W. Rogers.
Description: Grand Rapids, Michigan : Reformation Heritage Books, 2019. | Includes bibliographical references and index.
Identifiers: LCCN 2018046077 (print) | LCCN 2018050836 (ebook) | ISBN 9781601786494 (epub) | ISBN 9781601786487 (hardcover : alk. paper)
Subjects: LCSH: Ryle, J. C. (John Charles), 1816-1900. | Church of England—Bishops—Biography. | Bishops—England—Biography.
Classification: LCC BX5199.R9 (ebook) | LCC BX5199.R9 R64 2019 (print) | DDC 283.092 [B] —dc23
LC record available at https://lccn.loc.gov/2018046077

For additional Reformed literature, request a free book list from Reformation Heritage Books at the above regular or e-mail address.

To Christie,
for your patience and encouragement

and to

Henry and Hugh,
for your love and laughter

Contents

Tables

Preface

J. C. Ryle is the most popular and the most neglected evangelical Anglican of the Victorian era. He became the undisputed leader and spokesman of the evangelical party within the Church of England in the last half of the nineteenth century, and his works continue to be read by evangelicals of various denominational stripes more than a century after his death. Despite this popularity, he has been virtually ignored. An illuminating comparison can be made between Ryle and one of his most famous contemporaries, Charles Haddon Spurgeon. In the year that Spurgeon died (1892), at least eighteen biographies were written about him. Fewer than half that many have been written about Ryle in the 118 years since his death in 1900.

M. Guthrie Clark (1947) and G. W. Hart (1963) produced the first biographies of Ryle, but they are brief and based on minimal research. Marcus Loane published a short biography in 1953 and enlarged it in 1967 and again in 1983. Loane's biographies present Ryle as a model Christian and an example of evangelical continuity within the Church of England. While Loane's works utilize more primary- and secondary-source material than the works of either Clark or Hart, they tend to be more hagiographic and devotional than critical or scholarly.

In 1975 Reiner Publications released an autobiographical fragment Ryle composed for his family in 1873 that covered his life from 1816 to 1860. Peter Toon edited the volume, and Michael Smout added a biographical postscript that discussed Ryle's life after

1860.[1] Following its publication, Toon, Smout, and Eric Russell set out to write the definitive critical biography of Ryle but fell short of their goal. Russell was forced to abandon the project because of prior vocational commitments. Soaring production costs restricted the work to fewer than one hundred pages. Moreover, the authors concluded that a definitive life could not be written until more was known about evangelicalism in the Church of England and G. R. Balleine's *History of the Evangelical Party* was replaced. Despite these setbacks, their work remained the fullest treatment of Ryle until Eric Russell's biography replaced it in 2001.

Russell's biography, *J. C. Ryle: That Man of Granite with the Heart of a Child*, is the fullest treatment of Ryle to date. Russell presents Bishop Ryle as an exemplary church leader—one who was able to combine leadership, conviction, and compassion. Russell delves more deeply into Ryle's thought than previous biographers and uncovers new and valuable material (especially in Liverpool), but in the end Russell's work has more in common with the work of Clark, Hart, and Loane than that of Toon and Smout.

Iain H. Murray published a new biography, *J. C. Ryle: Prepared to Stand Alone*, in 2016 to commemorate the two-hundredth anniversary of Ryle's birth. It is the first major biography of Ryle written by a non-Anglican. Though it is less comprehensive than Russell's work, Murray draws new attention to Ryle's love of Puritanism; his relationship with his favorite son, Herbert Edward Ryle; and the abiding emphases of his teaching. Murray presents Ryle as a champion of biblical orthodoxy in an age of doctrinal decline. He was an exemplary evangelical, as opposed to an Anglican, for Murray is clearly unsympathetic to Ryle's churchmanship. This approach may make Ryle more accessible to some non-Anglicans, but it tends to minimize important church-related aspects of his thought and ministry.

---

1. Peter Toon and Michael Smout, *John Charles Ryle: Evangelical Bishop* (Swengal, Pa.: Reiner Publications, 1976), 5.

Several other studies deserve mention. Ian D. Farley's outstanding work *J. C. Ryle, First Bishop of Liverpool: A Study in Mission amongst the Masses* focuses exclusively on Ryle's episcopacy in Liverpool. John Newby systematized Ryle's theology under the traditional theological loci in an unpublished dissertation titled "The Theology of John Charles Ryle." J. I. Packer penned an appreciative and insightful survey of Ryle's life and work in *Faithfulness and Holiness: The Witness of J. C. Ryle.* David Bebbington evaluated Ryle's ministry and outlook in *The Heart of Faith: Following Christ in the Church of England.* Alan Munden contributed a short but remarkably comprehensive account of Ryle's life to the Day One Travel Guide series titled *Travel with Bishop J. C. Ryle: Prince of Tract Writers.* Andrew Atherstone has edited and published a new edition of Ryle's autobiography titled *Bishop J. C. Ryle's Autobiography: The Early Years.* It is based on the original text recently rediscovered in December 2015 among the private family archives of John Charles, prince of Sayn-Wittgestein-Berleburg, grandson of Edward Hewish Ryle and named for his great-great grandfather, Bishop John Charles Ryle. It is now the definitive edition of this critically important primary source, and it includes an expansive appendix containing a number of extremely rare documents that shed light on Ryle's early years. And Lee Gatiss has recently edited and introduced three new volumes on Ryle: *Distinctive Principles for Anglican Evangelicals* (2014), *Christian Leaders of the Seventeenth Century* (2015), and *Stand Firm and Fight On: J. C. Ryle and the Future for Anglican Evangelicals* (2016). Gatiss's introduction to *Christian Leaders* on Ryle as a historian is particularly illuminating and is the first study of its kind.

The purpose of this work is to produce the first intellectual biography of J. C. Ryle. Toon and Smout were unable to produce such a work in 1975, and in many respects, this work seeks to complete what they started. Thankfully, a number of excellent studies have shed new light on Anglican evangelicalism,[2] and Balleine's

---

2. See David Bebbington, *Evangelicalism in Modern Britain: A History from*

work has been replaced by Kenneth Hylson-Smith's *Evangelicals in the Church of England: 1734–1984*. Therefore, an undertaking of this kind is now possible.

The primary question of this work is, Who is J. C. Ryle? The typical answer is epitomized by the nom de plume he used in the correspondence columns of the evangelical press—"an old soldier." Both friend and foe alike regard him as an "icon of unbending traditionalism."[3] I argue that he is far more dynamic and complex, progressive and pragmatic, and creative and innovative than is often realized. Ryle simply defies simple categorization. He could be traditional, moderate, and even radical—and was called such at different times by different groups during his fifty-eight-year ministry. Perhaps the difficulty in understanding the man is attributable to the many and varied roles he played in the Victorian Church. He began his ministerial career as a rural parish priest; he ended it as the bishop of the second city of the British Empire. In the time between, he became a popular preacher, influential author, effective controversialist, recognized party leader, stalwart

---

the 1730s to the 1980s (Grand Rapids: Baker, 1989); Grayson Carter, *Anglican Evangelicals: Protestant Sessions from the Via Media, 1800–1850* (Oxford: Oxford University Press, 2001); Christopher J. Cocksworth, *Evangelical Eucharistic Thought in the Church of England* (Cambridge: Cambridge University Press, 1993); Boyd Hilton, *The Age of Atonement: The Influence of Evangelicalism on Social and Economic Thought* (Oxford: Oxford University Press, 1991); John Kent, *Holding the Fort: Studies in Victorian Revivalism* (London: Epworth Press, 1978); Doreen Roseman, *Evangelicals and Culture*, 2nd ed. (Eugene, Ore.: Pickwick Publications, 1992); Mark Smith and Stephen Taylor, eds., *Evangelicalism in the Church of England c.1790–c.1890: A Miscellany* (Woodbridge, U.K.: Boydell Press, 2004); Peter Toon, *Evangelical Theology 1833–1856: A Response to Tractarianism* (Atlanta: John Knox, 1979); Martin Wellings, *Evangelicals Embattled: Responses of Evangelicals in the Church of England to Ritualism, Darwinism, and Theological Liberalism 1890–1930* (Carlisle, U.K.: Paternoster Press, 2003); and Anne Bentley, "The Transformation of the Evangelical Party in the Church of England in the Latter Nineteenth Century" (PhD diss., University of Durham, 1971).

3. Martin Wellings, introduction to "J. C. Ryle: 'First Words.' An Opening Address Delivered at the First Liverpool Diocesan Conference, 1881," in *Evangelicalism in the Church of England c.1790–c.1890: A Miscellany*, ed. Mark Smith and Stephen Taylor (Woodbridge, U.K.: Boydell Press, 2004), 286.

Church defender, and radical Church reformer. Much of the work that has been done on Ryle has focused on certain aspects of his ministry or has treated the whole more generally. As a result, some aspects of Ryle's life and work have never been discussed in detail, and others have never been discussed at all. The aim of this work is to present J. C. Ryle's thought, life, and ministry in its fullness and in context. In so doing, I hope to provide a more thorough answer to the central question of this work than has hitherto been given and shed further light on Victorian evangelicalism in general and evangelicalism within the Church of England in particular.

This volume is organized chronologically and topically. Each chapter focuses on a particular period of Ryle's life and analyzes an aspect of his thought and work, building on the previous chapter thematically. For example, Ryle's preaching in Helmingham, which is the subject of chapter 2, created a market for his pastoral writings, which is the subject of chapter 3. The work concludes with a summary of Ryle's thought and life.

Acknowledgments

I would like to thank *some* of the people who helped turn this dream into a reality. I would like to thank Dr. David Puckett, my doctoral supervisor, for pointing me in Ryle's direction and for his advice and encouragement along the way. Dr. Michael Haykin's interest and example has spurred me on as well.

I owe a debt of gratitude to an army of librarians in Liverpool, Oxford, Cambridge, Bristol, Glasgow, and London for granting me access to sources that are not available in the United States, and to Southern Seminary for generously giving me a field-study grant that allowed me to visit them. Ben Ruppert and his predecessors at the Southern Seminary Interlibrary Loan Office have been a tremendous help in tracking down obscure Victorian sources. I would like to thank Dr. Miles Van Pelt and Reverend John McCarty for giving me a research room in the RTS Jackson Library and allowing me to camp out there for the last three years. I would also like to thank Jay Collier and Annette Gysen at Reformation Heritage Books for believing in this project and helping me see it to completion.

I have been blessed by the love and support I have received from my family and good friends. The Davises of Vicksburg, Mississippi, have been a great source of encouragement. The Shearers of Anchorage, Kentucky, were our home away from home. Ben Bailie has been a sounding board, wise counselor, and sympathetic listener since my first day on campus. And Joe Hillrich, Tim Walker, and Nathan Cummins have walked with me through the highs and lows of this project—and life, more generally—over the last eight years. Their support has been incalculable.

No words can adequately express my appreciation to my wife, Christie, and my boys, Henry and Hugh. Your sacrifice, encouragement, and faith in me have made this dream a reality.

Christian and Clergyman

John Charles Ryle was born on May 10, 1816, at Park House, Macclesfield. He was the fourth of six children and the eldest son. The Macclesfield of Ryle's birth was a growing factory village with a population of 17,746, according to the census of 1821.[1] It was situated on a main route from London to the northwest and was linked to the major industrial centers of Manchester and Liverpool by canals. It was home to a copper works and a number of cotton mills, but the silk industry dominated all others. The silk trade prospered during the closing decades of the eighteenth century, and that prosperity was accelerated by the Napoleonic Wars, which made French silks scarce. During these years many industrialists made a fortune in silk. John Ryle (1744–1808), Ryle's grandfather, was one of them.

Shortly before Ryle's birth, the religious character of Macclesfield was strongly Protestant, Anglican, and evangelical. Lollardy took root in Macclesfield during the fifteenth century, its forest providing a safe haven for worshipers. There is no available evidence about the town's response to the Reformation, but based on subsequent history, it was probably well received. Puritanism

---

1. For the history of Macclesfield, see C. Stella Davies, *A History of Macclesfield* (Manchester: Manchester University Press, 1961); J. P. Earwaker, *East Cheshire Past and Present: A History of the Hundred of Macclesfield, in the County of Palatine of Chester*, 2 vols. (London: J. P. Earwaker, 1877, 1880); George Ormerod, *The History of the County of Palatine and the City of Chester*, 3 vols. (London: George Routledge and Sons, 1882).

flourished in Cheshire in general and Macclesfield in particular. As early as the late sixteenth century, Puritan services, the Geneva gown, and popular religious lectures could be found in the Macclesfield church. Roman Catholicism, on the other hand, almost vanished altogether after the Reformation; it survived only in the households of a few wealthy Roman Catholic families. Given the town's Puritan sympathies, it is not surprising that it supported the Parliamentarians during the Civil War, nor is it surprising that ten ministers within the deanery of Macclesfield lost their livings as a result of the Great Ejection.

The reception of the evangelical revival in Macclesfield deserves special attention. Evangelical preaching and doctrines were first brought to the town by the itinerant John Bennet of Chinley in the early 1740s. John Wesley came in 1745 and then again in 1759. From that time on he visited regularly. One of the more remarkable features of Wesley's ministry in Macclesfield was his unusually strong relationship with the established church in the community. The vicar of St. Michael's, James Roe (1711–1765), became an evangelical late in life. David Simpson (1745–1799), the vicar of Christ Church, was an ardent and enthusiastic evangelical. He was an active pastor, prolific author, a local itinerant, and intimate friend of John Wesley. For a season, all the parish churches in Macclesfield were in evangelical hands, and local Methodists were all communicants in the Church of England.

Family

By all accounts John Ryle was a remarkable man. He became a successful silk manufacturer, prosperous landowner, and respected banker. When he died in 1808, he left his son, J. C. Ryle's father, somewhere between 250,000 and 500,000 pounds. John's success also extended to the political sphere. He was elected alderman and then mayor of Macclesfield. He was also a committed evangelical Christian, Methodist, and philanthropist. His mother had been converted after hearing John Wesley preach in 1745, and through her influence he became a Christian. Wesley and Ryle became intimate friends, and Wesley often stayed at Ryle's home when he visited Macclesfield, which he did regularly from 1759 until his death in 1791.[2] Ryle provided the site for the construction of a Methodist meetinghouse in 1764 and the land and the funds for another in 1779. J. C. Ryle never knew his grandfather or his grandmother; both died before he was born. He spoke of them and their evangelical faith with great admiration in his autobiography, however.[3]

The parents of J. C. Ryle, John Ryle (1783–1862) and Susanna Hurt, form an interesting contrast with his grandparents. Both Ryle's grandfather and father were professional successes. Ryle's father continued to run the lucrative family silk business. He purchased more land and properties and expanded the family's holdings. He also took over a failing bank in 1800 and made it profitable for decades. Both Ryle's grandfather and father were interested in politics and public service. Ryle's father was elected mayor of Macclesfield in 1809 and 1810. He became the first MP for Macclesfield elected under the reformed Parliament in 1832, and he held that seat until 1837.[4] He later became the high sheriff of Cheshire. Before his bank crashed in 1841, he was so excessively popular that he was practically the "king of the place."[5] Ryle's mother, Susanna, also came from a wealthy, land-owning family. She was related to Sir Richard Arkwright, the inventor of the

---

2. John Wesley often mentioned these visits in his journals. See *The Journal of the Rev. John Wesley, A.M. Sometime Fellow of Lincoln College, Oxford,* ed. Nehemiah Curnock, 8 vols. (London: Charles H. Kelly, 1909–1916), 4:310; 6:14, 100, 226, 411; 7:300. For more information about Methodism in Macclesfield, see Benjamin Smith, *Methodism in Macclesfield* (London: Wesley Conference Office, 1875); and R. B. Walker, "Religious Changes in Cheshire, 1750-1850," *Journal of Ecclesiastical History* 17 (1966): 77–94.

3. See J. C. Ryle, *Bishop J. C. Ryle's Autobiography: The Early Years,* ed. Andrew Atherstone (Edinburgh: Banner of Truth, 2016), 6.

4. Ryle, *Autobiography*, 5.

5. Ryle, *Autobiography*, 5.

spinning jenny. But neither John nor Susanna showed much interest in spiritual matters.

Ryle recorded in his autobiography that his home was destitute
of real spiritual religion. Family prayers were almost never said.
His father's spiritual instruction consisted of showing the children
pictures in an old Bible on sleepless Sunday nights. His mother's
spiritual instruction consisted of nothing more than occasionally
listening to the children recite the Church catechism in "a very grave
and rather gloomy manner."[6] Sometimes the elderly members of
the family read sermons silently on winter Sunday nights, but they
looked so "unutterably grave and miserable" that Ryle concluded
sermons must be dull and religion must be disagreeable.[7] His first
governess was a Socinian, and none of her successors had "any real
spirituality about them."[8] The Christian Sabbath was not kept, they
had no religious friends or family members, and no Christians ever
visited them or brought them any religious books or tracts.[9]

The family regularly attended Christ Church, which was one of
only two parish churches in Macclesfield. For a brief period, both
churches had evangelical incumbents, which was unusual for the
time.[10] They were not, however, succeeded by evangelical clergymen. Ryle described the incumbents of St. Michael's and Christ
Church of his childhood as "wretched high and dry sticks of the
old school" and remarked, "I can truly say that I passed through
childhood and boyhood without hearing a single sermon likely

---

6. Ryle, *Autobiography*, 62–66.

7. Ryle, *Autobiography*, 62.

8. Ryle, *Autobiography*, 64.

9. Ryle said that the only two books that affected him as a child were Bunyan's
Pilgrim's Progress and Mrs. Sherwood's *Conversations on the Church Catechism*.

10. Charles Row, the incumbent of St. Michael's, had an evangelical conversion
late in life. David Simpson, the minister of Christ Church from 1779 to 1799, was
an outspoken evangelical, popular preacher, and energetic pastor. He regularly
allowed John Wesley to preach in his pulpit. See Mark Smith, "David Simpson," in
Oxford Dictionary of National Biography, ed. H. C. G. Matthew and Brian Harrison
(Oxford: Oxford University Press, 2004), 683–84.

to do good to my soul."[11] He was brought up to regard evangelical clergymen as "well-meaning, extravagant, fanatical enthusiasts, who carried things a great deal too far in religion."[12]

Ryle summed up the spiritual condition of his family and childhood as follows:

> The plain truth is that neither in my own family nor among the Hurts or Arkwrights with whom I was most mixed up when young can I remember that there was a whit of what may be called a real spiritual religion. There was literally nothing to make us young people thorough Christians. We never heard the gospel preached on Sunday and vital Christianity was never brought before us by anybody from the beginning of the year to the end or on a weekday.[13]

Education

Ryle was a precocious child and an eager learner. Isaac Eaton, the clerk of St. Michael's, taught him to read, write, and cipher at an early age. Miss Holland, his sister's Unitarian governess, instructed him in the rudiments of Latin as well. By the age of four he had become a proficient reader and was extremely fond of books, especially books about travel, natural history, military battles, and shipwrecks.[14]

In 1824, at the age of eight, Ryle was sent to a preparatory school run by John Jackson, vicar of Over. This was not a happy time in his life. The accommodations were rough and uncomfortable. He was one of seventeen pupils who were lodged in two rooms and shared one washroom. He later remarked, "Of course at

---

11. Ryle, *Autobiography*, 63.

12. Ryle, *Autobiography*, 64.

13. Ryle, *Autobiography*, 64.

14. Ryle, *Autobiography*, 20. Military battles and seafaring remained a lifelong fascination for Ryle. He regularly used military and maritime illustrations in his sermons.

this rate we could not be very clean."[15] There was also a great deal of "petty bullying and tyranny." For example, with the master's permission, he was tossed in a blanket by the older boys for not rising with the rest of the students. He was thrown to the ceiling and then fell to the floor when a student let go of one corner of the blanket. He suffered a concussion and was sick for some time, but the incident was hushed up and his family was never told.[16] Furthermore, the pupils were often left unsupervised for long periods of time while Rev. Jackson attended to the needs of his parish.

In terms of academics, things were more tolerable. The students were well grounded in Latin and Greek. They were also taught writing, arithmetic, history, geography, French, and dancing. The two most popular sports were cricket and stone throwing, and Ryle excelled at both. Religious instruction was nonexistent, and as a result, the moral condition of the school was deplorable. He later recalled, "As to the religion at the private school there was literally none at all, and I really think we were nothing better than little devils. I can find no other words to express my recollection of our utter ungodliness and boyish immorality."[17]

Ryle's three and a half years at Jackson's preparatory school gave him a good grounding in Latin and Greek; produced a sturdy, independent, and combative young man;[18] and laid a good foundation for future academic success at Eton and beyond. From a moral and spiritual standpoint, however, his education was a complete failure. He recollected, "I am quite certain that I learned more moral evil in a private school then I ever did in my whole life afterwards and most decidedly got no moral good."[19]

---

15. Ryle, *Autobiography*, 23–24.

16. Ryle, *Autobiography*, 24.

17. Ryle, *Autobiography*, 66.

18. Ryle, *Autobiography*, 25: "I don't think I was an ill-natured, bad-tempered boy, but I was sturdy, very independent and combative. I had a very strong opinion of my own, and never cared a bit for being a minority, and was ready to fight anybody however big if necessary."

19. Ryle, *Autobiography*, 26.

The King's College of Our Lady of Eton beside Windsor was founded by Henry IV in 1440 to combat heresy and provide a clerical education for the middle class.[20] When Ryle entered in January 1828, it was doing neither. His classmates were hardly middle class. Most of them were the sons of noblemen, aristocrats, or the rich and well connected. Religion had no place in the curriculum. The headmaster of the school was the infamous Dr. John Keate, who stands out in the public mind as the supreme symbolic figure of the old unreformed Eton.[21] Keate was an excellent classical scholar, a poet, and an accomplished teacher, but he is probably best remembered for his savage floggings. The curriculum under Keate was exclusively, narrowly, and monotonously classical. Homer, Virgil, and Horace were read in extenso. Under Keate, a student could expect to read through the *Iliad* and *Aeneid* twice during his tenure at Eton. Translations from books of extracts, such as *Scriptores Graeci*, *Scriptores Latini*, and *Scriptores Romani* rounded out the curriculum. Mathematics was optional. History, English literature, and geography were studied only insofar as they had a bearing on the classics. The only natural science that was offered consisted of occasional guest lectures. Religious instruction was nonexistent and even discouraged until the Duke of Newcastle established a scholarship to encourage the study of divinity in 1829.[22]

---

20. For two of the best histories of Eton, see H. C. Maxwell Lyte, *A History of Eton College 1440–1875* (London: Macmillan, 1877); and Christopher Hollis, *Eton: A History* (London: Hollis and Carter, 1960). See also William Lucas Collins, *Etoniana, Ancient and Modern* (London: William Blackwood and Sons, 1865); Lionel Cust, *A History of Eton College* (New York: Charles Scribner's Sons, 1899); Wasey Sterry, *Annals of the King's College of Our Lady of Eton beside Windsor* (London: Methuen, 1898); and Francis St. John Thackeray, *Memoir of Edward Craven Hawtrey D.D., Headmaster and Afterward Provost of Eton* (London: George Bell and Sons, 1896).

21. Hollis, *Eton: A History*, 191.

22. Keate's antagonism to religious instruction has been well documented. John Bird Sumner, the archbishop of Canterbury, was forbidden "from saying a single word about God to his pupils" while serving as an assistant master at Eton from 1802 to 1817. Every Sunday afternoon between two and three all the boys

Upon entering Eton, students were divided into groups, or houses. Ryle was assigned to Hawtrey's House, which was named for the assistant master Edward Craven Hawtrey.[23] This assignment was extremely fortunate for the young student. By all accounts, Hawtrey's House was the best in Eton in every respect. It was comfortable, the boys were well cared for, and there was no positive cruelty. Moreover, Hawtrey was an attentive and encouraging tutor, which was unusual for Eton at the time. Though Eton had not yet adopted the private system pioneered by Thomas Arnold at Rugby, Ryle received something akin to it from him. Under Hawtrey's tutelage, Ryle studied French, history, and English literature, in addition to Keate's narrow selection of Greek and Latin authors. Hawtry also personally helped him prepare for Oxford. Under Hawtry's guidance, Ryle read nearly every book in which he was later examined for first-class honors at Oxford. Although Ryle had almost nothing positive to say about Keate, he remained grateful to his tutor for the rest of his life. In 1890, Bishop Ryle said, "I am certain that if it had not been for Hawtrey, I should never have been a First-class man side by side with Dean Stanley in classics, or Craven University Scholar."[24]

---

of the upper school were required to hear "prayers" read by the headmaster. The "prayers" turned out to be discourses on abstract morality from *Blair's Sermons*, the *Spectator*, or a pagan moral philosopher like Epictetus. Eton historian Henry Maxwell Lyte said, "It seems incredible that there should ever have been an entire absence of religious teaching at the greatest school in Christian England; yet such, from all accounts, must have been the case at Eton until about sixty years ago." See Lyte, *History of Eton College*, 361.

Ryle later returned to Eton to rectify this deficiency personally. He was invited to preach at chapel in 1871, and though the sermon has not survived, according to his friend Rev. C. W. Furse he proclaimed the uselessness of "high morality" and "gentlemanly conduct" apart from the saving grace of God. See the *Authorized Report of the Church Congress Held at Nottingham* (London: W. Wells Gardner, 1871), 414–15.

23. Edward Craven Hawtrey was assistant master from 1814 to 1834, headmaster from 1834 to 1853, and provost from 1853 to 1862. See Thackeray, *Memoir of Edward Craven Hawtrey.*

24. Thackeray, *Memoir of Edward Craven Hawtrey*, 51.

Ryle described his first year and a half at Eton as "thoroughly miserable." He did not know any of the six hundred boys at the school. He was awkward, shy, younger than many first-year students, and felt out of place in the South. Shortly thereafter, he began to flourish. He made steady academic progress during his six and a half years at Eton. He rose to the top of his class by the time he reached the fifth form. He placed fourth in the Newcastle Scholarship, to the surprise of many. He joined the debating society and took a prominent part in its proceedings as well. By his sixth year, he was regarded as one of the most prominent boys in the school. He believed he could have achieved even more academically if his tutor was ill less frequently.

Ryle's academic success was equaled by his athletic prowess. He was blessed with a tall, robust, and athletic frame, which earned him the nickname Magnus.[25] He took fencing lessons, enjoyed rowing, and excelled in hockey, but cricket was his great love.[26] He was a member of Eton's cricket club. The top eleven cricketers—known as the XI—were chosen to represent Eton in matches against Harrow and Winchester. He earned a place on the team and went on to become its captain. He later said that his time as captain of the XI helped prepare him for leadership in the Church.[27]

---

25. Ryle's size and stature were impressive even later in life. For example, at the Swansea Church Congress (1876), one of the speakers said the following of the sixty-three-year-old Ryle: "Canon Ryle dropped a hint that he was ready to turn up his sleeves, and double his fists, and square his shoulders, against any one who should say a word in favour of confession. It seemed that at this point he drew the line. Certainly I should not like to accept battle with him for I am afraid, judging from the Canon's build, I should get, in plain English, an awful drubbing." *The Official Report of the Nineteenth Annual Church Congress Held at Swansea* (London: John Hodges, 1879), 397.

26. "Nothing did I enjoy so much as cricket when I was in the XI and as long as I live I think I shall say, that the happiest days I ever spent in a simple, earthly way were the days when I was captain of the XI in Eton playing-fields." Ryle, *Autobiography*, 36.

27. Ryle, *Autobiography*, 36–38.

Ryle's years at Eton also proved to be a time of limited spiritual awakening. Though Headmaster Keate discouraged religious instruction and gave it no place in the school's official curriculum, the founding of the Newcastle Scholarship in 1829 encouraged the study of divinity. Those competing for the prize—fifty pounds a year for three years—had to demonstrate proficiency in Greek and Latin and submit three papers: one on the Gospels, one on Acts, and one on general divinity and church history. Preparing for the Newcastle examination exposed Ryle to dogmatic Christianity for the first time, and he traced the beginning of his first clear doctrinal views back to his preparation for this exam. He later wrote, "It is a simple fact, that the beginning of any clear doctrinal views I have ever attained myself, was reading up the Articles at Eton, for the Newcastle Scholarship."[28]

Ryle completed his education in 1834 and left with unfeigned regret. His last two years at Eton were some of the happiest of his life, but he felt compelled to leave. He was ready to compete for first-class honors in the classics at either Oxford or Cambridge. He decided on Christ Church, Oxford, and entered in October 1834.

Christ Church was founded as Cardinal College by Cardinal Wolsey in 1525 for the education of the youth in virtue and the maintenance of the Christian church and faith.[29] It received a new name, Christ Church, and a new royal foundation from King Henry VIII in 1546. Under the leadership of Cyril Jackson (dean from 1783 to 1809), Christ Church became preeminent among the colleges of Oxford. Jackson's success, however, was not maintained by

---

28. J. C. Ryle, *Who Is the True Churchman? or, The Thirty-Nine Articles Examined* (London: William Hunt, 1872), 38.

29. For the history of Christ Church, see Judith Curthoys, *The Cardinal's College: Christ Church, Chapter and Verse* (London: Profile Books, 2012). See also W. G. Hiscock, *A Christ Church Miscellany* (Oxford: Oxford University Press, 1946); and Henry L. Thompson, *Christ Church* (London: F. E. Robinson, 1900). For a superb study of nineteenth-century Oxford, see M. G. Brock and M. C. Curthoys, eds., *Nineteenth-Century Oxford, Part 1*, vol. 6 of *The History of the University of Oxford* (Oxford: Oxford University Press, 2007).

his successors. When Ryle entered Christ Church in October 1834, Thomas Gaisford was dean. Though his scholarship was legendary, he opposed all reform, and as a result Christ Church suffered.

Ryle's tutors at Christ Church were Augustus Short and Henry Liddell. Ryle had nothing positive to say about Short. "Short as a tutor was perfectly useless," he complained, "and I never learned anything from him."[30] Liddell, on the other hand, was "a very good tutor and I heartily wished I had been under him during the whole time I was at Oxford." He later remarked that "if I had only had such a wise and kind tutor as Liddell was all the time I was there, I believe I might have carried off three times as many honors as I did."[31]

As it was, Ryle managed to carry off a number of honors during his three years at Oxford. He won a Fell Exhibition at the end of his first year. He won the Craven University Scholarship at the end of his second year. At the end of his third and final year he won a "very brilliant" first class in *Literae Humaniores*, an achievement that remained a source of pride for the rest of his life.[32] Following his spectacular first, he was urged to come forward as a candidate for a fellowship at Christ Church, Brasenose, or Balliol, but declined all such offers, believing his future was in politics, not academia.

In addition to academic success, Ryle continued to excel in cricket. He made the University XI all three years he was at Oxford and was the captain of the team during his second and third years.

---

30. Ryle, *Autobiography*, 51.

31. Ryle, *Autobiography*, 51–52, 59. For a life of Liddell, see Henry L. Thompson, *Henry George Liddell: A Memoir* (New York: Henry Holt, 1899). Ryle is specifically mentioned on p. 27 as one of Liddell's first thirteen pupils. Liddell described this first group of students as "a very good set who will keep all my wits at work." His relationship with his students was also described as "more directly pastoral." See Thompson, *Henry George Liddell*, 28–29.

32. There were eleven first-class honors awards in 1837, but the examinations of Ryle, Arthur Stanley, and Henry Heighton so far exceeded the rest that making a small class of these men was discussed.

He also helped revive the old Oxford versus Cambridge matches by contacting his former Etonian classmates at Cambridge.[33]

Despite his success, Ryle was not happy during his time at Oxford. He disliked the tone of society among the undergraduates. The "miserable idolatry" of money and aristocratic connection disgusted him so completely that he contemplated becoming a republican. His classmates were distant and cold, and he missed the camaraderie he had experienced at Eton. And the tutors, with the exception of Liddell, gave him no help, counsel, or advice and seemed generally disinterested. As a result, he developed a "rather soured misanthropical view of human nature" and concluded that the whole system needed reform. Though Ryle's academic and athletic careers at Christ Church were, by all accounts, outstanding, he said, "I left Oxford with a brilliant reputation for the honors which I had taken but with very little love for the university and very glad to get away from it."[34]

Before moving forward, something should be said about Ryle's spiritual and theological development during this period of his life. Ryle entered Oxford as the first of the *Tracts for the Times* were being published by the leaders of the Oxford movement. In fact, E. B. Pusey, one of the movement's principal leaders, was the Regius Professor of Hebrew at Christ Church. Ryle appears to have been completely indifferent to Tractarianism at the time.[35] Nor was he drawn to evangelicalism. Ryle noted that there were a good number of evangelical men at Oxford at the time, but their preaching

---

33. Toon and Smout, *John Charles Ryle*, 30n3.

34. Ryle, *Autobiography*, 54.

35. Tractarianism had little influence in Christ Church. J. H. Newman complained to H. W. Wilberforce that "Christ Church alone is immobile." Oriel, Trinity, and Exeter were the Tractarian strongholds. See Peter B. Nockles, "Lost Causes and…Impossible Loyalties: The Oxford Movement and the University," in *Nineteenth-Century Oxford, Part 1*, vol. 6 of *The History of the University of Oxford*, ed. M. G. Brock and M. C. Curthoys (Oxford: Oxford University Press, 2007), 232.

was "very defective."[36] He did, however, speak positively of the preaching of Edward Denison and Walter Hamilton at St. Peter's in the East, who were sympathetic to evangelicalism at this point in their ministries.[37] Ryle also wrestled with skepticism for a time—which he omitted in his autobiography.[38] He was delivered from it by reading George Stanley Faber's *The Difficulties of Infidelity*.[39] For the most part, Ryle was generally indifferent to religion during his time at Oxford until midsummer 1837.

Despite his personal indifference, Ryle was compelled to study divinity as part of the requirements for his degree. The new examination statute of 1800, which introduced the concept of honors degrees, required that every candidate demonstrate a knowledge of the Gospels in Greek, the Thirty-Nine Articles, and Bishop Butler's *Analogy* (William Paley's *Natural Theology* could be substituted). Ryle's account of the viva voce portion of his examination sheds further light on his reading. In addition to the Articles, Bible, and Butler/Paley, Ryle was examined on the prayer book, church history and tradition, the fathers, the creeds, Augustine, and Pelagius.[40]

---

36. Ryle's comment about the noticeable presence of evangelical men seems to confirm J. S. Reynolds's contention that evangelicals were well represented at Oxford at this time, and their strength should not be gauged exclusively by their response to the *Tracts*. He wrote, "Thus the evangelicals at Oxford were not content with defending their theological views. They were still busy extending their spiritual work. During a critical period they can be said to have neglected neither doctrine nor practice." J. S. Reynolds, *The Evangelicals at Oxford 1735–1871: A Record of an Unchronicled Movement with the Record Extended to 1905* (Oxford: Marcham Manor Press, 1975), 115.

37. Hamilton later became an Anglo-Catholic.

38. Years later he recalled, "I can remember the days when I tried hard to be an unbeliever, because religion crossed my path, and I did not like its holy requirements. I was delivered from that pit, I believe, by the grace of God leading me to...Faber's *Difficulties of Infidelity*. I read that book, and felt that it could not be answered." J. C. Ryle, *Unbelief a Marvel* (London: William Hunt, 1880), 17.

39. George Stanley Faber, *The Difficulties of Infidelity* (Philadelphia: Thomas Kite, 1829).

40. Ryle, *Autobiography*, 55–57. For more information, see James Pycroft, *The Student's Guide to a Course of Reading Necessary for Obtaining University Honours by*

Through his pursuit of first-class honors at Oxford, Ryle unintentionally, and perhaps to some degree unwillingly, received a substantial theological education.

Conversion

In autumn 1837, before he took his degree, Ryle underwent an evangelical conversion. He described it as a gradual process as opposed to a sudden change. This process began with the Newcastle Scholarship, preparing for an honors degree at Oxford, and the preaching of Denison and Hamilton. In his autobiography Ryle mentions a number of significant events that he believed the Holy Spirit used in a special way to convert him.

The first was a rebuke from a friend. While out hunting with a group of friends about a year after leaving Eton, Ryle swore in the presence of Algernon Coote, who proceeded to rebuke him sharply. The rebuke pricked his conscience and made a deep and lasting impression on him. It made him consider the sinfulness of sin for the first time, and it was the first time someone ever told him to think, repent, and pray. He later said that this rebuke "was one of the first things that I can remember that made a kind of religious impression upon my soul."[41]

The second was the evangelical ministry of a newly opened church in Macclesfield—St. George's in Sutton. St. George's was originally opened as a Congregational chapel in 1824, but it was reopened for Church of England services in 1828 after a dispute divided the congregation. The bishop of Chester was asked to bring St. George's under episcopal authority. It was officially consecrated

---

a Graduate of Oxford (Oxford: Henry Slatter, 1837). This is practically a CliffsNotes to honors degrees, but even this condensed reading list shows how much divinity Ryle would have been responsible for. This anonymous graduate encourages students to make an outline of Jewish history from the Old Testament; memorize the Thirty-Nine Articles; familiarize themselves with the major arguments of Butler, Paley, and Sumner; and read the Bible thoroughly.

41. Ryle, *Autobiography*, 68.

in 1834, and the land for the church and the churchyard was donated by Ryle's father. The newly appointed bishop of Chester, the evangelical John Bird Sumner, appointed an evangelical clergyman, William Wales, to be its first minister.[42] He was succeeded by another evangelical in 1834, John Burnet. According to Ryle, the "gospel was really preached" by these men, and they introduced "a new kind of religion" into the Church of England in that part of Cheshire.[43] He attended St. George's with his family while home on holiday, and its evangelical ministry began to "set him thinking about religion."

The third was the conversion of Harry Arkwright, Ryle's first cousin. He was converted while preparing for ordination with Rev. Burnet of St. George's. Ryle was struck by the "great change" that took place in Harry's character and opinions. Shortly thereafter, Ryle's sister Susan "took up Mr. Burnet's opinions" and was converted as well. As a result, evangelical religion became the subject of many family conversations, and he began to think more deeply about it.

The fourth was a severe illness that struck in midsummer 1837 as he was preparing for his exams. He was confined to his bed for days and was brought "very low for some time." During this "very curious crisis," he began to read the Bible and pray for the first time. He later credited these new habits with helping him go through his exams "very coolly and quietly."[44]

The fifth and final event was hearing a lesson read from Ephesians 2 one Sunday morning.[45] Around the time of his examinations, Ryle attended Carfax Church, formally known as St. Martin's, feeling somewhat depressed and discouraged. The reader

---

42. For a solid biography of John Bird Sumner, see Nigel Scotland, *John Bird Sumner: Evangelical Archbishop* (Leominster, U.K.: Gracewing Books, 1995).

43. Ryle, *Autobiography*, 68.

44. Ryle, *Autobiography*, 68–70.

45. For a more detailed analysis of the dating and the circumstances of Ryle's conversion, see Appendix 4: "Canon Christopher on Ryle's Conversion," in Ryle, *Autobiography*, 199–213.

of the lesson made some lengthy pauses when he came to verse 8: "By grace—are ye saved—through faith—and that, not of yourselves—it is the gift of God." This unusual and emphatic reading of Ephesians 2:8 made a tremendous impact on him and led to his own evangelical conversion.[46] By year's end, J. C. Ryle was "fairly launched as a Christian."

The beginning of Ryle's Christian pilgrimage was not easy. He had no spiritual mentors or guides. He was left to "fight out everything" for himself and, as a result, "made sad blunders."[47] Through this process of trial and error, he finally found the guidance he so desperately wanted in books. Those that helped him most were William Wilberforce's *Practical View of Christianity*, John Angell James's *Christian Professor*, Thomas Scott's *Remarks on the Refutation of Calvinism by George Tomline*, John Newton's *Cardiphonia*, Joseph and Isaac Milner's *History of the Christian Church*, and Edward Bickersteth's *The Christian Student*.[48]

Moreover, his new evangelical convictions were challenged almost as soon as they were embraced. The opponents of evangelicalism within his family, and his cousin Canon John Ryle Wood in particular,[49] were horrified by his evangelical conversion, and they tried to convince him to abandon his new religious principles.

---

46. Ryle had Ephesians 2:8 engraved on his gravestone.

47. Ryle, *Autobiography*, 70.

48. William Wilberforce, *A Practical View of the Prevailing Religious System of Professed Christians, in the High and Middle Classes in this Country, Contrasted with Real Christianity*, 17th ed. (London: T. Cadell, 1829); John Angell James, *The Christian Professor* (London: Hamilton, Adams, and Company, 1837); Thomas Scott, *Remarks on the Refutation of Calvinism by George Tomline, D.D., F.R.S., Lord Bishop of Lincoln, and Dean of St. Paul's, London*, 2nd ed. (London: A. Macintosh, 1817); John Newton, *Cardiphonia: or, The Utterance of the Heart: In the Course of Real Correspondence* (Edinburgh: Waugh and Innes, 1824); Joseph Milner and Isaac Milner, *The History of the Church of Christ* (London: R. B. Seeley and W. Burnside, 1836); and Edward Bickersteth, *The Christian Student* (London: R. B. Seeley and W. Burnside, 1829).

49. Rev. John Ryle Wood was canon of Worcester from 1841 to 1886. He also served as tutor to Prince George.

Contending for his newly found evangelical faith only rooted him more deeply in it and attached him more firmly to it. He explained, "The whole result was that the more they argued, the more I was convinced that they were wrong and I was right, and the more I clung to my new principles. Nothing I believe roots principles so firmly in people's minds as having to fight for them and defend them…. What is won dearly is prized highly and clung to firmly."[50]

His refusal to abandon his evangelical faith came with heavy personal costs. It caused "great uncomfortableness" in his family. He was estranged from friends and relatives, and this "miserable state of things" continued for a period of about three and a half years. Though he lost many friends at this time as a result of his conversion, he made some new ones in evangelical circles, which he described as a "kind of immediate free-masonry."[51] Among them were John Thornycroft and his two sisters, Harry Arkwright, Mr. Massey, the two Misses Leycesters of Toft, Admiral Harecourt and his wife, Admiral Sir Harry Hope, and Mrs. Georgina Tollechmache. Ryle said these friends "strengthened me in my principles, encouraged me in my practice, solved many of my difficulties, assisted me by their advice, counseled me in many of my perplexities, and cheered me generally by showing me that I was not quite alone in the world."[52]

Religious Opinions

By winter 1837, Ryle had developed "strongly marked, developed, and decided" religious opinions. He said his new views "seemed to flash out before my mind, as clearly and sharply as the pictures on a photographic plate when the developing liquid is poured over it."[53] He summarized them as follows:

---

50. Ryle, *Autobiography*, 71–72.
51. Ryle, *Autobiography*, 74.
52. Ryle, *Autobiography*, 75.
53. Ryle, *Autobiography*, 72.

The extreme sinfulness of sin, and my own personal sinfulness, helplessness, and spiritual need: the entire suitableness
of the Lord Jesus Christ by His sacrifice, substitution, and
intercession to be the Saviour of a sinner's soul; the absolute
necessity of anybody who would be saved being born again
or converted by the Holy Ghost; the indispensable necessity
of holiness of life, being the only evidence of a true Christian;
the absolute of coming out from the world and being separate
from its vain customs, recreations, and standards of what is
right, as well as its sins; the supremacy of the Bible as the only
rule of what is true in faith, or right in practice, and the need
of regular study and reading it; the absolute necessity of daily
private prayer and communion with God if anyone intends
to live the life of a true Christian; the enormous values of
what are called Protestant principles as compared to Romanism; the unspeakable excellence and beauty of the doctrine of
the Second Advent of our Lord and Saviour Jesus Christ; the
unutterable folly of supposing that baptism is regeneration or
formal going to church Christianity or taking the sacrament
a means of wiping away sins, or clergymen to know more of
the Bible than other people or to be mediators between God
and men by virtue of their office.[54]

Though this quotation provides a good summary of J. C. Ryle's
theology, some clarification is desirable. Ryle's theology is best
described as Protestant, Reformed, Puritan, evangelical, Anglican,
and premillennial.

It is difficult to overstate the importance of the Protestant Reformation for Ryle. According to him, it saved English Christianity,
gave birth to the Reformed Church of England, and was the source
of all of England's spiritual and material prosperity under God.
His view of the English Reformation will be discussed at greater
length in chapter 4. In terms of his religious opinions, however,
there are three doctrines that he particularly associated with the

---

54. Ryle, *Autobiography*, 72–73.

Reformation. The first is the sufficiency and supremacy of the Holy Scriptures, which make it the only rule of faith and practice. The second is the right, duty, and necessity of private judgment. The third is justification by faith alone. These three doctrines were the "principles which won the battle of the Protestant Reformation" and the "keys of the whole controversy between the Reformers and the Church of Rome."[55]

In terms of soteriology, Ryle is best described as a moderate, or evangelical, Calvinist. He wrote, "In a word, I believe that Calvinistic divinity is the divinity of the Bible, of Augustine, and of the Thirty-nine Articles of my own Church."[56] He believed that as a result of the fall, man was dead in sin and had no power to turn to God.[57] He believed that election was unconditional.[58] He believed that God's saving grace worked monergistically and efficaciously. He believed in the perseverance of the saints. Yet he believed that

---

55. J. C. Ryle, *Prove All Things: A Tract on Private Judgment* (Ipswich: Hunt and Son, 1851), 3.

56. J. C. Ryle, *The Christian Leaders of the Last Century; or, England a Hundred Years Ago* (London: T. Nelson and Sons, 1869), 379.

57. J. C. Ryle, "Your Election," in *Home Truths: Being Miscellaneous Addresses and Tracts by the Rev. J. C. Ryle, B.A.* (Ipswich: W. Hunt, 1872), 8:151.

58. Ryle, "Your Election," 148:

> The true doctrine of election I believe to be as follows. God has been pleased from all eternity to choose certain men and women out of mankind, whom by His counsel secret to us, He has decreed to save by Jesus Christ. None are finally saved except those who are thus chosen. Hence the Scripture gives to God's people in several places the name of "God's elect," and the choice or appointment of them to eternal life is called "God's election." Those men and women whom God has been pleased to choose from all eternity, He calls in time, by His Spirit working in due season. He convinces them of sin. He leads them to Christ. He works in them repentance and faith. He converts, renews, and sanctifies them. He keeps them by His grace from falling away entirely, and finally brings them safe to glory. In short God's eternal election is the first link in that chain of a sinner's salvation of which heavenly glory is the end. None ever repent, believe, and are born again, except the elect. The primary and original cause of a saint's being what he is, is in one word, God's election.

Christ's death was sufficient for the whole world, that He "tasted death for every man," and that He bore the sins of the whole world.[59] He believed that God loves all mankind, not just the elect. He denied that the doctrine of election destroys human responsibility or the free offer of the gospel. He rejected the doctrine of double predestination. Such are the contours of Ryle's Calvinism.

In terms of personal piety, Ryle's view of the Christian life is definitely cast in the Puritan mold.[60] He believed that the Holy Spirit is the source and sustainer of all spiritual life. Like the Puritans, he believed that the Spirit always works in a similar manner or pattern, and thus he stressed the importance of "marks" or "evidences" of the Spirit's work. His spirituality was also Christocentric. More specifically, it was focused on Christ's atonement, ongoing intercession, and second advent.[61] He also stressed the importance of the diligent use of the means of grace. These included Bible reading, private prayer, regularly attending public worship, regularly hearing the preaching of God's word, and regularly receiving

---

59. J. C. Ryle, *Do You Believe?* (London: William Hunt, 1860), 12–13:

> I confess, boldly, that I hold to the doctrine of particular redemption, in a certain sense, as strongly as any one. I believe that none are effectually redeemed but God's elect. They and they only are set free from the guilt, and power, and consequences of sin. But I hold no less strongly, that Christ's work of atonement is sufficient for all mankind. There is a sense in which He has tasted death for every man, and has taken upon Him the sin of the world. I dare not pare down, and fine away, what appear to me the plain statements of Scripture. I dare not shut a door which God seems, to my eyes, to have left open. I dare not tell any man on earth that Christ has done nothing for him, and that he has no warrant to apply boldly to Christ for salvation. Christ is God's gift to the whole world.

60. Ryle admired the Puritans and published approving biographical sketches of a number of them when they were generally very unpopular among churchmen. For Ryle's defense of the Puritans, see *Light from Old Times; or, Protestant Facts and Men with an Introduction for Our Own Days*, 2nd ed. (London: Chas. J. Thynne, 1898), xiv–xviii. Furthermore, he quoted from Puritan divines extensively in *Holiness*.

61. The Christocentrism of Ryle's hymnals, which are an excellent and neglected source of his spirituality, will be discussed in chapter 3.

the Lord's Supper. Finally, he stressed the importance of observing the Christian Sabbath as well.

J. I. Packer argues that Ryle's ministerial agenda, as well as his spirituality, was also influenced by the Puritans. Ryle's desire to evangelize the English people, purify and reform the national church, unite all English Christians, and promote the holiness of English believers matches what Packer calls the "Puritan quadrilateral."[62]

Ryle regularly and repeatedly identified himself as an "evangelical," and evangelical religion, according to Ryle, was characterized by five leading features.[63] First, evangelicals assign absolute supremacy to the Holy Scripture and regard it as the only rule for faith and practice. Second, evangelicals emphasize the doctrine of human sinfulness and corruption and the need for a radical cure. Third, evangelicals attach paramount importance to the person and work of Christ and the necessity of faith in Him. Fourth, evangelicals stress the importance of the inward work of the Spirit in the heart of the believer and an experimental acquaintance with it. Finally, evangelicals insist that the inward work of the Spirit will always be manifested outwardly by a holy life. For Ryle, these points constituted the essence of the evangelical gospel and the Christian faith.

Ryle was a committed Anglican churchman. He regarded the Thirty-Nine Articles, the Church's confession of faith, as the greatest human doctrinal standard. He loved the prayer book, its liturgy, and its forms of prayers. He affirmed, with the thirty-fifth article, that the homilies contain "godly and wholesome Doctrine." He repeatedly quoted from the Church catechism with approbation. Furthermore, Ryle was firmly attached to the episcopal form of church government. He considered it to be the most scriptural form of church government and the best means of providing pastoral oversight for the nation. In short, when properly administered, the

---

62. J. I. Packer, *Faithfulness and Holiness: The Witness of J. C. Ryle* (Wheaton, Ill.: Crossway, 2002), 37–43.

63. J. C. Ryle, *Evangelical Religion: What It Is, and What It Is Not* (London: William Hunt, 1867).

Church of England was the best church on earth. This deeply held conviction led Ryle to become an enthusiastic Church reformer and defender.

In terms of eschatology, Ryle was a premillennialist.[64] He summarized the chief articles of his "prophetical creed" as follows:

> (I) I believe that the world will never be completely converted to Christianity by any existing agency, before the end comes. (II) I believe that wide-spread unbelief, indifference, formalism, and wickedness, which are seen throughout Christendom, are only what we are taught to expect in God's Word. (III) I believe that the grand purpose of the present dispensation is to gather out of the world an elect people, and not to convert all mankind. (IV) I believe that the second coming of our Lord Jesus Christ is the great event which will wind up the present dispensation, and for which we ought daily to long and pray. (V) I believe that the second coming of our Lord Jesus Christ will be a real, literal, personal, bodily coming.... (VI) I believe that after our Lord Jesus Christ comes again, the earth shall be renewed, and the curse removed; the devil shall be bound, the godly shall be rewarded, the wicked

---

64. I would have liked to address this aspect of Ryle's thought (as well as the other ones), but space did not permit a more extensive treatment. See Alan Munden, "The 'Prophetical Opinions' of J. C. Ryle," *Churchman* 125 (2011): 251–62, for a helpful summary of Ryle's eschatology.

Ryle apparently began reading works on eschatology shortly after his ordination. In 1853 he specifically mentioned having read the following works: *The Mystery of Israel's Salvation* by Increase Mather; *Prophetical Landmarks* by Horatius Bonar; *Redemption Drawing Nigh* by Alexander Bonar; *Popular Objections to the Premillenial Advent Considered* by George Ogilvy; *Sermons on the Second Advent* by Hugh M'Neile; *The Restoration of the Jews* and *A Practical Guide to the Prophecies* by Edward Bickersteth; and *Isaiah as It Is: Judah and Jerusalem the Subject of Isaiah's Prophesying* by Alexander Keith. His interest in this subject appears to have peaked in the 1850s. Ryle preached a number of sermons on the subject at that time and later published them as tracts. He also attended the annual Lent sermons at St. George's, Bloomsbury, at the invitation of Henry Montagu Villiers, later bishop of Carlisle, which focused on unfulfilled prophecy. Ryle addressed this gathering in 1851, 1853, and 1855. But the second advent of Christ and the future gathering of the Jews remained prominent emphases for the rest of his ministry.

shall be punished; and that before he comes there shall neither be resurrection, judgment, nor millennium, and that not till after he comes shall the earth be filled with the knowledge of the glory of the Lord. (VII) I believe that the Jews shall ultimately be gathered again as a separate nation, restored to their own land, and converted to faith in Christ, after going through great tribulation. (VIII) I believe that the literal sense of the Old Testament prophecies has been far too much neglected by the Churches, and is far too much neglected at the present day, and that under the mistaken system of *spiritualizing* and *accommodating* Bible language, Christians have too often completely missed its meaning. (IX) I do not believe that the preterist scheme of interpreting the Apocalypse, which regards the book as almost entirely *fulfilled*, or the futurist scheme, which regards it as almost entirely *unfulfilled*, are either of them to be implicitly followed. The truth, I expect, will be found between the two. (X) I believe that the Roman Catholic Church is the great predicted apostasy from the faith, and is Babylon and antichrist, although I think it highly probable that a more complete development of antichrist will yet be exhibited in the world. (XI) Finally, I believe that it is for the safety, happiness, and comfort of all true Christians, to expect as little as possible from Churches or Governments under the present dispensation,—to hold themselves ready for tremendous convulsions and changes of all things established,—and to expect their good things only from Christ's second advent.[65]

Ryle was a moderate premillennialist.[66] He refused to speculate about dates and times, and he did not discuss controversial

---

65. J. C. Ryle, *Coming Events and Present Duties*, 2nd and enlarged ed. (London: William Hunt, 1879), viii–xi.

66. His premillennialism, coupled with his pessimism about the future, place Ryle in the "Recordite" or "extreme" faction within Anglican evangelicalism according to Boyd Hilton's taxonomy. See Hilton, *Age of Atonement*; and *A Mad, Bad, and Dangerous People? England 1783–1846* (Oxford: Oxford University Press, 2006), 174–84, 401–5. Hilton argues that a division emerged in Anglican

subjects publicly. He insisted that his prophetical views were not articles of faith but private opinions, and acknowledged that "holier and better men than myself do not see these subjects with my eyes, and think me utterly mistaken."[67] But he believed his "prophetical creed" was scriptural and consistent with church history and personal experience.

Ordination

After graduating from Oxford, Ryle moved back to Macclesfield and lived with his family at Henbury. His father purchased the estate in 1837, and by all accounts it was beautiful. It was three miles west of the city center and closer to the more congenial, high-class country society. It consisted of a thousand acres, a large house, woods, and water. He quickly became attached to it and, as the eldest son, was destined to become the lord of the manor.

In 1838 he moved to London to read the law at Lincoln's Inn. He stayed only six months because of illness. He believed he had not yet fully recovered from preparing for his degree at Oxford. This London interlude was not a happy time. He made no friends, felt isolated, and was shocked by the immorality of the city.[68] While

---

evangelicalism in the 1820s between two groups: the Claphamites and the Recordites. The Claphamite evangelicals were respectable, enlightened, rationalist, postmillennial, and moderate, but the Recordites were Pentecostal, premillenarian, adventist, revivalist, and extreme. J. C. Ryle, John Bird Sumner, and Edward Bickersteth were premillennialists, but hardly extremists, and were closer to the moderate strand of Claphamite evangelicalism than Hilton's taxonomy allows.

67. Ryle, *Coming Events and Present Duties*, vi.

68. In an address to the Liverpool YMCA in 1889, Ryle discussed his time in London:

> When I had finished my college education I was launched in London all by myself, and went there to read law. It was only a comparatively small circumstance which prevented me from following the law altogether; however, when I was there I remember that I thought that it was impossible for a man to serve Christ and be a true Christian when living in a great wicked and corrupt city such as London, the metropolis of the world, is sure to be. The thought came across my mind,—How can a man serve and follow Christ and be able to resist

in London, however, he became a communicant member of Baptist Noel's chapel, St. John's, Bedford Row, Holborn.[69]

He returned to Henbury later in the same year and went to work at his father's bank in order to learn the family business. Over the next four years, he became a prominent man in Macclesfield. He became a county magistrate. He was made captain of the Macclesfield troop of the Cheshire Yeomanry, which was comprised of six hundred men, and most of the leading men in Cheshire were his officers. He began his career as a public speaker and addressed both religious and political gatherings. He also began reading in preparation for going into Parliament. His parents urged him to marry, and his father offered him eight hundred pounds a year and a house, but he was not ready to do so.

From a spiritual perspective, these four years were not satisfying. His religious convictions continued to be a source of tension in

---

the world, the flesh, and the devil, when he does not know any one, and there is no one to help him or encourage him? How can it be done? Is it possible? The doubt came across my mind again and again, and it was only by the great mercy of God that I was able to resist it.

J. C. Ryle, "Daniel the Prophet," in *The Rule of Life and Conduct: Discourses Delivered before the Members of the Liverpool Young Men's Christian Association* (Liverpool: Young Men's Christian Association, 1889), 8.

69. St. John's was an important evangelical proprietary chapel. Richard Cecil and Daniel Wilson, both prominent evangelical clergymen, served as its ministers. Baptist Wriothesley Noel became its minister in 1827 and attracted large and influential congregations. He became an early leader of the evangelical party but abandoned the Church of England in 1848 as a result of the Gorham controversy. The stir his secession caused was almost as great as John Henry Newman's. He became critical of the union of church and state but never joined the disestablishment movement. He later defended evangelical clergymen from attacks by C. H. Spurgeon in *Baptismal Regeneration*. For more information on Baptist Noel, see Grayson Carter, "Baptist Wriothesley Noel," in *Oxford Dictionary of National Biography*, ed. H. C. G. Matthew and Brian Harrison (Oxford: Oxford University Press, 2004), 969–70; Grayson Carter, "Evangelicals and Tractarians: Baptist Noel and the Evangelical Response to the Gorham Affair," in *Anglican Evangelicals: Protestant Sessions from the Via Media, 1800–1850* (Oxford: Oxford University Press, 2001); and David Bebbington, "The Life of Baptist Noel: Its Setting and Significance," *The Baptist Quarterly* 24 (1972): 389–411.

the home, and he had the uncomfortable feeling that he was merely being tolerated. The estrangement from former friends and family members continued. But Rev. John Burnet and his future brothers-in-law, both evangelicals and both students for ordination under Burnet, were a source of encouragement. During this period he admitted that he was too focused on his own spiritual conflicts and difficulties and did not sufficiently "aim at works of active usefulness to the souls of others."[70] He did, however, read prayers in the housekeeper's room and occasionally visited a sick or dying person, but his parents' objections kept him from regular teaching, preaching, visiting, and evangelizing. Ryle later described this period of his life as a time of "patient learning and not active doing."[71]

Everything changed in 1841. Ryle's grandfather had taken over the first and only bank in Macclesfield in 1800 and made it profitable. After his passing, Ryle's father took it over. He was not well suited to banking. He was too easygoing, too good natured, and too careless about details. He loaned his brother-in-law Charles Wood two hundred thousand pounds to start manufacturing cotton in Macclesfield. The plan failed, and the money was lost. Wood encouraged John to open a second branch of his bank in Manchester to cover the losses. The Manchester branch was initially successful, but it was not properly supervised by John and his business partner, Mr. Daintry. To make matters worse, they left it in the hands of a bad manager, who chronically made unwise loans to unfit applicants. When the situation became known, John and Daintry's banking associate in London stopped payment, their banks went bankrupt, and the Ryles were ruined. J. C. remarked, "We got up one summer's morning with all the world before us as usual, and went to bed that same night completely and entirely ruined."[72]

---

70. Ryle, *Autobiography*, 83.
71. Ryle, *Autobiography*, 84.
72. Ryle, *Autobiography*, 88.

Limited liability was not applied to the banking industry until 1858, and thus everything had to be sold to pay the creditors. Henbury was sold immediately. The household servants and staff were dismissed. Ryle sold his two horses, Yeomanry uniform, sword, saddle, and accoutrements for 250 pounds. The children were left with nothing but their personal property and clothes. In short, "everything was swept clean away."[73] But his mother's dowry, which was worth thirty thousand pounds, could not be touched by the bankruptcy. His parents, along with his unmarried sisters, moved to Hampshire and lived off the interest for the rest of their lives. Over the next twenty years, both father and son made payments to settle the debts of the bank. The last payment of nine thirty-seconds of a penny was made in 1861. It was observed that Ryle went around in threadbare clothing to save as much money as he could to pay off his father's debt—for which he was not legally responsible.[74]

Embarrassed and humiliated, Ryle went to live with a family friend, Colonel Thornhill, in New Forest to contemplate his future. He had no desire to be a private tutor. The learned professions— engineering and the law—would not allow him to support himself for several years. He was approached about being a private

---

73. Ryle, *Autobiography*, 87.

74. A few days after the death of J. C. Ryle, Canon Alfred Christopher (1820–1913), rector of St. Aldate's, Oxford, published his reminiscences of the late bishop in *The Record* (June 15, 1900):

> When the beloved veteran, the late Canon Bardsley, Rector of St. Ann's, Manchester, was in Oxford many years ago as deputation for the Church Pastoral-Aid Society, he told me he knew that for many years, when Mr. Ryle was rector of Helmingham, he wore threadbare clothes, and denied himself many things, in order to pay off, so far as possible, the small depositors at his father's bank. He was not himself a partner in the bank, and was not legally liable for anything.... When I next saw Bishop Ryle, I asked him if Canon Bardsley's story was in all respects correct, and he was obliged to acknowledge that it was so.

See appendix 4: "Canon Christopher on Ryle's Conversion," in Ryle, *Autobiography*, 211–12.

secretary to William Gladstone, but he declined. He wrote, "I felt no confidence in him, and would not have it for a moment."[75] He became a clergyman because he "felt shut up to do it, and saw no other course of life open to me."[76]

Ordination was a process that involved a number of steps.[77] First, the candidate had to contact the bishop or his secretary, declare his intentions, and receive instructions regarding requirements. The second step in the process was usually an interview with the bishop. If that meeting was satisfactory, the candidate would be asked to submit a series of documents that included evidence of an academic degree, testimonials of the moral character of the candidate, a baptism certificate that demonstrated the candidate was of canonical age (twenty-three), the *Si Quis*,[78] and a nomination by an incumbent who offered a title to orders in the form of a curacy with a specified stipend. Once the paperwork was in order, the candidate had to pass a series of episcopal examinations, which usually took place from Thursday to Saturday. Having passed the exam, the candidate was ordained on Sunday.

Ryle sought ordination at the hands of Charles Sumner, the evangelical bishop of Winchester, in December 1841.[79] Sumner's candidates for ordination were housed in Farnham Castle, and the examination process followed the typical Thursday to Sunday plan. Examinations began each morning at ten. The candidate's

---

75. Ryle, *Autobiography*, 98. Ryle remained a lifelong opponent of W. E. Gladstone both in politics and religion. Gladstone and Ryle collided on a number of issues discussed below, most notably the disestablishment of the Irish church and Ryle's leadership of the diocese of Liverpool.

76. Ryle, *Autobiography*, 98.

77. I am deeply indebted to Alan Haig's explanation of the ordination process in *The Victorian Clergy* (London: Croom Helm, 1984), 183–92.

78. The *Si Quis* was a notification of the candidate's intention to present himself for ordination to inquire whether any impediment may be alleged against him. This was usually publicly read at the candidate's home church.

79. Charles Sumner's ordination process is discussed in detail in George Henry Sumner, *Life of Charles Richard Sumner, D.D. Bishop of Winchester* (London: John Murray, 1876), 142–45.

paperwork was reviewed by one examining chaplain, and after that a viva voce examination took place with another. Each candidate was then personally interviewed by Bishop Sumner, who typically discussed any concerns he had about the exams, the candidate's previous ministerial work, or the sample sermons candidates were required to submit. The exams ended each day around four or five o'clock and dinner was served at seven. Sumner typically invited outstanding clergymen to dine with the candidates to give them advice and encouragement. A final service was held at ten at night in which the bishop expounded an appropriate Scripture text for candidates for the ministry. For the ordination service, which was held on Sundays in an intimate chapel in the castle, Sumner selected a well-known preacher to deliver a stirring charge to the candidates at this important moment of their lives.

Ryle was ordained a deacon on December 12, 1841, and preached his first sermon a week later on December 19. He was later ordained a priest on December 11, 1842.

Early Ministry

After ordination, Ryle became the curate of Rev. William Gibson, the evangelical rector of Fawley. Gibson was kind to Ryle and held him in high esteem, but for most of Ryle's curacy, Gibson was away in Malta and offered little guidance. When Gibson did reside, Ryle complained that he was too cautious and unduly influenced by his wife, who thought he was dangerous and extreme.

Fawley was a large rural parish that occupied a triangular section of New Forest between Southampton Water and the Solent. Ryle was given charge of St. Katherine's, a chapel of Ease, in the district of Exbury, which contained around seven hundred people. Exbury offered a number of challenges for the new curate. Many of the inhabitants were poor and unaccustomed to an active, evangelical ministry. The district was home to a number of poachers and smugglers and almost no gentlemen. Drunkenness abounded. The Baptists and the Methodists carried off many of the more serious

Christians. Snakes infested the wetlands; thus snakebites were common and resulted in a number of deaths. Ague, typhus, and especially scarlet fever were persistent problems as well.

Ryle went to work in Exbury with uncommon zeal. He prepared two written sermons for Sundays.[80] He delivered two extempore expository lectures each week in cottages. He taught and supervised the parish Sunday school. He kept up an aggressive system of pastoral visitation, which included visiting every home in the district each month, amounting to nearly sixty visits per week. In addition to his pastoral labors, necessity compelled him to serve as a doctor and policeman.[81]

The impact of Ryle's ministry on the town was difficult to determine, and Ryle later said that two years is not enough time to really get to know the people. The church was full on Sundays and people seemed interested in his teaching, but the farmers were "a rich, dull, stupid set of people," and the laborers were set in their ways.[82] He took unpopular stands against late-night cricket on Saturday nights and refused to play cards and dance, which caused some to regard him as "an enthusiastic, fanatical mad dog."[83] And he continued to struggle with the transition from riches to poverty. Nevertheless, Ryle learned two valuable lessons in Exbury that served him moving forward. First, he learned "what power one man has against a

---

80. Ryle's earliest extant sermon, "The Compassion of Christ," dates from this period. It was preached to raise money for foreign missions, which remained a lifelong priority. It can be found in *The Christian Race and Other Sermons* (London: Hodder and Stoughton, 1900), 219–30.

81. For a description of Ryle's work as a doctor and police officer, see *Autobiography*, 101–3. Also, Ryle's experience "doctoring the people's bodies" gave him great respect for the medical profession. On July 31, 1883, he gave the opening address at the annual conference of the British Medical Association in Liverpool. In his address, "Luke, the Beloved Physician," he said, "Next to the office of him who ministers to men's souls, there is none really more useful and honourable than that of him who ministers to the soul's frail tabernacle—the body." J. C. Ryle, *The Upper Room: Being a Few Truths for the Times* (London: William Hunt, 1888), 31.

82. Ryle, *Autobiography*, 102.

83. Ryle, *Autobiography*, 103.

multitude as long as he has right on his side."[84] Second, preaching to agricultural laborers taught him the value of simplicity in preaching and the importance of a "good lively delivery."[85]

In November 1843, Ryle resigned the curacy of Exbury due to illness after ministering there less than two years. He blamed it on the climate of the district, but his symptoms—"constant headache, indigestion, and disturbances of the heart"—are consistent with anxiety or depression, which could have been caused by isolation, being overworked, a lack of rest, and grief over his recent personal losses. After resigning, he traveled to Leamington Spa to recuperate under the supervision of Dr. Henry Jephson.

Shortly thereafter, Bishop Sumner offered Ryle the rectory of St. Thomas, Winchester. He accepted it immediately and began in early December. Winchester was a cathedral town of three thousand inhabitants. It was home to the famous Winchester School, whose headmaster was George Moberly, the future bishop of Salisbury. John Keble, one of the fathers of the Oxford movement, lived nearby and exerted considerable influence in the town. Samuel Wilberforce, a canon of the cathedral, was an influential figure as well. He took an interest in Ryle and unsuccessfully attempted to convince him to abandon his evangelical views on baptism. He was, however, much more successful with Ryle's family, who lived in his parish at the time.[86]

From Ryle's perspective, the whole place was in a "very dead state."[87] The cathedral body was worldly. Most of the seven parishes were occupied by unsatisfactory incumbents. Even the evangelical clergymen were cautious and fearful. The previous rector of

---

84. Ryle, *Autobiography*, 103.

85. J. C. Ryle, *Simplicity in Preaching* (London: William Hunt, 1882), 6, 47.

86. Ryle's younger brother, Frederick William, was Wilberforce's curate in Alverstoke. Samuel Wilberforce, Henry Manning, and Henry Wilberforce frequently visited the Ryles and eventually carried everyone in Ryle's family, except his father, into the "tide" and "current" of ritualism. Ryle, *Autobiography*, 122–23.

87. Ryle, *Autobiography*, 109.

St. Thomas, an evangelical, had grown increasingly inactive before
his retirement. Ryle went to work immediately. He preached two
services on Sunday, started a popular weekday expository lecture
in the infant school, made house-to-house pastoral visits during
the week, and supervised a district visitors' society. As a result of
his work, St. Thomas, which could hold six hundred people, was
filled to capacity and the whole parish was turned upside down.

Five months into his ministry in Winchester, Ryle received an
offer he could not refuse. He was offered the rectory of Helmingham in Suffolk. It was a small, rural parish of only three hundred
people, but he was offered five hundred pounds per annum, which
was five times more than he was earning in Winchester. Though
Ryle was flourishing in Winchester, poverty constrained him to
take the offer. The new position made him financially independent
of his father and allowed him to help pay back his father's creditors.

Conclusion

Ryle began his ministry in Helmingham on Easter Sunday, 1844,
and he would remain there for the next seventeen years. While in
Helmingham, Ryle would become well known in evangelical circles
as a preacher and a writer. But the substance of his sermons and
works, as well as the character of his entire ministerial outlook,
was shaped during the formative years discussed in this chapter.

Ryle embraced evangelical principles and experienced an
evangelical conversion sometime in fall 1837. By the winter of that
same year, his religious opinions were firmly settled and remained
virtually unchanged in every point for the rest of his life. New
circumstances brought out new emphases in his works, but the
substance remained the same. Moreover, that Ryle was forced
to defend his new evangelical convictions almost as soon as he
embraced them helped turn him, a person who was already naturally competitive and perhaps combative to some degree, into a
formidable evangelical controversialist.

Ryle frequently lamented that he had no one to guide him spiritually during the first twenty-eight years of his life. His parents showed almost no interest in his soul. The church of his childhood did him no good. Religious instruction was nonexistent at Rev. Jackson's preparatory school and at Eton. The tutors at Christ Church, with the exception of Liddell, showed little interest in him. His only spiritual guides, until the Reverends Wales and Burnet came to St. George's, were books. Therefore, it is not surprising that he would begin publishing a wide variety of religious works almost as soon as he found the time to do so in Helmingham. Through those works, especially his tracts, he would become a spiritual guide and father to many.

Ryle's early ministerial experiences in Exbury and Winchester taught him to value an active, aggressive, and fearless evangelical ministry. With little guidance or oversight, he filled his churches in Exbury and Winchester by preaching, lecturing, visiting, distributing tracts, and running the parish machinery—that is, the Sunday school and district visitors' society. These were the means he discovered for doing good to souls. He would employ these same tactics in Helmingham, Stradbroke, and Liverpool.

Finally, Ryle was emerging as an independent thinker and actor. He was naturally independent as a child and became even more so as a result of his experiences at home and school and in his early years in the ministry. Speaking of his position in Winchester, Ryle made the following statement, which could, with some justice, be regarded as his life's motto:

> The story of my life has been such that I really cared nothing for anyone's opinion, and I resolved not to consider one jot who was offended and who was not offended by anything I did. I saw no one whose opinion I cared for in the place, and I resolved to ask nobody's counsel, in the work of my parish, or as to the matter or manner of my preaching, but just to do

what I thought the Lord Jesus Christ would like, and not to care one jot for the face of man.[88]

Ryle's independence would become a defining characteristic of his ministry. On occasion, it would cause him to run afoul of other churchmen, even those within his own party. It also helped propel him into national leadership and earned him the respect of churchmen of all schools of thought.

---

88. Ryle, *Autobiography*, 110.

2

Preacher

In 1844 Helmingham was a small agricultural village in the East Anglian county of Suffolk. It was dominated by John Lord Tollemache of Helmingham Hall.[1] John was an agriculturalist and a politician. He owned over thirty thousand acres in Cheshire and Suffolk, and he sat as a Tory MP for South Cheshire from 1841 to 1868 and for West Cheshire from 1868 to 1872. John and his wife, Georgina, were also committed evangelicals. Georgina befriended Ryle after his conversion and was probably responsible for securing the offer of this lucrative living.

Apart from the parish rectory, Ryle found the parish in good order. There were no public houses or beer shops. The church had recently been completely restored. All three hundred of Ryle's parishioners lived within a mile of the church. Church attendance was typically very high as well.[2] Ryle kept up his regular parish work—two written sermons for Sundays, weekly lecturing, pastoral

---

1. See E. D. H. Tollemache, *The Tollemaches of Helmingham and Ham* (Ipswich, U.K.: W. S. Cowell Butter Market, 1949).

2. Ryle completed, returned, and signed the questionnaire for the Religious Census of 1851. He recorded that on March 30, 1851, there were 96 adults and 27 Sunday school scholars present for morning worship and 145 adults and 27 scholars present for evening worship. This was slightly lower than the twelve-month average of 130 adults and 40 scholars for Sunday mornings and 200 adults and 40 scholars for the evening. St. Mary's had accommodation for only 150 worshipers (50 free sittings, 100 rented); thus many people sat on benches in the aisles. See T. C. B. Timmins, ed., *Suffolk Returns from the Census of Religious Worship, 1851* (Suffolk, U.K.: St. Edmundsbury Press, 1997), 87.

visits, and superintending the Sunday school—but because the parish was small and in good working order, he had more free time for reading and studying than at any point in his life.[3] It was at this time that Ryle developed his distinctive preaching style.

The purpose of this chapter is to examine Ryle's preaching. This is an appropriate starting point since he regarded preaching as the chief work of the Christian minister. Despite the importance Ryle attached to preaching, his biographers say surprisingly little about it.[4] The focus of this chapter will be on his homiletical theory. An examination of Ryle's preaching at Helmingham (1844–1861) reveals that he was deeply indebted to the classical rhetorical tradition he received at Eton and Oxford. It also reveals a willingness to depart from it, in certain respects, to win the attention of his congregation. This will be demonstrated by describing his homiletical development, examining his distinctive

---

3. Ryle, *Autobiography*, 117.

4. Ryle's earliest biographers say very little about his preaching. They briefly mention the failure of his early preaching experiments in New Forest, which led to the development of his crucified style, but then move on to other topics. Toon and Smout provide slightly more analysis than the previous biographers. They discuss his style, the impression his preaching made on others, and the different audiences he addressed, but their treatment is less than two pages in length. See Toon and Smout, *John Charles Ryle*, 46–47. Eric Russell is the first biographer to devote an entire chapter to Ryle's preaching. He addresses a number of preaching-related topics but does not treat the style or substance of his sermons in great detail. See Eric Russell, "Simplicity in Preaching," in *J. C. Ryle*, 57–74. J. I. Packer also treats Ryle's preaching in a chapter in *Faithfulness and Holiness*. Though he covers much of the same ground as earlier biographies, his chapter makes one important contribution: he argues that the themes of sin and grace were Ryle's hermeneutical key to the Scriptures and thus the focal point of his sermons and tracts. See Packer, "A Great Preacher," in *Faithfulness and Holiness*, 61–66. Farley's treatment of Ryle's preaching in his study of Ryle's episcopacy is the most extensive to date. He discusses important aspects of the style (Ryle's urgency and the techniques he employed to gain and hold the hearer's attention) and substance (evangelistic thrust and cry for evidences) of his sermons, as well as their popularity. See Ian D. Farley, "The Theology of J. C. Ryle, I: The Preacher," in *J. C. Ryle, First Bishop of Liverpool: A Study in Mission amongst the Masses* (Waynesboro, Ga.: Paternoster Press, 2000), 1–41. Farley's work represents a significant advancement in the study of Ryle's preaching, but more is needed.

crucified style, and comparing him to two of his most famous contemporary preachers."

Ryle's Homiletical Development

J. C. Ryle gave his first public address at the age of seven. At an annual dinner party hosted by Colonel Parker for the children of the most prominent families in east Cheshire, Ryle stood up on his chair and exclaimed at the top of his voice, "Well, Colonel Parker, I have had a good dinner."[5] The short speech impressed the colonel, who regarded it as a great compliment, but Ryle's earliest rhetorical training came at Eton.

Though the curriculum under Dr. Keate was classical, rhetoric received little attention apart from the occasional quote from a great orator in *Scriptores Graeci* and *Scriptores Latini*. But it is likely that Ryle's attentive tutor, Edward Craven Hawtrey, encouraged him to read Aristotle's *Rhetoric* and Cicero's rhetorical works in preparation for entering Oxford.

The chief source of Ryle's education in rhetoric came from the "Pop." In 1811 Charles Fox Townshend founded a debating club called the Eton Society.[6] It was later renamed the Pop after its meeting place—Mrs. Hatton's confectioner's shop (*popina* in Latin). Membership was originally restricted to the twenty best debaters, but that number was increased to thirty shortly thereafter. Debates took place every Saturday afternoon, and the subject matter was limited to history or literature; political questions and polemical subjects were strictly off limit. A number of famous orators made their debut at the Pop, including W. E. Gladstone, Sir Francis Doyle, and Lord Derby. Ryle joined the society during his time at Eton and became a prominent member. He, along with the future vice-chancellor of England, Sir John Wickens, and the

---

5. Ryle, *Autobiography*, 20.

6. For more information on the Eton Society, see Lyte, *History of Eton College*, 373–76; Hollis, *Eton: A History*, 208–9; and Cust, *History of Eton College*, 262–64.

future British peer and Liberal MP, Lord Edward Richard Littleton, were among its principal speakers. Ryle's first public speeches were prepared, delivered, and defended in this debating society.

Ryle joined no such society at Christ Church and focused exclusively on reading for his degree and cricket. In preparation for his degree, however, he read and studied some of the most important works of the classical rhetorical tradition. He specifically mentions being examined on Aristotle's *Rhetoric*,[7] and it is likely that he read Cicero's rhetorical works (*De Oratore, De Inventione,* and *De Partitione Oratoria*) and Quintilian's *Institutio Oratoria* as well.[8] This reading constituted the only formal homiletical training Ryle ever received.

After graduation, Ryle began speaking regularly in public. He was invited to speak to religious, presumably evangelical, meetings because of his recognized religious character, and he was invited to speak to political meetings because of his position as his father's eldest son and his speaking ability.[9] He continued to "come forward frequently on public occasions as a speaker" until his father's bankruptcy propelled him into the Church.

After ordination, Ryle was preaching at least four times a week in Exbury. Despite his zealous efforts, Ryle struggled to keep the attention of his rural congregation. Furthermore, with his rector gone to Malta, he, as a young preacher, had no one to guide him. Therefore he embarked on a series of pulpit experiments in an attempt to win the attention of his congregation. He began to model himself after the preaching of Canon Henry Melvill, "the

---

7. Ryle, *Autobiography*, 56.

8. Ryle quoted from both of these works in *Simplicity in Preaching*, 8, 23. Additionally, other Oxonians who were contemporaries of Ryle mentioned reading both authors. For an illuminating glimpse into the curriculum of Oxford, see *The Student's Guide to a Course of Reading Necessary for Obtaining University Honours by a Graduate of Oxford*. This anonymous author encouraged students to focus on Aristotle as opposed to Cicero and Quintilian, but he noted that the definitions from the latter must be "learned by rote."

9. Ryle, *Autobiography*, 80.

Evangelical Chrysostom," of St. Paul's,[10] but he quickly discovered that agricultural laborers did not appreciate Canon Melvill's florid language and grandiloquence.

Ryle continued to experiment for the next few years. In Winchester, he read written sermons with great earnestness and fire. Though they were thoroughly evangelical and filled the church to capacity, they were still "far too florid, and far less simple and direct" than the preaching style he later learned.[11] In Helmingham Ryle found his voice. As he began to "crucify," or rather simplify, his style, he began to win and keep his rural congregation's attention and quickly gained a reputation for being a powerful and engaging preacher.

The Crucified Style

Ryle's distinctive style of preaching has been described as the *crucified style*. This is an accurate designation as long as the term *style* is understood in its technical, classical sense. *Style* is the third of Cicero's five canons of rhetoric, and Ryle certainly crucified it, opting for a simpler and more direct approach instead of Cicero's ornamented style. But he hardly abandoned the classical rhetorical training of his youth. The classics provided the only homiletical training Ryle ever received, at least until ordination, and he continued to rely heavily on his classical education even as he experimented with style and delivery. Therefore, Ryle's crucified style may be described as classical rhetorical theory simplified stylistically.

Classical Influence

Several fundamental elements of the classical rhetorical tradition may be found in Ryle's preaching. The first parallel between Ryle's

---

10. Canon Henry Melvill (1798–1871) was regarded as the most popular preacher in London and one of the greatest rhetoricians of his generation. For a brief summary of his life and ministry, see G. C. Boast, "Henry Melvill," in *Oxford Dictionary of National Biography*, ed. H. G. C. Matthew and Brian Harrison (Oxford: Oxford University Press, 2004), 764–65.

11. Ryle, *Autobiography*, 113.

homiletical theory and the classical rhetorical tradition is the insistence that orations be persuasive. For both Aristotle and Cicero, the essence of rhetoric is persuasion.[12] Ryle agreed, but he went one step further. The goal of a sermon was not merely to persuade his audience to embrace certain theological propositions but to compel them to respond appropriately to his message, which typically meant "conversion for the unconverted, decision for the wavering, and growth in grace for the believer."[13]

In addition to agreeing with the classical rhetorical tradition on the goal of rhetoric, Ryle also agreed on the means of achieving this end. Classical rhetoricians believed that the means of persuasion are rhetorical proofs, which are divided into three categories: logical demonstration (*logos*), emotional appeal (*pathos*), and the speaker himself (*ethos*).[14] Ryle's Helmingham sermons provide numerous examples of each.

Logical demonstration was Ryle's primary method of persuasion, and he employed a variety of logical arguments to persuade his audience to act.[15] Appealing to authority is one of his most frequent tactics. For Ryle, the Bible was the supreme authority, but he

---

12. Aristotle defined the art of rhetoric as "the power to observe the persuasiveness of which any particular matter admits." *The Art of Rhetoric* 1.2, trans. H. C. Lawson-Tancred (London: Penguin Books, 1991), 74. For Cicero, it was "to speak in a manner suited to persuade an audience." *De Oratore* 1.31.138, in *Cicero in Twenty-Eight Volumes*, trans. E. W. Sutton (Cambridge, Mass.: Harvard University Press, 1976), 3:97.

13. See J. C. Ryle, *A Pastor's Address to His Flock at the Beginning of a New Year* (Ipswich: Hunt and Son, 1846), 28. Also J. C. Ryle, *Be Not Slothful, but Followers* (London: William Hunt, 1846), 21–22.

14. Aristotle, *Art of Rhetoric* 1.2, 74–75.

15. In classical rhetorical terminology, these arguments are called *commonplaces*, or *common topics*. Aristotle, for example, discusses them in *Art of Rhetoric* 2.18–26. Ryle's indebtedness to the classical rhetorical tradition can be seen by his use of this technical terminology in his preaching. In a sermon preached before his Helmingham congregation, he said, "I need not dwell long on this point. To say much in proof of it would only be multiplying truisms and heaping up common places which all allow." J. C. Ryle, *He Whom Thou Lovest Is Sick* (Ipswich: William Hunt, 1859), 5.

also appealed to authoritative documents such as the Articles, homilies, the prayer book, and the Church catechism, and authoritative theologians such as the English Reformers, the pre-Laudian divines, select Puritans, and the evangelical fathers. In addition to appealing to authorities, he frequently developed arguments from the definition of terms, drew conclusions by comparing and contrasting, employed examples from both the Bible and church history, and made inferences by using analogies.[16]

In addition to logical demonstration, Ryle also appealed to the emotions of his audience to persuade them to act. He once told his Helmingham congregation, "I do not want to fill your heads, but to move your hearts."[17] To this end, he frequently discussed happiness: the happiness of the true Christian and the misery of the unbeliever.[18] He also attempted to move the heart by appealing to fear. His sermons are not terrorizing or pressurizing, but they can be serious and sobering.[19] His goal in using fear was not merely

---

16. Rather than providing extensive examples of each type of argument, I will provide one for each type I discuss. For an example of an argument from the definition of terms, see Ryle's definition of *idolatry* in "Idolatry, A Predicted Sin of the Visible Church, with Its Abolition at Christ's Coming," in *Popish Darkness and Millennial Light: Being Lectures Delivered During Lent, 1851, at St. George's Bloomsbury* (London: James Nisbet, 1851), 56–57. For an example of an argument by comparison, see Ryle's comparison of Christ and the world in *I Have Somewhat to Say unto Thee* (London: William Hunt, 1845), 10. For an argument from example, see the biblical and historical examples Ryle employed to prove his assertion that the Holy Spirit can convert any person, no matter how wicked they may be in *Living or Dead?* (London: William Hunt, 1849), 19–21. For an argument by analogy, see Ryle argue that religious zeal is analogous to the habit of mind that makes men great scientists or very wealthy in *Be Zealous* (London: William Hunt, 1852), 5–6.

17. See J. C. Ryle, "Regeneration," in *The Christian Race and Other Sermons* (London: Hodder and Stoughton, 1900), 26.

18. This is especially true in his sermons to children. For example, see J. C. Ryle, *Seeking the Lord Early* (London: William Hunt, 1845). For a good example of a sermon to his regular congregations with an extended appeal to happiness, see J. C. Ryle, *Are You an Heir?* (London: William Hunt, 1852), 23–30.

19. J. C. Ryle, *Pastor's Address to His Flock*, 3:

You walk on with your eyes shut, and seem not to know that the end of your path is hell. Some dreamers fancy they are rich when they are

to frighten his listeners but to warn and awaken them. He also appealed to other emotions such as anger, peace, loneliness, and friendship. On rare occasions, he even used humor.[20]

Ryle also believed that the preacher's character contributes to the persuasiveness of sermons. This aspect of his preaching is difficult to demonstrate given the subtle and nonverbal nature of ethos. But the importance he attached to the character of the preacher can be seen in at least three ways. First, he frequently discussed the importance of the preacher's character when he addressed clerical meetings.[21] Second, according to Aristotle, expressions of goodwill to the audience contribute to the persuasiveness of the speaker, and these types of expressions are readily observable in Ryle's Helmingham sermons.[22] Finally, on rare occasions Ryle spoke from personal experience.

---

poor, or full when they are hungry, or well when they are sick, and awake to find it all a mistake. And this is the way that many of you dream about your souls; you flatter yourselves you will have peace, and there will be no peace; you fancy that you are all right, and in truth you will find that you are all wrong. Surely you are asleep! Dear brethren, what can I say to arouse you? Your souls are in awful peril: without a mighty change they will be lost. When shall that change once be?

20. Before a clerical audience, Ryle used humor to make a point about ministers being separate from the world. He said, "I trust we shall hear every year of fewer and fewer ministers of the Gospel who are magistrates, and fewer and fewer ministers who take part in agricultural meetings, and win prizes for fat pigs, enormous bullocks, and large crops of turnips. There is no apostolical succession in such avocations." J. C. Ryle, "Give Thyself Wholly to Them," in *Home Truths, Seventh Series* (London: William Hunt, 1859), 243.

21. For example, he frequently urged his fellow clergymen to guard their conversation, be wholly devoted to their calling as gospel ministers, and be separate from the world in order to be more faithful and fruitful ministers. See J. C. Ryle, *Be Thou an Example of the Believer in Word* (Weston-Super-Mare, U.K.: J. Whereat, 1853); and Ryle, "Give Thyself Wholly to Them."

22. For Aristotle's discussion of the causes of persuasiveness, see *Art of Rhetoric* 2.1, 141. One such example in Ryle can be found in a sermon with the provocative title "Living or Dead?" Ryle introduced the sermon with a searching question but then reminded his hearers: "If I say hard things, it is not because I do not love you. I write as I do, because I desire your salvation. He is your best friend, who tells you the most truth." Ryle, *Living or Dead?*, 3.

A third parallel between Ryle's homiletical theory and the classical rhetorical tradition is the structure of an oration. Cicero divided an oration into six parts: introduction (*exordium*), narrative (*narratio*), partition (*partitio*), confirmation (*confirmatio*), refutation (*refutatio*), and conclusion (*peroratio*).[23] Though many Victorian preachers abandoned the Ciceronian model and composed their sermons in accordance with literary conventions that governed nineteenth-century prose,[24] all of these elements are identifiable in almost every sermon Ryle preached.[25]

Ryle's use of the partition is of particular interest. The partition was considered unfashionable by Victorian homiletical theorists, and Ryle was aware of its unpopularity.[26] Nevertheless, he used the partition throughout his ministry. In 1882 Ryle could say, "For my own part, I honestly confess that I do not think I have preached two sermons in my life without divisions."[27] His use of the partition, despite its widespread unpopularity, is another indication of Ryle's indebtedness to his classical rhetorical training.

---

23. The *exordium* (introduction) introduces the oration, and its purpose is to bring the mind of the auditor into a proper condition to receive the speech. The narration follows the exordium and narrates what has happened or explains the nature of the case. In the partition, the third part of a speech, the orator previews or outlines the major arguments of his case. The fourth and largest part of a speech is the confirmation. In this part of the oration, the orator proves his case. The refutation, the fifth part of a speech, is devoted to refuting opponents. The peroration is the conclusion of the whole speech. See Cicero, *De Inventione* 1.20–109, 41–163.

24. Robert H. Ellison, *The Victorian Pulpit: Spoken and Written Sermons in Nineteenth-Century Britain* (London: Associated University Presses, 1998), 20.

25. It should be noted that refutation does not form a separate and distinct section in Ryle's sermons. Objections to specific arguments were typically answered as a part of the overall proof offered for a particular argument.

26. Ellison, *Victorian Pulpit*, 25. Ryle said, "There is a morbid dread of 'firstly, secondly, and thirdly' in many quarters. The stream of fashion runs strongly against divisions." Ryle, *Simplicity in Preaching*, 18.

27. Ryle, *Simplicity in Preaching*, 20. Examples of partitions abound in Ryle's printed sermons. For a few examples of partitions, see *Be Not Slothful, but Followers*; *Be Zealous*; *What Time Is It?* (London: William Hunt, 1854); *Have You Peace?* (London: William Hunt, 1854); and *He Whom Thou Lovest Is Sick*. It should be noted that when printed sermons were republished as tracts, the partitions were often removed.

A fourth parallel between Ryle's homiletical theory and the classical rhetorical tradition is the importance given to memory.[28] Classical rhetoricians tended to focus primarily on the orator and techniques he could use to help him recall his speech. Ryle's focus, however, was primarily on the hearer and techniques he could employ to help them recall his sermon. One of these techniques is the use of the partition. He defended the use of this unfashionable part of an oration precisely because it helped his audience remember his sermon.[29] Not only did he retain the partition but he made his main points short and simple, and he often repeated words or phrases to make them easy to remember.[30] His use of mnemonic devices was not limited to the partition. He used similar techniques to make important parts of his arguments memorable. For example, after arguing that true Christians come to God by faith in Christ, he defended his assertion in three successive paragraphs by arguing that "it is an old way," "it is a good way," and "it is a tried way."[31]

Finally, Ryle agreed with Cicero that the style and the substance of an oration must be audience appropriate. During his ministry in Helmingham, Ryle addressed a number of different audiences. In addition to his own congregation, he preached to clerical meetings, children, large working-class audiences, and supporters of various religious and charitable organizations. In each of these sermons, he

---

28. Memory was the fourth of Cicero's five canons of rhetoric, and he defined it as "the firm mental grasp of matter and words." His treatment of the subject in *De Inventione* and *De Oratore* focuses primarily on orators and techniques speakers can use to help them recall their speech. See Cicero, *De Inventione*, trans. H. M. Hubble, vol. 2, Loeb Classical Library (Cambridge, Mass.: Harvard University Press, 1976), 1.7.9. See also *De Oratore* 2.86.350–67.

29. Ryle, *Simplicity in Preaching*, 20: "I find it of the utmost importance to make people understand, remember, and carry away what I say, and I am certain divisions help me do so."

30. For example, the main points of his sermon "Be Not Slothful, but Followers" are (1) Warning Words, (2) Encouraging Words, (3) Quickening Words, (4) Words of Instruction, and (5) Words of Duty. Ryle, *Be Not Slothful, but Followers*, 9.

31. J. C. Ryle, "Able to Save," in *Home Truths, Seventh Series* (London: William Hunt, 1859), 171–72. Examples of this kind abound in Ryle's published sermons.

tailored his message specifically to these different groups of hearers. Perhaps the best example of this is his sermons for children.[32]

These sermons have the same persuasive goal, evangelical substance, and classical structure as the sermons he preached before his Sunday congregation in Helmingham. In terms of style, however, they are noticeably different. A number of typical elements are missing, such as multiple quotations from Scripture, allusions to the Old Testament, illustrations from church history, warnings against false teaching, and appeals to authorities outside the Bible. Instead, he spoke with greater warmness and tenderness, explained biblical terms and ideas by using illustrations and analogies from his listeners' world (like insects, animals, school, and family), and told memorable stories that often involved other children.

Attaining Simplicity in Preaching

Ryle discovered that his rural congregation in Exbury did not appreciate the ornamented style of Cicero, so he began to experiment with his style, language, and delivery. Through this process of trial and error, Ryle discovered how to capture the attention of his congregations, and he presented his findings years later in *Simplicity in Preaching*, a short manual on preaching.

In *Simplicity in Preaching*, Ryle offered five hints to young preachers to help them avoid his early mistakes and cultivate a simple preaching style. The first hint is to choose a text or topic that the preacher clearly understands. He warned them to avoid obscure passages and difficult subjects and to focus on the plain subjects of the Bible. Perhaps this explains why Ryle preached

---

32. See the following children's sermons by Ryle published at Helmingham: *Seeking the Lord Early* (1845); *Little and Wise* (London: William Hunt, 1851); *Children Walking in Truth* (1856); and *No More Crying* (1859). Ryle continued to preach and publish children's sermons as vicar of Stradbroke and as bishop of Liverpool. For published collections of Ryle's sermons for children, see *Sermons to Children* (New York: Protestant Episcopal Society for the Promotion of the Gospel, 1856); *The Two Bears, and Other Sermons for Children* (London: William Hunt, 1869); *Boys and Girls Playing, and Other Addresses to Children* (London: William Hunt, 1881).

topically and discouraged the practice of consecutive expository preaching. The second hint is to use simple words and plain common speech. "Dictionary words" may seem fine and sound grand, but they are rarely of any use to ordinary congregations.[33] The most powerful and forceful words are typically short, plain, and simple. The third hint is to aim for a simple style of composition. He urged preachers to beware of colons and semicolons and to never write long sentences or paragraphs. They should stick to commas and periods and write as if they were "asthmatical or short of breath." The fourth hint is to be direct. They should speak in terms of *I* and *you*, and not in vague plural numbers. Plain and direct speech is easily understood. The fifth hint is to make abundant use of anecdotes and illustrations, which shed light on the preacher's subject and grab people's attention. In short, they turn the ear into an eye.

Ryle's discovery of the virtue of simplicity was nothing new; it was a common feature of Victorian literature. Plainness, simplicity, and clarity were the basic principles of style for Victorian prose, and Victorian homileticians composed their sermons in accordance with these literary conventions.[34] In fact, the literary sermon became one of the distinguishing characteristics of Victorian preaching.[35] It is also noteworthy that at the end of *Simplicity in Preaching*, Ryle urged preachers to read and study works of literature such as John Bunyan's *Pilgrim's Progress*, the great speeches in

---

33. Ryle, *Simplicity in Preaching*, 23.

34. Ellison, *Victorian Pulpit*, 20, 30.

35. For surveys of Victorian preaching, see Edwin Charles Dargan, *From the Close of the Reformation to the End of the Nineteenth Century 1572–1900*, vol. 2 of *A History of Preaching* (New York: Hodder and Stoughton, 1912); Horton Davies, *Worship and Theology in England: From Watts and Wesley to Martineau, 1690–1900*, combined ed. (Grand Rapids: Eerdmans, 1996); O. C. Edwards Jr., *A History of Preaching* (Nashville: Abingdon, 2004); Robert H. Ellison, ed., *A New History of the Sermon: The Nineteenth Century* (Leiden: Brill, 2010); and especially *Victorian Pulpit*; Keith A. Francis, and William Gibson, eds., *The Oxford Handbook of the British Sermon 1689–1901* (Oxford: Oxford University Press, 2012); Hughes Oliphant Old, *The Modern Age*, vol. 6 of *The Reading and Preaching of the Scriptures in the Worship of the Christian Church* (Grand Rapids: Eerdmans, 2007).

Shakespeare, and the writings of William Cobbett and John Bright, in order to "attain a good style of composition in preaching."[36]

Ryle abhorred essay-like sermons. They were blunt swords and headless arrows that did not awaken sinners or edify saints. But his preaching was influenced by Victorian print culture more, perhaps, than he realized. Whether it was simply a result of trial and error or reading and study, or both, the simple preaching style Ryle developed at Helmingham was Victorian as well as classical. Perhaps his crucified sermons were able to keep and hold the attention of his hearers precisely because they resembled the other forms of literature his parishioners read on a regular basis.

A Rhetorical Comparison

At some point in each of their careers, John Henry Newman, Charles Haddon Spurgeon, and J. C. Ryle preached and published sermons on John 11:1–44. Newman preached "The Tears of Christ at the Grave of Lazarus" sometime between 1825 and 1843 and published it in volume 3 of *Parochial and Plain Sermons*. Spurgeon preached "A Mystery! Saints Sorrowing and Jesus Glad!" at the Metropolitan Tabernacle on August 7, 1864, and published it in volume 10 of the *Metropolitan Tabernacle Pulpit*. J. C. Ryle preached "He Whom Thou Lovest Is Sick" in October 1858 at St. Mary's, Nottingham, on behalf of the county hospital and published it as a tract in the following year under the same name. By comparing these three sermons on the same text, I hope to place Ryle in his rhetorical and homiletical context.

Even though all three sermons are based on the same well-known text, there is only one rhetorical feature common to all of them: each sermon concludes with an exhortation (application). Newman brought his sermon to a close by urging his hearers to "take to [themselves] these comfortable thoughts, both in the

---

36. Ryle, *Simplicity in Preaching*, 44.

contemplation of our own death, or upon the death of our friends."[37] Like Newman, Spurgeon and Ryle concluded their sermons with calls to action. Spurgeon concluded by reminding his congregation that the one thing needful to eternal life is faith in Christ. Ryle, on the other hand, concluded with applications directed at four different kinds of hearers.[38]

The structure of the sermons is considerably different. Apart from the conclusion, there are no discernible elements of the Ciceronian parts of an oration in Newman's sermon. It can be outlined as follows:

Question: why did our Lord weep at the grave of Lazarus?

1. First of all, as the context informs us, He wept from very sympathy with the grief of others.

2. But next, we may suppose (if it is allowable to conjecture), that His pity, thus spontaneously excited, was led forward to dwell on the various circumstances in man's condition which excite pity.

3. Here I have suggested another thought which admits of being dwelt upon. Christ was come to do a deed of mercy, and it was a secret in His own breast.

4. Alas! There were other thoughts still to call forth His tears. This marvelous benefit to the forlorn sisters, how was it to be attained? At His own cost. Joseph knew he could bring joy to his brethren, but at no sacrifice of his own. Christ was bringing life to the dead by His own death.

---

37. John Henry Newman, "Tears of Christ and the Grave of Lazarus," in *Parochial and Plain Sermons* (London: Rivingtons, 1877), 3:128–38.

38. Everyone is urged to consider what they will do when they are ill. Those who are not prepared to meet God are counseled to repent and believe in Christ immediately. Sick Christians are reminded how much they may glorify God in times of illness. Finally, all Christians are exhorted to keep up close communion with Christ, which alone can provide peace in times of sickness. See Ryle, *He Whom Thou Lovest Is Sick*, 18–24.

Conclusion: Let us take to ourselves these comfortable thoughts, both in the contemplation of our own death, or upon the death of our friends.[39]

Newman's sermon is essentially a literary essay. He began with a question and then provided answers to it that built on one another, which made his sermon both linear and progressive. He did not use mnemonic devices or address the audience until the conclusion. In sum, his sermon is a sustained meditation on the text with the application coming only at the end. Newman wrote complete sermon manuscripts beforehand, and his preaching consisted of reading them aloud to his congregation. His personal piety and theological insight, as opposed to rhetorical fireworks, made his sermons compelling.

Spurgeon's sermon, on the other hand, contains three of the six parts of an oration: introduction, exposition, and conclusion. It can be outlined as follows:

Introduction

I. Jesus Christ designed the death of Lazarus and his after resurrection FOR THE STRENGTHENING OF THE FAITH OF THE APOSTLES.

   a. Let us observe that *the trial itself would certainly tend to increase the apostles' faith.*
      i.   *Trial takes away many of the impediments of faith.*
      ii. Nor is *affection of small service to faith, when it exposes the weakness of the creature.*
      iii. Furthermore, trial is of special service to faith when *it drives her to God.*
      iv. And then *trial has a hardening effect upon faith.*

   b. But not to tarry here, let us notice that the *deliverance which Christ wrought by the resurrection of Lazarus, was calculated also to strengthen the faith of the apostles.*
      i.   Here *divine sympathy became most manifest.*

---

39. Newman, "Tears of Christ and the Grave of Lazarus," 128–38.

ii. What an exhibition these disciples had of *the divine power* as well as divine sympathy.

II. Jesus Christ had an eye also to THE GOOD OF THE FAMILY.

    a. Mary and Martha had faith, but it was not very strong, for they suspected Christ's *love*...[and] they certainly *doubted* his power.

    b. They were three *special favourites* upon whom very distinguishing regard was set, and therefore it was that he sent them a *special trial*.

        i. Special trial was attended with a *special visit*.

        ii. This special visit was attended with *special fellowship*.

        iii. And soon you shall have *special deliverance*.

III. Now I come to the third point.... This trouble was permitted for GIVING FAITH TO OTHERS.

    a. Afflictions often lead men to faith in Christ because *they give space for thought*.

    b. Afflictions lead men to faith full often *by preventing sin*.

    c. Troubles, again, often bring men to believe in Jesus because they compel them *to stand face to face with stern realities*.

    d. Trials *tend to make men believe in Christ when they are followed by deliverances*.

Conclusion[40]

Spurgeon introduced his sermon with a lengthy, two-page embellishment of the death of Lazarus, which he concluded by setting forth the main point of the sermon: "We have thus plainly before us the principle, that our Lord in his infinite wisdom and superabundant love, sets so high a value upon his people's faith, that he will not screen them from those trials by which faith is strengthened."[41] He presented his main points in the final paragraph

---

40. C. H. Spurgeon, "A Mystery! Saints Sorrowing and Jesus Glad!," in vol. 10 of *The Metropolitan Tabernacle Pulpit* (Pasadena, Tex.: Pilgrim Publications, 1969), 461–72. Italics original.

41. Spurgeon, "Mystery!," 463.

of the introduction, but they do not form a separate partition. The exposition of his sermon is built around three main points that demonstrate how trials benefit three different groups of people in the text of John 11. He apparently chose these main points based on their placement in the text and not on a logical relationship between each group of people. His conclusion, like Newman's, is a short, one-paragraph exhortation, but unlike Newman, Spurgeon spread personal applications throughout his sermon. Spurgeon also employed mnemonic devices in various places. The division of the sermon into heads or divisions that were announced ahead of time is itself a mnemonic device. He repeated words and phrases such as *faith*, *trials*, *affliction*, and *special*, and he frequently under-scored an important assertion by asking questions in different ways or restating the point in different terms.

Ryle's sermon is the most classical of the three. It contains all six parts of a Ciceronian oration. It can be outlined as follows:

Introduction
Narrative
Partition
Confirmation

    I. The *universal prevalence of sickness.*
      a. Sickness is everywhere.
      b. Sickness is among all classes.
      c. Sickness is of every sort and description.
      d. Sickness is often one of the most humbling and distressing trials that can come upon man.
      e. Sickness is not preventable by anything that man can do.
      f. Now what can we make of this great fact?...I answer, in a word, it is sin.
      g. [Digression: refutation of atheism and deism:] Reader, I pause for a moment at this point, and yet in pausing, I do not depart from my subject.
        i. Reader, you have doubtless heard of Atheists.
        ii. Reader, you have doubtless heard of Deists.
        iii. The universal prevalence of sickness is one of the indi-rect evidences that the Bible is true.

      iv. Reader, stand fast on the old ground that the Bible, and
          the Bible only, is God's revelation of Himself to man.

II. The *general benefits* which sickness confers on mankind.
    a. Sickness helps to *remind men of death*.
    b. Sickness helps to make man *think seriously* of God, and
       their souls, and the world to come.
    c. Sickness helps to *soften men's hearts*, and teach them
       wisdom.
    d. Sickness helps to *level and humble us*.
    e. Finally, sickness helps *to try men's religion*, of what sort it is.

III. The *specific duties* to which sickness calls us.
    a. One paramount duty which the prevalence of sickness
       entails on man, is that of *living habitually prepared to
       meet God.*
    b. Another paramount duty which the prevalence of sick-
       ness entails on you, is that of *living habitually ready to
       bear it patiently.*
    c. One more paramount duty which the prevalence of sick-
       ness entails on you, is that of *habitual readiness to feel
       with and help your fellow men.*

Conclusion[42]

    Ryle introduced the sermon by pointing out the uniqueness of
the text and then placed the sermon text in context in the narrative.
After the narrative, Ryle summarized the point of the sermon: "I
invite your attention this day to the subject of sickness. The subject
is one which we ought frequently to look in the face. We cannot
avoid it. It needs no prophet's eye to see sickness coming to each
of us in turn one day.… Let us turn aside for a few moments, and
consider sickness as Christians."[43] In the partition, he presented his
main points by listing them with roman numerals and indenting
them to set them off from the rest of the text. Ryle's main points are

---

42. J. C. Ryle, *He Whom Thou Lovest Is Sick*, 3–24. Italics original.
43. Ryle, *He Whom Thou Lovest Is Sick*, 4.

not specifically derived from the text of John 11, like Spurgeon's, but are related to the subject of sickness. Moreover, they build on each other, like Newman's, and flow from the general observations to particular duties. Under his first main point, Ryle digressed into an extended refutation of atheism and deism. His conclusion is more extensive than either Newman's or Spurgeon's. Ryle's extensive use of mnemonic devices is also noteworthy. The partition is an aid to memory, and it is made even more memorable by the repetition of the word *sickness* and the descending order of the points from "universal prevalence," to "general benefits," to "specific duties." The subpoints under each main point are framed to be easily remembered: they begin the same way and repeat words and phrases. Like Spurgeon, Ryle underscored important ideas by asking questions and restating the assertion with different words.

The style of the sermon is considerably different as well. Though all three sermons contain fairly simple speech and plain words, they differ in terms of topic complexity/simplicity, composition, and directness. Spurgeon's and Ryle's sermon topics are relatively simple. Spurgeon discussed how trials increase faith, and Ryle discussed sickness. Newman's topic, on the other hand, is considerably more complex. The central question of the sermon is motive. Why did Christ weep at the grave of Lazarus? In order to answer it he appealed to the *communicatio idiomatum*—the relationship between the divine and human attributes of Christ.[44] Though his answers are compelling, even a university audience might find this

---

44. For example, in explaining his second answer ("But next, we may suppose [if it is allowable to conjecture], that His pity, thus spontaneously excited, was led forward to dwell on the various circumstances in man's condition which excite pity") he said, "Here He had incommunicable thoughts with His Eternal Father. He would not tell them why it was; He chose another course for taking away their doubts and complaints. 'He opened not His mouth,' but He wrought wondrously." Newman, "Tears of Christ and the Grave of Lazarus," 134.

topic challenging. At the very least, it was not simple—which he readily acknowledged in the first paragraph.[45]

The composition of the sermons themselves provides a contrast. Both Newman and Ryle composed complete manuscripts before preaching and used them to various degrees in their delivery. Newman read his sermons aloud without oratorical display. Ryle, on the other hand, read them with a "good deal of earnestness and fire."[46] Spurgeon's sermons were delivered completely extempore, and he was mildly contemptuous of manuscript writers.[47] Their differing style of composition is even more revealing.

Table 1. An analysis of the composition of sermons preached by J. H. Newman, C. H. Spurgeon, and J. C. Ryle on John 11:1–44

	Word count	Number of paragraphs	Number of sentences	Avg. words per sentence
J. H. Newman	3,129	17	103	30.37
C. H. Spurgeon	7,093	27	293	24.21
J. C. Ryle	7,586	69	505	15.02

45. He wrote, "In attempting any answer to this inquiry, we should ever remember that the thoughts of our Saviour's mind are far beyond our comprehension." Newman, "Tears of Christ and the Grave of Lazarus," 128.

46. Ryle, *Autobiography*, 113.

47. *C. H. Spurgeon Autobiography*, rev. ed. (1897–1900; repr., Edinburgh: Banner of Truth, 2005), 1:268:

> But I do not see why a man cannot speak extemporaneously upon a subject which he fully understands. Any tradesman, well versed in his line of business, could explain it without needing to retire for meditation, and surely I ought to be equally familiar with the first principles of our holy faith; I ought not to feel at a loss when called upon to speak upon topics which constitute the daily bread of my soul. I do not see what benefit is gained, in such a case, by the mere manual labour of writing before speaking, because, in so doing a man would write extemporaneously, and extemporaneous writing is likely to be even feebler than extemporaneous speech.

First, both Spurgeon and Ryle were considerably more verbose than Newman. Their sermons were more than twice as long as his. This difference may be attributable to different attitudes toward the place of preaching in worship. For a high churchman like Newman (his conversion to Roman Catholicism took place in 1845), preaching was important but not preeminent. For evangelical Protestants with Puritan sympathies (Spurgeon and Ryle), the preached word was the chief means of grace and, thus, the single most important work of the Christian minister. Second, Ryle used more paragraphs than Newman and Spurgeon combined, and thus his were considerably shorter on average. Though Newman's sermon was about 41 percent the length of Ryle's, if his use of paragraphs remained constant, he would add only twenty-five more paragraphs if it were expanded to the length of Ryle's. That would still leave a deficit of twenty-seven. The comparison with Spurgeon is more illuminating. Though their sermons are fairly close in length, Ryle used two and a half times more paragraphs than Spurgeon. Finally, Ryle spoke and wrote in shorter sentences than either Newman or Spurgeon. Newman averaged more than thirty words per sentence, and Spurgeon was close behind, averaging more than twenty-four. Ryle averaged roughly fifteen words per sentence, which made them twice as short as Newman's and 1.6 times shorter than Spurgeon's. Ryle's use of short paragraphs and sentences sets him apart stylistically from both Newman and Spurgeon.

Ryle and Spurgeon were much more direct than Newman. The word *you* appears in Newman's sermon only three times. *We*, however, appears fifty-five times in his short sermon. Furthermore, he only specifically addressed his audience in the opening and closing sections, as previously noted. Ryle and Spurgeon, on the other hand, repeatedly and directly addressed their audience throughout their sermons. Second-person plural forms (*you*, *your*, *thee*, *thou*, and *reader*), searching questions, and direct commands abound in both sermons. Perhaps the only significant difference between Ryle and Spurgeon in this respect is their concluding exhortation. Ryle's is longer and more specific than Spurgeon's, but the difference could be explained by the different focus of each sermon. Spurgeon was focused more narrowly on Christians while Ryle addressed the topic of sickness more generally.

In sum, the structure of Ryle's sermon is more classical than that of either Newman or Spurgeon. Stylistically, in some respects he is like both men, but in others he is unique. Like Newman, Ryle wrote and read his Sunday sermons. Like Spurgeon, Ryle repeatedly addressed his audience throughout his message. Ryle's preaching, however, appears to be simpler in terms of composition than either Newman's or Spurgeon's. He used more and thus shorter paragraphs than either of them, and his sentences were, on average, considerably shorter as well.

Ryle's Popularity as a Preacher

After Ryle found his voice as a preacher, popularity soon followed. He quickly filled his church in Helmingham, and roughly 80 percent of the village population came to hear him preach each Sunday afternoon.[48] As his reputation grew, so did the crowds. Visitors came from neighboring villages to hear him preach, and benches had to be placed in the aisles to accommodate the crowds. During this time Ryle became acquainted with most of the leading evangelicals in Suffolk, and he began the habit of speaking and preaching wherever and whenever the opportunity presented itself.[49] He addressed various evangelical societies, such as the British Reformation Society, the Colonial Church and School Society, the Church of England Young Men's Society, and the London Society for Promoting Christianity among the Jews, as well as local and aggregate clerical meetings. He also helped found the Special Services for the Working Classes in 1856, which went on to become an organized institution of the Church of England.[50]

---

48. Timmins, *Suffolk Returns from the Census of Religious Worship, 1851*, xxvii.

49. Ryle, *Autobiography*, 118.

50. These special mission services were an experiment that was born out of a

Personal tragedy led to increased popularity. Ryle's first wife, Matilda Charlotte Louisa Plumptre, died in 1848, a year after giving birth to their first child, Georgina. He married Jessie Walker in 1850, but she was chronically ill for the duration of their marriage and died of Bright's disease in 1860. During the 1850s the Ryles frequently stayed in London for months at a time in order for Jessie to deliver babies or convalesce. As a result of these extended London residencies, Ryle became acquainted with the leading evangelical clergy and laymen in the city and was continually asked to preach and speak. He later reckoned that he spoke in more than sixty church pulpits in London during the 1850s.[51]

After Helmingham, Ryle's popularity as a preacher continued to grow. He became a regular platform speaker for most of the leading evangelical and missionary societies, such as the Church Missionary Society, the Church Pastoral Aid Society, the Colonial and Continental Church Society, and the Islington Clerical Conference. He was chosen to be the select preacher for the University of Cambridge in 1873 and 1874, and he was awarded the same honor by the University of Oxford in 1874, 1875, 1876, 1879, and 1880. As the bishop of Liverpool, he preached regularly and drew large crowds well into his eighties. In short, Ryle's preaching played an important part in his rise to party and then national church leadership.

In 1884 the editors of the *Contemporary Pulpit* asked readers to send in lists of the greatest living English-speaking Protestant

---

clerical meeting in 1856. Hugh M'Neile, canon of Chester (1845–1868), John Cale Miller, incumbent of St. Martin's Birmingham, and Ryle decided that the best way to economize their strength and reach the masses was to open a large church in one of the big manufacturing towns and conduct special services for the working classes for five or six consecutive nights. The first of these was held in Birmingham at St. Martin's Church, and all three men spoke. After Birmingham, they went on to organize similar services in Ipswich, Islington, and then at Exeter Hall. Though many people initially predicted failure, the services proved to be remarkably successful, ultimately becoming an organized institution of the Church of England. For a brief history of the origin of these services, see J. C. Ryle, "What Is Our Position?," in *Home Truths, Seventh Series* (London: William Hunt, 1859), 253–54.

51. Ryle, *Autobiography*, 132.

preachers. Ryle did not make the list.[52] Many of the top ten were
London ministers, and almost all preached in large cities. In 1884
Ryle was the bishop of a large city, but most of his ministerial career
up to that point had been spent in small, rural parishes. Furthermore, in that same year Gladstone was publicly denouncing the
diocese of Liverpool, and its bishop by implication, as a disgrace
to the nation. Nevertheless, with the exception of C. H. Spurgeon's
sermons, Ryle's sermons are probably more widely read than anyone's on the list. Moreover, his *Simplicity in Preaching* continues
to be used in seminary classrooms more than 130 years since its
publication. Ryle was by no means the most popular preacher of
Victorian Britain. He was, however, one of the most popular and
influential preachers of the evangelical party in the mid to late Victorian era, and his sermons, which make up most of the chapters
of his popular works, continue to be read today.

---

52. The rankings are as follows:

1. Henry Parry Liddon, canon of St. Paul's, London
2. C. H. Spurgeon
3. Joseph Parker of London's City Temple
4. Alexander Maclaren of Manchester's Union Chapel
5. Frederic William Farrar, canon of Westminster
6. Henry Ward Beecher
7. William Magee, bishop of Peterborough
8. William J. Knox-Litte
9. William Boyd Carpenter, canon of Windsor
10. R. W. Dale, Carr's Lane Birmingham

3

Pastor

Thanks to the small size and good working order of his parish, J. C. Ryle had time to begin a writing ministry at Helmingham. He began publishing sermons as early as 1845, and within four years he was publishing material regularly. It became a normal part of his regular pastoral work from that time forward. From 1849 until his death in 1900, Ryle published at least one work every year.

The transition from preacher to author went fairly smoothly. Ryle's growing popularity as a preacher, coupled with his evangelical connections in Suffolk and London, created a market for his works. Furthermore, his simple style of composition was well adapted to the tastes of Victorian readers. It also meant that he would not have to spend excessive amounts of time editing his sermons. Naturally, he began by publishing his sermons, but shortly thereafter he began converting them into evangelistic tracts. In 1849 he compiled and published his first hymnbook, and in 1856 he published the first installment of his *Expository Thoughts on the Gospels*. These new publishing ventures—tracts, hymnbooks, and commentaries—increased his popularity among evangelicals and expanded his influence outside his parish, but they were originally written to supplement his regular pastoral work and to provide spiritual guidance, and as such, they provide valuable insight into his pastoral theology.

Evangelical Tracts

After ordination, Ryle began distributing tracts as part of his regular program of pastoral care in Exbury. He distributed tracts published by the Religious Tract Society and discussed their contents with his parishioners when he made his weekly pastoral visits.[1] He purchased them in bulk in Southampton and circulated them among the families because he was too poor to give them away.[2] He continued to distribute tracts in conjunction with pastoral visits for the rest of his ministry. The pastoral advantages to tract distribution were many. They could be read by those who were unable or unwilling to come to church. They provided safe reading material for the faithful. They offered spiritual guidance to those who needed it. They promoted spiritual conversation within the home. They also served as edifying conversational topics for pastoral visits.

---

1. Hannah More (1745–1833) was one of the earliest and most influential evangelical tract writers. She wrote dozens of loyalist, moral, and Christian tales specifically for the lower classes to "supplant the multitude of vicious tracts circulated by hawkers, and to supply, instead of them, some useful reading, which may be likely to prove entertaining also." They were published anonymously as *Cheap Repository Tracts*. A total of 114 were sold for a halfpenny or a penny every month from 1795 to 1798. They were funded by subscriptions and distributed by booksellers across the country. More contributed forty-nine tracts and masterminded the whole operation. The tracts were wildly popular, and nearly two million were sold by the end of their first year of publication. The popularity of *Cheap Repository Tracts* paved the way for the creation of the Religious Tract Society, founded in 1799. While many evangelicals rejoiced in the wide diffusion of More's tracts, many regretted that they did not contain a "fuller statement of the great evangelical principles of Christian truth." Therefore, the Religious Tract Society was founded to produce cheap tracts of a more decidedly religious character. The founding committee insisted that good tracts are characterized by three qualities. They must contain "pure truth." There should be "some account of the way of a sinner's salvation in every tract." Finally, they must be plain: "Perspicuity here is, next to truth, the first quality of a good tract." By its jubilee memorial in 1850, the Religious Tract Society had distributed over 500 million copies of religious tracts and books in 110 languages and could boast of 1,202,242 pounds, 13 shillings, and 8 pence in total receipts. See [Hannah More?], *Cheap Repository Tracts: Entertaining, Moral, and Religious*, new ed. (London: Law and Gilbert, 1807), iv–v; and William Jones, *The Jubilee Memorial of the Religious Tract Society: Containing a Record of Its Origin, Proceedings, and Results AD 1799 to AD 1849* (London: Religious Tract Society, 1850), 12, 18–19.

2. Ryle, *Autobiography*, 101.

In November 1843 Ryle published his first tract, *A Minister's Parting Words to the Inhabitants of Exbury*, which was his farewell address to the district. When he came to Helmingham in 1844, he immediately began publishing his own material for the benefit of his parishioners. The first of these tracts was his inaugural address: *I Have Somewhat to Say unto Thee*. After penning a popular tract about the uncertainty of life following the Great Yarmouth disaster,[3] he was asked to edit a new evangelical magazine. He declined the offer but proposed a new series of tracts instead. Being unable to secure any financial assistance for this project, he continued alone and thus embarked on what would prove to be one of his most fruitful endeavors. He went on to publish more than two hundred tracts. Some, like *Do You Pray?* and *Living or Dead?*, sold more than one hundred thousand copies over the years. *What Do We Owe to the Reformation?* sold more than eighty thousand copies in a single year.[4] By 1897 it was estimated that more than twelve million copies of his tracts had been sold, and many had been translated into other languages.[5]

Ryle's tracts may be divided into three categories: published sermons, occasional tracts, and controversial writings. Most of Ryle's tracts were originally sermons. This was especially true of the tracts written in Helmingham. In a Christmas sermon in 1859, Ryle noted, "The old marble statues in Helmingham church have heard the substance of every tract I have ever written."[6] Therefore,

---

3. On May 2, 1845, a large crowd gathered to celebrate the opening of the Great Yarmouth suspension bridge over the River Bure. Hundreds flocked onto the bridge to see a circus clown in a geese-drawn tub pass by underneath, and the large number of people caused the bridge to collapse. Seventy-nine people died in the accident, including fifty-nine children. M. Guthrie Clark and Eric Russell incorrectly state the date and the number of fatalities of the Great Yarmouth disaster in their biographies.

4. Alan Munden, "J. C. Ryle—The Prince of Tract-writers," *Churchman* 119 (2005): 7.

5. G. R. Balleine, *A History of the Evangelical Party in the Church of England* (London: Longmans, Green, 1908), 278.

6. J. C. Ryle, *Come! A Christmas Invitation* (Ipswich: William Hunt, 1859), 10.

in terms of style and substance, they are identical to Ryle's sermons. In most instances, the only alteration that takes place is substituting "Dear Reader" for "My Dear Friends and Brethren." When he went beyond adjusting the title, he typically added quotes in footnotes from important Anglican authorities.[7]

In addition to publishing sermons as tracts, Ryle produced a number of tracts in response to noteworthy public events. As mentioned previously, one of his earliest tracts was occasional in nature. He wrote an anonymous evangelistic tract about the brevity of life in response to the Great Yarmouth disaster of 1845. In 1866 he wrote two similar tracts in response to the cattle plague and an outbreak of cholera.[8] He also wrote a tract in defense of clergymen who opposed Gladstone in the parliamentary elections of 1868 titled *Strike: But Hear!* Given the popularity of these kinds of tracts (*This Is the Finger of God* went through at least eight editions and sold at least forty thousand copies), it is surprising that Ryle produced so few of them.

The third category of tracts Ryle composed was controversial in nature. As his influence spread, he was regarded as an emerging leader of the evangelical party. As a party leader, it was only natural that he address the controversial issues facing evangelical churchmen. Tracts were his preferred method of addressing them. He published tracts written from an evangelical perspective to address ritualism, Church reform, diocesan conferences, Church congresses, Church-chapel relations, biblical inspiration, and

---

7. For example, in *Are You Forgiven?* (Ipswich: William Hunt, 1849), Ryle adds a number of fairly extensive quotes in footnotes from the Homilies, Richard Hooker, Bishop Latimer, Bishop Hooper, Bishop Beveridge, Bishop Hall, Archbishop Cranmer, Archbishop Usher, Archbishop Leighton, and Archbishop Sandys. Ryle's purpose in doing so seems obvious—he wanted to demonstrate that his view of human depravity and justification was the view of the leading theological authorities of the Church of England.

8. See J. C. Ryle, *This Is the Finger of God! Being Thoughts on the Cattle Plague* (London: William Hunt, 1866); and J. C. Ryle, *The Hand of the Lord! Being Thoughts on Cholera* (London: William Hunt, 1866).

competing systems of holiness. Ryle was involved in nearly every Church controversy of his day, and he typically laid out his position to the public in the form of tracts.

Many of Ryle's tracts went on to become the chapters of his books. From 1851 to 1871, his publisher, William Hunt, published collections of his tracts in an eight-volume series titled *Home Truths*.[9] Alan Munden argues that this series represents Ryle's most significant publication, for "it represented the essence of Ryle's Reformed theology."[10] While the place of *Home Truths* in Ryle's corpus is debatable, these volumes contain perhaps the clearest and fullest presentation of his theology in a noncontroversial context. Many of the tracts that were included in *Home Truths* reappeared in his more well-known works such as *Knots Untied*, *Old Paths*, *Practical Religion*, and *Holiness*.[11]

Before considering the contributions of the tracts, it is worth asking what made Ryle's tracts so popular. They were solidly evangelical and cheap (they typically cost a penny), but there were many other cheap, evangelical tracts that were far less popular. The popularity of Ryle's tracts is probably attributable to three primary factors. The first is their style. Like his sermons, the tracts were simple, easily understood, and direct. They communicated the essentials of the evangelical gospel in a way that could be understood by ordinary people. For example, George Everard, vicar of St. Mark's Wolverhampton, discovered that Ryle's tracts were particularly useful in reaching the working classes in his large, industrial parish. Captain Hedley Vicars distributed them among his troops during the Crimean War. *The Christian Observer* even encouraged Christian writers who labored for the poor and young to model the style and

---

9. See J. C. Ryle, *Home Truths: Being Miscellaneous Addresses and Tracts by the Rev. J. C. Ryle, B.A.* 8 vols. (Ipswich: W. Hunt and Sons, 1852–1872).

10. Munden, "J. C. Ryle," 10.

11. Munden points out that of the seventy-nine chapters that appear in the aforementioned works, forty-eight were originally published in *Home Truths*. Munden, "J. C. Ryle," 10.

diction of Ryle's tracts.[12] In short, Ryle's simple style of composition was able to win the attention of readers as well as hearers.

Second, Ryle's written sermons proved to be remarkably well suited to the Religious Tract Society's (RTS) product design and selling strategy.[13] The RTS insisted that a quality tract have three ingredients: pure evangelical truth, an evangelistic thrust, and simplicity. Ryle's sermons, both in terms of style and substance, met these criteria with little to no alteration. Therefore, it is not surprising that the evangelical publisher William Hunt was interested in publishing his sermons as tracts.[14]

Third, as Joseph Stubenrauch has noted, in order to provide meaningful profit for the seller, a religious tract needed to catch a potential customer's attention and be entertaining enough to encourage the customer to make repeat purchases. Therefore, the most popular tracts among tract hawkers were those that had catchy titles, discussed calamitous events, and were tailored to a variety of social and cultural niches.[15] Again, Ryle's sermons were easily adaptable to this selling strategy. He gave his sermons catchy, direct, and often confrontational titles.[16] He discussed sensational current events, such as the cholera outbreaks and plagues, as well as hot-button theological issues and political events. Furthermore, he addressed a variety of sermons to social and cultural niches such as parents, young men, children, and churchmen.

---

12. *Christian Observer*, January 1851: 64.

13. For an excellent study of the RTS's product design and selling strategy, see Joseph Stubenrauch, "Silent Preachers in the Age of Ingenuity: Faith, Commerce, and Religious Tracts in Early Nineteenth-Century Britain," *Church History* 80 (2011): 547–74.

14. For a brief history of Ryle's relationship with his publisher William Hunt, see Alan Munden, *Bishop J. C. Ryle: Prince of Tract Writers* (Leominster, U.K.: Day One Publications, 2012), 83.

15. Stubenrauch, "Silent Preachers in the Age of Ingenuity," 555, 567.

16. Note the titles of the following tracts by Ryle: *Living or Dead?*; *Are You Forgiven?*; *Wheat or Chaff?*; *Shall You Be Saved?*; *Peace! Be Still!*; *Strive!*; *Keep It Holy!*

So what did tract writing contribute to Ryle's ministry? There are at least three noteworthy contributions. First and foremost, tract writing and distribution helped him fulfill his pastoral responsibilities to his district. He began circulating tracts as part of his regular pastoral work in Exbury, and he continued to do so in Helmingham and beyond. Tracts reached people his sermons did not, and by publishing and distributing his own tracts, he could provide spiritual guidance throughout the week. Unfortunately, I have been unable to find any record of the impact Ryle's tracts had on his own parishioners, although there is abundant testimony about the impact they had on readers beyond the boundaries of his parish. But his continuing to write and distribute tracts throughout his ministry is a good indicator of his estimate of their usefulness. Practical usefulness—doing good to souls—was the standard by which he judged everything in ministry. If tract writing and distributing was not practically useful, he probably would have abandoned the practice. In many respects, the question of effectiveness is beside the point. Tracts provided spiritual guidance—guidance he did not receive at home, church, or school. Books, it must be remembered, were his only spiritual guides and companions for a formative portion of his pilgrimage. Through tracts Ryle provided spiritual guidance for those, like him, who had no guides.

Second, Ryle's tracts were the means of converting many souls to Christ. Testimonies abound to the converting power of his tracts. For example, a ritualist clergyman, Canon W. J. Knox-Little, told the Swansea Church Congress, "When I was a lad awakening to the deeper thoughts of spiritual things…groping about in the dark for something to get hold of, it was one of those beautiful tracts of Canon Ryle's that was my guide, and as long as I live I shall respect and love him for the sake of the tract that did me so much good."[17]

Perhaps the most memorable of these accounts is the conversion of a Dominican priest who read one of Ryle's tracts (*Are*

---

17. *Nineteenth Annual Church Congress Held at Swansea*, 397.

You Forgiven?) on his way to stamp out a reform movement in the Roman Catholic Church in Mexico. He was converted after reading the tract and continued to foster the movement he originally intended to destroy. The Protestant church that was born as a result grew to over forty thousand members by the end of the nineteenth century.[18] Even years after Ryle's death, his successor in Liverpool, Bishop F. J. Chavasse, received letters from all over the world thanking Ryle for the spiritual guidance his tracts provided.

Third, the tracts Ryle published at Helmingham brought him almost immediate fame. He became a well-known clergyman in Suffolk and London as a result of his preaching, but his tracts made him a household name, especially in evangelical households throughout Great Britain and its colonies. As early as 1851, *The Christian Observer* was praising his tracts and holding them out as a model for style and diction. By 1853 it was discussing "the great charm of these tracts" and "the spell which binds the eyes and thoughts and feelings to every page."[19] By the time Ryle left Helmingham in 1861, he was a bona fide evangelical celebrity. By the time of his death in 1900, he was regarded as the "Prince of Tract-writers."[20]

Expository Thoughts on the Gospels

In addition to distributing tracts, Ryle delivered two midweek expository lectures as part of his regular pastoral work in Exbury. He continued the practice in Winchester and lectured regularly in Helmingham and beyond. In the early 1850s, Ryle began a new publishing venture: he wrote a series of expository tracts that would go on to become his *Expository Thoughts on the Gospels*. This commentary series ran to seven volumes and was finally completed

---

18. A. R. M. Finlayson, "Address on the Church and the Printing Press," in *The Official Report of the Church Congress Held at Portsmouth* (London: Bemrose and Sons, 1885), 374.

19. *Christian Observer*, January 1851: 64; April 1853: 221–22.

20. Balleine, *History of the Evangelical Party*, 272.

in 1873. A commentary on the Acts of the Apostles was planned but never completed. The purpose of this project was to provide suitable reading for family prayers, aid those who visited the sick and poor, and furnish devotional readers of the Gospels with a profitable companion. His "chief desire" was to lead his readers to "Christ and faith in Him, to repentance and holiness, and to the Bible and to prayer."[21] Though Ryle maintained this focus throughout, the series evolved considerably over time.

The first installment, *Expository Thoughts on the Gospel of St. Matthew*, appeared in 1856. In the preface he explained that the work is not a "learned, critical commentary," nor is it a "continuous and homiletic exposition." Ryle divided the biblical text into short sections (usually around twelve verses), provided a brief explanation of the main scope and purpose of the passage, and then selected a few prominent doctrinal or practical points to draw plainly and vigorously to the reader's attention.[22] He generally limited himself to "things needful to salvation" and thus passed over secondary matters.[23] The style and composition of the commentaries are nearly identical to his sermons and tracts. He endeavored to be "plain and pointed" and chose "picked and packed words" to arrest the attention of his audience. His aim was to "say something that might strike and stick in consciences" because he was convinced that "a few points, well remembered and fastened down, are better than a quantity of truth lying loosely and thinly scattered over the mind."[24]

A good example of Ryle's exposition can be found in his commentary on the miracle of the feeding of the five thousand in Matthew 14:13–21. He began with a brief summary of the miracle and its significance: "These verses contain one of our Lord

---

21. J. C. Ryle, *St. Mark, Expository Thoughts on the Gospel: For Family and Private Use* (Ipswich: William Hunt, 1857), vi.

22. J. C. Ryle, *St. Matthew, Expository Thoughts on the Gospel: For Family and Private Use* (Ipswich: William Hunt, 1856), iv.

23. Ryle, *St. Matthew*, iv.

24. Ryle, *St. Matthew*, iv–v.

Jesus Christ's greatest miracles.... Of all the miracles worked by our Lord, not one is so often mentioned in the New Testament as this." Therefore, "it is plain that this event in our Lord's history is intended to receive special attention. Let us give it that attention, and see what we may learn."[25] The rest of the commentary is devoted to listing, explaining, and applying three expository thoughts that are derived from the miracle. They are as follows:

> In the first place, this miracle is *an unanswerable proof of our Lord's divine power.*
>
> In the second place, this miracle is a *striking example of our Lord's compassion toward men.*
>
> In the last place, this miracle is a *lively emblem of the sufficiency of the Gospel to meet the soul-wants of all mankind.*[26]

Each expository thought is both doctrinal and practical. With his first point, Ryle argued that this miracle provides conclusive proof of Christ's full divinity. He warned the reader, however, to see more in it than the "cold, orthodox, and unconverted" man. True believers must commit it to memory and thank God for an almighty Savior.[27] In his second point he urged readers to consider the compassion of Christ toward sinners. His compassion should lead people to repentance and serve as an example that Christians should follow. In his third and final thought, Ryle argued that this miracle is an emblem of the sufficiency of the gospel. The doctrine of Christ crucified for sinners as their vicarious substitute is sufficient to meet the wants of every soul, and he invited his reader to eat and be filled.

Expository Thoughts on the Gospel of St. Mark appeared the following year. Its purpose and structure is identical to the previous volume. The only difference is the introduction of occasional

---

25. Ryle, *St. Matthew*, 162.

26. Ryle, *St. Matthew*, 162–65.

27. Ryle, *St. Matthew*, 163.

explanatory footnotes.[28] Some of these footnotes are simply quotations from other commentators or respected theologians. Others contain Ryle's own thoughts about difficult subjects, difficult expressions, and important topics. Still others include both.

One such example can be found in Ryle's extended discussion of the unpardonable sin, which can be found in a footnote in his exposition of Mark 3:22–30. The footnote begins with an expression of pastoral concern: "It [the unpardonable sin] is confessedly one of the hard things of Scripture, and has often troubled the hearts of Bible readers." He acknowledged, though, "it seems that there is such a thing as an *unpardonable* sin."[29] After refuting opposing interpretations, he offered his own definition and illustrated it with the case of Judas Iscariot. He then provided a few pastoral words to relieve tender consciences and concluded the discussion with a reassuring quote from *The Cause and Cure of a Wounded Conscience* by Thomas Fuller.

Expository Thoughts on the Gospel of St. Luke was published in two volumes in 1858–1859. It follows the general design of the previous volumes, with one important exception. Ryle's explanatory notes are no longer occasional; they are appended to each portion of exposition. The purpose of this addition is fourfold. First, they offer additional insight on difficult passages. Second, they aid readers who do not know Greek. Third, they provide illuminating quotations from approved authors on important and pressing subjects. Finally, they give Ryle the opportunity to refute false teaching from the text at hand.[30] Ryle's notes on the penitent thief of Luke 23:39–43 provide an example of each of these.

The first note following the exposition resolves an apparent contradiction between Luke's account of the crucifixion and those

---

28. There are sixty-seven such footnotes in *Expository Thoughts on the Gospel of St. Mark.*

29. Ryle, *St. Mark*, 57.

30. J. C. Ryle, *St. Luke, Expository Thoughts on the Gospels: For Family and Private Use* (Ipswich: William Hunt, 1858–1859), 1:iv–v.

of the other Synoptic Gospels. In the notes on verse 40, Ryle admitted that the translation of the Authorized Version had not given the full sense of the Greek words, and then he explained the actual meaning. He supplied quotations from a number of approved writers, including Chrysostom, Luther, Rollock, and Baxter. His notes on this text also contain strenuous refutations of baptismal regeneration, purgatory, and Roman Catholic exegesis that attempt to defend them.

Ryle began work on *Expository Thoughts on the Gospel of St. John* shortly after finishing the previous volumes. He published his commentary on the first four chapters in 1860, but the death of his second wife, "domestic anxieties," a change of residence, and the pastoral demands of a new parish more than four times as large as his previous one brought the project to a halt. The first volume was finally completed and published in 1865, followed by the second in 1869, and the third in 1873. While these volumes are a continuation of the series that began in 1856, they are significantly different from all that came before them.

Like the previous volumes, they contain a continuous series of short expositions for family reading, visiting the sick or poor, or to use as a companion to private reading. Unlike the previous volumes, this volume included a full commentary on every verse of John's gospel, forming, what Ryle called, a "complete commentary."[31] This new commentary is so extensive that it dwarfs his "expository thoughts" and forms the principal part of the work.[32] Ryle's treatment of John 19:1–16 illustrates this well. His expository thoughts on Christ's trial before Pilate take up only four pages, but his commentary on this text is more than twenty-one pages in length. Why did Ryle drastically change the format of his commentary? In the preface of the first volume he explained:

---

31. J. C. Ryle, *St. John, Expository Thoughts on the Gospels: For Family and Private* (Ipswich: William Hunt, 1865, 1869, 1873), 1:iv.

32. Ryle, *St. John,* 1:iv.

The circumstances of the times are my justification. We live in a day of abounding vagueness and indistinctness on doctrinal subjects in religion. Now, if ever, it is the duty of all advocates of clear, well-defined, sharply-cut theology, to supply proof that their views are thoroughly borne out by Scripture. I have endeavoured to do so in this Commentary. I hold that the Gospel of St. John, rightly interpreted, is the best and simplest answer to those who profess to admire a vague and indistinct Christianity.[33]

In short, new pastoral concerns called for a new commentary.

What did *Expository Thoughts* contribute to Ryle's ministry in Helmingham and beyond? First, it provided another literary platform to provide spiritual guidance. In fact, the entire series should be seen as an expression of pastoral concern. The original threefold purpose of the series must not be forgotten. *Expository Thoughts* was born out of a desire to promote regular family worship, aid district visitors, and provide spiritual guidance for readers of the Gospels. The addition of footnotes, then occasional notes, and then a full verse-by-verse commentary should be seen, primarily, as a pastoral response to changing circumstances. These additions allowed him to address pressing pastoral issues in greater depth without significantly altering the project's pastoral purposes.

Second, the series proved to be exceptionally popular and further increased Ryle's popularity. *Expository Thoughts* was warmly received by evangelical churchmen. *The Christian Observer* reviewed a number of the volumes and repeatedly gave their author high praise.[34] One reviewer said, "In this matter of exposition for the family circle, Mr. Ryle appears to us to stand almost unrivalled."[35] Evangelical churchmen, like the philanthropist George Moore and Bishop Frederic Barker of Sydney, bought them in bulk

---

33. Ryle, *St. John*, 1:iv.

34. See *Christian Observer*, June 1859: 423–29; July 1860: 504–6; September 1865: 723.

35. *Christian Observer*, June 1859: 424.

and distributed them alongside Ryle's tracts. The series proved to be popular among Dissenters as well. Charles Spurgeon remarked, "We prize these volumes.... Mr. Ryle has evidently studied all previous writers upon the Gospels, and has given forth an individual utterance of considerable value."[36] Even high churchmen appreciated his work. Rev. William Benham told the Croydon Church Congress, "We do not all agree with Canon Ryle, but all I hope have his work on St. John—it is full of excellent reading."[37] *Expository Thoughts* remains popular even today. It was republished throughout the twentieth century; the most recent republication took place in 2013. Ryle's commentaries on Matthew, Mark, and Luke were recently included in the Crossway Classic Commentaries series, alongside commentaries by John Calvin, Martin Luther, and John Owen.

Hymnbooks

The length of my treatment of Ryle's hymnbooks warrants an explanation. Of the three types of pastoral writings discussed in this chapter, the hymnbooks have been the most neglected. It is not overstating the case to say that they have been almost completely ignored by his biographers. When they are discussed, they are frequently mentioned only in passing. During the course of my research, I have been unable to find a single bibliography that includes all of them. Most only include one or two. This neglect is unfortunate. Ryle believed hymns were a valuable pastoral resource, and he spent a considerable amount of time and energy compiling hymnbooks for his congregations. Because of this neglect, and because the hymnbooks provide valuable insight into Ryle as a pastor, I have treated this group of writings more extensively than the tracts and commentaries, which generally receive more attention.

---

36. C. H. Spurgeon, *Commenting and Commentaries* (London: Passmore and Alabaster, 1876), 149.

37. W. Benham, "Address on Nonconformity," in *The Official Report of the Seventeenth Annual Meeting of the Church Congress, Held at Croydon* (Croydon: Jesse W. Ward, 1877), 498.

As Ian Bradley notes, hymn singing was a novel experience for most Victorian churchmen.[38] The reason for its late arrival in the established churches of the British Isles can be traced back to a dispute that arose between Lutheran and Reformed Protestants in the sixteenth century. In addition to introducing congregational singing in the vernacular to the German Mass, Martin Luther summoned German poets to compose "pious poems" and "spiritual songs" for use in worship.[39] Reformed churches permitted congregational singing of the Psalms but regarded the use of uninspired hymns to be a violation of the regulative principle of worship. Ultimately Calvin's influence prevailed over Luther's in Britain, and thus English and Scottish churches became psalm singers instead of hymn singers.

The nucleus of the English Psalter was Calvin's *Form of Church Prayers*, which was brought to English soil by returning Marian exiles.[40] The completed form, known as the *Old Version* of Thomas Sternhold and John Hopkins, appeared in 1562. It contained "the whole Booke of Psalmes, collected to Englysh metre" along with nineteen authorized hymns appended to it.[41] A *New Version* of the English Psalter was produced by Nahum Tate and Nicholas Brady and published in 1696. It achieved semiofficial status because Tate and Brady's psalms were frequently bound together with the Book of Common Prayer, but a century would pass before it enjoyed widespread popularity.[42] By this time, the hymns of Watts and Wesley were beginning to make significant inroads into the established church via evangelical clergymen.

---

38. Ian Bradley, *Abide with Me: The World of Victorian Hymns* (Chicago: GIA Publications, 1997), 1.

39. See *Liturgies of the Western Church*, selected and introduced by Bard Thompson (Philadelphia: Fortress Press, 1980), 119.

40. Louis F. Benson, *The English Hymn: Its Development and Use in Worship* (1915; repr. Richmond, Va.: John Knox Press, 1962), 27.

41. These included versifications of New Testament texts (such as the Magnificat, Benedictus, Nunc Dimittis, and the Lord's Prayer), the Ten Commandments, two ancient hymns ("Veni Creator" and "Te Deum"), and a number of prayers.

42. Bradley, *Abide with Me*, 2.

Before this took place, a new musical tradition emerged in country parish churches in the late eighteenth century that deserves notice. Before the middle of the eighteenth century, the metrical psalms were sung without musical accompaniment and were led by a precentor, who "lined out" each stanza before the congregation joined in. Because of this, psalm singing often proved to be a lengthy (and sometimes tedious) affair, and consequently, precentors often found themselves singing alone, and parish churches found themselves losing parishioners to hymn-singing Dissenting chapels. This led many parish churches to abandon unaccompanied, precentor-led psalm singing and introduce a choir and instrumentalists, who were installed at the west end of the gallery. Though metrical psalms continued to be used exclusively, these aesthetic changes helped breathe new life into the old practice. Ian Bradley suggests that this west gallery music, as it was called, was the dominant tradition in English country churches when Victoria came to the throne.[43]

Metrical psalm singing and west gallery music soon gave way to the hymn and the organ. In the eighteenth century, Dissenters began to write and introduce their own hymns and hymn tunes for their services. Isaac Watts and Charles Wesley were the most prolific and popular hymn writers of the eighteenth century. Watts composed six hundred hymns for his congregation at Mark Lane Chapel, London, and Charles Wesley composed sixty-five hundred for the Methodists. Their hymns proved to be wildly popular, and though the Church initially regarded them as "enthusiastical," they gradually gained nearly full acceptance. Evangelical clergymen were instrumental in this respect. Theologically, they were closer to Dissenters and Methodists than other churchmen and thus were more willing to experiment with hymns in worship. Furthermore, there were a number of talented hymn writers within the evangelical ranks, such as Augustus Toplady, John Newton, and William

---

43. Bradley, *Abide with Me*, 3.

Cowper. They were instrumental in making hymn singing palatable to more dignified congregations by the quality of their poetry. Oddly enough, it was the staunch opponents of the evangelicals who secured a place for hymn singing within the Church of England. The Tractarians were enthusiastic supporters of hymn singing, though they had different reasons and different aims. For the Tractarians, metrical psalm singing was a relic of the Reformation, and they wanted to abandon it to return to the hymns of the early church. They produced a number of talented hymn writers, such as John Henry Newman and John Keble, and a number of talented hymn translators, most notably, John Mason Neal. Their acceptance of hymn singing removed many of the final objections to the practice and established it as an accepted part of Anglican worship.

Ryle considered the acceptance of hymn singing in the Church of England to be a positive development—a sign of spiritual vitality. He wrote, "I regard with deep satisfaction the growing taste for hymn-singing and praise, as an essential part of worship. It is one of the healthiest signs of our times. There is an old and quaint, but most true saying, 'When the sun begins to rise, the birds begin to sing.'"[44] Why was Ryle so encouraged by this development? In short, hymns do a tremendous amount of spiritual good. He wrote:

> Good hymns are an immense blessing to the Church of Christ. I believe the last day alone will show the world the real amount of good they have done. They suit all, both rich and poor. There is an elevating, stirring, soothing, spiritualizing effect about a thoroughly good hymn, which nothing else can produce. It sticks in men's memories when texts are forgotten. It trains men for heaven, where praise is one of the principal occupations. Preaching and praying shall one day cease forever; but praise shall never die. The makers of good ballads are said to sway national opinion. The writers of good

44. J. C. Ryle, *The Additional Hymn-Book: Being Three Hundred Hymns for Public Worship. Most of Them Not Found in the Collections Commonly Used* (London: William Hunt, 1875), vii.

hymns, in like manner, are those who leave the deepest marks on the face of the Church. Thousands of Christians rejoice in the Te Deum and "Just as I am," who neither prize the Thirty-nine Articles, nor know anything about the first four councils, nor understand the Athanasian Creed.[45]

Given his estimation of the value of hymns, it is not surprising that Ryle would produce hymnbooks for his own congregation.

What constituted a good hymn for Ryle? He had five criteria. First, good hymns must be universal—that is, nonsectarian. Second, good hymns are Christocentric, meaning they are "full of Jesus Christ, whether living, dying, rising, interceding, sympathizing, or coming again."[46] Third, good hymns are experimental in nature and contain the full range of Christian experience: "their crosses, hopes, fears, sorrows, and joys."[47] Fourth, good hymns are characterized by simple poetry. He acknowledged that simplicity and plainness might offend the tastes of the highly educated and literary classes, but they represent only a small minority of churchmen. The majority of worshipers, however, desire "simple, manly, [and] plain hymns."[48] Finally, good hymns are warm and full of life. Ryle did not defend "vulgarity, irreverence, or nonsensical jingles and repetition in our hymns: all this I abhor."[49] But hymns that are filled with "warmth," "fire," "life," and "unction" move the affections and "come home to the heart of all true Christians." They are the opposite of "cold, stiff, chilling, and ungenial" hymns.[50]

---

45. Ryle, *Christian Leaders of the Last Century*, 382.

46. J. C. Ryle, *Hymns for the Church on Earth: Being Three Hundred Hymns and Spiritual Songs (for the Most Part Modern Date)* (Ipswich: William Hunt, 1860), v.

47. Ryle, *Hymns for the Church on Earth* (1860), v.

48. Ryle, *Additional Hymn-Book*, vii. Ryle could be a harsh critic of poetry. Of the hymns of John Berridge, he said, "The Vicar of Everton was no more a poet than Cicero or Julius Caesar; and although the doctrine of his hymns is very sound, the poetry of them is very poor, while the ideas they occasionally present are painfully ludicrous." Ryle, *Christian Leaders*, 217.

49. Ryle, *Additional Hymn-Book*, vi.

50. Ryle, *Additional Hymn-Book*, vi.

Ryle published his first hymnal, *Spiritual Songs: Being Twenty-Six Hymns Not to Be Found in the Hymn Books Most Commonly Used*, in 1849. It contains no preface or introduction, nor is there any discernible thematic arrangement.[51] As the subtitle suggests, it does not include well-known and popular hymns. Most of the hymns were relatively modern, although there are four exceptions.[52] The subtitle also provides a clue as to the purpose of the work. This collection of hymns was intended for private and family worship, not congregational use. Ryle chose one hymn for every day of the month except Sundays. He explained the purpose of this series in a later edition: "The comfort of invalids and the edification of Christians in private, have been the two principal objects I have had in view in preparing this collection."[53] In order to comfort and edify, he selected hymns that focused on the person and work of Christ, the Christian life as a difficult pilgrimage, trust in God and resignation to His will in trying circumstances, and heaven as the Christian's home and rest.

He enlarged *Spiritual Songs* the following year.[54] He kept the original twenty-six hymns and added thirty-six more. Though the size of the hymnal changed, the purpose and the preference for modern hymns did not. Private worship and devotional meditation remain the primary focus of the work. Adding to the title *For a Month* makes this even more explicit. Ryle apparently selected two hymns for each day of the month for this edition. The themes of the newly added hymns are consistent with the pastoral priorities of the first edition. Assurance, resignation, pilgrimage, death,

---

51. The last three hymns are an exception. They focus specifically on death and dying.

52. Ryle included one hymn from Richard Baxter, a Gerhardt hymn translated by John Wesley, and two obscure hymns by Charles Wesley.

53. Ryle, *Hymns for the Church on Earth*, iv.

54. The new edition was titled *Spiritual Songs for a Month: Being Sixty-Two Hymns, Not to Be Found in the Hymn Books Most Commonly Used*. It was the third edition of the original *Spiritual Songs* (Ipswich: Hunt and Sons, 1849), which may indicate that his hymnal proved to be popular outside his parish.

and heaven remain prominent themes. There seems to be a new emphasis on doxology and Christology in this edition, however.[55] It is also worth noting that this enlarged edition contains a considerable number of hymns written by women. The first edition contained only two; the enlarged edition contains ten.[56]

Ryle published a tenth and enlarged edition of *Spiritual Songs* in 1858. This hymnal contained all the hymns of the previous editions and included thirty-eight new selections, bringing the total number of hymns to one hundred. As was the case with the previous enlargement, the purpose and the preference for modern hymns remained unchanged. Thematically, the hymnal was only slightly altered. Doxology, Christology, and assurance are even more prominent among the new additions.[57] Hymns that focus on new topics, such as prayer, missions, and spiritual warfare, were added. Ryle continued to add hymns written by women, and this edition included hymns written by American women such as Fanny J. Crosby, Mary S. B. Schindler, and Phoebe Cary.[58]

In 1860 Ryle published *Hymns for the Church on Earth: Being Three Hundred Hymns and Spiritual Songs (For the Most Part Modern Date)*. Despite the change in title, this hymnal is essentially a third expansion of *Spiritual Songs*. All the hymns from the previous editions of *Spiritual Songs* are included in their original order except one.[59] The new selections are simply added to the previous ones. Ryle's pastoral concerns and preference for modern hymns

---

55. I do not mean to suggest that these emphases were wholly absent in the first edition of *Spiritual Songs*. That is certainly not the case. But there does appear to be a greater emphasis on praising God and the person and work of Christ in this enlarged edition. Perhaps this represents an attempt to remedy an oversight in the original.

56. These include hymns by Charlotte Elliott, Mary Bowley Peters, Julian Anne Elliott, Ann Taylor Gilbert, and Sarah Flower Adams.

57. The name Jesus appears in eight of the thirty-eight new hymns.

58. Eighteen of these one hundred hymns were written by women.

59. Ryle substituted one Ann Taylor Gilbert hymn for another. "When I Listen to Thy Word" was hymn 52 in the third and tenth editions of *Spiritual Songs*. In *Hymns for the Church*, he replaced it with "Thou, Who Didst for Peter's Faith."

remained the same. The spiritual themes and emphases that were present in previous hymnals are present in this one,[60] and he continued to include hymns written by women. Despite these similarities, there are some important new additions. The first and maybe most important addition is the preface. In the preface Ryle provided valuable insight into the purpose of his hymnals, his preference for modern hymns, the criteria he used to select material, and the sources he used. Second, this new hymnal contains a number of Communion hymns, which are absent from previous hymnals. The inclusion of these hymns indicates that Ryle was concerned about the corporate life of the Christian, as well as the private life. Finally, in this hymnal Ryle added a considerable number of German hymns from the translations of Catherine Winkworth (*Lyra Germanica*), Jane Borthwick (*Hymns from the Land of Luther*), and Richard Massie (*Lyra Domestica*).

Twelve years later Ryle published a small hymnbook titled *Special Hymns for Special Occasions*. It contains thirty-one hymns: six are new selections; the rest were taken from previous hymnals.[61] The hymns were selected, as the title suggests, to be used on special occasions. At least two appear to be chosen for use on specific days of the church calendar.[62] Others seem to be intended for use on more regular religious occasions, such as morning prayer, the meeting of friends (presumably for spiritual conference), missionary assemblies, or the opening of Sunday worship. Still others

---

60. Doxology, Christology, assurance, death, and resignation are all prominent and recurring themes. But there does appear to be a greater emphasis on the Christian life as a pilgrimage and heaven as the Christian's home and rest among the newly added hymns. Given the new title (and focus) of this hymnal—the church militant—this is hardly surprising.

61. The precise breakdown is as follows: seven are new, four come from the first edition of *Spiritual Songs* (1849), three come from the third edition (1850), four come from the eighth edition (1858), and fourteen come from *Hymns for the Church on Earth*.

62. "Spirit Divine, Attend Our Prayers" is a Good Friday hymn, and "Come, O Thou All-Victorious Lord" is a Lenten hymn.

appear to be selected for other types of special occasions. For example, "Blest Be My God That I Was Born" celebrates the blessings of being born in a Christian home and land. "When Languor and Disease Invade" comforts the sick and suffering Christian who may be anticipating death. Though this hymnal is small and contains little new material (and no new spiritual emphases), it underscores the importance Ryle attached to hymns and hymn singing. If this little hymnbook accurately reflects its author's wishes, and if it was strictly followed (i.e., used on the special occasions the hymnal calls for), Ryle's parishioners would sing at least one hymn every day of their lives. The only other daily spiritual duties Ryle urged on his parishioners were Bible reading and prayer.

In 1875 Ryle published a new hymnal titled *The Additional Hymn-Book: Being Three Hundred Hymns for Public Worship, Most of Them Not to Be Found in the Collections Commonly Used.* This hymnal differs from its predecessors in a number of important respects. Unlike the previous compilations, this hymnal was intended for use in the context of public worship, but only as a supplement to the general collections already in use.[63] He used (and endorsed) Charles Kemble's *A Selection of Psalms and Hymns, Arranged for the Public Services of the Church of England.*[64] Together these two volumes provide an illuminating glimpse into Ryle's use of hymns in worship.[65] He also cut material for the first time in a major hymnbook.

---

63. Ryle, *Additional Hymn-Book*, iii: "In a word, it is not meant to take the place of any of the general Collections which already exist. It is simply, as its name indicates, an 'Additional' or 'Supplementary' hymn-book."

64. The following testimonial from Ryle can be found in a number of places: "I have decided on introducing Mr. Kemble's Hymn Book in my Parish Church. After a careful examination, I find no collection which combines *soundness, fullness,* and *cheapness* so thoroughly as it does." See *The Ecclesiastical Gazette*, June 13, 1865.

65. Kemble's collection is more traditional and Anglican than the *Additional Hymn-Book*. It contains versifications of all the Psalms. It includes far more hymns from the great hymn writers, such as Watts, Wesley, Newton, Cowper, and Toplady, than Ryle's supplement. Moreover, the hymns are arranged according to the church calendar. The *Additional Hymn-Book*, on the other hand, contains more modern hymns that are loosely arranged, if intentionally arranged at all. It does, however,

In previous hymnals new hymns were simply added to the old ones. In this work, however, many of the hymns that made up the previous hymnals were not included.[66] He also chose a different kind of hymn for this work. In his previous hymnals, he selected "the best modern hymns, and a few old hymns, which are not so well known as they deserve to be."[67] In this work, he chose modern hymns that are "already deservedly popular,"[68] which included American gospel songs written by Philip Bliss and Ira Sankey. Many of these new hymns emphasize spiritual themes that are not prominent in previous hymnals, including a desire for revival, polemics, invitation, missions and evangelism, and the second advent of Christ. Despite these changes, the work is not entirely new. More than a third of the hymns appeared in the earlier hymnals. All the spiritual themes and emphases of the earlier hymnals are present in this one. He continued to include a significant number of hymns written by women. As was the case with earlier hymnals, pastoral concerns remain paramount. Ryle said he sent forth the *Additional Hymn-Book* "with an earnest prayer that it may be found useful, and may help forward Christ's cause in the world."[69]

Ryle published a final expansion of *Hymns for the Church on Earth* in 1876.[70] In the preface he explained that though this work

---

contain more hymns with subscripts connecting those hymns to certain days on the church calendar than his other hymnals.

66. Ryle included only eight of the original twenty-six hymns that made up the first edition of *Spiritual Songs*. He retained only sixteen of the thirty-six hymns that were added to its first expansion, and only nineteen of the thirty-eight hymns of the second. Of the two hundred new additions found in *Hymns for the Church on Earth*, only seventy-eight were included in the *Additional Hymn-Book*. Of the six new hymns in *Special Hymns for Special Occasions*, he kept only three. Roughly 60 percent (176) of the hymns that appeared in the *Additional Hymn-Book* were new.

67. J. C. Ryle, *Hymns for the Church on Earth: Containing Four Hundred Hymns (for the Most Part Modern Date)* (London: William Hunt, 1876), iv.

68. Ryle, *Additional Hymn-Book*, iii–iv.

69. Ryle, *Additional Hymn-Book*, vii.

70. I found another edition of *Hymns for the Church on Earth* published in New York by A. D. F. Randolf. Though Ryle may have consented to its publication,

bears the same title as the first edition, it is "so much altered, enlarged, and improved, that it is almost a new book."[71] Ryle omitted a number of hymns that appeared in the first edition because they became popular over the intervening fifteen years, and a number of "truly beautiful" hymns appeared during that same period which he felt compelled to include.[72] Unlike the *Additional Hymn-book*, this hymnal was not intended to be used in public worship but, like the first edition, was published for private worship and devotional reading.[73] Once again, pastoral, not liturgical, concerns are primary: "The comfort of invalids, and the edification of Christians in private, have been the two principal objects I have had in view in preparing this collection."[74] Since Ryle added only two new hymns to this collection, there are no new spiritual themes or emphases. But since this final compilation contains most of the hymns of the previous hymnals, it serves as an excellent one-volume collection of Ryle's favorite hymns, spiritual emphases, and pastoral concerns.

---

it is not a new hymnal strictly speaking, and thus I have not included it in this discussion of hymnals.

71. Ryle, *Hymns for the Church on Earth*, iii.

72. All but two of the new hymns can be found in *The Additional Hymn-book*. The exceptions are hymn 390, "I Am Hast'ning Homeward, to the Land I Love," by Emma G. Denning, and hymn 394, "Help Me to Hear Aright the Chastening Rod," anonymous. Twenty-six hymns come from *Spiritual Songs* (1849); twenty-seven come from *Spiritual Songs* (1850); thirty-seven come from *Spiritual Songs* (1858); 194 come from the first edition of *Hymns for the Church on Earth* (1860); one comes from *Special Hymns for Special Occasions* (1872); and 115 come from *Additional Hymn-Book* (1875).

73. Ryle admitted that some of these hymns are "admirably adapted" for congregational singing, but many are better suited for private reading because of their highly experimental character, and others are "shut out of public usefulness" by their irregular meters. Ryle, *Hymns for the Church on Earth*, v.

74. Ryle, *Hymns for the Church on Earth*, vi. He went on to say, "If the four hundred hymns which I now send forth, shall do good to the weakest lamb in Christ's flock, and shall comfort, cheer, stablish, or build up one suffering member of Christ's mystical body, the labour which I have expended in collecting them will be more than repaid." Ryle, *Hymns for the Church on Earth*, viii.

Though these hymnals were less popular than his tracts and commentaries,[75] and though they have been almost universally neglected by Ryle's biographers, they provide valuable insight into Ryle as a pastor. First, they demonstrate the importance Ryle attached to hymns, hymnbooks, and hymn singing in general. He was convinced that hymns suit all classes; are uniquely spiritualizing, didactic, and memorable; and train Christians for heaven. Given these numerous spiritual benefits, it is hardly surprising that he would commend daily hymn singing to his people and compile hymnbooks for them. It is also noteworthy that Ryle published his first hymnal in 1849 and his last in 1876. With the exception of tract writing, no other publishing endeavor spanned such a large part of his ministry.

Second, the hymnals also provide additional insight into Ryle's pastoral concerns. The stated purpose of six of his seven hymnals was to edify Christians in private and comfort invalids. Given Ryle's esteem for good hymns, it is hardly surprising that he would use them as a means of private edification. Like his tracts and commentaries, they allowed him to provide spiritual guidance outside the parish church walls. His focus on invalids, however, needs more explanation. Though providing pastoral care for invalids and those unable to regularly attend church would probably be a priority for many evangelical clergymen, it was personal for Ryle. During his ministry in Helmingham (when he published four of his seven hymnals), Ryle married and buried two wives. His first wife, Matilda, became extremely ill after the premature birth of their

---

75. Of all Ryle's pastoral works, his hymnbooks proved to be the least popular of the three genres. Though *Spiritual Songs* and *Hymns for the Church on Earth* went through a number of editions, none of the hymnbooks have been republished since 1883. Henry Edward Bickersteth consulted Ryle's collections, however, in compiling his popular hymnbook, *The Hymnal Companion to the Book of Common Prayer*. The *Additional Hymn-Book* is mentioned in the hymnologist John Julian's famous *Dictionary of Hymnology*. Though they never achieved the publishing success of his tracts and commentaries, Ryle's hymnbooks proved to be moderately popular during his lifetime.

first child in 1847. She suffered from extreme postnatal depression, which included delusions and other psychotic symptoms, and died the following year. He married his second wife, Jessie, in 1850, but she became ill shortly thereafter. Though she lived for another ten years, she was never well for more than three months at a time, and in the last five years of her life she had "painfully little enjoyment of life."[76] Perhaps Ryle's wives and their caretakers may have found comfort in hymns and hymnbooks written specifically for invalids, such as those published by one of Ryle's favorite hymn writers, Charlotte Elliot.[77] Maybe the explanation for this emphasis lies elsewhere. In either case, providing spiritual guidance for invalids was one of Ryle's pastoral priorities, and he was convinced good hymns could help him do so.

Third, the hymnals provide an excellent glimpse into Ryle's spirituality. Christology is clearly Ryle's favorite theme. The person and work of Christ dominate all other spiritual emphases in every hymnal. It typically occurs more than twice as many times as its nearest rival. He also selected a large number of hymns that describe the Christian life as a difficult pilgrimage. Ryle was not a killjoy; he did not believe that the Christian life was nothing but "losses and crosses." But he was convinced that the world, the flesh, and the devil harass every pilgrim and seek to impede their progress. Therefore trials are a normal part of the Christian life until the pilgrim reaches heaven, which is another prominent theme in Ryle's hymnals that is frequently associated with pilgrimage. Assurance in the face of fear and doubt is another prominent spiritual emphasis in these hymnals. It should be noted that these hymnals know nothing of the so-called Victorian crisis of faith. The fears that need calming and the doubts that need reassuring

---

76. Ryle, *Autobiography*, 133–34.

77. See Charlotte Elliott, *The Invalid's Hymn-Book* (Dublin: John Robertson, 1834); and Charlotte Elliott, *Hours of Sorrow Cheered and Comforted: Thoughts in Verse, Chiefly Adapted to Seasons of Sickness, Depression, and Bereavement* (London: James Nisbet, 1836).

arise not from the discoveries of science or higher criticism, but from sickness, suffering, and loss. Though Ryle may have emphasized this theme for the comforting and encouraging of invalids, it remained a prominent theme in the *Additional Hymn-Book*, which was not written specifically for that purpose. Finally, these hymnals serve as a reminder that Ryle's Protestant, Puritan, and evangelical spirituality was cast in a decidedly Anglican mold. This is most evident in the *Additional Hymn-Book*. As previously mentioned, this is the only hymnal Ryle published to be used in public worship, and it was used to supplement Kemble's *Selection of Psalms and Hymns*. The *Additional Hymn-Book* contains a number of hymns that have subscripts connecting a particular hymn to a particular day in the church calendar (Lent, Advent, and Easter), a particular rite (confirmation), or a particular part of the liturgy (Holy Communion, Sunday morning, Sunday evening). His use of Kemble's hymnal is even more revealing. Kemble's hymns are specifically arranged around the church calendar and include special selections for saints' days, confirmations, and the consecration of churches, which many Dissenters would find unacceptable.

Fourth, the hymnals reveal that Ryle's taste for hymns was eclectic and modern. The following are the eleven most frequently cited hymn writers in Ryle's hymnals:

1. Horatius Bonar (1808–1889)
2. James George Deck (1807–1884)
3. Charles Wesley (1707–1788)
4. James Montgomery (1771–1854)
5. Charlotte Elliot (1789–1871)
6. Thomas Kelly (1769–1855)
7. Paul Gerhardt (1607–1676)
8. Karl Johann Phillip Spitta (1801–1859)
9. Tie: John S. B. Monsell (1811–1875), Isaac Watts (1674–1748), Mary Bowley Peters (1813–1856)

This list is interesting in a number of respects. It reveals, first of all, an overwhelming preference for modern hymns. Ryle regarded

Isaac Watts, Charles Wesley, John Newton, William Cowper, and Augustus Toplady as the writers of the "best English hymns," and he specifically held Toplady in high esteem.[78] Yet with the exception of Watts and Wesley, their hymns are noticeably absent from Ryle's hymnbooks. Eight of these eleven authors wrote during his lifetime. Second, it reveals Ryle's appreciation of non-Anglican hymn writers: five are Dissenters, one is a Methodist, two are Lutherans, and three are churchmen. Third, it reveals that Ryle appreciated the contribution women were making to Victorian hymnody. Charlotte Elliot and Mary Bowley Peters were among his favorite authors, and many of the German hymns that were included in his hymnals were translations made by Catherine Winkworth and Jane Borthwick.

Ryle's somewhat unusual taste in hymns made his hymnals significantly different from the most popular hymnals in use in the Church of England. In the *Additional Hymn-Book*, Ryle observed, "I believe that out of the three-hundred hymns in this volume at least two hundred and fifty will not be found in Kemble's, Bickersteth's, Windle's, Mercer's, the Christian Knowledge Society, or the 'Ancient and Modern' Collections."[79] A comparison between this

---

78. Ryle, *Christian Leaders of the Last Century*, 383:

> Of all English hymn-writers, none, perhaps, have succeeded so thoroughly in combining truth, poetry, life, warmth, fire, depth, solemnity, and unction, as Toplady has. I pity the man who does not know, or knowing, does not admire those glorious hymns of his beginning, "Rock of Ages, cleft for me"; or, "Holy Ghost, dispel our sadness"; or, "A debtor to mercy alone"; or, "Your harps, ye trembling saints"; or, "Christ, whose glory fills the skies"; or, "When languor and disease invade"; or, "Deathless principle arise." The writer of these seven hymns alone has laid the Church under perpetual obligations to him.

79. Ryle, *Additional Hymn-Book*, iii. The hymnals he refers to are *Psalms and Hymns, Selected by the Rev. Charles Kemble* (1853); Henry Edward Bickersteth, ed., *The Hymnal Companion to the Book of Common Prayer*, annotated ed. (London: Sampson Low, Son, and Marston, 1870); *The Church and Home Metrical Psalter and Hymnal*, edited by Rev. W. Windle (1870); *Church Psalter and Hymn Book*, edited by Rev. William Mercer (1863); *Hymn-book for the Society for Promoting Christian*

hymnal and *Hymns Ancient and Modern* (1867) is particularly illuminating. Both hymnals are roughly the same size (300 hymns vs. 265 hymns) and both were intended to be used for worship in the Church of England, and yet they have only four hymns in common. The hymnal edited by the evangelical Henry Edward Bickersteth, *Hymnal Companion to the Book of Common Prayer*, tells a similar tale. Though it contains four hundred hymns, it shares only thirteen with the *Additional Hymn-Book*. When it came to hymnbook publishing, Ryle went his own way.

Conclusion

By the end of the 1850s, Ryle's ecclesiastical star was on the rise. He had established himself as a popular preacher. He was an in-demand platform speaker for various evangelical societies and meetings. His pastoral writings, particularly his tracts and commentaries, were enormously popular as well. In short, he was quickly becoming one of the young leaders of the evangelical party. Despite his growing influence, the 1850s were one of the most difficult decades of his life—they were "years of singular trials."[80]

Ryle's first wife died in 1848, and in the following years death would make "great gaps" in his circle of friends and family.[81] He lost his mother, sister Caroline, brother-in-law William Courthope, and many of his best friends in the 1850s. His second wife, Jessie, lost her mother, father, sister, and brother during the same period. The worst trial was Jessie's continued illness. As previously mentioned, she became ill less than six months after her marriage to Ryle, and she remained ill for the majority of their ten-year marriage. She gave birth to five children during this time: Isabella (1851), Reginald (1854), Herbert (1856), Arthur (1857), and an unnamed daughter

Knowledge (1863); Henry Williams Baker and Louis Coutier Biggs, eds., *Hymns Ancient and Modern, for Use in the Services of the Church* (London: Novello, 1861).

80. Ryle, *Autobiography*, 130.

81. Ryle, *Autobiography*, 130.

who was either stillborn or died shortly after birth in 1853. Jessie died of Bright's disease in 1860 and was buried in the Helmingham churchyard at the north side of the church. Ryle was left a widower with five children—one from his first marriage and four from his second—ranging in age from three to thirteen.

To complicate matters further, Ryle's relationship with John Tollemache broke down around 1857. The precise cause of the falling out is unknown, but conflicts of this nature between squires and parsons were not uncommon.[82] It resulted in a suspension of all friendly relations between the two men and made Ryle's position in Helmingham "extremely uncomfortable" at a difficult time.[83] Tollemache asked Ryle to leave as soon as another living was offered to him. Fortunately, a generous offer from Stradbroke came in the autumn of 1861, and Ryle happily accepted.

------

82. For an excellent summary of the complex relationship between the squire and the parson, see chapter 1 of Owen Chadwick, *Victorian Miniature* (Cambridge: Cambridge University Press, 1960).

83. Ryle, *Autobiography*, 133.

4

Controversialist

John Pelham, the evangelical bishop of Norwich, appointed Ryle to All Saints, Stradbroke, in the fall of 1861. It was only about fifteen miles north of Helmingham, but in many respects, it was worlds apart. It was one of the most prestigious livings in the entire diocese of Norwich. His income exceeded one thousand pounds per year, which was twice as much as Helmingham. For the first time since his father's bankruptcy, Ryle was financially independent. Among other things, this allowed him to hire a curate to assist him.[1] There was no resident landlord like John Tollemache to contend with, which freed him to manage his new parish as he saw fit. Life in Stradbroke proved to be much happier than it had been in Helmingham. In October 1861 Ryle married Henrietta Clowes. By all accounts, she was a remarkable woman, a devoted wife, and a loving stepmother.[2] She brought much happiness to Ryle and his family.

---

1. His curates in Stradbroke were Adam Washington, Robert Washington, John Toolis, Clement Sneyd, Edward Stead, and Charles Mules, the future bishop of Nelson (New Zealand).

2. Henrietta was the daughter of Lieutenant Colonel W. L. Clowes of Broughton Old Hall, Lancashire. She was a talented organist and photographer. Some of her surviving photographs can be seen in Stradbroke or at www.stradbrokearchive .org.uk. J. C. Ryle is the subject of a number of them. More importantly, she was a "true helpmeet to her husband, and a true mother to her step-children," according to Herbert Edward Ryle—J. C.'s third child. See chapter 2, "Home and School: 1861–1869," in Maurice H. Fitzgerald, *A Memoir of Herbert Edward Ryle: K.C.V.O., D.D., Sometime Bishop of Winchester and Dean of Westminster* (London: Macmillan, 1928), 10–22.

Stradbroke was a large village by Suffolk standards. It extended for more than thirty-seven hundred acres, which included a number of isolated hamlets as well as a central village. Most of the thirteen hundred inhabitants were poor agricultural laborers, and the nearest railway stations were eight (Harleston) and nine (Diss) miles away. There was one Baptist chapel, but the majority of the inhabitants were churchmen. Ryle befriended the young Baptist minister shortly after his arrival, and the two got along quite well.[3]

Ryle went to work in Stradbroke as he had previously done in Exbury, Winchester, and Helmingham. He continued to preach twice on Sundays to large crowds. It was not unusual for people to travel up to twenty miles to hear him preach. By 1870 All Saints needed to be completely restored, in part to accommodate the large crowds. He continued to lecture and hold midweek religious meetings. In the winter, he held cottage meetings for three successive weeks at a time in different parts of the parish in order to provide access to everyone in the district. In the summer, the congregation met in the open air. He continued his regular program of pastoral care. He founded and supervised a flourishing Sunday school. He regularly visited house to house. He continued to write tracts and commentaries and compile hymnbooks. In Stradbroke, however, Ryle added "controversialist" to his ministerial résumé.

---

3. In a discussion on Nonconformity, Ryle told the Croydon Church Congress:

I found when I first went to my parish of Stradbroke, that there was a clever and lively young Baptist minister settled there. He was about to deliver a lecture on poetry, and he sent to me to ask if I could lend him Chaucer, as he happened not to have it. I lent it him, and told him he was quite welcome to any other books I had in my library. He availed himself of my offer, and the result was he would never allow a word to be said against me, and always treated me with the greatest respect.

J. C. Ryle, "Address on Nonconformity," in *The Official Report of the Seventeenth Annual Meeting of the Church Congress Held at Croydon* (Croydon: Jesse W. Ward, 1877), 497.

Refuting false teaching had always been part of Ryle's ministry. In his ordination vows he promised to be "ready, with all faithful diligence, to banish and drive away all erroneous and strange doctrines contrary to God's Word."[4] But in the 1860s and 1870s Ryle began to come forward publicly to oppose three different theological movements—ritualism, neologianism, and Keswick spirituality—that he believed undermined essential elements of the evangelical gospel.

Ritualism

Ritualism was a movement within the Church of England to restore the forgotten worship of the Roman Catholic Church into the divine service. Eucharistic vestments, high ceremonial, the adoption of the eastward position in the celebration of Holy Communion, and other forms of ornamentation began to be introduced into parish worship in the early 1850s. The ritualists, however, were concerned with more than aesthetic expression. In addition to beautifying worship, these ritualistic innovations, they believed, gave expression to Roman Catholic truth that had been lost since the Reformation.

The relationship of ritualism to Tractarianism has been the subject of revision in recent decades.[5] The traditional interpretation is that ritualism naturally developed out of Tractarianism.[6] But more recent studies emphasize the discontinuity between the Oxford movement and the ritualists. Nigel Yates argues that ritual

---

4. See "The Form and Manner of Ordering of Priests," in The Book of Common Prayer (1662).

5. See Nigel Yates, *Anglican Ritualism in Victorian Britain 1830–1910* (Oxford: Oxford University Press, 1999); and W. S. F. Pickering, *Anglo-Catholicism: A Study in Religious Ambiguity* (London: SPCK, 1989). See also Chadwick, *Victorian Church*.

6. For example, P. T. Marsh argues that ritualism was an aesthetic expression, the tangible poetry, of the Oxford movement. See *The Victorian Church in Decline: Archbishop Tait and the Church of England 1868–1882* (London: Routledge and Kegan Paul, 1969), 112. See also Kenneth Hylson-Smith, *Evangelicals in the Church of England: 1734–1984* (Edinburgh: T&T Clark, 1989), 123. This is the position of most of the older studies of the Victorian Church before Chadwick's work.

innovation was taking place before the publication of the *Tracts for the Times* and that Tractarians and ritualists should be seen as overlapping elements of the broader picture of high churchmanship in the second quarter of the nineteenth century.[7] Owen Chadwick contends that ritualism emerged from Cambridge, not Oxford, and that the leaders of the Oxford movement neither supported nor encouraged ritual innovation. They regarded it as a potential distraction to their primary mission: the reassertion of Roman Catholic truth.[8]

In the public eye, especially the evangelical public, the two were indistinguishable. After the first major ritualism controversy in 1842, several writers attempted to expose the connection between Tractarianism and ritualism. Perhaps the most influential came from the evangelical vicar of Cheltenham, Francis Close, titled *The Restoration of Churches Is the Restoration of Popery*.[9] Evangelicals were not alone in equating ritualism with Tractarianism. Some ritualists, like Richard Frederick Littledale, referred to themselves as "Tractarians,"[10] and some Tractarians, like E. B. Pusey, acknowledged that Tractarian doctrine was the bulb from which the flower of ritualism sprang.[11]

Ryle had no doubts about the connection between Tractarianism and ritualism. More than a decade after the supposed death of Tractarianism (1845), Ryle argued that Tractarianism, in the form of ritualism, was one the greatest dangers facing the Church:

---

7. Yates, *Anglican Ritualism in Victorian Britain 1830–1910*, 40–69.

8. Chadwick, *Victorian Church*, 2:212. Chadwick argues that ritualism was caused by (1) the taste of the age; (2) the widespread belief that this was the way to draw in the working classes; (3) the growing congregationalism of town parishes; and (4) the strong Anglican desire for due obedience to authority. See Chadwick, *Victorian Church*, 2:310.

9. Francis Close, *The Restoration of Churches Is the Restoration of Popery* (London: Hatchard and Son, 1844).

10. Richard Frederick Littledale, *Innovations: A Lecture* (London: Simpkin and Marshall, 1868), 28.

11. Pusey said, "What we taught in word, they teach in deed." Thomas O. Beeman, *Ritualism: Doctrine Not Dress. Notes of Lectures on Ritualism, the Development of Tractarianism* (Cranbrook, Kent: George Waters and Sons, 1868), 5.

One of the chief dangers of the day is the firm hold which Tractarianism has on a large portion of the clergy, and not a small portion of the laity. We must not suppose that Tractarianism is extinct. Newman and Manning, and Oakley, and Ward, have gone to Rome, but they have left behind a leaven which still works, and will work, in the hearts of many of the clergy and laity. I believe that people do not sufficiently estimate the power which Tractarianism has over a large body in the Church of England. It does not come forward as prominently as it once did, but it is not less dangerous. Its influence just now, is seen in the unscriptural doctrines put forth respecting the Lord's Supper, in the secret efforts that are made in some quarters to introduce the Romish confessional, and in the wide-spread taste for histrionic ceremonies, and Popish habiliments in the performance of public worship.[12]

Ryle was not primarily concerned over ceremonial trifles. Nor was the ritualistic controversy merely a new incarnation of the old disputes between high and low churchmen. Ritualism represented an organized attempt to eliminate Protestantism from the Church of England and to reintroduce the doctrines of the Church of Rome.[13] Ryle touched on some of the major areas of controversy in the previous quote: the Lord's Supper, auricular confession, and ritualistic innovation. These issues, together with differing interpretations of Anglicanism, constituted the heart of the ritualist controversy.

The Lord's Supper
It is difficult to overstate the importance the Lord's Supper played in the controversy between Ryle and the ritualists. He believed that unsound views of the sacrament were the "foundation" and

---

12. J. C. Ryle, "What Is Our Position?," in *Home Truths, Seventh Series* (London: William Hunt, 1859), 255–56.

13. J. C. Ryle, *Reasons for Opposing Ritualism* (London: Church Association, n.d.), 2.

"hidden root of nine-tenths" of Romanizing ritualism.[14] The Tractarian position developed over time and was not discussed in detail in the *Tracts for the Times*. But its mature articulation can be found in the works written after 1845 of E. B. Pusey, Archdeacon Denison, and Robert Wilberforce. Wilberforce provided an excellent summary of the main elements of their Eucharistic teaching in *The Doctrine of the Holy Eucharist* (1854):

> But that Christ's presence in the Holy Eucharist is a real presence; that the blessings of the new life are truly bestowed in it through communion with the New Adam; that consecration is a real act, whereby the inward part or thing signified is joined to the outward visible sign; and that the Eucharistic oblation is a real sacrifice—these points it will be attempted to prove by the testimony of Scripture and of the ancient Fathers.[15]

---

14. J. C. Ryle, *Knots Untied: Being Plain Statements on Disputed Points in Religion* (London: William Hunt, 1874), 164. Ryle wrote extensively on the subject in Stradbroke. He published the following works during this period of his ministry: *The Sacrament of the Lord's Supper: Its True Intention and Rightful Position in the Church of Christ* (London: William Hunt, 1866); *Why Were Our Reformers Burned?* (London: Office of the Church Association, 1867); *The Real Presence: What Is It?* (London: William Hunt, 1869); *Why, and Why Not? Being Questions about the Lord's Supper* (London: William Hunt, 1869); *His Presence: Where Is It?* (London: William Hunt, 1873); two chapters of *Knots Untied* (1874) are devoted to it; and it is discussed in *Church Principles and Church Comprehensiveness: Being Two Papers* (London: William Hunt, 1879).

15. Robert Isaac Wilberforce, *The Doctrine of the Holy Eucharist*, 3rd ed. (London: John and Charles Mozley, 1854), 5–6. William Goode provided another helpful summary of the Tractarian position:

> The doctrine of Archdeacon Denison and Dr. Pusey, then, is, that, in the Lord's Supper, the Bread and Wine are so influenced and operated on by the act of consecration, that though bread and wine remain, yet there is by consecration a real though spiritual presence of the Body and Blood of Christ so united to the Bread and Wine as to form with them one compound whole; and hence that the Body and Blood of Christ are received by *all* communicants, whatever their state of mind may be. Whether they are present by transfusion or conjunction, they do not clearly state—and the difference is unimportant except as affecting the terms used—but it is maintained that that which the communicant puts

Wilberforce's quote highlights the three major areas of disagreement between Ryle and the ritualists with respect to the Supper: the status of the minister, the purpose of the Supper, and the nature of Christ's presence.[16]

According to the ritualists, the celebrant was nothing less than a sacrificing priest. The ritualist catechism, *The Ritual Reasons Why*, states that the reason why the prayer of consecration is to be said standing before the altar (in the eastward position) is because "this is the position of a sacrificing Priest."[17] The use of the controversial Eucharistic vestments was meant to communicate this truth

---

into his mouth consists of two parts, one bread and wine, the other the Body and Blood of Christ present in a spiritual and supernatural manner in conjunction with the bread and wine.

William Goode, *The Nature of Christ's Presence in the Eucharist* (London: T. Hatchard, 1856), 1:2. Ryle also provided extracts from the sermons of Archdeacon Denison that affirmed the real presence of Christ in the consecrated elements and a Eucharistic sacrifice in *Knots Untied*, 169–71.

16. Another area of contention was the efficacy of the Supper. It will not be addressed below because the purpose of the Supper and the nature of Christ's presence in it were significantly more important to the debate between Ryle and the ritualists. Ryle often said something about it in his controversial writings on the Supper, however, so I will provide an excerpt that presents his position:

The Lord's Supper was never meant to confer benefits on communicants *ex opera operato*, or by virtue of a mere formal reception of the ordinance. We were not intended to believe that it does good to any but those who receive it with faith and knowledge. It is not a medicine or a charm which works mechanically, irrespective of the state of mind in which it is received. It cannot of itself confer grace, where grace does not already exist. It does not convert, justify, or convey blessing to the heart of an unbeliever. It is an ordinance not for the dead but for the living,—not for the faithless but for the believing,—not for the unconverted but the converted,—not for the impenitent sinner but for the saint. I am almost ashamed to take up time with such trite and well-known statements as these. The Word of God testifies distinctly that a man may go "eat and drink damnation to himself" (1 Cor. xi.27, 29). To such testimony I shall not add a word.

Ryle, *Knots Untied*, 168.

17. Charles Walker, ed., *The Ritual Reason Why* (London: J. T. Hayes, 1866), 117.

symbolically as well.[18] Ryle abhorred the notion that the celebrant is a sacrificing priest and rejected sacerdotal understanding of the Christian ministry as a dangerous error. He argued that this idea is entirely foreign to the New Testament, and he believed that the silence of the Pastoral Epistles, where this might naturally be discussed, is a "speaking silence."[19] The formularies of the Church of England repudiate it as well. He argued that there is nothing in the Thirty-Nine Articles that could possibly justify the idea of a sacrificing priesthood or a sacerdotal ministry. Even the language of *priest* in the prayer book offers the ritualist no safe haven. In the Latin version of the Articles, the Roman priest is called a *sacerdos* (a sacrificing priest), but the English priest is specifically called a *presbyteri* (elder). Therefore, the word "priest" in the prayer book means only "presbyter" or "elder."[20] In short, the Christian minister is preeminently a preacher of the word and is in no sense a sacrificing priest.

For ritualists, the Eucharistic oblation was real sacrifice as well as a sacrament.[21] Ryle stated the purpose of the Supper positively and negatively. Positively, the Supper was ordained to be a continual remembrance of Christ's atoning death on the cross and a merciful provision for the quickening, strengthening, and refreshing of the believer's faith.[22] Negatively, the Supper was never intended to be a sacrifice of any kind. To prove his assertion, Ryle appealed to the New Testament and formularies of the Church of England.

---

18. For example, Walker explained that the reason the choir wears the alb is because it is engaged in assisting the priest in the offering of the sacrifice. Walker, *Ritual Reason Why*, 16.

19. J. C. Ryle, *The Distinctive Principles of the Church of England* (London: William Hunt, 1878), 32.

20. Ryle argued that the rejection of any sacerdotal or sacrificial character in the Christian ministry is one of the distinctive principles of the Church of England. Ryle, *Distinctive Principles* (London: William Hunt, 1879), 30–31.

21. See Robert Isaac Wilberforce, "The Holy Eucharist Regarded as a Sacrifice," in *Doctrine of the Holy Eucharist*, 299–338.

22. Ryle, *Sacrament of the Lord's Supper*, 5–7. This chapter went on to become the eighth chapter in *Knots Untied*, which I will refer to from this point.

After surveying the accounts of the institution of the Lord's Supper in the Synoptic Gospels and in 1 Corinthians, Ryle concluded that the idea of a real Eucharistic sacrifice is entirely absent.[23] The Church's formularies were in precise harmony with the teaching of Scripture in this respect as well.

Regarding the sacraments, Ryle held the Church catechism in particularly high esteem for its logical preciseness and theological accuracy.[24] It specifically addresses the purpose of the sacrament of the Lord's Supper by asking the following question: "Why was the sacrament of the Lord's Supper ordained?" It supplies the following answer: "For the continual remembrance of the sacrifice of the death of Christ, and of the benefits which we receive thereby."[25] Like the catechism, the prayer book teaches that the purpose of the sacrament is remembrance, not sacrifice. He noted that the word *altar* is entirely absent from the Communion service, as is the word *sacrifice*, but it repeatedly emphasizes that the Supper is a "remembrance" of Christ's death.[26] In short, the idea of a real Eucharistic sacrifice is repugnant to both the Scriptures and the Church's formularies.

The nature of Christ's presence in the sacrament is the third major area of disagreement between Ryle and the ritualists. The ritualists, while denying transubstantiation, affirmed that Christ is really and truly present in the elements of bread and wine after consecration. Ryle affirmed a real, spiritual presence of Christ

23. For Ryle's interpretation of the institution of the Lord's Supper in the Synoptic Gospels, see his commentary on Matthew 26:26–35; Mark 14:17–25; and Luke 22:14–23 in *Expository Thoughts on the Gospels*. Elsewhere he wrote, "Not one of the writers of the New Testament ever speaks of the sacrament as a sacrifice, or calls the Lord's table an altar, or even hints that a Christian minister is a sacrificing priest. The universal doctrine of the New Testament is that after the one offering of Christ there remains no more need of sacrifice." Ryle, *Why, and Why Not?*, 7.

24. Ryle, *Knots Untied*, 164: "Rightly used, I hold the Church Catechism to be a most powerful weapon against semi-Romanism. Fairly interpreted, it is utterly subversive to the ritualistic system."

25. *The Book of Common Prayer*, 350th anniversary ed. (New York: Penguin Books, 2012), 304.

26. Ryle, *Why, and Why Not?*, 7.

within the hearts of all believing and faithful communicants in the Lord's Supper. He explained, "Every right-hearted believer, who ate that bread and drank that wine in remembrance of Christ, would in so doing find a special presence of Christ in his heart, and a special revelation of Christ's sacrifice of His own body and blood to his soul."[27] He utterly rejected the notion that Christ was bodily present in the Supper, however.

First and foremost, Ryle rejected the ritualists' doctrine of real presence because it is not taught in Scripture. In the three accounts of the institution of the Lord's Supper in the Gospels, Christ referred to the bread and wine as "My body" and "My blood," but Ryle insisted that cannot be literally true. The bread and wine are simply "lively emblems" or "visible sermons" that represent or signify Christ's sacrificial death.[28] It is simply taken for granted that *is* and *are* frequently mean "represent" in Scripture, especially in the parables.[29] This interpretation is confirmed by the fact that Paul refers three times in 1 Corinthians 11:26–28 to the consecrated bread simply as *bread*, and not the body of Christ. John 6 is a particularly critical text in the debate between Ryle and the ritualists. Wilberforce devoted an entire chapter of *The Doctrine of the Holy Eucharist* to proving that this chapter taught a real and not merely a symbolic or virtual presence of Christ in the Supper.[30] Ryle devoted a considerable amount of space defending his position in his commentary on John as well.[31] He denied that this text has any reference whatsoever to the sacrament of the Lord's Supper. Christ's "flesh and blood" refers to His upcoming sacrificial and substitutionary death on the cross for sinners. Moreover, "eating and drinking" is not a bodily act, but an inward and spiritual act of the heart—that

---

27. Ryle, *Knots Untied*, 199.

28. Ryle, *St. Luke*, 2:396.

29. The parable of the sower in Matthew 13 was one of Ryle's favorite proof texts for this method of interpretation.

30. See chapter 7 of Wilberforce, *Doctrine of the Holy Eucharist*.

31. See his comments on John 6:52–59.

is, faith. Faith, and faith only, in Christ's atonement is absolutely necessary for salvation. In sum, "the atonement of Christ, His vicarious death and sacrifice, and faith in it—these things are the key to the whole passage."[32] This interpretation is supported by "weighty reasons." To suggest that this passage refers to a literal eating of Christ's body and blood in the Supper would be revolting to Jews and a violation of their purity laws regarding the eating of blood. It would interpose a bodily act between the soul and its salvation, which is without precedent in Scripture. It would make Communion absolutely necessary to salvation, which would condemn all noncommunicants (including infants, children, and the penitent thief) to hell; raise ignorant, godless, and faithless communicants to heaven; and open the floodgates of superstition and idolatry.[33]

Ryle vehemently opposed the ritualists' doctrine of the real presence for theological as well as exegetical reasons. First, though the ritualists denied transubstantiation, their doctrine of the real bodily presence of Christ was identical to that of the Roman Catholic Church.[34] Second, by suggesting that Christ's body can be present in two places at the same time, the ritualists destroyed the true humanity of Christ and embraced the ancient heresy of the Apollinarians.[35] Third, by asserting that Christ is truly present and actually resacrificed during the celebration of the Lord's Supper, they dishonor the doctrine of the finished work of Christ's atonement.[36] Fourth, by suggesting that a human priest can offer acceptable sacrifices to God, Christ, the Great High Priest, is robbed of His glory.[37] Finally, by exalting sinful men into the position

---

32. Ryle, *St. John*, 1:399.

33. Ryle, *St. John*, 1:394.

34. Ryle, *Knots Untied*, 171.

35. Ryle, *Knots Untied*, 167.

36. "A sacrifice that needs to be repeated is not a perfect and complete thing." J. C. Ryle, *Why Were Our Reformers Burned?* (London: William Macintosh, 1871), 21.

37. Ryle, *Why Were Our Reformers Burned?*, 21.

of mediators between God and man, the ritualists destroyed the scriptural doctrine of the Christian ministry.[38]

Ryle was also convinced that the ritualists' doctrine of the real presence was incompatible with the formularies of the Church of England. The Thirty-Nine Articles cannot be harmonized with the ritualists' doctrine of the real presence. Ryle flatly stated, "If the language of the Twenty-eighth Article can be reconciled with the doctrine of Archdeacon Denison and his school, I can only say that words have no meaning at all."[39] The liturgy of the Church of England is incompatible with the ritualist teaching as well. The words *altar* and *sacrifice* were purposely excluded from the Communion service, and the rubric at the end of that service specifically condemns the doctrine of a real presence in no uncertain terms.[40] The catechism of the Church of England agrees with the Articles and the liturgy against the ritualists. It affirms the spiritual presence of Christ in the Supper to every faithful communicant but not a local, corporeal presence in the bread and wine. The homilies of the Church of England that address the sacrament also agree with the Articles, liturgy, and catechism. They affirm that the sacrament is a memorial of Christ's death and that it must be received with faith and knowledge; but they deny that the Supper is a sacrifice, that the minister is a sacrificing priest, and that Christ is bodily present in the elements.[41]

---

38. Ryle, *Why Were Our Reformers Burned?*, 21.

39. Ryle, *Knots Untied*, 171.

40. Ryle, *Knots Untied*, 173. *Book of Common Prayer*, 276: "It is here declared, that thereby no Adoration is intended, or ought to be done, either unto the Sacramental Bread or Wine there bodily received, or unto any Corporal Presence of Christ's natural Flesh and Blood. For the Sacramental Bread and Wine remain still in their very natural substances, and therefore may not be adored; (for that were Idolatry, to be abhorred of all faithful Christians;) and the natural Body and Blood of our Saviour Christ are in Heaven, and not here; it being against the truth of Christ's natural Body to be at one time in more places than one."

41. Ryle, *Knots Untied*, 174–75.

Ryle also provided a catena of quotations from a broad spectrum of Anglican authorities to support his position. He quoted Jeremy Taylor, the famous nonjuror Dr. Brett, Archbishop Ussher, Archbishop Cranmer, Bishop Ridley, Bishop Hooper, Bishop Jewel, Dr. Waterland, Dean Aldrich, Bishop Henry Philpotts, and Archbishop Longley. Furthermore, he repeatedly recommends Dean Goode's "masterly" and "unanswerable" work *The Nature of Christ's Presence in the Eucharist*, which defends the sound Protestant views of the Lord's Supper.[42]

Auricular Confession

Auricular confession—people confessing their sins to God in the presence of a priest authorized to forgive them in God's name—was one of the most controversial practices revived by the ritualists. E. B. Pusey adopted the practice during the early stages of the Oxford movement and advocated its regular and systematic use. The ritualists quickly embraced it and made it a cornerstone of their spirituality. Habitual confession was urged on parishioners as a vital element of the spiritual life and a means of being reconciled to God after a lapse into sin after baptism.[43] Ritualists published a number of confessor's manuals to encourage the practice.[44] Some went as far as making confession a precondition to confirmation and Communion.

Evangelicals were not opposed to spiritual conferences. They encouraged them. Ryle probably engaged in these regularly during his house-to-house visits. The major problem evangelicals had with confession, aside from its obvious connections to Roman Catholicism, was its imposition of a human mediator between the sinner and the Savior. Ryle expressed the concern of many evangelicals

---

42. Ryle, *Knots Untied*, 176.

43. E. B. Pusey published *Advice for Those Who Exercise the Ministry of Reconciliation Through Confession and Absolution: Being the Abbe Gaume's Manual for Confessors*, 2nd ed. (Oxford: James Parker and Company, 1878).

44. The most famous was *The Priest in Absolution: A Manual for Such as Are Called unto the Higher Ministries in the English Church* (London: Joseph Masters, 1866). It caused a public outcry and was denounced in the House of Lords.

when he wrote, "All religious systems which put anything between the heavy-laden sinner and Jesus Christ the Saviour, except simple faith, are dangerous and unscriptural."[45]

Ryle believed that confessing sin is absolutely necessary for salvation and inward peace, but he insisted that this confession must be made directly to Christ alone, for He alone is the "great High Priest" who is able and willing to absolve every sinner who confesses to Him.[46] There is no better high priest, and Christians need no other mediator or priest.[47] Therefore, people who turn away from Christ to confess to anyone else rob their own soul.[48]

Ryle opposed the confessional because it lacks all scriptural warrant. He noted that there is no evidence that anyone in the New Testament ever confessed sin privately to a minister or was privately absolved. Moreover, in the Pastoral Epistles, where one might expect to find the subject mentioned, it is entirely absent.[49] He acknowledged that John 20:23 is often quoted in defense of priestly absolution, but he was unconvinced. He believed that this commission gave the apostles declarative authority, not judicial authority, and thus he denied that Christ meant to delegate to the apostles, or any others, the power of absolutely pardoning or not pardoning, absolving or not absolving, anyone's soul.[50]

The formularies of the Church of England offer no support for it either. The homily of repentance specifically condemns auricular confession as having "not the warrant of God's Word" and acknowledges no other priest for deliverance from sin "but our

---

45. Ryle, *Knots Untied*, 381.

46. Ryle, *Knots Untied*, 266.

47. Ryle pointed out that Christ is a high priest of almighty power, of infinite willingness to receive confession of sin, of perfect knowledge, of matchless tenderness, who can sympathize with all those who confess to Him. Ryle, *Knots Untied*, 266–67.

48. Ryle, *Knots Untied*, 268.

49. Ryle, *Knots Untied*, 257–58. See also Ryle, *St. John*, 3:399.

50. See Ryle, *St. John*, 3:398.

Saviour Jesus Christ."[51] Ryle admitted that there are two passages in the prayer book which appear to support confession: the exhortation in the Communion service and the visitation of the sick. But when honestly interpreted and read in light of the Reformers' intentions, there was no evidence suggesting that the Church of England sanctions auricular confession.

The exhortation in the Communion service is directed toward those who cannot quiet their conscience. Such a person is exhorted to come to a "discreet and learned Minister of God's Word, and open his grief; that by the ministry of God's holy Word he may receive the benefit of absolution, together with ghostly counsel and advice, to the quieting of his conscience, and avoiding of all scruple and doubtfulness." This, according to Ryle, is nothing more than an exhortation for a person to seek spiritual counsel from a minister in order to have his or her difficulties explained by texts from the Bible.

The language in the "Order for the Visitation of the Sick" is stronger. The sick person is urged to make a special confession of his sins, and the priest "shall absolve him" after his confession. Ryle insisted that the most that can be said of this absolution is that it is declarative—that is, if he repents and believes, he will be forgiven as the Scriptures declare. Therefore, when the minister says, "I absolve thee," he can only mean, "I declare thee absolved."[52]

Ryle was also concerned about the pastoral implication of habitual confession. First, it dishonors Christ by undermining the glory and uniqueness of His office as high priest. Christ alone is the Christian's priest, confessor, absolver, and spiritual director.[53] Second, it destroys Christian liberty. It makes the confessor little less than a god, and it makes those who confess little better than slaves.

---

51. As quoted in Ryle, *Knots Untied*, 275.

52. After discussing these passages, Ryle said that he deeply regrets that these passages in the formularies contain expressions that seem to support his opponents' position, and he should rejoice to see them removed. See Ryle, *Knots Untied*, 269–70n1.

53. Ryle, *Knots Untied*, 259.

He warned, "If we love Christian liberty, and value inward peace, let us beware of the slightest approach to the Romish confessional!"[54] Finally, church history shows that the confessional is a practice of a "most vile and evil tendency." It has often led to the "grossest and most disgusting immorality," and for every soul it reclaimed it has destroyed thousands.[55] He was so alarmed by the practice that he warned fathers and husbands not to allow a clergyman to draw their wives and daughters into private confessionals, and he urged them to refuse to send their sons to schools that permit it.[56]

In summer 1873, an anticonfessional meeting was held at Exeter Hall. While Ryle was unable to attend, he sent a brief letter expressing his regrets for not attending. He wrote, "It is my deliberate conviction that habitual private confession is absolutely without warrant of scripture—manifestly dishonouring to the priestly office of Christ—most injurious to the minister—most useless to the laity—and most mischievous and immoral in its tendency. I would rather see the Church of England perish than see habitual auricular confession sanctioned in our pale. God bless the meeting."[57] This short statement provides an excellent summary of Ryle's problems with auricular confession, and it gives some indication of the intensity of his opposition to it.

Ritualistic Innovation
Ritualistic innovation in public worship was another area of disagreement between Ryle and the ritualists. The ritualists were

---

54. Ryle, *Knots Untied*, 271.

55. Ryle, *Knots Untied*, 270. In a footnote Ryle specifically pointed the reader to Charles Elliott's *Delineation of Romanism* and the discussion of "solicitants." He then remarked, "If then they are not convinced of the immoral tendency of the confessional, I shall be surprised." See Charles Elliott, *Delineation of Roman Catholicism Drawn from Authentic and Acknowledged Standards of the Church of Rome* (New York: G. Lane and P. P. Sandford, 1842), 314.

56. See J. C. Ryle, *What Do We Owe to the Reformation?* (London: Church Association, n.d.), 21–22; and Ryle, *Reasons for Opposing Ritualism*, 4.

57. *The Church Association Monthly Intelligencer*, July 1873: 171.

attempting to restore the forgotten worship of the primitive church to the Church of England by introducing a variety of ancient ritual practices into its worship services.[58] These included the use of incense, distinctive clerical vestments, lights on the altar, and a number of other controversial symbols and practices.[59] The purpose of these ritual acts was twofold: to uphold the dignity of divine worship, and to "shadow forth" by outward deed and gesture certain truths that worshipers might otherwise lose sight of.[60] Ryle, on the other hand, regarded the reintroduction of these ritual practices as great evils that must be resisted by all faithful churchmen. They were without scriptural warrant, and they were nothing less than an unveiled attempt to Romanize the Church of England from within.

Ryle believed that the leading principles of worship were clearly presented in the Bible. True worship must be directed to God alone, which rules out praying to dead saints or angels or adoring the Communion elements. It must be directed to God through the atonement and mediation of Christ, which excludes all other human or angelic mediators. It must be explicitly scriptural, deducible from Scripture, or in harmony with Scripture. Therefore, nothing may be required which is contrary to God's Word, no matter how ancient the practice. It must be intelligible, and thus worship in which the mind takes no part is useless and unprofitable. Above all, it must be worship of the heart. The heart is the principal thing, not gestures, postures, bowing, and bodily service.[61]

---

58. Littledale, *Innovations: A Lecture*, 27.

59. Littledale specifically listed twelve: prayers for the dead, the choral service, the sign of the cross, the weekly offertory, daily celebration of Holy Communion, the elevation of the host, turning eastward to pray or say the creed, the division of the sexes, the mixed chalice in Holy Communion, incense, vestments, and lights on the altar. Littledale, *Innovations: A Lecture*, 8–13.

60. Walker, *Ritual Reason Why*, 1. Walker's catechism is an excellent resource for the study of ritualism, especially for those who are unfamiliar with many of the elements used in Anglo-Catholic worship.

61. J. C. Ryle, *How Do You Worship?* (London: William Hunt, 1868), 9–15.

The essential elements of worship, like the leading principles of worship, were easily discerned in the New Testament as well.[62] The Sabbath must be honored. There should be a minister to conduct the worship of Christian congregations. The preaching of God's word must occupy a prominent place. There should be united public prayers. The Scriptures should be publicly read. There should be united praise. The two sacraments should be used regularly.[63] In short, simplicity ought to be the "grand characteristic" of Christian worship as well as preaching.[64]

For Ryle, the problems with the ritualistic innovations went beyond faulty exegesis. There was an unmistakable Romeward tendency in the ceremonial novelties of the ritualists.[65] He was concerned about three in particular. The first was the growing trend of using an excessive number of decorations and ornaments in

---

62. Ryle's emphasis on the New Testament is worth noting. He saw very little continuity between Old Testament and New Testament worship. He wrote, "There is a wide difference…between the law of Moses and the law of Christ. The Jew's religion was full of strict and minute directions about worship: the Christian's contains very few directions, and those of the simplest and most general descriptions." Ryle, *How Do You Worship?*, 15–16. The ritualists, on the other hand, saw almost universal continuity between Old Testament and New Testament worship. They frequently appealed to the directions related to the decoration of the tabernacle to justify their innovations, as well as Christ's pronouncement that He came not to abolish the law, but to fulfill it. Walker, *Ritual Reasons Why*, 2–3.

63. Ryle, *How Do You Worship?*, 15–20.

64. Ryle, *Evangelical Religion*, 24.

65. J. C. Ryle, *Lessons from English Church History* (London: William Hunt, 1871), 35:

They have all been in one direction, whether of dress, or gesture, or posture, or action, or anything else. They have all been as unprotestant as possible. They have all been borrowed or imitated from Popery. They have all exhibited one common bias, and animus,—an anxious desire to get as far as possible from the ways of the Reformers, and to get as near as possible, whether legally or illegally, to the ways of Rome. They have all shown one common systematic determination to unprotestantize, as far as possible, the simple worship of the poor old Church of England, and to assimilate it, as far as possible, to the gaudy and sensuous worship of Popery.

worship. Though he did not despise good ecclesiastical architecture, a well-conducted service, or reverent worship, he believed that the excessive use of "gaudy dressing, candle-lighting, and theatrical ceremonial" in divine service defeats the very purpose of worship.[66] It distracts people from Christ, encourages people to walk by sight instead of by faith, and emphasizes outward appearances at the expense of the heart.[67] Moreover, there was no warrant for gorgeous and decorated ceremonies, nor were there any symbols except water, bread, and wine in the Gospels or the Epistles.[68] The New Testament unequivocally asserts, however, that human nature is easily led astray and thoroughly inclined to idolatry. Therefore, ornamentation and ceremony, if used at all in worship, must be used sparingly.

The second ritualistic innovation that concerned Ryle was the use of Eucharistic vestments in the celebration of the Lord's Supper.[69] They included the amice, alb, cope, girdle, stole, maniple, tunic, dalmatic, and chasuble.[70] The ritualists insisted that these vestments are apostolic in origin and mark the dignity of the service by symbolizing the passion of Christ.[71] Ryle saw the use of them as an overt attempt to undermine the Protestant principles of the Church of England and opposed them on the following grounds. First, there is no proof that Eucharistic vestments were used in apostolic times to celebrate the Lord's Supper, nor is there any suggestion that they are necessary for the proper celebration of the Lord's Supper. They are entirely without warrant in Scripture.

---

66. Ryle, *How Do You Worship?*, 23.

67. Ryle, *Evangelical Religion*, 25.

68. Ryle, *How Do You Worship?*, 23.

69. Ryle was particularly concerned about the use of distinctive vestments in worship. He wrote at least three tracts to specifically warn the public about this issue. See *Distinctive Vestments* (London: Church Association, n.d.); *Twelve Reasons against the Distinctive Vestments* (London: Church Association, n.d.); and *The Ornaments Rubric* (London: Church Association, n.d.).

70. For a description of these vestments, see Walker, *Ritual Reason Why*. Ryle specifically singles out the alb, cope, and chasuble in *Distinctive Vestments*, 3.

71. Walker, *Ritual Reason Why*, 18.

Second, Eucharistic vestments imply that the Christian minister is a sacrificing priest, the Lord's Table is an altar, the Supper is a real sacrifice, and that the elements contain Christ's real presence. In short, there is an inseparable connection between distinctive vestments and the sacrifice of the Mass.[72] Third, the history of the Church of England provides no warrant for their use.

Ryle acknowledged that during the beginning of the English Reformation, "when our Reformers were only half enlightened," the use of distinctive vestments was ordered in the first prayer book of Edward VI (1549).[73] Nicholas Ridley and Thomas Cranmer even had their fellow Reformer John Hooper imprisoned for refusing to wear episcopal vestments.[74] But once they saw scriptural truth more fully and clearly, they expressly forbade the use of these vestments altogether in the second prayer book of Edward VI (1552).[75] In the first year of her reign, Elizabeth issued a series of injunctions and advertisements requiring ministers to wear a "comely surplice," but the alb, cope, and chasuble were omitted.[76] Archbishop Parker, the first primate under Elizabeth, only mentioned the surplice in the Articles of Inquiry of 1569. In 1576, Archbishop Grindal referred to Eucharistic vestments as "relics and monuments of superstition and idolatry" in his Articles of Inquiry and ordered them to be

---

72. Ryle, *Distinctive Vestments*, 3.

73. Ryle, *Distinctive Vestments*, 3.

74. Though Ryle appreciated all three English Reformers, he believed Hooper was right to refuse the vestments, and Ridley and Cranmer were in the wrong. He called Hooper more "far-sighted" than his fellow laborers and suggested that if Hooper's views had been allowed to prevail, "one half of the Ritualistic controversy would never have existed at all." For Ryle's discussion of the vestment controversy, see *Bishops and Clergy of Other Days* (London: William Hunt, 1868), 23–26.

75. Ryle quoted from the words at the beginning of the morning service: "The priest shall wear neither alb, vestment, nor cope,—but shall have and wear a surplice only." Ryle, *Distinctive Vestments*, 3.

76. Ryle, *Distinctive Vestments*, 3–4. Also, in *The Ornaments Rubric* Ryle provided specific quotations from various documents (e.g., the prayer book, acts of Parliament, visitation articles) to support many of the historical claims he makes in *Distinctive Vestments*.

"defaced, broken, and destroyed."[77] The Canons of 1604 say nothing about distinctive vestments and simply order the minister to wear a "decent and comely surplice" when performing his public duties.[78] During the last prayer book revision (1662), distinctive vestments were not restored, and nothing was added to justify their use. In sum, in the parish churches of the Church of England, Eucharistic vestments (specifically the alb, cope, and chasuble) had not been used or sanctioned since the first days of Elizabeth.

The third ritualistic innovation that concerned Ryle was the use of the "eastward position," which refers to the position of the celebrant of the Eucharist, standing on the same side of the altar as the people with his back to them. Ryle opposed this practice for the same reason he opposed distinctive vestments: it was an outward and visible sign of the sacrifice of the Mass; it lacked all scriptural warrant;[79] it was without warrant of the prayer book, fairly interpreted;[80] and it was a direct step toward Roman Catholicism.[81]

---

77. Ryle, *Distinctive Vestments*, 4; Ryle, *Ornaments Rubric*, 2.

78. Ryle acknowledged, with regret, that the twenty-fourth canon orders the cope to be worn in cathedrals by those who administer Communion. He pointed out, however, that the chasuble, and not the cope, was regarded as the sacrificial garment, and it was not ordered to be used. See Ryle, *Distinctive Vestments*, 4; and Ryle, *Ornaments Rubric*, 2–3.

79. The four accounts of the institution of the Lord's Supper in the New Testament make no mention of it. Ryle was convinced that any plain, impartial, and unprejudiced person, reading the simple narrative of the New Testament for the first time, would say unhesitatingly that Christ broke the bread and gave the cup in full view of the whole congregation of the apostles. Why should clergymen make a mystery where Christ made none? See J. C. Ryle, *The Eastward Position* (London: Church Association, n.d.), 2.

80. The Communion office never calls the minister a sacrificing priest, the table an altar, and the Supper a sacrifice. The rubric that directs the minister's position specifically says that the elements are to be consecrated "before the people." Ryle pointed out that this statement, "before the people," is even more remarkable because it first directs the minister to stand before the table and order the bread and wine so that he may do what he does with order and decency. Only after he has properly ordered the elements, he is to consecrate them "before the people"—that is, standing in such a position that everyone can see what he does. Ryle, *Eastward Position*, 2.

81. Ryle, *Eastward Position*, 2.

Interpreting Anglicanism

In addition to significant doctrinal differences, Ryle and the ritualists interpreted Anglicanism and its relationship to the Protestant Reformation very differently. For ritualists like Richard Frederick Littledale, the English Reformers were traitors and scoundrels who ushered in an era of unprecedented despotism, misery, and spiritual destitution.[82] They destroyed the true worship of God, ruined the church of their forefathers, and made religion cold, sordid, and dismal.[83] The ritualists were the faithful sons of the Church of England. They were simply attempting to restore the Church of England to its primitive purity. The Reformers were the true ecclesiastical innovators.[84]

For Littledale, the Protestant Reformation was a tragedy and a curse, but Ryle considered it to be the greatest blessing God had ever bestowed on England.[85] Before the Reformation, when the

---

82. Littledale's hatred for the English Reformers and the English Reformation is palpable. He said that Robespierre, Danton, Marat, St. Just, and Couthon merit as much admiration and respect as Cranmer, Ridley, Latimer, and Hooper, "who happened to have the ill-luck to be worsted in a struggle wherein they meant to serve their adversaries as they were served themselves" (15). In fact, these Reformers out-sinned these Jacobins in terms of cruelty, impiety, and licentious foulness (31). The so-called Marian martyrs were neither "true nor brave." Hugh Latimer was a coarse, profane, unscrupulous, persecuting bully and coward (44). John Hooper was a sacrilegious perjurer (46). Nicholas Ridley was the least criminal of the English Reformers, "but he by no means rises to the level of a good man or a good citizen" (48). John Foxe, the infamous author of *Acts and Monuments*, was a lying bigot (21). Littledale, *Innovations: A Lecture*.

83. For Littledale's catalogue of Protestant innovations, see *Innovations: A Lecture*, 22–24.

84. Littledale, *Innovations: A Lecture*, 27: "The Reformers destroyed the worship of God, and set up the Abomination of Desolation in its place. We are trying to restore the forgotten worship.... The religion we teach is an old one. The newfangled ways have all failed, and we think it worth while to try the old ones again. They succeeded thoroughly once, and they may not have lost their virtue yet. We are not innovating."

85. Ryle, *Lessons from English Church History*, 13. For an excellent treatment of Ryle as a historian, see Lee Gatiss's introduction to *Christian Leaders of the Seventeenth Century*, ed. Lee Gatiss (London: Church Society, 2015), 7–20. I have also

Church of England was completely and entirely Roman Catholic, English religion was at its worst.[86] Gross religious ignorance and spiritual darkness dominated the land. The English Bible was banned. There was little preaching. Worship services were carried out in an unknown tongue.[87] Being destitute of scriptural knowledge, Englishmen adopted "the most groveling, childish, and superstitious practices in religion."[88] They worshiped images, bowed down to statues, and venerated the relics of dead saints. Furthermore, Englishmen groaned under the degrading tyranny and swindling impostures of the Romish priesthood. Through their tricks, lying wonders, and impositions, the priests enriched themselves and maintained their power and influence at the expense of the people.[89] In terms of morality, the clergy were generally immoral and unholy in the extreme. As a result, the moral tone of the laity was at its lowest ebb.[90] In short, there was an utter famine of vital Christianity in the land.

The Protestant Reformation delivered England from all these evils and conferred a number of positive blessings. It gave Englishmen the Bible in their own language and liberty to read it. It restored the apostolic doctrine of the forgiveness of sins by simple faith in Christ. It provided intelligible religious services for every parish in the land. It produced a true standard of practical holiness. It asserted the supremacy of the Holy Scriptures as the sole rule of faith and practice. It revived the true preaching of the gospel. It led to the creation of the greatest Protestant confession of faith: the Thirty-Nine Articles of Religion. It simplified, purified,

---

discussed Ryle's historical understanding and defense of evangelical identity in Bennett W. Rogers, "Ryle and Evangelical Identity," *Foundations: An International Journal of Evangelical Theology* 70 (2016): 94–111.

86. Ryle, *Lessons from English Church History*, 7.

87. Ryle, *What Do We Owe to the Reformation?*, 4–5.

88. Ryle, *What Do We Owe to the Reformation?*, 6.

89. Ryle, *What Do We Owe to the Reformation?*, 7.

90. Ryle, *What Do We Owe to the Reformation?*, 9.

and popularized the whole Christian religion in the realm.[91] Ryle concluded, "Whatever England is among the nations of the earth, as a Christian country, whatever political liberty we enjoy, whatever freedom we have in religion, whatever safety for life and property there is among us, whatever purity and happiness there is in our homes, whatever protection and care for the poor, we owe it, in very great measure, to the Protestant Reformation."[92]

The English Reformers were hardly "unredeemed villains."[93] They delivered England from antichrist (Roman Catholicism), founded the Reformed Church of England, and cemented its foundations with their blood.[94] They were not perfect men, and Ryle was unwilling to defend everything that was said and done in the heat of conflict. Given the difficulties they had to contend with—the tyrannical and inconsistent conduct of Henry VIII, the early and untimely death of Edward VI, the persecuting cruelty of Queen Mary, and the compromising policy of Queen Elizabeth— it is a marvel that they accomplished so much.[95] He believed that no group of Englishmen, in spite of their faults, did more good in their day, lived better, died better, and left a better mark on England than the English Reformers.[96]

In addition to differing interpretations of the Protestant Reformation, Ryle and the ritualists disagreed about the Church's formularies as well. Should the Articles interpret the prayer book, or should the prayer book interpret the Articles? The ritualists had little love for the Articles. They pejoratively referred to them as "forty stripes save one" or the "Calvinistic Articles" and often

---

91. For discussions of the positive blessings of the Protestant Reformation, see Ryle, *Lessons from English Church History*, 15–16; and Ryle, *What Do We Owe to the Reformation?*, 11–15.

92. Ryle, *Lessons from English Church History*, 16.

93. J. C. Ryle, *Principles for Churchmen: A Manual of Positive Statements on Doubtful or Disputed Points* (London: William Hunt and Company, 1884), 365.

94. Ryle, *Church Principles and Church Comprehensiveness*, 13.

95. Ryle, *Lessons from English Church History*, 17.

96. Ryle, *Lessons from English Church History*, 17.

ignored them altogether.[97] The prayer book, more specifically the first prayer book of Edward VI (1549), was the true test of church-manship for the ritualists.

For Ryle, the Thirty-Nine Articles were the Church's confession of faith and the first, foremost, chief, and principal test of church-manship, not the prayer book.[98] To support his assertion, he offered the following proofs. First, the title of the Articles that was prefixed to every complete prayer book suggests that they were intended to be the true test of churchmanship.[99] Second, he appealed to the statute law of the realm. In two unrepealed Acts of Parliament (the 13th of Elizabeth, cap. 12, and the 28th and 29th of Victoria, cap. 122), the Thirty-Nine Articles were held up as the tests of minis-terial soundness and were to be publicly read and assented to by every minister on the first Sunday after being instituted to any liv-ing.[100] Third, Ryle pointed to the royal declaration prefixed to the Articles in 1628 by Charles I, which declared that the Articles "do contain the true doctrine of the Church of England agreeable to God's Word."[101] Fourth, he appealed to a circular letter issued by the Crown in 1721 to uphold the doctrine of the Trinity. It forbade clergymen from teaching anything about the Trinity that is not con-tained in Holy Scripture and is not agreeable to the three creeds and the Thirty-Nine Articles.[102] Fifth, his position appears to be supported by Thomas Rogers, who published the first exposition of

---

97. Ryle, *Knots Untied*, 69.

98. For Ryle's examination of the Thirty-Nine Articles and their place within the Church of England, see *Who Is the True Churchman? Or, the Thirty-Nine Articles Examined* (London: William Hunt, 1872); "The Thirty-Nine Articles," in *Knot Untied*, 62–86; and *Church Principles and Church Comprehensiveness*, 12–20.

99. The complete title reads as follows: "Articles agreed upon for the avoiding of Diversities of Opinion, and for the establishing of Consent touching true Religion." This title was originally written by Archbishop Cranmer and was retained by Arch-bishop Parker in the second edition of the prayer book.

100. For more information on these two acts, see Ryle, *Knots Untied*, 72–73.

101. Ryle, *Knots Untied*, 74.

102. Ryle, *Knots Untied*, 74.

the Articles in 1607. According to Rogers, the Articles are the doctrine that the Church of England professes, and other doctrines not expressed therein the Church "neither hath nor holdeth."[103] Finally, he provided a catena of quotations from Anglican authorities belonging to different schools, who all agreed that the Thirty-Nine Articles were the Church's doctrinal standard.[104]

Though Ryle considered the Articles to be the Church's doctrinal standard, he insisted that he did not undervalue the prayer book. He wrote, "In loyal love to the Prayer-book, and deep admiration of its contexts, I give place to no man. Taken for all in all, as an uninspired work, it is an incomparable book of devotion for the use of a Christian congregation."[105] The Reformers never intended the prayer book to hold the same office as the Articles. It is a manual of public devotion, not a confession of faith. Though Ryle's position may have seemed extravagant to some ritualists, it was vindicated in the Voysey judgment, which declared that "pious expressions of devotion are not to be taken as binding declarations of doctrine."[106]

The Church Association

Any discussion of Ryle's campaign against ritualism would be incomplete without mentioning his involvement with the London Church Association. In 1859 the ritualists formed the English Church Union in order to "defend and maintain unimpaired the doctrine, discipline, and ritual of the Church of England against Erastianism, Rationalism, and Puritanism, and to afford counsel and protection to all persons, lay and clerical, suffering unjust aggression or hindrance in spiritual matters."[107] Shortly thereafter

---

103. Ryle, *Knots Untied*, 74.

104. He provided quotes from Bishop Hall, Bishop Stillingfleet, Bishop Beveridge, and Bishop Tomline. Ryle, *Knots Untied*, 75–76.

105. Ryle, *Church Principles and Church Comprehensiveness*, 19–20.

106. Ryle, *Knots Untied*, 77.

107. Eugene Stock, *The History of the Church Missionary Society: Its Environment, Its Men, and Its Work* (London: Church Missionary Society, 1899), 2:348.

they initiated a series of prosecutions. The first were directed at evangelical clergymen who held missionary services in theaters. In 1862 it attempted to institute legal proceedings against Samuel Waldegrave, the evangelical bishop of Carlisle, for heresy.

Evangelicals responded by forming the Church Association in 1865. It was established to "uphold the Doctrines, Principles, and Order of the United Church of England and Ireland, and to counteract the efforts now being made to pervert her teaching on essential points of the Christian faith, or assimilate her Services to those of the Church of Rome, and further to encourage concerted action for the advancement and progress of Spiritual Religion."[108]

To effect these objectives, the Church Association published tracts, sponsored lectures, and held meetings. Nearly one hundred local chapters were opened throughout the country, its membership grew to nearly ten thousand, and *The Church Association Monthly Intelligencer* was widely read. But the group quickly became known primarily for its legal actions, which earned it the nickname "Persecution Society Limited."

The Church Association initiated a series of legal actions against clergymen for introducing ritualistic worship into their parish churches.[109] One of the most notorious cases was that of A. H. Mackonochie. Mackonochie was charged with elevating the elements of the Lord's Supper, using lighted candles on the Communion table (when they were not needed for light), using incense, and mixing water with wine. The Judicial Committee of the Privy

---

108. *Church Association Tracts* (London: Church Association, 1865–?), 1:1. The Church Association was originally intended to be an inclusive body. It sought to unite all moderate churchmen who were prepared to stand by Reformation principles, and efforts were made to include men on its council who were not usually identified with the evangelical school. The founders abstained from asking Lord Shaftesbury to be president in order to preserve the association from a party character. Stock, *Church Missionary Society*, 2:348.

109. For an excellent description of the ritual cases in the later nineteenth century, see Bentley, "Transformation of the Evangelical Party," 124–71. See also Marsh, *Victorian Church in Decline*, 111–34, 218–41.

Council condemned him on all points and ordered him to pay court costs.[110] Another prominent case involved Rev. John Purchas. In 1869, the Church Association began proceedings against Purchas for a long list of ritual offenses, including the adoption of the eastward position in celebration of the Lord's Supper and wearing Eucharistic vestments. The following year the Judicial Committee ruled against Purchas on all offenses except wearing a biretta.[111] Other prosecutions followed, and the Church Association won a number of judgments against the ritualists.[112] Some ritualists, like Arthur Tooth and Mr. Green of Miles Platting, were even imprisoned. These judgments proved to be Pyrrhic victories. Ultimately, they failed to suppress ritualism, made evangelicals unpopular, and divided the party.

Ryle was deeply involved with the Church Association from its founding. He wrote a number of tracts on its behalf.[113] He delivered lectures on the Reformation and evangelicalism.[114] He frequently spoke at regional and national meetings. His name appeared regularly in *The Church Association Monthly Intelligencer*. He became a vice president in 1870. He also labored to make

---

110. Bentley, "Transformation of the Evangelical Party," 127.

111. Bentley, "Transformation of the Evangelical Party," 127.

112. Some of the more noteworthy are the Bennett judgment, Folkestone judgment, and Ridsdale judgment.

113. All the following were published in London by the Church Association: *The Teaching of the Ritualists Not the Teaching of the Church of England* (tract 4, n.d.); *Eastward Position* (tract 30); *Distinctive Vestments* (tract 33); *Reasons for Opposing Ritualism* (tract 55); *What Do We Owe to the Reformation?* (tract 56); *What Practical Course of Action Should Now Be Taken to Give Effect to the Various Judgments on Disputed Points of Ceremony in the Church?* (tract 61, 1877); *Distinctive Principles of the Church of England* (tract 68); *Eastward Position no. 2* (tract 136); *Twelve Reasons against the Distinctive Vestments* (tract 137); *The Priesthood of Christ* (tract 140); *What Do the Times Require?* (tract 147, 1879); *Ornaments Rubric* (tract 148); *Church Reform: The Position of the Laity* (tract 191); *Regeneration and Baptism* (tract 193); and *Why Were Our Reformers Burned?* (tract 56).

114. See the following publications by Ryle: *Why Were Our Reformers Burned?*; *Evangelical Religion*; and *Archbishop Laud and His Times: A Lecture* (London: Hatchards, 1869).

the Church Association the basis of a league of Protestant and evangelical churchmen.[115]

When the Church Association met in Manchester to contemplate legal action in 1867, Ryle expressed "a good deal of doubt" about the policy.[116] It could be useful to ascertain the meaning of the law, but no effort should be made to enforce it. For voicing his concerns about prosecuting the ritualists, he was quickly shouted down and accused of being "only two-thirds of a Protestant." The large assembly, according to one attendee, erupted.[117] A new policy of prosecution was immediately adopted, a general fund was created to finance it, and fifty thousand pounds was donated to assist the new work. Though the Church Association did not follow his advice about litigation, he continued to support it and served as a moderating voice.

The Church Association tested the law and established that it upheld the evangelical position on forty-four points of ritual. It raised Protestant feeling in some quarters, especially in the House of Commons,[118] but legal action proved to be an ineffective weapon against ritualistic innovation. Despite the judgments against them, many ritualists evaded (Mackonochie) or simply ignored (Purchas) the ruling of the courts. With each new ritual prosecution the Church Association grew more and more unpopular. By imprisoning their opponents, they made martyrs of them. Simply put, litigation popularized ritualism instead of suppressing it. Furthermore, it ultimately proved corrosive to the unity of the evangelical party as well. Some wanted to continue the prosecutorial campaign against the ritualists while others, like Ryle, believed such a policy

---

115. See J. C. Ryle, *We Must Unite! Being Thoughts on the Necessity of Forming a Well Organized Union of Evangelical Churchmen* (London: William Hunt, 1868). Ryle's quest for evangelical unity will be discussed in the next chapter.

116. Evelyn R. Garratt, *The Life and Personal Recollections of Samuel Garratt* (London: James Nisbet, 1908), 298.

117. Garratt, *Life and Personal Recollections of Samuel Garratt*, 299.

118. Bentley, "Transformation of the Evangelical Party," 130, 144.

must be abandoned. The Church Association, which was originally founded to suppress ritualism and unite supporters of the Reformation, failed on both counts.

Ryle's struggle with ritualism, which began in earnest in Stradbroke, lasted for the rest of his life. It intensified over time as ritualism continued to grow and spread. It became more personal, as will be seen in the case of Rev. James Bell Cox of St. Margaret's, Liverpool. During his ministry in Stradbroke, Ryle emerged as one of the leading evangelical opponents of ritualism. He attacked ritualism through every means available to him: the pulpit, lectern, platform, and press. He produced a considerable body of work during these two decades. Many of these works proved to be remarkably popular. *What Do We Owe to the Reformation?* sold eighty thousand copies in a single year, and *Knots Untied* went through ten editions in eleven years. Aside from increasing Ryle's popularity (or unpopularity, in some quarters), what does his role in this controversy reveal about him?

First, it provides insight into Ryle as a theologian. The ritualist controversy was not merely a debate about ceremonies. It included exegetical debates about the meaning of critical biblical texts such as John 3:5 or 6:53; theological debates about the nature of the church, Christian ministry, and the sacraments; historical debates about the nature of Anglicanism and its relation to the Protestant Reformation; and debates about the pastoral utility of a variety of ritual practices. Ryle entered into every aspect of this debate with unusual thoroughness and zeal. His antiritualist writings from 1865 to 1875 are probably his most rigorous works. They certainly are his most passionate. No single issue facing the Church concerned Ryle more than ritualism. Therefore, he threw his energy into this debate as a theologian, historian, and pastor like no other.

Second, Ryle's antiritualist writings provide valuable insight into his understanding of Anglicanism. More specifically, they reveal his attitude toward the English Reformation and the English Reformers, his understanding of the relationship between the various formularies of the Church, and his interpretation of specific prayer book statements that were central to this debate. His assault on ritualism was simultaneously a defense of the Protestant and evangelical character of the Church of England. Therefore, these writings provide the best insight into Ryle's interpretation of Anglicanism of all his works.

Third, the antiritualist writings reveal Ryle's romantic streak and sensibility. The romantic movement in England awakened a new appreciation for history in the early nineteenth century. This new historical sensibility is easily discernible in Tractarianism and then in ritualism. The ritualists wanted to return to the "Merrie Olde England" of the Middle Ages or, beyond that, to the heroic age of the fathers and martyrs. Ryle offered churchmen a romantic alternative. The Middle Ages were hardly merry—they were a time of unprecedented spiritual and moral darkness. The Reformation delivered England from the thrall of antichrist and brought with it unprecedented spiritual, moral, and temporal blessings. The golden age to which the Church must return is the era of the Protestant Reformation.

Finally, Ryle's participation in the ritualist controversy revealed his moderation. As previously noted, he questioned the wisdom of taking ritualist clergymen to court, and when the Church Association adopted the policy anyway, he urged them to use the courts only to ascertain the meaning of the law and not to imprison clergymen. When asked to preach for high churchmen, he did so and even donned the surplice to honor the customary usage—a move that earned him fierce denunciations in the evangelical periodical *The Rock*.[119] He also urged churchmen of all three schools to pursue more unity.[120] Ryle's campaign against ritualism was not a veiled

---

119. See James Whisenant, "Anti-Ritualism and the Moderation of Evangelical Opinion in England in the Mid-1870s," *Anglican and Episcopal History* 70 (2001): 451–77.

120. See J. C. Ryle, *Can a Greater Amount of Unity Be Obtained among Zealous and Pious Churchmen of Different Schools of Thought?* (London: William Hunt, 1872).

attempt to drive out all those who were not evangelicals or narrow the Church's comprehensiveness beyond the Articles, prayer book, and homilies.

Neologianism

In 1859, the year the ritualists formed the English Church Union, a series of monumental works were published that unsettled the faith of many Englishmen.[121] The first of these was *On the Origin of Species* by Charles Darwin. Darwin was by no means the first to call into question the historicity of Genesis 1 or to propound a doctrine of evolution. In *Principles of Geology* (1830), Charles Lyell argued that the earth's surface developed gradually and uniformly over an immense span of time. Six years later he called into question the universality of Noah's flood by suggesting it was merely a local disaster. In 1844 the anonymous author of *Vestiges of the Natural History of Creation* denied the special creation of animals, claiming that all animal life, like the earth's surface, was the product of a lengthy evolutionary process. Darwin simply expanded the concept of evolution in *Origin of Species* by arguing that life on earth evolved over generations through a process of natural selection. He

---

121. Midcentury movements of thought and evangelical responses are discussed in Bentley, "Transformation of the Evangelical Party"; L. E. Binns, *The Evangelical Movement in the Church of England* (London: Methuen, 1928); L. E. Binns, *Religion in the Victorian Era*, 2nd ed. (London: Lutterworth Press, 1946); S. C. Carpenter, *Church and People, 1789–1889: A History of the Church of England from William Wilberforce to "Lux Mundi"* (London: SPCK, 1933); Chadwick, *Victorian Church*; K. Theodore Hoppen, *The Mid-Victorian Generation 1846–1886* (Oxford: Clarendon Press, 1998); Hylson-Smith, *Evangelicals in the Church of England*;Timothy Larsen, *Contested Christianity: The Political and Social Contexts of Victorian Theology* (Waco, Tex.: Baylor University Press, 2004); Marsh, *Victorian Church in Decline*; John Rogerson, *Old Testament Criticism in the Nineteenth Century: England and Germany* (London: Fortress Press, 1985); George W. E. Russell, *A Short History of the Evangelical Movement* (London: A. R. Mowbray, 1915); Nigel Scotland, *'Good and Proper Men': Lord Palmerston and the Bench of Bishops* (Cambridge: James Clark, 2000); D. C. Somerveil, *English Thought in the Nineteenth Century*, 2nd ed. (London: Methuen, 1929); Anthony Symondson, ed. *The Victorian Crisis of Faith* (London: SPCK, 1970); and Wellings, *Evangelicals Embattled*.

purposely avoided the controversial topic of human origins in this work, but in *The Descent of Man* (1871), he applied his evolutionary theory to humanity and sexual selection. Though Darwin did not discuss the religious implications of his theories, many of his militant supporters, such as T. H. Huxley and the X Club, were more than willing to do so. Thanks in large part to their efforts, Darwin became a symbol for the incompatibility of science and religion.

In addition to new scientific theories, biblical criticism began to undermine popular faith in the Bible. In 1860 *Essays and Reviews* was published by seven eminent liberal churchmen.[122] Frederick Temple urged the free study of the Bible. Rowland Williams presented the results of several critical studies of the Old Testament. Baden Powell denied the possibility of the miraculous and warmly welcomed the work of Darwin. A. B. Wilson called for a broadening of the Church's subscription policy and suggested that the Bible contained errors. C. W. Wilson critiqued attempts to harmonize Genesis and geology and called on theologians to accept the discoveries of modern science. Mark Pattison provided a historical survey of the tendencies of religious thought in the eighteenth century. Benjamin Jowett, in what proved to be the most important essay of the work, argued that the Bible should be studied and interpreted like any other book. These essays did not mark a significant advancement in critical method. Their importance is that six of the seven contributors were clergymen of the Church of England, and they were willing to openly question traditional orthodox views.[123]

Shortly after the publication of *Essays and Reviews*, the bishop of Natal, John William Colenso, published *St. Paul's Epistle to the Romans* and the first installment of *The Pentateuch and Book of Joshua Critically Examined*.[124] Colenso embraced a low view of inspiration, denied eternal punishment, judged parts of the

---

122. See *Essays and Reviews* (London: John W. Parker and Son, 1860).

123. Rogerson, *Old Testament Criticism*, 209.

124. See John William Colenso, *St. Paul's Epistle to the Romans: Newly Translated and Explained from a Missionary Point of View* (Cambridge: Macmillan,

Pentateuch to be unhistorical, declared that Anglican doctrine must be broadened to appeal to intelligent people, and asserted that the essential truths of the Bible did not depend on the historical truth of its narratives.[125] These conclusions shocked the nation.[126] Colenso and the essayists were attempting to restate the Christian faith in light of new scientific and historical thought. They sought to bridge a perceived gap between Christian doctrine and the views of educated Englishmen. The evangelicals pejoratively referred to this enterprise as *neology*. These "new views" in theology were simply expressions of rationalism, skepticism, and infidelity. Evangelicals believed that the faith of millions was at stake, and they responded in three different ways.

First, they appealed to the ecclesiastical courts. Evangelicals supported the prosecution of Rowland Williams and A. B. Wilson, both ordained clergymen and *Essays and Reviews* contributors, for teaching doctrines that were contrary to the formularies of the Church of England. They were unwilling to support the demotion of Bishop Colenso by Bishop Gray of Cape Town, however, fearing that the move was actually a subtle ritualist plot to establish in the colonies a form of "spiritual supremacy fashioned after the mode of Hildebrand."[127] In 1869 Gladstone nominated Frederick Temple, the author of the introductory article of *Essays and Reviews*, to succeed Henry Phillpotts as the bishop of Exeter. Though evangelicals opposed the nomination and the Church Association prepared a memorial in protest, the party was divided on the appropriate response, and Temple was made a bishop without much resistance. As was the case with ritualism, the prosecutions achieved noth-

---

1861); *The Pentateuch and Book of Joshua Critically Examined* (London: Longmans, Robert, and Green, 1862).

125. Hylson-Smith, *Evangelicals in the Church of England*, 137. For an excellent summary of Bishop Colenso's criticism of the Old Testament, see Rogerson, *Old Testament Criticism*, 220–37.

126. Carpenter, *Church and People*, 504.

127. Bentley, "Transformation of the Evangelical Party," 104.

ing. The teaching of Williams and Wilson was deemed to be not inconsistent with the Church's formularies in 1864. Despite the best efforts of Bishop Gray and Samuel Wilberforce, John Colenso remained the bishop of Natal.

Second, there were a number of failed attempts to unite evangelicals with high churchmen and ritualists in opposition to neologianism. After the *Essays and Reviews* judgment, a temporary alliance was formed between the Protestant Lord Shaftsbury and the Tractarian E. B. Pusey, and a joint declaration condemning the book was signed by evangelicals and high churchmen. The union proved short-lived. If Church Association fund-raising is any indication of the party's priorities, evangelicals were much more concerned about suppressing ritualism than neologianism. In 1869 the Church Association created a new fund for prosecuting neologians, and 709 pounds was raised.[128] This pales in comparison to the fifty thousand pounds that was raised two years prior for the prosecution of ritualists. Furthermore, during the Athanasian Creed controversy of the early 1870s, evangelicals sided with broad churchmen against the high churchmen in order to preserve an opening for Dissenters to return to the established church.[129]

Third, evangelicals assaulted neology in print. Though they produced a large number of books and pamphlets attacking neologianism, there were relatively few substantial academic works. Anne Bentley attributes this to a lack of scholars among their ranks. But Kenneth Hylson-Smith points out that there was a solid phalanx of evangelical scholars among the seniors at Oxford whose scholarship was acknowledged by the frequency with which they were invited to deliver the famous Bampton Lectures.[130] Thomas Rawson Birks published *The Bible and Modern Thought* in 1861, which was

128. Bentley, "Transformation of the Evangelical Party," 106.

129. Bentley, "Transformation of the Evangelical Party," 111.

130. See Bentley, "Transformation of the Evangelical Party," 117; and Hylson-Smith, *Evangelicals in the Church of England*, 139. See also Reynolds, *Evangelicals at Oxford*.

possibly the most important evangelical response to new critical
views. In the same year, Edward Garbett delivered the Boyle Lectures on "The Bible and Its Critics" and argued for the objective
reality of Christian revelation, which admitted neither addition nor
diminution. In his Bampton Lectures (1867), he contended for the
absolute necessity of a dogmatic faith and championed the supremacy of revealed truth over subjective human reasoning. Payne Smith,
a Syriac scholar, took part in the debate as well. Despite these contributions, most evangelical responses tended to be popular polemics.
Ryle's antineologian writings fall into this latter category.[131] They
indicate that he was primarily concerned about three issues in particular: the inspiration of Scripture, the importance of dogmatic
Christianity, and the eternal punishment of the impenitent.

The Inspiration of Scripture

Ryle's treatment of the inspiration of Scripture was popular, pastoral, and, to some degree, polemic. His aim was to supply simple

---

131. See the following by J. C. Ryle: Preface to *Moses, or the Zulu? A Detailed
Reply to the Objections Contained in Parts I and II of Bishop Colenso's Work*, by W.
Wickes (London: Wertheim, Macintosh, and Hunt, 1863); *Are We Not in Perilous
Times?* (London: William Hunt, 1868); *Be Not Carried About* (London: William
Hunt, 1869); "What Does the Earth Teach?," in *Shall We Know One Another, and
Other Papers* (London: Cassell, Petter, and Galpin, 1870); "Pharisees and Sadducees"
and "Divers and Strange Doctrines" in *Knots Untied*; *Bible Inspiration: Its Reality
and Nature* (London: William Hunt, 1877); *Whose Word Is This?* (London: William
Hunt, 1877); *I Fear! A Caution for the Times* (London: William Hunt, 1877); "Eternity," in *Practical Religion: Being Papers on the Daily Duties, Experiences, Dangers,
and Privileges of Professing Christians* (London: William Hunt, 1877); *Dogma: A
Paper for the Times, Being Thoughts on the Importance of Distinct and Definite Views
of Religious Truth* (London: William Hunt, 1878), first published as "The Importance of the Clear Enunciation of Dogma in Dispensing the Word, with Reference
to Instability among Modern Christians," in *Be Thou a Faithful Dispenser of the
Word of God and His Holy Sacraments: Being Papers Read at the Islington Clerical
Meeting, 1878* (London: William Hunt, 1878); *What Do the Times Require?*; *Unbelief
a Marvel*; *The Oracles of God* (London: William Hunt, 1881); *Thoughts on Immortality* (London: William Hunt, 1883); *What Canst Thou Know?* (Stirling: Drummond's
Tract Depot, 1884); *Is All Scripture Inspired? An Attempt to Answer the Question*
(London: William Hunt, 1891).

antidotes to skeptics and show the unreasonableness of their position and to invigorate Christians by making them see the strength of their position and to help rid them of a doubting spirit.[132] In his defense of the plenary verbal inspiration of Scripture, he typically addressed four related issues: the proofs of divine inspiration, the extent of divine inspiration, new scientific discoveries, and biblical criticism.

Proving divine inspiration. In order to prove divine inspiration, Ryle appealed to internal evidence. He believed that the Bible is the best witness to its own inspiration, and he pointed to six undeniable facts that ought to satisfy every reasonable inquirer.[133] First, the extraordinary depth, fullness, and richness in the contents of the Bible are proof of divine inspiration. It provides more spiritual light on the most important subjects than all other books combined. The Bible alone provides a reasonable account of the beginning and end of history, a true and faithful account of humanity, and true views of God. It alone teaches that God has made a full, perfect, and complete provision for the salvation of fallen people by Christ, and it alone explains the state of things we see in the world around us. The extraordinary contents of the Bible are a great fact that can be explained only by admitting its inspiration.[134]

Second, the extraordinary unity and harmony of the Bible is proof of divine inspiration. The Bible was written by more than thirty authors who came from every rank and class in society over the span of fifteen hundred years. Their writing styles may differ, but the mind that runs through their work is always the same. They all give one account of humanity, God, the way of salvation, and the human heart. Though readers see spiritual truth unfold

---

132. Ryle, *What Canst Thou Know?*, 5.

133. Ryle, *Bible Inspiration*, 10: "Nothing can possibly account for the Bible being what it is, and doing what it has done, except the theory that it is the Word of God."

134. Ryle, *Bible Inspiration*, 11–19.

progressively, they never detect any real contradiction. Chance could not produce such unity; the only satisfactory account is divine inspiration.[135]

Third, the extraordinary wisdom, sublimity, and majesty in the style of the Bible are proof of divine inspiration. Nothing in literature compares with the Bible, and to speak of comparing the Bible with other so-called sacred books, such as the Koran, the Shasters, or the Book of Mormon, is positively absurd. Ryle suggested that God allowed the existence of these pretended revelations simply to prove the immeasurable superiority of His own word.[136] To suggest that the Bible differs only in degree from the works of Homer, Plato, Shakespeare, Dante, and Milton is blasphemous folly. Every unprejudiced reader must see that there is an unfathomable gulf between the Bible and every other book. Furthermore, it must be remembered that the human authors of the Bible had no special advantages. They lived in the remotest corners of the earth, and most of them had little leisure, few books, and no great learning. Yet the book they wrote is unrivaled. The only reasonable explanation is that they wrote under the direct inspiration of God.[137]

Fourth, the extraordinary accuracy in the facts and statements of the Bible prove that the Bible is inspired. In the eighteen hundred years since the closing of the canon of Scripture, there have been enormous changes, discoveries, and improvements, but the Bible remains perfect, fresh, and complete. The march of intellect has not overtaken it. Science has never proven it wrong. The discoveries of travelers never convict it of mistakes. In short, nothing is found that overturns one jot or tittle of the Bible's historical facts or the Bible's account of the human heart. Only divine inspiration can account for this fact.[138]

---

135. Ryle, *Bible Inspiration*, 19–21.
136. Ryle, *Bible Inspiration*, 22.
137. Ryle, *Bible Inspiration*, 21–24.
138. Ryle, *Bible Inspiration*, 24–26.

Fifth, the Bible is extraordinarily suited to the spiritual wants of humanity. It meets the heart of individuals in every rank or class, in every country and climate, in every age and period of life. It suits all. Other books become obsolete and old-fashioned, but the Bible remains evergreen. It has been studied and prayed over by fathers, schoolmen, Reformers, Puritans, and modern divines, and it has yet to be exhausted. It is the book for every heart because He who inspired it knows every heart and what all hearts require.[139]

Finally, the Bible has had the most extraordinary effect on the condition of those nations in which it has been known, taught, and read. The countries where there is the greatest amount of idolatry, cruelty, tyranny, impurity, misgovernment, or disregard for life and liberty and truth are those countries where the Bible is forbidden, neglected, or unknown. The countries where liberty and morality have attained the highest pitch are those countries where the Bible is free to all. Ryle challenged the neologian to compare the fruit of his principles with his own: "The Neologian, the Socinian, the Deist, the skeptic, or the friends of mere secular teaching, have never yet shown us one Sierra Leone, one New Zealand, one Tinnevelly, as the fruit of their principles. We only can do that who honour the Bible and reverence it as God's Word."[140]

The extent of inspiration. There are two questions related to the extent of inspiration. The first question is how far and to what degree the biblical authors were assisted by divine aid. Ryle acknowledged this was a difficult question that even the best Christians were not entirely agreed on. Inspiration is a miracle, and miracles, by definition, are mysterious. He refused to speculate about the exact manner of inspiration. He abhorred the mechanical theory of inspiration, which makes men like Moses or Paul no better than organ pipes or ignorant secretaries who wrote by

---

139. Ryle, *Bible Inspiration*, 26–29.

140. Ryle, *Bible Inspiration*, 31. The places Ryle mentions are examples of successful evangelical missionary endeavors.

dictation what they did not understand.[141] Instead, in some marvelous manner, the Holy Ghost made use of their natural faculties and capacities, put into their minds thoughts and ideas, and then guided their pens in writing and expressing them. The result is that the finished product is not the work of erring men, but the thoughts and words of God.[142]

The second question is related to the Bible itself. To what extent is the Bible inspired? Again, Ryle acknowledged that all Christians are not agreed on this subject, but he stated his position as follows: "The view which I maintain is that every book, and chapter, and verse, and syllable of the Bible was given by inspiration of God."[143] Though it was painful to disagree with able and gifted men on religious questions, "in matters like these," he said, "I dare not call any man master."[144]

Ryle admitted that the doctrine of verbal plenary inspiration is not accepted by many good Christians and is bitterly opposed in some quarters. He offered six practical arguments for his position. First, if the Bible contains flaws and imperfections, it cannot be a perfect rule of faith and practice. Second, the language that the Bible uses to describe itself is incomprehensible if it is not fully inspired. For example, the Bible refers to itself as "the oracles of God" and frequently equates its words with God's words. Third, the New Testament's use of the Old supports the position that every word was inspired by God. In many of these quotations, the force of the passage turns on a single word or the use of the singular instead of the plural number (Matt. 22:44; Gal. 3:16). Fourth, if the words of the Bible are not inspired, then the Bible is not an effective weapon in controversy. Adversaries could evade every argument by replying that the text is faulty and therefore has no authority. Fifth, abandoning verbal plenary inspiration destroys the usefulness of

---

141. Ryle, *Bible Inspiration*, 37.
142. Ryle, *Bible Inspiration*, 39.
143. Ryle, *Bible Inspiration*, 41. Ryle is referring to the original autographs.
144. Ryle, *Bible Inspiration*, 39–40.

the Bible as an instrument for preaching and instruction. Every scriptural reproof and exhortation could be dismissed as a mistake. Finally, the denial of verbal plenary inspiration destroys the usefulness of the Bible as a source of comfort and instruction in private reading. The value of many cherished texts depends on a single phrase or a verb tense.[145]

He also answered a wide variety of objections to his position.[146] These include objections to statements that seem incredible or absurd (Balaam's ass speaking or Jonah's sojourn in the belly of a whale); the presence of trifling details that appear unworthy to be called inspired (Paul's request for his cloak, books, and parchments); difficulties in harmonizing gospel accounts; the theological errors present in the speeches of Job's miserable counselors; the implications of Paul's statements "Not I, but the Lord" and "I, not the Lord"; the issue of various readings; and the Bible's use of uninspired writings. The two most important objections that he discussed relate to new scientific discoveries and biblical criticism.

New scientific discoveries. Ryle's attitude toward new scientific discoveries is remarkably positive. He wrote, "I shall always hail the annual discoveries of physical science with a hearty welcome. For the continual progress of its students by experiment and observation, and for the annual accumulation of facts, I am deeply thankful."[147] Thus he had no sympathy for "those weak-kneed Christians who seem to think that science and religion can never harmonize, and that they must always scowl and look askance at one another, like two quarrelsome dogs."[148] Simply put, scientific progress does not make people unbelievers. Creation, as well as

---

145. Ryle, *Bible Inspiration*, 44–51.

146. See Ryle, *Bible Inspiration*, 51–64. In 1891 Ryle updated and republished this treatise under the title *Is All Scripture Inspired?* In the new edition, he expanded the objection section. See pages 62–69.

147. Ryle, *What Canst Thou Know?*, 12–13.

148. Ryle, *What Canst Thou Know?*, 12.

revelation, was given by God for humanity's instruction.[149] There is a close harmony between them, and they throw mutual light on each other if both are read with a spiritual eye.[150] He confidently asserted that he had no fear that science would ever finally contradict the Bible: "I am firmly convinced that the words of God's mouth, and the works of God's hands, will never be found to really contradict one another. When they appear to do so, I am content to wait. Time will untie the knot."[151]

Despite his confidence in the ultimate compatibility of science and revelation, he acknowledged that there was a growing suspicion that new scientific discoveries were disproving the Bible and undermining the "old creed" of verbal plenary inspiration. Therefore, he offered a number of simple antidotes to cure spiritual skepticism regarding science and the Bible. First, wise Christians ought to admit there are many things in religion that of necessity cannot

---

149. J. C. Ryle, "What Does the Earth Teach?," in *Shall We Know One Another, and Other Papers* (London: Cassell, Petter, and Galpin, 1870), 25.

150. In "What Does the Earth Teach?" Ryle provided six examples of this. The earth, as well as the Bible, teaches the wisdom and power of God, the doctrine of the fall of humanity, the great truth that life comes out of death, God's sovereignty in giving life where He wills ("whatever men may please to say about the doctrine of election in theology, they cannot deny its existence in vegetation"), the importance of the diligent use of means, and the great truth of the resurrection of the body.

151. Ryle, *What Canst Thou Know?*, 13. "Time will untie the knot" is an excellent summary of Ryle's overall position. Great principles in theology should not be abandoned because of difficulties. He encouraged Christians to wait patiently, for the difficulties might melt away. His favorite illustration of this principle is drawn from astronomy. Before the discovery of the planet Neptune, certain aberrations of the planet Uranus perplexed astronomers, and some even suggested that the whole Newtonian system might be untrue. But one French astronomer, Leverrier, argued before the Academy of Science that men of science should not abandon a principle because of difficulties that could not be explained. Time would vindicate the Newtonian system. Shortly thereafter, the planet Neptune was discovered, which explained the aberrations associated with Uranus and vindicated the Newtonian system. Ryle concluded, "Let us not give up the great principle of plenary verbal inspiration because of apparent difficulties. The day may come when they will all be solved." Ryle, *Bible Inspiration*, 62–64.

be fully understood.[152] Creation, the fall of humanity, the doctrine of the Trinity, the incarnation of Christ, the person and work of the Holy Spirit, the inspiration of Scripture, and the reality of miracles cannot be fully explained because they are above the reach of human faculties of comprehension. But it does not follow that they ought to be rejected because they cannot be fully understood. Humanity's grasp of any subject is always small and incomplete. Therefore, no Christians ought to be ashamed of admitting that there are many things in revealed religion they do not fully understand, while believing them fully and living in this belief.[153]

Second, wise Christians ought to remember that there are many things in the material world which are not fully understood. The heaven over our head and the earth beneath our feet supply deep questions that have not been answered by astronomers and geologists. There are deadly viruses and poisons that the best chemists and doctors have been unable to cure. There are questions related to light, heat, electricity, and magnetism that have yet to be answered. Nevertheless, people do not reject the work of Isaac Newton, Edward Jenner, and Michael Faraday because they cannot explain the material world in its entirety. In short, science, like faith, contains hard things.[154]

Third, while it is true we cannot know the Almighty to perfection, it is not true to say that we can find out nothing at all in religion.[155] In fact, we know enough to make unbelief and agnosticism inexcusable. We know the universality of suffering and death. We find that the majority of human beings have a settled, rooted, inward feeling that this life is not all and there is a future state beyond the grave.[156] We find that faith in Christ is the only thing that has ever enabled men and women to look forward to the

152. Ryle, *What Canst Thou Know?*, 5.
153. Ryle, *What Canst Thou Know?*, 7.
154. Ryle, *What Canst Thou Know?*, 8–9.
155. Ryle, *What Canst Thou Know?*, 15.
156. Ryle, *What Canst Thou Know?*, 16.

future without fear and has given them peace and life and hope in death.[157] Above all, we find that Jesus Christ Himself is the great fact that has never been able to be explained away. His purity, teaching, resurrection, and influence are simple matters of history and demand the attention of every honest person who wishes to inquire about the great subject of religion.[158]

Fourth, though skepticism and agnosticism were the most common spiritual diseases of his generation, Ryle insisted that intellectual difficulties were but one source of unbelief, and probably not the greatest. For many, the real source of unbelief was the heart. They loved sins the Bible condemns and refused to give them up, and so they took refuge from an uneasy conscience by trying to persuade themselves that the Bible is not true. In short, the measure of their creed was their affections.[159] For others, the root of their unbelief was a lazy, indolent will. They disliked self-denial, cross bearing, and "taking pains" in spiritual matters, and so they refused to make up their minds and be decided about anything in religion. Thus, they were tossed to and fro, not knowing what they believed about religion.[160]

Finally, many professing Christians were continually shaken in their minds by doubts about the truth of Christianity because they were utterly ignorant of the evidences of Christianity and the enormous difficulties of infidelity.[161] Ryle lamented that not one in a hundred churchgoers ever read a page of Leslie, Leland, Watson, Butler, Paley, Chalmers, M'Ilvaine, Daniel Wilson, Porteus, or Whately.[162] Therefore, it was no surprise that the minds of such

---

157. Ryle, *What Canst Thou Know?*, 16.

158. Ryle, *What Canst Thou Know?*, 18.

159. Ryle, *What Canst Thou Know?*, 20–21.

160. Ryle, *What Canst Thou Know?*, 21–22.

161. Ryle, *What Canst Thou Know?*, 25–26.

162. Ryle, *What Canst Thou Know?*, 26. Though Ryle did not mention specific works, it is likely he was referring to the following: Charles Leslie, *A Short and Easy Method with the Deist* (1698); John Leland, *A View of the Principal Deistical Writers* (1754); Richard Watson, *An Apology for the Bible* (1796); Joseph Butler, The *Analogy*

people were unable to resist the attacks of the most commonplace infidelity, much less the refined and polished skepticism of these latter days.[163] The remedy for this state of affairs was obvious. All professing Christians ought to arm their minds with the elementary evidences of revealed religion and the difficulties of infidelity. Every minister should preach occasionally on evidences, and every educational institution that made any pretense to be Christian should never leave this subject out in its instruction of the young.

Old Testament criticism. Ryle's attitude toward Old Testament criticism was wholly negative. He wrote, "I can find no words to express my entire disagreement with such theories."[164] The implications of biblical criticism were blasphemous and undermined the very foundations of Christianity.[165] One of Ryle's earliest controversial works was a short critique of Bishop Colenso's infamous work on the Pentateuch, which appeared as a preface to Rev. W. Wicks's work *Moses, or the Zulu? A Detailed Reply to the Objections Contained in Parts I and II of Bishop Colenso's Work* (1863). In his estimation, Colenso's work was so exceedingly weak and open to criticism that he did not expect it to do much harm. It would shake the faith of only the weakest and most credulous person, and it would convince only those who were looking for an

of Religion, Natural and Revealed, to the Constitution and Course of Nature, 2nd ed. (Cambridge: Hilliard and Brown, 1736); William Paley, *A View of the Evidences of Christianity* (1794); Thomas Chalmers, *A Series of Discourses on the Christian Revelation, Viewed in Connection with the Modern Astronomy* (1817); Thomas Chalmers, *On the Power, Wisdom and Goodness of God as Manifested in the Adaptation of External Nature to the Moral and Intellectual Constitution of Man* (1833); Charles Pettit M'Ilvaine, *The Evidences of Christianity, in Their External, or Historical Division* (1832); Daniel Wilson, *The Evidences of Christianity* (1828–1830); Beilby Porteus, *A Summary of the Principal Evidences for the Truth and Divine Origin of the Christian Revelation* (1801); and Richard Whately, *Christian Evidences* (1837).

163. Ryle, *What Canst Thou Know?*, 26.
164. Ryle, *Is All Scripture Inspired?*, 63.
165. Ryle, *Is All Scripture Inspired?*, 65.

excuse for unbelief.[166] He provided a brief, six-point critique of the bishop's findings. First, Colenso found difficulties where none exist. Second, many of the alleged difficulties had been considered and answered by previous commentators. Third, his treatment was one-sided in the extreme. Fourth, he denied the possibility of God's miraculous agency as a solution to many of his difficulties. Fifth, Colenso ignored the evidence that did not support his conclusions. Finally, someone who held such views should not be a bishop of the Church of England.[167] Ryle concluded his critique by confidently asserting, "I have no fear for the cause of Christ's truth from Bishop Colenso's attack. The Word of God has passed through furnaces seven times hotter than that which the Bishop has heated, and come out unscathed, unharmed, and purer than before. The same thing will happen again."[168] Though he did not fear for "Christ's truth," he feared for the establishment of the Church of England. If Bishop Colenso was allowed to continue to minister in the Church of England "unchallenged, unrebuked, and undisturbed," the Church would be disgraced and the enemies of the establishment would act.[169] Englishmen would come to one of the following conclusions: one may believe anything about the Bible and be a churchman; the bishops consider Colenso's work unanswerable; there is no ecclesiastical discipline in the established church; and the bishops are afraid of controversy and love peace more than truth.[170] Though prosecutions for heresy were "hateful things," the present circumstances made them not merely necessary but a positive duty.[171]

With the exception of the reply to Colenso's work, Ryle typically focused his attack on the practical and pastoral implications

---

166. Ryle, preface to *Moses, or the Zulu?*, v.

167. Ryle, preface to *Moses, or the Zulu?*, vi–vii.

168. Ryle, preface to *Moses, or the Zulu?*, vii.

169. Ryle, preface to *Moses, or the Zulu?*, ix.

170. Ryle, preface to *Moses, or the Zulu?*, ix.

171. Ryle, preface to *Moses, or the Zulu?*, viii.

of Old Testament criticism. First, he pointed out that the Old and New Testaments stand or fall together.[172] Both are equally inspired. Both are equally authoritative. The New Testament continually quotes the Old as the word of God.

Second, Old Testament criticism dishonors Christ and the apostles. They regarded the events recorded in the Pentateuch as real, historical, and true.[173] If this is not the case, then people must conclude that they were either fallible or fallacious.[174] If they were mistaken on these important subjects, then they may be mistaken on others as well. Their authority as religious writers is at an end.[175]

Third, Old Testament criticism "strikes a deadly blow at the very roots of Christianity"—the person and work of Christ.[176] If Christ was ignorant about the true authorship and historicity of the Penta-teuch, he is an insufficient Savior.[177] How could an ignorant Christ judge the secrets of people on the last day? How could an ignorant Christ be a suitable savior for sinners? An ignorant Christ destroys the Christian's confidence in Christ and His peace. He wrote, "That blessed Saviour to whom I am taught to commit my soul, in the very week that He died for my redemption, spoke of the Flood and the days of Noah as realities! If He spoke *ignorantly,* with Calvary in full view, it would shake to the foundation my confidence in His power to save me, and would destroy my peace."[178]

Finally, higher criticism had never been able to explain away the three great facts: the historical person of Jesus Christ

---

172. Ryle, *Is All Scripture Inspired?*, 63.

173. Ryle, *I Fear!*, 10; See also Ryle, *Knots Untied*, 352.

174. Ryle, *Is All Scripture Inspired?*, 64.

175. Ryle, *I Fear!*, 11.

176. Ryle, *Is All Scripture Inspired?*, 65.

177. Ryle, *Is All Scripture Inspired?*, 65. This is precisely what the editor of Lux Mundi, Charles Gore, argued in his chapter "The Holy Spirit and Inspiration." See Lux Mundi: *A Series of Studies in the Religion on the Incarnation*, 4th ed. (London: John Murray, 1889).

178. Ryle, *Is All Scripture Inspired?*, 66.

Himself, [179] the Bible itself,[180] and the effect that Christianity has had on humanity.[181]

The Rejection of Dogma

Ryle believed that the proliferation of new views in theology were symptoms of a larger problem: the rejection of dogmatic theology. Dogmatic theology, simply put, is the statement of positive truth in religion. Dogmatism in science is presumptuous, but in religion it is a duty. Scientists have no inspired book to guide them, but Christians have an infallible guide in the Bible. When the Bible speaks plainly, clearly, and unmistakably on any point, Christians have a right to form positive and decided conclusions and to speak positively and decidedly. To refuse to be positive when God has spoken positively is a symptom of ignorance, timidity, and unbelief.[182]

Ryle attributed the growing dislike for dogma to a variety of causes. The first was the idolization of education and great learning. Second, there was a general tendency to elevate "free thought" and "free inquiry," and many people liked to prove their independence of mind by believing novelties.[183] Third, there was a widespread desire to appear charitable and liberal. Fourth, there was a morbid

179. Ryle, *Unbelief a Marvel*, 14: "How He can have been what He was on earth, lived as He lived, taught as He taught, and made the mark He has certainly made on the world, if He was not very God, and One miraculously sent down from heaven, is a question which those who sneer at Balaam's ass find it convenient to evade."

180. Ryle, *Unbelief a Marvel*, 14: "How this Book, with all its alleged difficulties, written by a few Jews in the corner of the earth…can be the Book that it is, so immeasurably and incomparably superior to anything else penned by man, and hold the position it holds after 1900 years' use,—how all this can be, if the Book was not miraculously given by inspiration of God, is a knot which cannot be untied."

181. Ryle, *Unbelief a Marvel*, 14–15: "The amazing change which has taken place in the state of the world before Christianity, and since Christianity,—and the difference at this day between those parts of the globe where the Bible is read, and those where it is not known. Nothing can account for this but the Divine origin of Scriptural religion. No other explanation will stand."

182. Ryle, *Dogma*, 4–5. This paper was originally read at the annual Islington clerical meeting in January 1878.

183. Ryle, *Be Not Carried About*, 8.

dread of controversy and an ignorant dislike of party spirit. Fifth was a widespread gullibility and silly readiness to believe everyone who spoke cleverly, lovingly, and above all, earnestly. Finally, original sin was ultimately behind the growing dislike for Christian dogma. Natural man hates the gospel and all its distinctive doctrines and delights in any excuse for refusing it.[184]

The evidence of the growing dislike for dogmatic theology was ubiquitous. English newspapers, when they were willing to discuss religious subjects, praised Christian morality but ignored Christian dogma. School boards jettisoned dogmatic theology under the name of sectarianism. Popular novels that attempted to describe the lives of Christians avoided doctrinal subjects and ended up presenting Christian character as a flower without roots. Liberal speakers were constantly urging popular audiences to abandon denominational Christianity and throw aside creeds and confessions, which unnecessarily bound modern Englishmen.[185] In short, the modern dislike of dogma was a widespread evil of the times that desired the fruits of Christianity without its roots, to have Christian morality without Christian dogma.[186]

What were the consequences of the growing dislike for dogmatic theology? Ryle believed it was creating and fostering a great instability in religion—that is, "jelly-fish" Christianity. "Jelly-fish" Christianity is a kind of Christianity "without bone, or muscle, or power."[187] Its leading principle is "no dogma, no distinct tenets, no positive doctrine."[188] And it was producing "jelly-fish" clergymen, young men, and worshipers.[189]

---

184. Ryle, *Dogma*, 12.

185. Ryle, *Dogma*, 6–7.

186. Ryle, *Dogma*, 7.

187. Ryle, *Dogma*, 12.

188. Ryle, *Dogma*, 13.

189. Ryle, *Dogma*, 13–14:

> We have hundreds of jelly-fish clergymen, who seem not to have a single bone in their body of divinity. They have no definite opinions;

Though dogmatic theology was growing increasingly unpopular, especially among young people, Ryle encouraged every loyal churchman to embrace it unashamedly for several reasons. First, the Bible teaches dogma.[190] Opponents of dogma asserted that the chief object of the New Testament was to teach morality rather than doctrine, but this was so utterly contrary to the facts that it was "absurdly untrue." The Gospel of John and the Epistles to the Romans, Galatians, Ephesians, and Hebrews are rife with dogmatic theology. Moreover, the moral precepts of the New Testament are undergirded by and inseparable from dogma and doctrine. In sum, he who gives up teaching dogma must give up teaching the Bible.

---

they belong to no school or party: they are so afraid of "extreme views" that they have no views at all. We have thousands of jelly-fish sermons preached every year, sermons without an edge, or a point, or a corner, smooth as billiard balls, awakening no sinner, and edifying no saint. We have legions of jelly-fish young men annually turned out from our Universities, armed with a few scraps of second-hand philosophy, who think it a mark of cleverness and intellect to have no decided opinions about anything in religion, and to be utterly unable to make up their minds as to what is Christian truth. They live apparently in a state of suspense, like Mahomet's fabled coffin, hanging between heaven and earth. Their souls are not satisfied with arguments which satisfied Butler, and Paley, and Chalmers, and M'Ilvaine, and Whately, and Whewell, and Mozley. Their only creed is a kind of "Nihilism." They are sure and positive about nothing. And last, and worst of all, we have myriads of jelly-fish worshippers, respectable church-going people, who have no distinct and definite views about any point in theology. They cannot discern things that differ, any more than colour-blind people can distinguish colours. They think every body is right and nobody wrong, everything is true and nothing is false, all sermons are good and none are bad, every clergyman is sound and no clergyman is unsound. They are "tossed to and fro, like children, by every wind of doctrine"; often carried away by any new excitement and sensational movement; ever ready for new things, because they have no firm grasp on the old; and utterly unable to "render a reason of the hope that is in them."

190. Ryle, *Dogma*, 17: "Do we not, then, all know and feel, as we read our New Testaments, that dogma meets us in every book from Matthew down to Revelation?"

Second, the Thirty-Nine Articles plainly teach dogma. Ryle asked, "What are these Articles but a wise compendium of dogmatical statements?"[191] Moreover, every incumbent is required by law and vow to declare publicly that he will teach and preach nothing contrary to the Articles. How then can a clergyman remain faithful to his ordination vows and reject dogmatic theology as narrow and illiberal?

Third, the prayer book teaches dogma. Ryle pointed out that there is an immense amount of dogmatic theology in the prayer book. It contains doctrinal statements about the Trinity, the deity of Christ, the personality of the Holy Ghost, the sacrifice and mediation of Christ, the work of the Spirit, and many other points. In short, the person who uses the prayer book and diminishes the importance of dogma holds an unreasonable and untenable position.[192]

Fourth, church history supports the use of dogma. Ryle confidently asserted, "There never has been any spread of the Gospel, any conversion of nations or countries, any successful evangelistic work, excepting by the enunciation of dogma."[193] He challenged his opponents to point to any English village, parish, city, or district that has been evangelized by their principles. Christianity without dogma is powerless, childless, and barren.[194]

Fifth, the lives of the most eminent and useful saints illustrate the importance of dogma. The holiest fathers, schoolmen, Reformers, Puritans, Anglicans, Dissenters, and churchmen have one common stamp and mark—"they have had certain systematic, sharply-cut, and positive views of truth."[195] Christian fruit never appears without Christian roots. Without dogma there can be no eminent holiness.

---

191. Ryle, *Dogma*, 18.
192. Ryle, *Dogma*, 19–20.
193. Ryle, *Dogma*, 20.
194. Ryle, *Dogma*, 21.
195. Ryle, *Dogma*, 22–23.

Finally, dogma is needed to die well.[196] Appealing to the personal experience of ministers, Ryle asked, "Can any of us say that he ever saw a person die in peace who did not know distinctly what he was resting on for acceptance with God and could only say, in reply to inquiries, that he was earnest and sincere?"[197] Christian morality will never smooth down a dying pillow.[198] Something more is needed. We want "the story of Christ dying for our sins, and rising again for our justification. We want Christ the mediator, Christ the substitute, Christ the intercessor, Christ the redeemer, in order to meet with confidence the King of terrors."[199] In the hour of death, "broad theology" is a miserable comforter.

Eternal Punishment

In addition to "new views" about inspiration, Ryle was also concerned about "new views" of eternal punishment.[200] In 1877, Frederic W. Farrar, canon of Westminster and chaplain in ordi-

---

196. Ryle, *Dogma*, 23. Geoffrey Best seems to confirm Ryle's assertion in his chapter "Evangelical and the Victorians," in *The Victorian Crisis of Faith*, ed. Anthony Symondson (London: SPCK, 1970), 55. After a scathing (and, in my opinion, biased) critique of Victorian evangelicalism, he concluded, "Death had no terrors for the Evangelical.... I am suggesting that the Evangelical's confidence in the face of death was unusually comforting and homely; that it lay at the heart of Evangelical religion; and that it helps to explain both the boldness of the Evangelical enterprise and the way, the sometimes maddening way, in which they set about those enterprises—the mixture of apparently admirable faith and goodness with an inaccessible and irrefutable self-assurance."

197. Ryle, *Dogma*, 23.

198. Ryle, *Dogma*, 23.

199. Ryle, *Dogma*, 23.

200. Though Ryle was clearly more concerned about inspiration, the issue of eternal punishment is briefly discussed in a number of his works that deal with the spread of false doctrine in general. See *Be Not Carried About!*; "Pharisees and Sadducees," in *Knots Untied*; and *Dogma*. He devoted two works specifically to the subject of eternal punishment. See "Eternity," in *Practical Religion: Being Papers on the Daily Duties, Experiences, Dangers, and Privileges of Professing Christians*, and *Thoughts on Immortality* (London: William Hunt, 1883). In the latter work, Ryle critiques Cannon Farrar's *Eternal Hope*, which specifically denies eternal punishment, and addresses the issue of conditional immortality.

nary to the queen, preached a series of sermons denying eternal punishment and affirming a form of universal reconciliation.[201] The publication of these sermons triggered a number of responses from clergymen, including Ryle.[202] His *Thoughts on Immortality* is a general defense of the traditional view of the future state and a specific refutation of Canon Farrar's work. Though "new views" about the future state seem appealing at first glance, they do not stand the test of calm investigation in the light of the Bible. Simply put, "the old is better."[203]

Ryle's thesis is that the future happiness of the saved and the future misery of the lost are eternal. The two stand or fall together, for the same temporal language is applied to each. Therefore, it is impossible to distinguish the duration of one from the other. If the joys of heaven are eternal, so must be the sorrows of hell.[204] In order to prove his assertion, he appealed to the Bible, the prayer book, and practical considerations.

The opponents of eternal punishment asserted that this doctrine is incompatible with the love, charity, and compassionate character of God. Ryle did not deny these attributes, but he insisted that the Scriptures reveal more about God's character than his opponents allowed. He pointed his opponents to the words of Christ. No one ever spoke "such loving and merciful words as our Lord Jesus Christ," and yet on three occasions he described the consequences of final impenitence as "the worm that never dies and the fire that is not quenched."[205] He pointed them to the apostle

---

201. See Frederic W. Farrar, *Eternal Hope: Five Sermons Preached in Westminster Abbey* (New York: E. P. Dutton, 1878).

202. See C. F. Childe, *The Unsafe Anchor: Eternal Hope a False Hope, Being Strictures on Canon Farrar's Westminster Abbey Sermons* (London: William Hunt, 1878); Edward Hayes Plumptre, H. Allon, Rev. J. H. Rigg, T. R. Birks, and David Gracey, *The Future: A Series of Papers on Cannon Farrar's Eternal Hope* (Detroit: Rose-Belford, 1878).

203. Ryle, *Thoughts on Immortality*, 10.

204. Ryle, *Thoughts on Immortality*, 23.

205. Ryle, *Thoughts on Immortality*, 24.

Paul. While the apostle wrote extensively about the preeminence of charity in 1 Corinthians 13, he also said that the wicked "shall be punished with everlasting destruction in 2 Thess. 1:9."[206] He also pointed to the apostle John. Though "the spirit of love" permeates his writings, he dwells most strongly in his Apocalypse on the reality and eternity of future woe.[207]

Second, the idea that punishment is not eternal cannot be reconciled with the language of the prayer book. The first petition of the litany asks "from everlasting damnation, good Lord, deliver us." The catechism teaches every child who repeats it that we desire our heavenly Father to "keep us from our ghostly enemy and from everlasting death." During the burial services, mourners at the graveside pray, "Deliver us not into the bitter pains of eternal death." Ryle asked, "Shall we teach our congregations that even when people live and die in sin we may hope for their future happiness in a remote future?" Such a suggestion would offend their common sense and lead them to conclude that the words of the prayer book are meaningless.[208]

Finally, Ryle was also concerned about the practical implications of denying the reality of eternal punishment. One practical consequence of denying eternal punishment is that it undermines the whole system of revealed religion.[209] Why did Christ suffer and die if people can be saved without Him? Why should people be urged to repent and believe if sinners may be converted after death? Why is the Spirit's work necessary if people may enter into heaven without being born again? A second practical concern is that denying eternal punishment is destructive to public morality and personal holiness.[210] Nothing is as pleasant to flesh and blood as the theory that sinners may live in sin and yet escape eternal perdition. No one

---

206. Ryle, *Thoughts on Immortality*, 25.
207. Ryle, *Thoughts on Immortality*, 25–26.
208. Ryle, *Thoughts on Immortality*, 27.
209. Ryle, *Thoughts on Immortality*, 29.
210. Ryle, *Thoughts on Immortality*, 30.

would repent, deny themselves, and take up the cross if they can get to heaven at last and escape punishment without trouble. Finally, every blow struck at the eternity of punishment is an equally heavy blow at the eternity of reward.[211] The Bible uses the same language and figures of speech to describe either condition. Thus, every attack on the duration of hell is an attack on the duration of heaven. Ryle pointed out, "With the sinner's fear our hope departs."[212]

Ryle admitted that the doctrine of eternal punishment is a "hard subject to handle lovingly."[213] While he abhorred "hard, austere, and unmerciful theology," Christians must not be wise above that which is written nor reject anything God has revealed about eternity out of a morbid love of liberality.[214]

Following his general treatment of the future state, Ryle dealt specifically with the claims made by Canon Farrar in *Eternal Hope*. He began with his general impression of the work: "I laid down the volume with regret and dissatisfaction, unconvinced and unshaken in my opinions."[215] Then he offered the following critique. First, the canon offered no new arguments for his position. Most of his claims had been made and refuted before.[216]

---

211. Ryle, *Thoughts on Immortality*, 31.

212. Ryle, *Thoughts on Immortality*, 32.

213. Ryle, *Thoughts on Immortality*, 32.

214. Ryle, *Thoughts on Immortality*, 32. The "hard, austere, and unmerciful theology" is probably a reference to supralapsarian theology, which attributes the cause of damnation ultimately to God's decree of reprobation. In the following sentence he provided clarification: "If men are not saved it is because they will not come to Christ (Jn. 5:40)."

215. Ryle, *Thoughts on Immortality*, 52.

216. He directed the reader to five works on the subject of eternal punishment that are "far sounder, and more Scriptural" than *Eternal Hope*: Horbery's *Enquiry into the Scripture Doctrine of the Duration of Future Punishments*, Girdlestone's *Dies Irae*, Childe's *Unsafe Anchor*, a volume of American essays by various authors titled *The Future Life*, and Bishop Pearson's *On the Creed*. According to Ryle, these works remained unanswered.

Second, the author ignored "vast difficulties" bound up with the subject of eternal punishment.[217] While he handled the love and compassion of God with characteristic rhetoric, he ignored other attributes of God's character like His infinite holiness and justice, His hatred of evil, and the unspeakable vileness and guilt of sin in His sight.

Third, the canon adopted a position that was identical to the one first taken up by Origen, which was rejected and condemned by his contemporaries. Moreover, his position was repudiated by prominent theologians in both the Eastern and Western churches, the Second Council of Constantinople (553), and by almost all theologians from the time of the Reformation to the present, including Lutherans, Calvinists, Arminians, Episcopalians, Presbyterians, and Independents.[218]

Fourth, Ryle admitted there were difficulties with the traditional view of eternal punishment that he could not entirely explain. Mystery should be expected in revealed religion, especially when dealing with subjects like "eternity," which human beings have "no line to fathom."[219]

Fifth, Ryle also acknowledged that many Roman Catholic theologians, as well as some Protestants, had made extravagant and offensive statements about the bodily suffering of the lost in another world.[220] He was probably referring to what the canon called the "abominable fancy" that the joy of the saved is increased by their permission to watch the suffering of the damned.[221] He pointed out that it is unfair to make Christianity responsible for the mistakes of its advocates. Moreover, the errors of Aquinas, Dante, Milton, Boston, and Edwards do not remove the mass of

---

217. Ryle, *Thoughts on Immortality*, 54–55.
218. Ryle, *Thoughts on Immortality*, 57–58.
219. Ryle, *Thoughts on Immortality*, 59–60.
220. Ryle, *Thoughts on Immortality*, 61–62.
221. Farrar, *Eternal Hope*, 66.

scriptural evidence for the doctrine of eternal punishment, which has never been explained away.

Sixth, while the Bible clearly teaches that there will be degrees of suffering (as well as degrees of glory), there is no indication that the punishment of the wicked will come to an end, nor is there any indication that there will be conversions beyond the grave.[222]

Seventh, Ryle addressed the argument from "common opinion."[223] The argument from common opinion is both dangerous and unsound. It is dangerous because it undermines Scripture as the only rule of faith and practice, and it is unsound because it ignores the effects of sin on the mind and heart. Furthermore, it is not altogether certain that the argument from common opinion would not support eternal punishment.[224]

Finally, Ryle addressed Canon Farrar's attempts to redefine terms.[225] For example, the canon argued that the terms *eternal* and *everlasting* do not always mean "endless." While it is true that *everlasting*, when applied to physical subjects like the hills, means nothing more than enduring, when it is applied to God and the human soul, it always denotes an endless eternity. In short, "from the beginning of Matthew down to the end of Revelation, the word can only bear one meaning. Whether applied to 'God,' or to the 'Spirit,' or to 'redemption,' or to 'consolation,' or to 'glory,' or 'punishment,' or 'fire,' it can only bear one interpretation. It always signifies that which has no end."[226]

---

222. Ryle, *Thoughts on Immortality*, 63–64.

223. The argument from "common opinion" simply states that eternal punishment cannot be true because the inward feeling of the multitudes revolt against it. Ryle, *Thoughts on Immortality*, 64.

224. Ryle specifically mentioned the Greek and Roman writers and said, "If anything is clearly taught in the stories of their mythology it is the endless nature of the suffering of the wicked." Ryle, *Thoughts on Immortality*, 67.

225. Ryle, *Thoughts on Immortality*, 68–71.

226. Ryle, *Thoughts on Immortality*, 71.

Another challenge to the traditional view came from those who advocated conditional immortality.[227] Proponents of this school of thought argued that immortality, in the fullest sense, is the privilege of the believer only. This misery of those who die in sin will come to an end after a period of punishment. Its advocates insisted that endless suffering is incompatible with the character of a loving and merciful God. Ryle offered a brief refutation.

First, human beings are poor judges of what is suitable for God's character.[228] Human ideas of the sinfulness of sin and the unutterable holiness of God are thoroughly inadequate and defective. No amount of misery could satisfy that breach of God's law for which the blood of Jesus Christ, the eternal Son of God, was needed to provide atonement. "It is the blood, and not the length of time that alone exhausts the sinfulness of sin."[229] Second, the alleged distinction between the duration of the future blessedness of the godly and the future misery of the ungodly is a distinction without a difference.[230] The language the Bible uses for both is one and the same. You cannot limit or shorten one without limiting or shortening the other. They stand or fall together. Finally, Ryle addressed the objection that it is shocking that God would call so many beings into existence who will finally come to everlasting misery.[231] He replied by quoting Butler's *Analogy*, which argues that the fact that many perish everlastingly is no proof that this was the end of God's design. God designed people for joy, not misery, but this does not prevent them from ruining themselves by vice.

---

227. It is not clear why Ryle addresses this subject here, given that Cannon Farrar rejects conditional immortality in *Eternal Hope*. See Farrar, *Eternal Hope*, xvi–xvii. It is likely that Ryle included this discussion simply because it was (1) related to the overall subject (the future state); (2) more plausible than annihilation; (3) being espoused by other clergymen (Farrar specifically mentions E. White, Mr. Minton, and Prebendary Constable on xvii), and (4) growing in popularity.

228. Ryle, *Thoughts on Immortality*, 73.

229. Ryle, *Thoughts on Immortality*, 74.

230. Ryle, *Thoughts on Immortality*, 74.

231. Ryle, *Thoughts on Immortality*, 79.

Ryle's controversy with neologianism provides an illuminating contrast with ritualism. There are at least three similarities between Ryle's antiritualist and antineologian writings. First, Ryle responded to each with similar types of arguments. He typically began with exegesis and then discussed the theological implication of particular ideas. Afterward, he appealed to church history in general and the formularies of the Church of England in particular. Finally, he pointed out the pastoral and practical implications. Second, Ryle's attitude toward new scientific discoveries was relatively moderate. He was not antagonistic to science. He acknowledged that there were difficulties with his position. He urged Christians to be content to wait for greater light. Third, the intensity of Ryle's opposition to biblical criticism was exceeded only by his opposition to ritualism.

There are also significant differences between Ryle's engagement with ritualism and with neologianism. During his ministry in Stradbroke, Ryle seemed far more concerned about ritualism than neologianism, if publishing is a reliable indicator of his level of concern. The works themselves have a different focus. Ryle's antineologian writings typically focus on popular arguments and pastoral implications instead of exegesis, theology, and history. The nature of the debate may be partly responsible for this shift. Ryle was not a scientist nor did he read German works on Old Testament criticism. He was, however, a pastor and popular writer, so it is not surprising that he would focus on popular arguments and pastoral concerns as opposed to the technical argument of specialists. It is hard not to fault Ryle for underestimating the threat of neology. For example, he said almost nothing about Darwinism in any of his works. He was hardly the exception in this respect. Evangelicals were much more concerned about the threat of ritualism than neologianism. Nevertheless, neology, especially in the form of biblical criticism and Darwinism, posed a serious threat to the orthodoxy of the Church of England, and many evangelicals, including Ryle, were slow to respond to it.

Keswick Spirituality

In the mid-1870s Ryle became involved in a third major controversy over Keswick spirituality. The Mildmay Conference functioned as a spiritual forerunner to Keswick. The first of these conferences was held at Barnet from 1856 until 1863, and then they moved to Mildmay Park in 1864. They were first organized by William Pennefather for the purpose of promoting personal holiness, brotherly love, and increased interest in the work of the Lord.[232] The conference typically began with morning prayer, intercession, and Bible reading; in the evening attendees heard addresses on foreign and home missions, the second advent, and personal holiness. Pennefather personally selected the conference speakers for their prowess as spiritual teachers and purposely avoided controversial topics in order to promote unity. Lord Radstock, the brothers Horatius and Andrew Bonar, Reginald Radcliffe, and Hay Aitken were regular speakers in the early years of the conference.[233] In the later years, Keswick leaders such as Evan Hopkins and Hanmer William Webb-Peploe were frequently asked to address the annual meeting. Pennefather died in 1873, but the Mildmay Conference lived on and continued to grow in popularity. It never became an official organ of the Keswick message, however. It allowed critics of Keswick, as well as its advocates, to address its audiences. Yet it proved to be fertile soil for the message of Keswick to take root in at least three respects. First, Pennefather gave a platform to speakers who first promoted the doctrine of sanctification by faith outside of Methodism. Second, it brought together a body of zealous Christian workers who were keenly interested in personal holiness, which formed a natural

---

232. William Pennefather, *The Church of the First-born: A Few Thoughts on Christian Unity* (London: John F. Shaw, 1865), 97.

233. Bentley suggests that Pennefather chose them because they were favorably inclined to revivalism and their denominational ties were loose. Bentley, "Transformation of the Evangelical Party," 389.

constituency for new holiness teaching. Third, Mildmay created a network of connections for the early Keswick teachers.[234]

The new holiness teaching that became the nucleus of early Keswick spirituality was imported from America.[235] In 1858 William Edwin Boardman, an itinerant Presbyterian minister, published *The Higher Christian Life*, which urged Christians to embrace a superior form of spiritual life immediately, by faith. A second conversion experience, full salvation, and deliverance from sin are offered to all Christians on the sole condition of full trust in Jesus.[236] Boardman's book generated interest and criticism on both sides of the Atlantic. He was invited to speak at the Mildmay Conference in 1869 and later moved to England permanently, where he continued to speak and contribute articles on holiness to periodicals such as *The Christian*. Boardman's impact as an author and speaker was limited, but a husband-and-wife ministry team from Philadelphia would spread and popularize his gospel of sanctification by faith.

Robert Pearsall Smith was a Quaker glass manufacturer from Philadelphia. Both he and his wife, Hannah Whitall Smith, received the second blessing of entire sanctification at a Methodist camp meeting in 1867. Shortly thereafter the Smiths began writing of their experience and traveling around the eastern United States, proclaiming immediate and complete victory over sin by faith, not

---

234. David Bebbington, *Holiness in Nineteenth-Century England* (Carlisle, U.K.: Paternoster, 2000), 75.

235. The history, teaching, and progress of the Keswick Convention are discussed in Balleine, *History of the Evangelical Party in the Church of England*; Bentley, "Transformation of the Evangelical Party"; Bebbington, *Holiness in Nineteenth-Century England*; Hylson-Smith, *Evangelicals in the Church of England*; Kent, *Holding the Fort*; H. C. G. Moule, *The Evangelical School in the Church of England: Its Men and Its Work in the Nineteenth Century* (London: James Nisbet, 1901); J. C. Pollock, *The Keswick Story: The Authorized History of the Keswick Convention* (London: Hodder and Stoughton, 1964).

236. William Edwin Boardman, *The Higher Christian Life* (Boston: Henry Hoyt, 1859), vi–vii.

by works or effort.[237] Robert was a persuasive platform speaker, but his wife made an even greater impact than he did. Her personal piety was genuine, her gifts for biblical exposition were evident, and she became a popular author. Her book *The Christian's Secret of a Happy Life* (1874) is considered to be the most influential book in the origins of Keswick.

The Smiths came to England to convalesce in 1873. They carried letters of introduction and were soon meeting with clergymen and influential laymen in private gatherings to promote holiness through faith. These meetings led to a series of conventions that ultimately gave birth to the Keswick Convention. The first was held at Broadlands Park in July 1874 at the invitation of Lord Cowper-Temple to explore the scriptural possibilities of faith as a means of achieving an unbroken walk with God and securing victory over all known sin. The success of this meeting led to the creation of another conference for the promotion of scriptural holiness, which was held in Oxford six weeks later.[238] Several smaller meetings followed in various parts of the country, but the next major event was the Brighton Convention, which was held in May 1875.[239] More than six thousand people attended the convention, and another was planned for the end of June, but before this meeting could take place, Pearsall Smith lost the leadership of the movement. He had a mental breakdown shortly after the conclusion of the Brighton Convention. The orthodoxy of his private teaching was called into question, and it was rumored that he committed adultery. The leadership of the movement fell to three evangelical clergymen: Canon Harford-Battersby, Evan Hopkins, and H. C. G. Moule.

---

237. See Robert Pearsall Smith, *Holiness through Faith: Light on the Way of Holiness*, rev. ed. (New York: Anson D. F. Randolf, 1875).

238. For an account of this meeting, see Robert Pearsall Smith, ed., *Account of the Union Meeting for the Promotion of Scriptural Holiness Held at Oxford, August 29 to September 7, 1874* (London: Daldy, Isbister, 1874).

239. For an account of the Brighton Convention, see *Record of the Convention for the Promotion of Scriptural Holiness Held at Brighton May 29th to June 7th, 1875* (London: S. W. Patridge, 1875).

Harford-Battersby presided over the first official Keswick Convention in July 1875 and held the movement together after the fall of the Smiths. Evan Hopkins emerged as a leading theologian of the movement. He succeeded Pearsall Smith as the editor of *The Pathway of Power* and later renamed it *The Life of Faith*. His works, such as *The Holy Life* (1881) and *The Law of Liberty in the Spiritual Life* (1884), helped rescue Keswick teaching from the charge of perfectionism and gave respectability to the movement. But it was H. C. G. Moule, the future bishop of Durham, who would make Keswick theology palatable to a large swath of evangelical churchmen. Moule joined the movement in 1884 and provided it with a first-rate theologian and scholar, an able exponent, and an influential writer.[240] According to Pollock, Moule saved the movement from fizzling out or exploding into heresy.[241]

The leaders of the evangelical party responded to the early phases of the new movement with deep suspicion. In spring 1873, G. T. Fox published *Perfectionism*, which was a refutation of the teaching of Boardman and Pearsall Smith. The *Record* and *The Christian Observer* published lengthy critical views of *Holiness through Faith*.[242] Evangelical leaders such as Edward Garbett, Canon Hoare, and Canon Money defended the traditional doctrine of progressive sanctification at various clerical meetings, but there were few more determined opponents than J. C. Ryle.

The importance of personal holiness had been a central theme of Ryle's ministry since his ordination. In a letter to the *Record*, he wrote,

To promote deep views of sin, to glorify and exalt our Lord Jesus Christ in all his offices, to maintain and uphold the duty and privilege of Scriptural holiness, self-consecration,

---

240. H. C. G. Moule's views on sanctification are set forth in *Thoughts on Christian Sanctity* (London: Seeley, 1885).

241. Pollock, *Keswick Story*, 68.

242. *Holiness through Faith* received a two-part review in the *Christian Observer*. The first appeared in November 1875; the second appeared in January 1876 (60–75).

and entire separation from the world, has been the main objects of my life for nearly thirty-five years. To promote these objects I have spent and been spent, suffered loss, and endured reproach. I have never flinched from supporting any movement from any quarter which I thought would promote them. God is my witness that I lie not.[243]

Despite the growing interest in personal holiness, Ryle was unable to support the movement. He initially attempted to redirect this renewed interest in personal holiness into more orthodox channels. He suggested that evangelical churchmen hold a rival conference on scriptural holiness, which took place in February 1875. According to the *Record*, it was well attended. Following the Brighton Convention, Ryle wrote a scathing critique of the meeting in which he compared the teaching of Moody and the Smiths to sunshine and fog.[244] This infamous letter was later reprinted and distributed at convention meetings without Ryle's knowledge or consent.[245] In February of the following year, he delivered an address at the second evangelical holiness conference for churchmen, which was held at St. James's Hall.[246] In 1877 he published the first edition of *Holiness: Its Nature, Hindrances, Difficulties, and Roots*, which was enlarged in 1879. It proved to be one of the most extensive critiques of early Keswick spirituality and one of Ryle's most popular and enduring works.

Ryle had five major concerns with Keswick's new teaching on holiness. He was concerned about the use of mass meetings to promote practical holiness and its teaching on sin, perfection, the role of faith in sanctification, and entire consecration.

---

243. J. C. Ryle, *A Letter on Mr. Pearsall Smith's Brighton Convention* (London: James Nisbet, 1875), 4.

244. Ryle, *Letter on Mr. Pearsall Smith's Brighton Convention*, 1.

245. Bentley, "Transformation of the Evangelical Party," 404. For the published version of this letter, see Ryle, *Letter on Mr. Pearsall Smith's Brighton Convention*.

246. The address was later published. See *About Sin!* (London: William Hunt, 1877).

Mass Meetings

One of the distinguishing characteristics of the Keswick movement was the use of mass meetings to promote its message. Evangelical churchmen were no strangers to religious meetings. Many evangelical clergymen attended local clerical meetings and the annual Islington Clerical Conference, and every May evangelicals flocked to Exeter Hall in London for the yearly meeting of their favorite societies. The early holiness meetings were different in at least three respects. First, they were more narrowly focused than other meetings. The sole purpose of these meetings was to promote scriptural holiness by "an ordered scheme of teaching out of the Holy Scriptures."[247] A second novel feature of these meetings was the extensive use of personal testimonies to bear witness to the results of one's own experience.[248] The Smiths encouraged these personal testimonies, especially from clergymen, because they were convinced that they were "most effective in encouraging others to avail themselves of the same grace."[249] Third, the stated purpose of these meetings was to encourage "a genuine spiritual experience"— namely, "a truly Scriptural experience of sanctification."[250]

---

247. Robert Pearsall Smith explained the precise method of instruction:

> The aim of the speakers therefore was to bring about this result by an ordered scheme of teaching out of the Holy Scriptures. There was a gradual progress in the truths brought forth. The promises of a condition of abiding holiness; examples of the manner in which it had been sought and attained; the contrast between such a state, and that of the larger portion of the professing Church at the present day; the satisfaction and peace enjoyed by those who have attained to the one, and the unsatisfied state of soul of those who stop short of it; these, and other kindred topics, were pressed home, with every variety of appeal to the hearts of the hearers, and each person was invited to self examination as to his and her state, to a renunciation of all idols of the flesh and spirit, and to a willing surrender of all to Christ, with a full trust in Him for the bestowal of the blessing asked.

Robert Pearsall Smith, *Account of the Union Meeting*, vi.
248. Robert Pearsall Smith, *Account of the Union Meeting*, vii.
249. Robert Pearsall Smith, *Account of the Union Meeting*, vii.
250. *Record of the Convention for the Promotion of Scriptural Holiness*, 5–6.

Ryle had no objections to large meetings in general or large meetings to promote holiness in particular. But he feared that these meetings did not produce lasting results.[251] More specifically, he doubted that these meetings produced real, practical holiness. He wrote, "I cannot withhold a growing suspicion that the great 'mass meetings' of the present day, for the ostensible object of promoting spiritual life, do not tend to promote private home religion, private Bible-reading, private prayer, private usefulness, and private walking with God."[252] If these meetings were of any real value, they would produce better husbands and wives, fathers and mothers, sons and daughters, brothers and sisters, and masters and mistresses and servants.[253] Ryle frankly admitted that he had not seen proof that they did. In short, it is easier to be a consistent Christian in a consecration meeting than in an uncongenial home.[254] Holiness meetings promoted the former but not the latter.

Sin

The Smiths' doctrine of sin is notoriously difficult to define. They purposely avoided theological and metaphysical distinctions, preferring to define sin "intuitively" or "experimentally."[255] At the

---

251. Ryle wrote, "Sensational and exciting addresses by strange preachers or by women, loud singing, hot rooms, crowded tents, the constant sight of strong semi-religious feeling in the faces of all around you for several days, late hours, long protracted meetings, public professions of experience—all this kind of thing is very interesting at the time and seems to do good. But is the good real, deeply-rooted, solid, lasting? That is the point." J. C. Ryle, *Holiness: Its Nature, Hindrances, Difficulties, and Roots*, revised and enlarged edition (1879; repr., Moscow, Idaho: Charles Nolan Publishers, 2001), xiv.

252. Ryle, *Holiness*, xiv.

253. Ryle, *Holiness*, xiv.

254. Ryle, *Holiness*, xiv–xv.

255. Robert Pearsall Smith argued that in defining sin, metaphysical distinctions must be avoided because the Scriptures do not employ them. Instead, these terms should be used only in the "intuitive sense," which is that sense which is comprehensible to most Christians. But he did not provide an intuitive definition in that work. *Holiness through Faith*, 92–93. Hannah Whitall Smith admitted that she had neither the desire nor the ability to treat the doctrines concerning sin:

Oxford Convention, Pearsall Smith offered three different definitions of sin: (1) that which in its moral quality is short of the infinite holiness of God; (2) the outbreaking of moral evil; and (3) those actual and known sins which are intended in the prayer "vouchsafe to keep us this day without sin."[256] The Smiths proclaimed deliverance from sin in the last two senses, and thus when they spoke of sin they were usually referring to definitions 2 and 3. Perhaps their clearest statement about sin came at the Brighton Conference when Robert defined sin as "disobedience to, or violation of the Divine law as is not inevitable in this world."[257] In sum, without denying original sin and the effects of the fall, when the Smiths spoke of sin, they usually were referring to known, actual, and voluntary sin.

Ryle complained in the *Record*, with some justification, that it was hard to know what the Smiths meant when they spoke about sin: "I frankly confess that I cannot understand the distinctive theology which is the foundation of the Brighton Convention."[258] For Ryle, any biblical definition of sin had to take into account original sin and guilt, as well as actual sin. It is both a "vast moral disease which affects the whole human race" and "doing, saying, thinking, or imagining, anything that is not in perfect conformity with the mind and law of God." [259] Anything less than this is unbiblical and inconsistent with the Thirty-Nine Articles.[260]

"These I will leave with the theologians to discuss and settle, while I speak only of the believer's experience in the matter." Hannah Whitall Smith, *The Christian's Secret of a Happy Life* (London: E. F. Longley, 1876), 145.

256. Robert Pearsall Smith, *Account of the Union Meeting*, 78–79.

257. *Record of the Convention for the Promotion of Scriptural Holiness*, 209.

258. Ryle, *Letter on Mr. Pearsall Smith's Brighton Convention*, 1.

259. See Ryle, *About Sin!*, 3–4. See also Ryle, *Holiness*, 2.

260. He appealed to the ninth article of the Church of England, which states that original sin is "the fault and corruption of the nature of every man, that naturally is engendered of the offspring of Adam; whereby man is very far gone from original righteousness, and is of his own nature inclined to evil, so that the flesh lusteth always contrary to the Spirit; and therefore in every person born into this world, it deserveth God's wrath and damnation."

It is evident that Ryle's and the Smiths' doctrine of sin differed in terms of emphasis. The Smiths almost completely ignored the doctrines of original sin and human depravity and focused exclusively on known, voluntary sin and its remedy. Ryle, on the other hand, focused on the extent of humanity's "vast moral disease" and its "guilt, vileness, and offensiveness." It would be inaccurate, however, to say that the difference was only a matter of emphasis. Ryle disagreed with the Smiths about the guilt of unknown sin in particular. The Smiths drew a distinction between intentional, conscious, voluntary acts of sin and unintentional, unconscious, involuntary acts of sin.[261] The former break the believer's communion with God and defile his or her conscience, but the latter do not. Pearsall Smith explained, "An unknown fault in a child will not prevent full joyous confidence in intercourse with the parent.... So an unknown, undesigned sin of ignorance, in one seeking the will of God, will not destroy communion."[262] Ryle rejected this distinction entirely as being without scriptural warrant. In both Leviticus and Numbers, Israel was distinctly taught that sins of ignorance rendered the people unclean and required atonement.[263] Moreover, Christ expressly taught in a parable (Luke 12:48) that an ignorant servant was not excused on account of his ignorance, but was punished.[264] In sum, "we shall do well to remember that when we make our own miserably imperfect knowledge and consciousness the measure of our own sinfulness, we are on very dangerous ground. A deeper study of Leviticus might do us much good."[265] Ultimately, Ryle and the Smiths could not agree on a precise definition of sin.

---

261. Robert Pearsall Smith, *Account of the Union Meeting; Record of the Convention for the Promotion of Scriptural Holiness*, 209; Hannah Whitall Smith, *Christian's Secret of a Happy Life*, 145.

262. Robert Pearsall Smith, *Account of the Union Meeting*, 78.

263. Ryle, *Holiness*, 3.

264. Ryle, *Holiness*, 3. See also his notes on Luke 12:48 in *St. Luke*.

265. Ryle, *Holiness*, 3.

Perfection

Differing definitions of sin led to different understandings of perfection. The Smiths did not actually teach absolute sinless perfection "in the flesh."[266] They did, however, make enough unguarded statements about it to ensure that they were frequently charged with promoting the Oberlin heresy of perfectionism.[267] They promised deliverance from all known sin, and full, unbroken, and uninterrupted communion with God by believing and resting in God's promises. It was not uncommon for their supporters to claim to live without sin (presumably *known* sin) for weeks or months or years at a time. For example, at the Oxford Convention, a man associated with George Muller in Bristol arose to testify to the veracity of the Smiths' teaching by stating that he "had lived in unbroken unclouded communion with Jesus for very many years."[268] In short, the perfectionism of the Smiths consisted in complete deliverance from all known sin, but not absolute sinless perfection.

Ryle was entirely unsympathetic to their doctrine of Christian perfection and regarded it to be an unscriptural delusion. In rejecting the Smiths' perfectionism, Ryle insisted that he was not advocating a defeatist approach to the Christian life. The life of a believer should be a life of victory, not failure.[269] He encouraged all Christians to aim for a *comparative* perfection, for "an all-round

---

266. For an explicit denial of absolute sinless perfection, see Robert Pearsall Smith, *Account of the Union Meeting*, 149–50.

267. In 1840 the American revivalist Charles Finney published *Views on Sanctification*, in which he argued that human beings had the ability to fulfill God's commands to be perfect. This was later labeled the Oberlin heresy because of Finney's connection with Asa Mahan, the president of Oberlin College, who held similar views. Some of the statements Hannah Whitall Smith made in *Christian's Secret of a Happy Life* are close to Finney's ideas. For example, she said that temptation is a blessed instrument that God uses to "complete our perfection" and suggested that "the heights of Christian perfection" can be reached by being "perfectly pliable," which enables perfect obedience. Hannah Whitall Smith, *Christian's Secret of a Happy Life*, 142, 178.

268. Robert Pearsall Smith, *Account of the Union Meeting*, 342.

269. Ryle, *Holiness*, 7.

consistency in every relation of life, [and] a thorough soundness in every point of doctrine."[270] But he denied that a *literal* perfection, a complete and entire freedom from sin, is attainable in this life. Sin no longer has dominion, but the heart of even the best Christian "is a field occupied by two rival camps."[271] More specifically, Ryle had three objections to their doctrine of perfection.

First, it was thoroughly unscriptural. The critical text at the heart of the controversy was Romans 7. The Smiths believed that Romans 7 describes the experience of either the unregenerate or unestablished, failing Christian—that is, one who has not achieved the higher spiritual life.[272] Ryle, on the other hand, believed that it describes the experience of the best saints in every age and that Paul says things in the chapter that no unregenerate person or weak Christian would ever or could ever say.[273] With few exceptions, this has been the interpretation of the best commentators in every age, especially the Reformers, Puritans, and modern evangelical divines.[274] Conversely, the Smiths' interpretation is generally that of the Romanists, Socinians, and Arminians.

Second, the Smiths' teaching on Christian perfection cannot be harmonized with the formularies of the Church of England. The ninth article says that infection of sin remains "in them that are regenerate." The fifteenth article declares that Christ alone is without sin and those who say they have no sin deceive themselves and the truth is not in them. The first homily declares that the regenerate "offend in many things" and have "many and great imperfections." Furthermore, it is difficult to see how someone

---

270. Ryle, *Holiness*, xxi.

271. Ryle, *Holiness*, 26.

272. See Robert Pearsall Smith, *Holiness through Faith*, 149; *Record of the Convention for the Promotion of Scriptural Holiness*, 91.

273. For Ryle's treatment of Romans 7, see *Holiness*, xxii–xxiii, 26.

274. Ryle specifically pointed readers to the commentaries of Andrew Willet, Elton, Thomas Chalmers, Robert Haldane, Stafford, and John Owen on *Indwelling Sin*.

who believed they have been delivered from all known sin could recite the general confession of sin in the Communion service.

Third, the Smiths' teaching was dangerous and positively harmful. It depresses many of the best Christians because they are unable to attain perfection. It "puffs up" weak and immature Christians by making them believe they have achieved something they have not. It discourages and keeps back inquirers after salvation. It disgusts and alienates unbelievers who know that it is incorrect and untrue.[275]

Finally, the Smiths' teaching is incompatible with the experience of the best Christians of all ages. Not one great saint in the Bible claimed to attain to perfection. On the contrary, men like David, Paul, and John declared in the strongest terms that they felt weakness and sin in their own hearts.[276] The same is true of the holiest men of modern times. The autobiographies and journals of men like John Bradford, Richard Hooker, Archbishop Ussher, Richard Baxter, Samuel Rutherford, and Robert Murray M'Cheyne all testify to the same fact—they considered themselves to be "debtors to mercy and grace" every day, and the last thing they ever laid claim to was perfection.[277]

The Role of Faith

According to the Smiths, Christians are sanctified by the same means by which they are justified—by faith alone without works or effort.[278] God and human beings have distinct and contrasting roles to play in sanctification. God's role is to accomplish the work of sanctification in people; people's role is simply to trust God to do it. Hannah Whitall Smith explained,

> There is a certain *work* to be accomplished. We are to be delivered from the power of sin, and are to be made perfect

275. Ryle, *Holiness*, xxi–xxii, 15.
276. Ryle, *Holiness*, xxi.
277. Ryle, *Holiness*, xxi.
278. Robert Pearsall Smith, *Holiness through Faith*, 15.

in every good work to do the will of God. "Beholding as in
a glass the glory of the Lord," we are to be actually "changed
into the same image from glory to glory even as by the Spirit
of the Lord." We are to be transformed by the renewing of our
minds that we may prove what is that good and acceptable
and perfect will of God. A real work is to be wrought in us
and upon us. Besetting sins are to be conquered. Evil habits
are to be overcome. Wrong dispositions and feelings are to be
rooted out and holy tempers and emotions are to be begot-
ten. A positive transformation is to take place. So at least the
Bible teaches. Now somebody must do this. Either we must
do it for ourselves or another must do it for us. We have most
of us tried to do it for ourselves at first, and have grievously
failed; then we discover from the Scriptures and from our
own experience that it is a work we are utterly unable to do
for ourselves, but that the Lord Jesus Christ has come on purpose to do it, and that He will do it for all who put themselves
wholly into His hand and trust Him to do it. Now under
these circumstances what is the part of the believer and what
is the part of the Lord? Plainly the believer can do nothing
but trust; while the Lord, in whom he trusts, actually does the
work entrusted to Him.[279]

As the titles of the Smiths' most famous books indicate, holiness
comes through faith—this is the Christian's secret to a happy life.

Ryle did not deny that faith played an important role in sanctification. It is the "root" of all holiness, and without it no one
possesses a single "jot" of it.[280] He did, however, reject the Smiths'

---

279. Hannah Whitall Smith, *Christian's Secret of a Happy Life*, 9–10.

280. See Ryle, *Letter on Mr. Pearsall Smith's Brighton Convention*, 2; Ryle, *Holiness*, xviii. In *Holiness* he wrote,

That faith in Christ is the root of all holiness; that the first step towards
a holy life is to believe on Christ; that until we believe we have not a jot
of holiness; that union with Christ by faith is the secret of both beginning to be holy and continuing holy; that the life that we live in the
flesh, we must live by the faith of the Son of God; that faith purifies the
heart; that faith is the victory which overcomes the world; that by faith

doctrine of sanctification by faith alone for three reasons. First, their teaching was without biblical warrant, and he offered an exegetical critique of many of the catchphrases of the movement. The phrase "holiness by faith" does not occur in the New Testament at all. "Sanctified by faith" appears only once (Acts 26:18), and upon closer inspection it does not actually teach sanctification by faith.[281] The oft-repeated exhortation to passively "yield yourself to God" occurs in Romans 6 only, and it does not support the meaning the Smiths gave it.[282] But the New Testament repeatedly summons Christians to "arise and work." It insists that faith without works is dead and stresses the importance of personal exertion and work in the pursuit of holiness.[283] In short, the Smiths were not promoting *scriptural* holiness.

Second, he accused the Smiths of confounding justification and sanctification. He acknowledged that justification and sanctification agree in certain respects. Both proceed originally from the free grace of God. Both are part of that great work of salvation that Christ accomplished for His people. Both are always found in the same persons. Both begin at the same time—conversion. Both are necessary to salvation.[284] Justification and sanctification differ in critical respects, however. Justification is the "reckoning and counting" a man to be righteous for the sake of another; sanctification is the actual making a man righteous. The righteousness

---

the elders obtained a good report—all these are truths which no well-instructed Christian will ever think of denying.

281. Ryle urges the reader to compare the account of Paul's conversion in Acts 26:18 to an earlier one in Acts 20:32. The true sense of the phrase "sanctified by faith in [Christ]" is this: "that by faith in Me they may receive forgiveness of sins and inheritance among them that are sanctified." Ryle, *Holiness*, xviii.

282. Ryle said, "Any Greek student can tell us that the sense is rather that of actively 'presenting' ourselves for use, employment, and service (see Romans 12:1)." *Holiness*, xxvii.

283. He pointed the reader to the following texts: James 2:17; Gal. 2:20; 1 Cor. 9:26–27; 2 Cor. 7:1; Heb. 4:11; 12:1.

284. Ryle, *Holiness*, 36–37.

that believers have by justification is an imputed righteousness; the righteousness that believers have by sanctification is imparted and inherent. In justification, works have no place at all; in sanctification, works are vastly important. Justification is a finished, complete, and immediate work; sanctification is an imperfect and progressive work. Justification admits no growth or increase; sanctification is eminently progressive and admits continual growth and enlargement. Justification has special reference to the Christian's person and status before God; sanctification has special reference to the Christian's heart and its moral renewal. Justification gives the Christian a title for heaven; sanctification prepares the Christian for it. Justification is not easily discerned by others; sanctification cannot be hidden.[285]

Third, Ryle's conception of the Christian life was very different from that of the Smiths. Christianity is a fight.[286] More specifically, it is a fight against the world, the flesh, and the devil. He acknowledged that this may sound extreme to some, but it is the unvarying testimony of the Bible.[287] Therefore the person who condemns fighting and insists that Christians must "sit still and yield ourselves to God" misunderstands the Bible and makes a great mistake.[288] This is also the testimony of the formularies of the Church of England. He quoted the Baptismal Service, which summons the baptized to "manfully fight under [Christ's] banner against sin, the world, and the devil, and to continue Christ's faithful soldier and servant unto life's end."[289] In short, "we must either fight or be lost."[290]

Finally, the Smiths' teaching on faith undermined practical exhortations. It was too vague and general; true holiness consists of

---

285. Ryle, *Holiness*, 37–38.

286. See Ryle's chapter "The Fight" in *Holiness*.

287. These include 1 Tim. 6:12; 2 Tim. 2:3; Eph. 6:11–13; Luke 13:24; John 6:27; Matt. 10:34; Luke 22:36; 1 Cor. 16:13; 1 Tim. 1:18–19.

288. Ryle, *Holiness*, 66.

289. Ryle, *Holiness*, 66.

290. Ryle, *Holiness*, 67.

more than simply trusting and resting. For Ryle the practical exhortations of the Bible were the true "pathway to a higher standard of holiness."[291] The three best sources are the Ten Commandments, the Sermon on the Mount, and the latter part of the Pauline Epistles.[292] Vague notions about resting in faith and generalities about holy living prick no conscience and give no offense. The details and specific ingredients in these portions of the Bible ought to be fully set forth and pressed on all believers in discussing scriptural holiness.[293]

Entire Consecration

The early Keswick teachers divided the Christian life into three distinct phases: the unconverted unbeliever, the converted but struggling believer, and the consecrated and victorious believer. Their primary concern was to usher believers from phase 2 to phase 3. Though they employed slightly different language, they all agreed that entire self-consecration was the secret to experiencing the higher Christian life.[294] In her how-to chapter on entering in to the higher Christian life, Hannah Whitall Smith explained how God bestows the gift of full salvation:

> In order to enter into this blessed interior life of rest and triumph you have two steps to take. First, entire abandonment; and, second absolute faith. No matter what may be the complications of your peculiar experience, no matter what your difficulties, or your surroundings, or your associations, these two steps definitely taken and unwaveringly persevered in, will certainly bring you out sooner or later into the green pastures and still waters of this higher Christian life. You may be sure of this. And if you will let every other consideration go and simply devote your attention to these two points, and be very

---

291. Ryle, *Holiness*, 362.

292. Ryle, *Holiness*, 362.

293. Ryle, *Holiness*, xix.

294. W. E. Boardman used the phrase "full trust"; Robert Pearsall Smith simply spoke of "faith"; and Hannah Whitall Smith used the phrase "full consecration."

clear and definite about them, your progress will be rapid, and your soul will reach its desired haven far sooner than now you can think possible.[295]

W. E. Boardman described this arrival into the "green pastures and still waters of this higher Christian life" as a second conversion.[296] Though the Smiths generally avoided this language, they referred to the same experience when they spoke of "full salvation" or "second consecration." In short, they promised a second blessing of rest and triumph to the "fully consecrated soul."

Ryle was not opposed to entire self-consecration. The necessity of being entirely devoted to Christ was classic evangelical teaching. Therefore, to charge evangelicals with ignoring the importance of self-consecration or to suggest that it had been newly discovered is simply inaccurate.[297] But he did have problems with certain aspects of the Keswick teaching about entire consecration that departed from the old paths.

First, Ryle rejected Keswick's threefold division of the Christian life. He believed that their divisions were identical to the Church of Rome, which placed all Christians into one of three categories: sinners, penitents, and saints.[298] More importantly, their threefold

---

295. Hannah Whitall Smith, *Christian's Secret of a Happy Life*, 47–48.

296. By speaking of the attainment of the higher life as a second conversion, Boardman denied that this meant a literal second regeneration. But he then muddied the water by stating that he was simply referring to what President Edwards called remarkable conversions. If he was referring to Jonathan Edwards's *Faithful Narrative*, then he has misunderstood the author's doctrine of conversion. This lends credit to Ryle's charge that his opponents confused consecration with conversion.

297. In *The Record* he wrote, "I never in my life heard of any thorough Evangelical minister who did not hold the doctrine and press it upon others…. That the common standard of holiness is deplorably low, and that there may be some so-called Evangelicals whose whole creed consists in justification by faith and opposition to Popery, I do not deny. But that the duty and privilege of entire self-consecration is systematically ignored by Evangelicals, and has only been discovered, or brought into fresh light, by the new theologians, I do not for a moment believe." Ryle, *Letter on Mr. Pearsall Smith's Brighton Convention*, 3.

298. Ryle, *Holiness*, xxvi.

division is patently unscriptural. The Bible speaks of only two classes of people: the believer and the unbeliever, the converted and the unconverted. Within each of these classes are various measures of sin and grace, but this is only the difference between the higher and lower end of an incline plane.[299] Between these two classes there is an enormous gulf that is as distinct as "life and death, light and darkness, heaven and hell."[300] In short, the early Keswick teachers made distinctions without scriptural warrant.

Second, Ryle rejected the notion of second conversions. More specifically, the Keswick teachers' stress on the second conversion revealed an inadequate understanding of true conversion. He denied that a person could be converted but not consecrated. He wrote, "More consecrated he doubtless can be, and will be as his grace increases; but if he was not consecrated to God in the very day that he was converted and born again, I do not know what conversion means."[301] Additionally, by emphasizing the need for a second conversion experience, the Keswick teachers were depreciating the more profound and foundational first "great change"—the new birth.[302] Furthermore, Ryle suspected that many of those who experienced the second conversion of consecration were actually converted for the first time. Finally, the tendency of the doctrine of second conversion was positively dangerous. It was likely to depress the meek and humble-minded and puff up the shallow, ignorant, and self-conceited.[303]

Third, Ryle believed that sanctification was a gradual and progressive work, not one that admitted instantaneous leaps from conversion to consecration.[304] One of the most attractive features of Keswick teaching about the higher Christian life was the ease and

299. Ryle, *Holiness*, xxvi.
300. Ryle, *Holiness*, xxvi.
301. Ryle, *Holiness*, xxvi.
302. Ryle, *Holiness*, xxvi.
303. Ryle, *Holiness*, xxvii.
304. Ryle, *Holiness*, xxvi.

speed with which one could reach it. The attendees at the Oxford Convention were promised the victory over sin "easily and without pain or effort."[305] At the Brighton Convention "instant deliverance" was offered for "instant trust,"[306] and many people testified that they experienced immediate and wonderful "rest and liberty" after fully surrendering to God.[307] Ryle, on the other hand, regarded this teaching to be nothing more than a "man-made invention" that was wholly without scriptural foundation.[308] Converted people need growth in grace, not a second conversion.[309]

Ryle defined growth in grace as the "increase in the degree, size, strength, vigour, and power of the graces which the Holy Spirit plants in a believer's heart."[310] Growth in grace is the plain teaching of the Bible, the best evidence of spiritual health and prosperity, the key to being happy in religion, the secret of usefulness to others, and the way to please God.[311] It is evidenced by increased humility, faith, and love toward Christ; holiness of life and conversion; spirituality of taste and mind; charity; and zeal and diligence in trying to do good to souls.[312] The means of growth in grace are the diligent use of private and public means of grace, watchfulness over one's conduct in the little matters of everyday life, caution about the company one keeps and the friendships he or she forms, and regular and habitual communion with Christ.[313] In sum, there are no shortcuts on the way to holiness—scriptural holiness is a gradual and progressive work.

---

305. Robert Pearsall Smith, *Account of the Union Meeting*, 292.

306. *Record of the Convention for the Promotion of Scriptural Holiness*, 382.

307. These testimonies abound in the official records of the Oxford and Brighton meetings. To read one of these accounts, see Smith, *Account of the Union Meeting*, 292.

308. Ryle, *Holiness*, xxvi.

309. Ryle, *Holiness*, xxvi.

310. Ryle, *Holiness*, 101.

311. Ryle, *Holiness*, 101–4.

312. Ryle, *Holiness*, 105–8.

313. Ryle, *Holiness*, 109–13.

Ryle played an important but limited role in this debate. He became involved in the controversy in May 1875 after the Brighton Convention and published a few influential critiques over the next five years, but after being appointed to the bishopric of Liverpool in 1880, he said little about it. He never discussed the controversy in his diocesan charges and addresses. He published *Thoughts and Questions about Holiness* in 1884, but it is merely a repackaging of the introduction and second chapter of *Holiness*. So why did he practically abandon this issue after becoming bishop of Liverpool?

The answer lies, in part, in the magnitude of the task before him in Liverpool. Ryle's new diocese provided more than enough work for him to do. In addition to the demands of the new diocese, Keswick theology was evolving. As previously mentioned, H. C. G. Moule joined the movement in 1884 and helped make Keswick's teaching more acceptable to evangelical churchmen. He still spoke in terms of a second spiritual crisis, but this crisis led to a process, not perfection. Under his leadership many evangelicals were won over. By 1901 Moule could say, "I do not think that any word would be heard from the Keswick platform really alien to the Evangelical Churchman's heart."[314] Ryle never attended the Keswick Convention or spoke on its behalf. It is safe to say that he remained an opponent, albeit an increasingly quiet one. He did, however, make Moule one of his examining chaplains in 1882, and Moule continued to serve him in some capacity for the rest of his life. This should not be seen as a tacit endorsement of the movement, however. Ryle's refusal to support this increasingly popular movement alienated him from many evangelicals, especially younger ones.

Ryle's most important contribution to this controversy was undoubtedly *Holiness*. It went through five editions during his lifetime, and it has been republished regularly since John Clarke republished it at the prompting of D. Martyn Lloyd-Jones in 1952. It is probably Ryle's most popular work at present. It and *Practical*

---

314. Moule, *Evangelical School in the Church of England*, 82.

Religion provide an excellent summary of Ryle's spirituality and were intended to be read as such.[315]

Holiness makes its own unique contribution to our understanding of Ryle's spirituality. It, more than any other work, reveals his indebtedness to the English Puritans. Though he occasionally quotes from Anglican authorities like Richard Hooker and Bishop Jewell and evangelical fathers like William Romaine, the vast majority of the extensive quotes of this work come from Puritan authors such as John Owen, John Bunyan, Thomas Goodwin, Samuel Rutherford, Richard Sibbes, Thomas Manton, John Flavel, William Gurnall, Thomas Watson, Thomas Brooks, Robert Traill, and Richard Baxter. Ryle's spirituality was cast in a Puritan mold, and nowhere is this more evident than in *Holiness*.

Ryle's Reputation as a Controversialist

During his ministry at Stradbroke, J. C. Ryle took part in every major theological controversy in which the evangelical party participated. Ritualism was the most important of these debates, and Ryle took a leading role. He offered a popular and pastoral critique of neology to strengthen the faithful and challenge the skeptic. He also provided a devastating critique of the early Keswick teaching. Perhaps no other evangelical played such an important role in each of these major controversies.

In 1874 Ryle published *Knots Untied: Being Plain Statements on Disputed Points in Religion*. It consists of a series of nineteen papers that address the major theological disputes of the day from an evangelical standpoint. Issues related to ritualism dominate the work, but neology is addressed as well. Keswick teaching is not discussed because the movement was still in its infancy, at least with respect to the Church of England. *Knots Untied* proved to be tremendously popular—the thirty-first edition was published in 1954. The publication of this work did more than simply increase

---

315. Ryle, *Practical Religion*, vi.

Ryle's popularity as a theologian and writer; it elevated him to the status of a party spokesman, at least in controversial matters. *The Christian Observer* reviewed the work in December 1874 and made the following observation: "Mr. Ryle is careful to explain that he does not pretend to be a mouthpiece of the Evangelical party; but we imagine that there are but few who would not accept him as their able advocate and intelligent apologist."[316]

Ryle's preaching made him a sought-after speaker. His tracts and commentaries made him a trusted spiritual guide. But his work as a controversialist made him a leader whom evangelicals could rally behind. This reputation was solidified by his work as a party uniter, Church defender, and Church reformer.

---

316. *Christian Observer*, December 1874, 947.

5

A National Ministry

As Ryle rose through the evangelical ranks, his concern for the evangelical party and the Church as a whole broadened. "Erroneous and strange doctrines" needed to be banished and driven away, but there were other challenges facing the party and the Church that had to be addressed. Evangelicals, as a body, were divided. The disestablishment movement was gaining momentum. It was necessary to reform the Church as well.

Around 1870 Ryle's ministry assumed a national character as he began to address each of these issues. He attempted to unite the evangelical body. He became a stalwart defender of the union of church and state. And he proposed a number of radical reforms to make the Church of England more pastorally effective.

Uniting Evangelicals

According to John Wesley, the evangelical body in the Church of England was nothing more than a rope of sand, and the history of the evangelical party in the nineteenth century did little to refute that claim. At the beginning of the century, the evangelicals enjoyed considerable unity under the leadership of William Wilberforce and the Clapham Sect, as well as through the network of the great societies, such as the Church Missionary Society (CMS), the Church Pastoral Aid Society (CPAS), the Bible Society, and the Jew's Society. The Islington Clerical Meeting, founded in 1827 by Daniel Wilson, gradually became another important center of unity for evangelical clergymen. This unity was shattered by debates over the Irvingites, eschatology, Catholic emancipation, the Reform Act, relations with Dissenters, and social action.[1]

Tractarianism in the 1830s and 1840s and then ritualism in the 1850s and 1860s helped reunite the party in opposition to a common enemy, at least in theory. In practice, unity remained elusive. Evangelicals had no Wilberforce or Simeon to rally around, and it was generally agreed that the great societies were no longer able to function as centers of unity. There were a number of attempts to unite the party under a single banner, but for the most part, these attempts failed miserably.

One such attempt was the creation of the Evangelical Alliance in 1846. It arose, in part, out of the proceedings of the Anti-Maynooth Committee in the spring of that year, and its purpose was to oppose the Maynooth Grant[2] and to unite all evangelical Christians around their common principles.[3] The Alliance enjoyed the support of a few prominent evangelical clergymen, such as Edward Bickersteth, but most refused to support it.[4] Many clergymen believed that Dissenters were obsessed with politics, especially the issue of disestablishment, and were losing their spiritual vitality. Others believed that cooperation was simply a practical impossibility.[5] Simply

---

1. Hylson-Smith, *Evangelicals in the Church of England*, 177.

2. In response to an appeal from Roman Catholic bishops in Ireland for assistance in repairing their college for training priests, the Tory government under Peel raised the annual grant to Maynooth from nine thousand pounds to twenty-seven thousand pounds and gave thirty thousand pounds for capital expenditure. Hylson-Smith, *Evangelicals in the Church of England*, 178.

3. John William Ewing, *Goodly Fellowship: A Centenary Tribute to the Life and Work of the World's Evangelical Alliance, 1846–1946* (London: Marshall, Morgan and Scott, 1946), 16. This is an excellent history of the Evangelical Alliance. See also James William Massie, *The Evangelical Alliance: Its Origin and Development* (London: John Snow, 1847).

4. Bickersteth was one of the founders of the Alliance and proposed its doctrinal basis. See Edward Bickersteth, *Five Letters on Christian Union* (London: Seeley, Burnside, and Seeley, 1845); and his letter to the *Christian Observer*, December 1845, 728–31.

5. Hugh M'Neile spoke for many evangelical clergymen when he said, "But though differences in worship and discipline, and national connexion, need not,

put, many evangelicals feared that an alliance with Dissenters would only magnify differences, "foment jealousies," and "multiply estrangements."[6] A true evangelical alliance would be possible in heaven, but not before. The Evangelical Association represented an attempt to create unity based on the spiritual union of all believers in Christ, but for many evangelical churchmen, unity based on doctrine, purpose, and action was preferable.[7]

Many evangelicals regarded the Church Association as the best potential source of unity for the party, although it was technically open to all churchmen who opposed ritualism.[8] It provided doctrinal unity, identified a common enemy, and summoned evangelicals to concerted action.[9] Furthermore, it provided organizational structure. The central association was headquartered in London, but it encouraged the formation of local associations throughout

---

and in point of fact do not, interfere necessarily with true Christian unity, they do and must interfere with manifest co-operation. Mutual recognition of one another as Christian brethren, notwithstanding such differences, is a duty. Co-operation, under such circumstances, appears to me to be an impossibility." Hugh M'Neile, *The Collected Works of the Very Rev. Dean M'Neile, D.D.* (London: Christian Book Society, 1877), 1:87. The *Christian Observer* took this position and discussed the Evangelical Alliance extensively in December of 1845 and throughout 1846.

6. M'Neile, *Collected Works*, 1:89.

7. For a good discussion of these two different approaches to unity and denominational identity, see Ralph Brown, "The Evangelical Succession? Evangelical History and Denomination Identity," *Evangelical Quarterly* 68 (1996): 3–13.

8. The Church Association was originally intended to be an inclusive body. It sought to unite all moderate churchmen who were prepared to stand by Reformation principles, and efforts were made to include men on its council who were not usually identified with the evangelical school. In fact, the founders abstained from asking Lord Shaftesbury to be president in order to preserve the association from a party character. Eugene Stock, *The History of the Church Missionary Society: Its Environment, Its Men, and Its Work* (London: Church Missionary Society, 1916), 2:348.

9. *Church Association Tracts*, 1:1: "The Church Association, established in 1865, to uphold the Doctrines, Principles, and Order of the United Church of England and Ireland, and to counteract the efforts now being made to pervert her teaching on essential points of the Christian faith, or assimilate her Services to those of the Church of Rome, and further to encourage concerted action for the advancement and progress of Spiritual Religion."

the country. Furthermore, there were many sympathetic lay and clerical associations already in existence that could easily join—all that was needed was a letter from a local association stating its desire to do so. Though the Church Association was a promising center of unity, its focus on legal action against ritualists made it unpopular with many people. This led some evangelicals to seek unity elsewhere—namely, in clerical and lay associations.

Clerical and lay associations brought together evangelical churchmen for fellowship, counsel, and encouragement. These conferences attracted many people who were turned off by the ritualist prosecutions and proved to be more comprehensive than the Church Association. Furthermore, they provided local nerve centers that could be linked together to unite the evangelical body as a whole.[10] Edward Garbett led the charge to unite the clerical and lay associations into a new union that would be independent of the older association. A conference on the subject was held at the Canon Street Hotel in January 1870. Though the meeting was well attended, some evangelicals, following the lead of men like Daniel Wilson and Joseph Bardsley, disapproved of the proposal for fear of undermining the Church Association and further dividing the party.[11] The Clerical and Lay Union was formed as a result of the conference, but the majority decided that the new union would injure the unity of the party. Therefore, it was decided that it would function as a branch of the Church Association. The Church Association now consisted of two branches: the old council and the union committees.[12] In 1873, after a resolution seeking an amicable separation failed, a small group of the union committee, led by Garbett, left the Church Association and formed a completely independent society—the Evangelical Union of the Church of England for the Promotion of Church Reform. As its title suggests,

10. Bentley, "Transformation of the Evangelical Party," 179.
11. Bentley, "Transformation of the Evangelical Party," 179–80.
12. Bentley, "Transformation of the Evangelical Party," 181–82.

it initially directed its attention to church reform, but the focus soon shifted to the Public Worship Regulation Act. Shortly after its passage in 1874, the new union faded from the scene.[13]

By the end of the 1870s, some evangelicals were convinced that a new, more decidedly evangelical union was needed. The opponents of the Reformation were becoming more aggressive as they increased in number and popularity, and the strength of the party was being sapped by the "time-serving and compromising policy" of many who professed to be loyal to evangelical principles but in reality were not.[14] The Church Association resolutely opposed ritualism, but it was open to all churchmen and thus lacked a sufficient doctrinal basis for union. What was needed was a new union made up of only "thoroughly decided men" who were willing to further the gospel and maintain the "distinctive, Evangelical Protestant Doctrines and Practices of the Reformation."[15] The Evangelical Protestant Union was formed to meet this need in 1879. It enjoyed the enthusiastic support of *The Rock* and grew to more than one thousand members by 1884, but its focus on secondary matters (surpliced choirs, preaching gowns) and its critical attitude toward fellow evangelicals ensured that it never became more than a fringe group.[16]

Partly as a response to the formation of the Evangelical Protestant Union and partly because of the Church Association's growing unpopularity, a second Union of Clerical and Lay Associations was formed in 1880. Ryle was one of its primary architects. This union proved to be more successful than the previous one. By 1884, it included nineteen associations and was represented in

---

13. Bentley, "Transformation of the Evangelical Party," 186–87.

14. "Is There Not a Cause? A Word to Evangelical Protestants in the National Churches of England and Ireland, on the Necessity Which Exists for the Evangelical Protestant Union," *The Irish Church Advocate*, May 1879: 142.

15. "Is There Not a Cause?," 142. The Evangelical Protestant Union also required that its clerical members abandon the use of surpliced choirs and preach only in the academic black gown.

16. Bentley, "Transformation of the Evangelical Party," 188.

twenty-seven dioceses out of thirty-two.[17] Despite Balleine's contention that this union was "never able to accomplish much," it is generally agreed that it did useful work in the provision of middle-class education, supplying guidelines to the Royal Commission on ecclesiastical courts, and promoting various church reforms with other churchmen.[18]

In summer 1889, a conference of Protestant churchmen was called to discuss the issue of organization once again. Thousands of representatives came from all parts of the country, and while the conference attendees gratefully acknowledged the past efforts of existing organizations, an entirely new union was needed.[19] So the Protestant Churchmen's Alliance was founded to unite "all Churchmen who desire to maintain the principles of the Reformation, the present Prayer-book and Articles, and the Acts of Uniformity, as their standards of doctrine and ritual, and especially, the non-sacerdotal character of the ministry of the Church of England."[20] Like the Church Association, this alliance was open to nonevangelical opponents of ritualism, but unlike the Church Association, the alliance was not favorably disposed to prosecutions. At its founding, two older societies, the Protestant Association and the Protestant Educational Institutes, were absorbed into it, and it carried on their work by sponsoring meetings and lectures as well as publishing literature to defend the Church's Protestant character. In 1893 the Alliance merged with the Union of Clerical and Lay Associations to form the National Protestant Church Union. This

---

17. Bentley, "Transformation of the Evangelical Party," 189.

18. Balleine, *History of the Evangelical Party in the Church of England*, 293. See also Toon and Smout, *John Charles Ryle*, 60; and Bentley, "Transformation of the Evangelical Party," 189–91.

19. Balleine, *History of the Evangelical Party in the Church of England*, 293.

20. Bentley, "Transformation of the Evangelical Party," 192. See also Norman D. J. Straton, *Why We Should Join the Protestant Churchmen's Alliance: Being an Address at a Conference of Churchmen in London, June 19th, 1889* (London: John Kensit, 1889).

new union adopted a policy of nonlitigation and decided instead to influence public opinion solely through education.[21]

Ryle was convinced that evangelical unity was a pressing need from his earliest days in the ministry. For example, in an early address titled "What Is Wanted," Ryle argued that one of the greatest "wants" of the time was a greater spirit of unity among evangelical churchmen:

> It is a shame and disgrace that there should be so little united action amongst men who in the main are so thoroughly agreed. Our enemies work together as one body. They never throw away a chance in carrying out their objects. They never lose an opportunity of advancing men who will pro-mote their cause. We, on the contrary, are like a rope of sand. We seldom meet together in large numbers to take counsel, and strengthen one another's hands. When we do meet, the excessive timidity of some, and the excessive crotchettiness of others, prevent anything being done. One class of excellent men will not allow a finger to be raised, lest by any chance the heads of the Church should be offended. Another class of men, no less excellent, will never consent to have anything done, unless every jot and tittle, and pin, and cord of the plan proposed is arranged in their own way. All this is very sad. It ought not so to be. I am sure there never was a period when union among Evangelical members of the Church of England was so much needed.[22]

Ryle continued to call for evangelical unity and worked on its behalf for the rest of his life. He championed a number of different centers for unity, but ultimately each one proved unable to sum-mon the evangelical body to united action.

Ryle, like many of his contemporaries, believed the great reli-gious societies that united earlier generations of evangelicals were

---

21. Balleine, *History of the Evangelical Party in the Church of England*, 293.

22. J. C. Ryle, *The Bishop, the Pastor, and the Preacher* (Ipswich: William Hunt, 1854), 45–46.

no longer able to do so. The membership of the societies increased significantly over the years, as had the number of societies evangelicals supported. The societies had their own important work to do—evangelization. Some people even complained that the societies were not what they once were and needed improvement.[23] They simply could not provide the needed adequate party organization, and involving them in controversy would inevitably distract them from their important, primary work. Though *The Christian Observer* still contended in 1870 that the great societies were "the strength" and the "true grounds and means of union among Evangelical Christians,"[24] most were convinced that they were unable to meet the needs of the time.

The Evangelical Association was not a solution either. Ryle appears to have supported this pan-evangelical body more than many of his fellow clergymen. He wrote a laudatory preface to Dr. A. Thomson's paper *The Sabbath*, which was originally read at the Conference of the Evangelical Alliance held in Geneva in 1861.[25] He presided over the jubilee celebration of the Alliance in Liverpool in 1896 and addressed the gathering.[26] In general, Ryle got along well with Dissenters. He joined them in support of the British and Foreign Bible Societies and the London City Mission.

---

23. Ryle noted that people continually complained about the character and conduct of the society meetings. It was generally agreed that they were no longer what they used to be in terms of interest, attendance, and results. Ryle offered two suggestions. First, the speakers should cooperate and address different but related points at the annual meetings. Second, the speakers should bring something to the meeting that "costs"—that is, spend greater time in preparing addresses. J. C. Ryle, "Closing Address," in *The Church: Its Duties, Claims, Perils, and Privileges. Being the Substance of the Addresses and Sermons Delivered at the Fifth Combined Clerical Meeting at Weston-Super-Mare* (Weston-Super-Mare, U.K.: J. Whereat, 1858), 68–69.

24. "Our Religious Anniversaries," *Christian Observer*, May 1870: 330.

25. J. C. Ryle, preface to *The Sabbath*, by Andrew Thomson (London: James Nisbet, 1863).

26. For Ryle's address, see A. J. Arnold, ed., *Jubilee of the Evangelical Alliance: Proceedings of the Tenth International Conference Held in London, June–July, 1896* (London: J. F. Shaw, 1897), 488–89.

He spoke with their ministers on various platforms on numerous occasions. He even preached for successive weeks in a Presbyterian pulpit. Like Hugh M'Neile, however, he regarded union with Presbyterians to be impractical. Their advocacy of disestablishment and secular education made it impossible to work with them to oppose ritualism. Ryle's advice was simple: "Let them go on in their own way: we can get on well enough without them. We are strong enough to go on with our own work ourselves."[27]

Before the founding of the Church Association, Ryle urged evangelical clergymen to unite around aggregate clerical meetings. Though they were originally formed for the encouragement and edification of the clergy, their "great value" lay in their ability to unite the evangelical clergy and summon them to collective action.[28] He urged his fellow ministers to form these meetings where there were none and to regularly attend those already in existence.[29] He looked forward to the day when the evangelical clergy of every county gathered annually to "take counsel together about the things of the common Gospel in which we are concerned."[30] These clerical meetings should appoint a secretary to correspond with other clerical societies in order to discuss matters that concerned the evangelical body and potential responses. In short, clerical societies could function as a kind of "electric telegraph" that would enable them to act with more power and success.[31]

---

27. J. C. Ryle, in *The Church Association Monthly Intelligencer* 7 (1873): 111: "In what manner can greater unity of action between the Council and the Branches of the Association be secured, in order to carry out the original objects of the Association as a centre of Union?"

28. As early as 1854, Ryle saw the potential for uniting the evangelical clergy through clerical meetings. J. C. Ryle, "What Is Wanted?," in *The Bishop, the Pastor, and the Preacher* (Ipswich: William Hunt, 1854), 47. See also Ryle, "Closing Address," 68.

29. Ryle, "What Is Wanted?," 47.

30. Ryle, "Closing Address," 68.

31. See "Address, by the Rev. Canon Hugh Stowell," in *The Church: Its Duties, Claims, Perils, and Privileges. Being the Substance of the Addresses and Sermons*

In Helmingham, Ryle regularly attended the combined clerical meeting held at Weston-Super-Mare. The comfort and edification of the clergy was the primary purpose of this annual meeting, but the various addresses often focused on pressing contemporary issues facing the Church, and calls for a united evangelical response were commonplace. For example, in Ryle's address to the meeting in 1858, he argued that the evangelical body must collectively respond to the challenges of the day by being more united, improving the conduct and character of religious society meetings, and demanding that the British government recognize Christianity in its governance of India.[32]

Ryle later reversed his position on clerical meetings. They did not provide a sufficient basis for union for a number of reasons.[33] First, like the great religious societies, clerical meetings had their own important work to do—encourage and edify the clergy. To involve them in controversy would only distract them from their primary purpose. Second, they were not yet numerous enough to provide sufficient unity to the body. Third, some of the clerical meetings did not include laymen. Finally, some clerical meetings, especially the large aggregate clerical gatherings, were not composed of purely evangelical men, which significantly hindered their usefulness.[34] In the mid-1860s Ryle pinned his hope of evangelical unity on the newly formed Church Association.

Shortly after its formation, Ryle became convinced that the best potential center for evangelical union was the London Church Association. It provided the truth-based, doctrinal unity that he valued. It was founded, in part, to promote unity and encourage

---

Delivered at the Fifth Combined Clerical Meeting at Weston-Super-Mare (Weston-Super-Mare, U.K.: J. Whereat, 1858), 40.

32. Ryle, "Closing Address," 68–71.

33. Ryle, *We Must Unite!*, 23–24.

34. As early as 1854, Ryle insisted that the usefulness of clerical meetings was dependent on the participants being like-minded. Clerical meetings composed of men of differing opinions inevitably lead to "constant constraint, or constant controversy, or constant triviality." Ryle, "What Is Wanted?," 47.

concerted action. It allowed evangelical laymen to play an active role in the life of the association. It offered the organizational structure needed to unify the party throughout the nation. It could enable the party to act, speak, and move as one if evangelicals rallied around it. In short, the Church Association, if properly supported, offered "a fulcrum for shaking the country and uniting all Evangelical Churchmen."[35]

Ryle championed the Church Association as the best hope for uniting the evangelical party for almost a decade. "United action" was the focus of the Islington Clerical Meeting of 1868, and Ryle argued in his address that the machinery for such union already existed in the Church Association.[36] After Edward Garbett and his followers seceded from the Church Association to form a new evangelical union in 1873, Ryle reaffirmed his commitment to the association and his conviction that it remained the best center for union.[37] As late as 1877 he summoned evangelicals to "unite boldly and confidently for the defense of our Protestant principles" by joining the Church Association.[38]

He acknowledged that there were problems with the Church Association as a center of union. In his address to the Islington Clerical Meeting in 1868, he admitted that the Church Association "undoubtedly began too much as a Negative Anti-Ritualist Society, and not sufficiently as a Positive Protestant and Evangelical Society."[39] He repeatedly urged the association not to give the public the impression that "the only thing we care for is going to

---

35. Ryle, We Must Unite!, 24.

36. This address was later published as We Must Unite! Being Thoughts on the Necessity of Forming a Well Organized Union of Evangelical Churchmen (London: William Hunt, 1868).

37. See J. C. Ryle, "In What Manner Can Greater Unity of Action between the Council and the Branches of the Association Be Secured, in Order to Carry Out the Original Objects of the Association as a Centre of Union?," The Church Association Monthly Intelligencer 7 (1873): 108–11.

38. Ryle, I Fear!, 23.

39. Ryle, We Must Unite!, 24.

the law and prosecuting" if it intended to be a center of union.[40] By
1880 Ryle appears to have reached the conclusion that the Church
Association was no longer able to function as the center of union.
It never became the "Positive Protestant and Evangelical Society"
he hoped it would become, and the ritual prosecutions made it
increasingly unpopular. In short, the Church Association was too
narrowly focused and too generally unpopular to unite the evangelical body. A new center of union was needed.

The Evangelical Protestant Union was ill-equipped to serve as
a center of union. In terms of both doctrine and practice, it was
even narrower than the Church Association. Ryle had already run
afoul of many of its supporters (especially in *The Rock*) in previous
years for attending Church congresses and wearing the surplice
when preaching in the pulpits of high churchmen. His new proposal was a second Union of Clerical and Lay Associations. This
union proved to be more representative of the evangelical body
as a whole, and, as previously mentioned, it stirred up interest in
middle-class education, supplied guidelines to the Royal Commission on ecclesiastical courts, and promoted various church reforms
with other churchmen. Ryle's duties as the first bishop of the newly
formed diocese of Liverpool kept him from being as active in the
life of the union as he was in the Church Association. But he continued to support the union he helped found and supported its
merger with the Protestant Churchmen's Alliance in 1893 to form
the National Protestant Church Union.

Uniting the rope of sand that was the evangelical body within
the Church of England was a lifelong quest for Ryle. From the
beginning of his ministry in Helmingham to his last days as the
bishop of Liverpool, he continually stressed the need for evangelicals to unite and worked toward that end. The evangelical body,
as Ryle discovered, proved notoriously difficult to unite. The party

---

40. Ryle, "In What Manner Can Greater Unity of Action between the Council
and the Branches of the Association Be Secured," 110. See also Ryle, *What Practical
Course of Action*, 4.

was diverse and contained a wide variety of personalities. Many of its clergy were so devoted to their parish work that they had little time for anything else. The evangelical creed was itself a hindrance to union. The right and duty of private judgment, one of the cherished legacies of the Protestant Reformation, made it difficult for evangelicals to submit their judgment to that of others. Among those who were willing to unite, there were a variety of opinions about the proper basis for union (spiritual or doctrinal), the distribution of authority (centralized or local), and the best means of achieving it (support existing centers of unity or form new ones). Ryle attempted to unite the party around clerical meetings, then the Church Association, and finally around the second Union of Clerical and Lay Associations. Clerical meetings of the 1850s and early 1860s showed promise, but they ultimately proved unable to provide the unity he believed the party needed. The Church Association provided the perfect center of union, at least in theory. It offered doctrinal unity without being excessively narrow. It identified a common enemy to oppose. It promoted the advancement of spiritual religion. It possessed strong and centralized leadership. In practice, however, the Church Association struggled to become more than an opposition party and was unable to shake its reputation for being excessively litigious. His final "scheme" for evangelical unity, as G. R. Balleine called it, the second Union of Clerical and Lay Associations, proved to be his most successful uniting endeavor. It opposed ritualism, but it made a number of positive contributions to the party and the Church as well. Despite the difficulties of uniting the evangelicals and despite opposition from some members of the Church Association, Ryle's "scheme" achieved what no other union could boast of—it became a party equivalent of a representative convocation.[41]

---

41. Bentley, "Transformation of the Evangelical Party," 191.

Defending the Establishment

According to Michael Watts, 1833 marked the arrival of a new era of militancy on the part of Dissenters.[42] At least four factors contributed to this growing militancy. First, dissent was growing. From its beginning to 1840 it had been growing faster than the population, and Dissenters continued to keep pace with population growth until the 1880s.[43] Second, the passage of a series of parliamentary acts simultaneously weakened the establishment and gave Dissenters more political power. The Tests and Corporation Acts were repealed in 1828. The Catholic Relief Act was passed in 1829. The Great Reform Act, which reorganized parliamentary representation and extended the franchise by 60 percent, was passed in 1832. The passage of these acts led many Dissenters to believe that they were riding the crest of a wave that would carry them to full religious equality with members of the established church.[44] Third, the rise of Tractarianism within the Church of England angered Dissenters and further alienated them from it.[45] The Tractarians considered Dissenters to be heretical and schismatic. Dissenters, on the other hand, regarded Tractarians as agents of Rome and harbingers of the Antichrist. The result was a deep religious divide between Church and chapel. Between 1828 and 1834, Christian England was more polarized than at any time

---

42. Michael R. Watts, *The Dissenters*, vol. 2, *The Expansion of Evangelical Non-conformity* (Oxford: Clarendon Press, 1995), 454.

43. David Bebbington, *Victorian Nonconformity*, rev. ed. (Eugene, Ore.: Cascade Books, 2011), 19. For information on the development and growth of Victorian Nonconformity, see 18–42.

44. Marsh, *Victorian Church in Decline*, 3.

45. The following comment from Spurgeon was typical of many Protestant Dissenters: "These Puseyites make good Churchmen turn to the Dissenters, and we who already dissent, are driven further and further from the Establishment. In the name of our Protestant religion, I ask whether a minister of the Church of England is allowed to bow before the altar of a Popish church? Is there no rule or canon which restrains men from such an outrage upon our professed faith, such an insult to our Constitution?" *Autobiography*, 2:370.

since the Civil War.[46] Finally, many Dissenters opposed the establishment on free-trade principles. The Anti-Corn-Law League, for example, opposed the Church's establishment as a form of religious monopoly, as a beneficiary of protection, and as a noxious example of aristocratic misrule.[47] Having freed themselves from the restrictions of the Clarendon Code and established their right to fully participate in the affairs of the state, Dissenters took the offensive and began to demand that their outstanding grievances be remediated[48] and challenged the position of the Church of England.

The church rate was the chief grievance of the Dissenters and the first target of their newfound aggression. It was a tax levied on all ratepayers for the repair and maintenance of parish churches. For churchmen, the justification for the rate was obvious: England was a Christian nation, and as such, it was the nation's first duty to provide for the true worship of God and the services of religion. The church rate, or something equivalent, was essential to achieve

---

46. Watts, *Dissenters*, 2:455. See also Marsh, *Victorian Church in Decline*, 3. Tensions between Church and chapel ran high again in 1862 as Dissenters celebrated the bicentennial of the Great Ejection of 1662 and seized the opportunity to attack the Church and the evangelical party. The *Christian Observer* noted that these celebrations were made "the occasion of a rude assault upon the Church of England, and especially upon the Evangelical clergy, who are charged with positive dishonesty and other misdemeanors of the baser kind." Preface to *Christian Observer* (London: Hatchard, 1862), iv. Articles addressing the celebration appeared in February and May 1862. Other evangelical clergymen, like Joseph Bardsley, published their own responses. See Joseph Bardsley, *Bicentenarians in Perplexity: Being an Examination of the Contradictory Reasons Assigned by Dissenters for the Commemoration of the Ejectment of Certain Ministers from the Church of England in 1662. With a Reply to the Charges of Dishonesty and Perjury Made against the Clergy of the Church of England* (London: Wertheim, 1862); and Joseph Bardsley, *The Nonconformist Commemoration of St. Bartholomew's Day, 1662* (Cambridge: Deighton and Bell, 1862).

47. See Richard Francis Spall Jr., "The Anti-Corn-Law League's Opposition to the English Church Establishment," *Journal of Church and State* 32 (1990): 123.

48. Chief among them were the payment of compulsory church rates, exclusion from degrees at Oxford and Cambridge, their inability to solemnize legal marriages, and the prohibition of all non-Anglican burial rites in parish graveyards.

this end.[49] For Dissenters, the rates essentially compelled them to pay for the upkeep of churches they were opposed to in principle. Dissenters had three avenues of redress. First, they could seek their abolition by an act of Parliament. This, however, proved largely unsuccessful until the passage of the Compulsory Church Rates Abolition Act of 1868.[50] Second, Dissenters could gain control of their local vestry and prevent money from being raised to repair the parish church.[51] This tactic proved to be highly successful, especially in large towns. Between 1831 and 1851, parish vestries comprised of Dissenting majorities successfully refused the church rate 484 times out of 632 attempts.[52] Third, they could simply refuse to pay and allow their goods to be seized and sold to cover the charge. Though seizures and imprisonment did little to change public policy, they aroused sympathy for the victims, embarrassed the established church, made the church rate even more odious to Dissenters, and transformed at least one Congregationalist minister into a mortal enemy of the establishment.

Edward Miall was the pastor of the prestigious Bond Street Congregational Chapel in Leicester.[53] He, along with the Baptist minister James Philippo Mursell, founded the Voluntary Church

---

49. John Brown M'Clellan, *Church Rates* (London: William Macintosh, 1868), 5. See also Churchman, *The Church, Church Rates, and Dissenters* (London: J. and C. Mozley, 1860); and *Church-Rates Vindicated: Together with Some Remarks on the Position and Prospects of the Present Ministry* (London: Whitaker, 1858).

50. Melbourne's government attempted to placate the Dissenters by meeting some of their lesser demands. The Marriage Act legalized marriages in Dissenting chapels. The establishment of the Civil Registry of Births, Marriages, and Deaths removed the legal disabilities attached to Dissenting baptism. The granting of a charter to the University of London gave Dissenters the opportunity of obtaining a degree at an English university. Yet the church rate remained.

51. The church rate was a local tax that had to be approved by the parish meeting in which every citizen had a right to vote.

52. Watts, *Dissenters*, 2:480.

53. See David Bebbington. "Edward Miall," in *Oxford Dictionary of National Biography*, ed. H. C. G. Matthew and Brian Harrison (Oxford: Oxford University Press, 2004), 12–14.

Society in 1835 to resist the local church rates and eventually disestablish the Church of England. In 1840 one of Miall's congregants, William Baines, was imprisoned for refusing to pay the church rate, and he left the ministry to devote himself wholly to the cause of disestablishment. In that same year, he became the editor of the *The Nonconformist*, which he hoped would replace the more cautious and deferential magazine *The Patriot*, edited by Josiah Conder.[54] In 1844 he helped found the Anti-State Church Association (later called the Liberation Society) in order to dissolve "the unhallowed union of Church and State."[55] It became one of the best organized and most powerful political lobbies in the country. His most influential work, *The British Churches in Relation to the British People*, was published in 1849.[56] He went on to champion the cause of disestablishment in Parliament as an MP for Rochdale in 1852 and Bradford in 1869. The greatest threat to the establishment, however, came not from a Dissenter but from a high churchman— William Ewart Gladstone.

William Gladstone was once a champion of the establishment. In his first work, *The State in Its Relations with the Church*, Gladstone argued that "the highest duty and highest interest of a body politic alike tend to place it in close relations of co-operation with the church of Christ."[57] On March 28, 1865, he announced to the Commons that he had converted to the principle of disestablishment in Ireland. There were a number of reasons for this conversion. First,

---

54. The leading articles of the early years of *The Nonconformist* can be found in Edward Miall's *The Nonconformist's Sketch Book: A Series of Views, Classified in Four Groups, of a State Church and Its Attendant Evils* (London: Nonconformists Office, 1842).

55. British Anti-State Church Association, *Proceedings of the First Anti-State-Church Association Conference* (London: British Anti-State Church Association, 1846), iv.

56. See Edward Miall, *The British Churches in Relation to the British People* (London: Arthur Hall, Virtue, and Company, 1849).

57. William Ewart Gladstone, *The State in Its Relations with the Church*, 3rd ed. (London: John Murray, 1839), 3.

the Church of Ireland was supported by only a small minority of
the Irish people[58] because most of them regarded it as an offensive
badge of English conquest.[59] Second, the Roman Catholic Church,
which regularly condemned the secret oaths and violent methods
of the Fenians, was the great bulwark against mass support for this
nationalist group.[60] Third, the English church would be in a stronger
position when it was no longer tied to its indefensible Irish counter-
part. Finally, the Reform Act of 1867, which extended the franchise
to all male heads of household, produced a large Liberal majority in
1868, and Irish disestablishment could potentially unite the various
factions of the party. Therefore, he made Irish disestablishment the
primary issue of the 1868 election.

Though they were often regarded as only half churchmen by
both high churchmen and Dissenters alike, evangelicals proved
to be the greatest defenders of the Irish church.[61] They organized
mass meetings in England and in Ireland, published articles in the
press, and engaged in a war of propaganda.[62] They argued that Irish
disestablishment was a national rejection of God, a violation of the
queen's coronation oath to defend the established church, and a
shield of straw against widespread popular agitation. It also set a
dangerous precedent that would soon be used against the Church
of England.[63] The evangelicals' defense rested on the essential unity
of the Church of England and Ireland and the danger of setting a

---

58. Marsh points out that in 1861, of Ireland's 5,798,967 people, only 693,357
were members of the Church of Ireland, but 4,505,265 were Roman Catholics. See
Marsh, *Victorian Church in Decline*, 19.

59. Chadwick, *Victorian Church*, 2:428.

60. David Bebbington, *William Ewart Gladstone: Faith and Politics in Victorian
Britain* (Grand Rapids: Eerdmans, 1993), 146–47.

61. Broad churchmen supported disestablishment as a means of pacifying
Ireland. High churchmen, the traditional defenders of the establishment, were
divided. Many were angered by the judgments of the judicial committee of the
Privy Council on certain aspects of ritualism. They were more fearful of Erastian
domination by the state than disestablishment.

62. Bentley, "Transformation of the Evangelical Party," 24–26.

63. Marsh, *Victorian Church in Decline*, 22.

precedent for English disestablishment. The only sure way to pre-serve the established church was to deny the validity of arguments based on numbers or utility and to rest the defense on the prin-ciple that it is the nation's duty to establish true religion.[64] Despite their efforts, the Irish Disestablishment Bill passed in 1869, and the Church of Ireland was severed from the state on January 1, 1871.

Energized by their recent victory, Dissenters began their assault on the Church of England in Parliament. Miall unsuccess-fully attempted to disestablish the English church in 1871, 1872, and 1873. But the Dissenters won a series of smaller victories that further undermined the principle of establishment.

The first was the passage of Forster's Education Bill of 1870. Before 1870, the parish church was primarily responsible for ele-mentary education. It was taken for granted that the church had a duty to educate, and that education ought to include instruction in the doctrines of Christianity. By 1870, however, there were not enough religious schools to cover the country. A national system of education was proposed, and board schools were to be created where voluntary schools were either inadequate or nonexistent. Dissenters welcomed an alternative to the single school parish (one of their chief grievances at this date), but they were divided over the nature of religious education in the newly formed board schools. Some, like Miall, wanted no religious instruction at all. Others, like Spurgeon, wanted only "undenominational" religious instruction. The famous Cowper-Temple clause, which prohibited the teaching of a religious catechism or religious formulary of any particular denomination in the newly created board school, united the divided Dissenters and ensured the passage of the bill. The result was that the Church was no longer England's schoolmaster.[65]

---

64. Bentley, "Transformation of the Evangelical Party," 26.

65. For more extensive discussions on this important subject, see Chadwick, *Victorian Church*, 2:299–308; Marsh, *Victorian Church in Decline*, 66–93; Watts, *Dissenters*, 2:535–58; and Bentley, "Transformation of the Evangelical Party," 54–102.

The second victory was the University Tests Act of 1871.[66] Legislation in 1854 and 1856 opened the education and lower degrees at Oxford and Cambridge to Dissenters but reserved the government of the university and its colleges to members of the Church of England. Dissenters and reformed-minded churchmen demanded that the religious tests be abolished. For conservatives in general and the evangelical party in particular, the question was whether the universities would remain Christian. If the religious tests were removed, non-Christians as well as non-Anglicans could be admitted to university privileges. In short, it struck at the root of the conception of the Church as the educator of the nation and the universities as the training centers of the clergy.[67] Gladstone's government passed the act in 1871, which opened all degrees and offices, except those tied to holy orders, to men of any religion or none at the universities of Oxford, Cambridge, and Durham.

The third victory was the passage of the Burials Act of 1880. Like the single parish school and university religious tests, burial laws were an outstanding grievance to Dissenters. Every baptized parishioner had a right to be buried in the parish churchyard, but the service had to be conducted by the incumbent and in accordance with the prayer book. Midcentury legislation created burial grounds for Dissenters, but these were not widespread and existed mainly in large towns, and tensions in the country parishes remained high.[68] In 1871 legislation was passed granting Dissenters the right to be buried in silence, but they were not pacified. They demanded the right to be buried by their own ministers using their own services in the parish churchyard. Evangelicals were opposed

---

66. For the history of the passage of this act, see Bentley, "Transformation of the Evangelical Party," 31–33; Chadwick, *Victorian Church*, 2:439–62; and Christopher Harvie, "Reform and Expansion, 1854–1871," in *Nineteenth-Century Oxford, Part 1*, ed. M. G. Brock and M. C. Curthoys, vol. 6 of *The History of the University of Oxford* (Oxford: Clarendon Press, 2007), 6:697–730.

67. Bentley, "Transformation of the Evangelical Party," 33.

68. Bentley, "Transformation of the Evangelical Party," 37.

to this proposal, but they could not agree on the proper response. For some, surrendering the churchyard would further undermine the establishment and move the Church one step closer to full-blown disestablishment. For others, surrender, though distasteful, was necessary and might prove in the end to strengthen the security of the establishment. In 1880 the Liberal Party regained a majority in Parliament and passed the Burials Act of 1880, which virtually conceded all of the Dissenters' demands but included safeguards against disorderliness to ease the fears of some churchmen. Churchmen and the establishment endured yet another defeat, and militant dissent won its last major political victory.

In 1870, the Congregationalist minister of Wrentham, John Brown, said the following about J. C. Ryle and his position as an evangelical churchman: "You are ministers of a church in which you only half believe, and are members of an order which does not half believe in you. The great body of the Clergy, and all the Dissenters, feel that you occupy a false position, and you only are blind to it."[69] Though kinder in tone, C. H. Spurgeon made a similar remark about Ryle in *The Sword and the Trowel*. He wrote, "He is a fearful instance of a Political Churchman. We believe the High Church party consider him to be a Dissenter, and we rejoice to believe that they are pretty near the mark, judging the good man doctrinally; and if they are right in their views Mr. Ryle is a political Dissenter himself, only he is out of his proper place."[70]

---

69. John Brown, *Dissent and the Church: The Substance of Three Letters to the Rev. J. C. Ryle in Reply to His Tract Entitled* "Church and Dissent" (London: James Clark, 1870), 14.

70. C. H. Spurgeon, "A Political Dissenter," in *The Sword and the Trowel* (London: Passmore and Alabaster, 1873), 108. Even today historians of the era continue to question evangelicals' attachment to the establishment. Anne Bentley argues that evangelicals were committed to the Church for pragmatic, as opposed to theological, reasons. G. F. A. Best suggests that evangelicals produced no arguments for the establishment except those drawn from high-minded expediency. See Bentley, "Transformation of the Evangelical Party," 14; and G. F. A. Best, "Evangelicals and the Established Church in the Early Nineteenth Century," *Journal of Theological Studies* 10 (1959): 65.

For Brown, Spurgeon, and many other Dissenters, evangelical convictions were simply incompatible with "Church principles," and they frequently charged evangelical churchmen with inconsistency and sometimes insincerity. Ryle was unmoved by such charges. He was deeply attached to the Church of England and the principle of establishment as well as evangelical doctrine. He wrote, "I care little for what men may think or say. Enough for me to know, that although I am considered a very low Churchman, I am as thorough a Churchman as any man alive. My Evangelicalism is very decided, but it never makes me blind to the merits of the Church of England."[71]

Though he respected Dissenters as fellow Christians and cooperated with them whenever possible, Ryle had no doubts about the superiority of the Church to the chapel. All things being equal, it was better for an Englishman to be a churchman than a Dissenter for six reasons.[72] First, the Church's confession of faith and standard of ministerial soundness, the Thirty-Nine Articles, was superior to all others.[73] Second, the Church's form of government (episcopacy) was more scriptural than presbyterianism, congregationalism, or the "anarchy of Plymouth Brethrenism."[74] Third, the Church's form

---

71. J. C. Ryle, *Church and Dissent: or, Why Do I Prefer Church to Chapel?* (London: William Hunt, 1870), 13.

72. This defense of Ryle's churchmanship was first published in *Church and Dissent*. It was republished under a new title, *I Am a Churchman! And Why?* (London: William Hunt, 1886) and was included in *Principles for Churchmen: A Manual of Positive Statements on Doubtful or Disputed Points* (London: William Hunt, 1884).

73. Ryle, *Church and Dissent*, 5.

74. Ryle, *Church and Dissent*, 5–6. Unfortunately, Ryle did not defend this claim at length here or anywhere else in his works. Perhaps he intended to discuss the subject more fully in his commentary on Acts, which never came to fruition. Or perhaps he thought that the New Testament's teaching was so clear on the subject that no defense was necessary. For a defense of the Church's form of government that Ryle would have likely endorsed, see J. B. Lightfoot, "Dissertation on the Christian Ministry," in *St. Paul's Epistle to the Philippians: A Revised Text with Introduction, Notes, and Dissertations* (London: Macmillian, 1868), 179–267.

of worship was superior to the chapel.[75] Fourth, the Church's system of fixed, settled, and independent endowments was a better mode of paying the minister than the voluntary system, which made a minister "entirely dependent on the whims, tastes, and fancies of his congregation."[76] Fifth, the Church's territorial system offered greater pastoral oversight than the congregational system of the chapel. It ensured the supervision of every soul in a district and assigned a minister to attend to the spiritual wants of every family.[77] Finally, the Church's system of admission, which "throws people on their own responsibility and bids them examine themselves whenever they repent and believe," did more good than the chapel's system of congregational endorsement.[78] He concluded:

> I respect many Dissenting ministers extremely. I admire their gifts, their graces, and their zeal. I have no doubt that they do a great deal of good, and save many souls. I never forget that English Dissent was mainly created by the abominable bigotry or shameful neglect of English bishops and clergymen. I always steadily refuse to unchurch Dissenters, to deny the validity of their orders, to ignore their sacraments, or to hand them over to the "uncovenanted mercies of God." I am always glad to meet them on common ground, and to co-operate with them whenever I can. But I never say that it is *just as good* for an Englishman to be a Dissenter as to be a Churchman, because, as an honest man, a Bible reader, and a close observer of human nature, I do not believe it.[79]

---

75. He explained, "The Prayer-book, no doubt, is not a perfect book, and has some blemishes. But I infinitely prefer Prayer-book prayers to extempore prayers. Above all, I prefer the large quantity of Scripture regularly read in our services, to one or two arbitrarily-selected chapters." Ryle, *Church and Dissent*, 6. See especially J. C. Ryle, *Thoughts on the Prayer Book and on Church and Dissent* (London: William Hunt, 1887).

76. Ryle, *Church and Dissent*, 6. Ryle added this quotation in *I Am a Churchman! And Why?*, 6.

77. Ryle, *Church and Dissent*, 7.

78. Ryle, *Church and Dissent*, 7.

79. Ryle, *Church and Dissent*, 8–9.

In short, Ryle was a convinced and committed churchman. He defended his attachment to the Church of England on scriptural, theological, liturgical, pastoral, and practical grounds, and he proved to be one of the Church's staunchest defenders.

Ryle was also committed to the principle of establishment and the lawfulness of the union of church and state. In his commentary on John 18:36, he presented the "leading principles" of established religion.[80] First, every government is responsible to God, and no government can prosper without His blessings. Every government is bound to do all that is in its power to obtain God's favor and blessing. Therefore, every government should promote true religion, and those that refuse to do so cannot expect God's blessing. Second, every government should strive to promote truth, charity, and high moral standards. True religion is the only root from which these virtues grow. Therefore, every government that does not strive to promote true religion is neither wise nor good. Third, it is absurd to suggest that government must leave religion alone because it cannot promote it without favoring one church over another. This is equivalent to saying that because we cannot do good to all, we must sit still and do good to none. Fourth, to suggest that no government can find out what true religion is, and thus it should regard all religions with equal indifference, is "an argument fit only for an infidel." In England, at any rate, belief in the truthfulness of the Bible is part of the Constitution, it is a crime to insult the Bible, and the testimony of an avowed atheist "goes for nothing in a court of law." Fifth, it is undoubtedly true that Christ's kingdom is independent of the rulers of the world, and they are unable to begin, increase, or overthrow it. But it is utterly false that the rulers of this world have nothing to do with Christ's kingdom, may safely leave religion entirely alone, and may govern their subjects as if they were beasts and had no souls at all. In sum, "the favorite theory of certain

---

80. Ryle, *St. John*, 3:288–89. This is the clearest articulation of Ryle's defense of the union of church and state. The date of publication, 1873, should also be noted. This was published at the height of the disestablishment controversy.

Christians that [Scripture] forbids Governments to have anything to do with religion, and condemns the union of Church and State, and renders all Established Churches unlawful, is in my judgment, baseless, preposterous, and utterly devoid of common sense."[81]

One of Ryle's earliest public defenses of the establishment came in 1858, when Ryle defended the church rate.[82] For Ryle, the church rate debate was about a principle, not money. Would England, as a nation, repudiate biblical religion and refuse to publicly acknowledge the Lord Jesus Christ? He was convinced that a nation ought to provide for the maintenance of God's worship and that there should be a charge on property for this purpose.[83] Though some churchmen were prepared to abandon the defense of the church rate for the sake of popularity or political expediency, he cautioned against it. It was morally and scripturally wrong.[84] It would lead to the separation of church and state.[85] Ultimately, it would displease God and provoke Him to judge the nation.[86] It is difficult to overstate the seriousness of this issue for Ryle. His warnings went largely unheeded. Churchmen were hopelessly divided on the issue, but Dissenters were not. The church rate was abolished in 1868, and the debate shifted from taxes to the establishment of the Church of Ireland.

---

81. Ryle, *St. John*, 3:287–88.

82. See Ryle, "Closing Address," in *Church: Its Duties, Claims, Perils, and Privileges*, 62–64.

83. Ryle, "Closing Address," in *Church: Its Duties, Claims, Perils, and Privileges*, 63.

84. Ryle, "Closing Address," in *Church: Its Duties, Claims, Perils, and Privileges*, 62: "No public opinion can make that right, which is wrong in the sight of God. A thing may be politically right, and expedient, and popular, but if scripturally wrong, we ought not to touch it with the tip of our fingers."

85. He called it "the thin edge of a wedge, which is to split in sunder the union of church and state in the land." Ryle, "Closing Address," in *Church: Its Duties, Claims, Perils, and Privileges*, 63.

86. Ryle, "Closing Address," in *Church: Its Duties, Claims, Perils, and Privileges*, 64: "I believe that God will be displeased; and that when God is displeased with a nation, he has but to put forth His finger, and that nation shall pass away. Amalek was the first among the nations, but his latter end shall be, that he perish for ever."

By 1868 Ryle was emerging as a leader of the evangelical party, and he threw the weight of his influence into defending the Irish church.[87] He opposed Irish disestablishment for six reasons. First, disestablishing the Irish church was tantamount to establishing a godless form of government in that country.[88] A presbyterian establishment in Ireland would be preferable to none at all. Second, disestablishment would be a direct breach of the Act of Union made between England and Ireland. The maintenance of the established church was an essential clause in the Act of Union, and therefore disestablishment would be a breach of national promise, constitute a national sin, and bring about the end of national good faith.[89] Third, to disestablish the Protestant Church of Ireland would give direct help and aid to popery. Fourth, disestablishment would do no real good. According to Ryle, Irish Catholics did not support it and had no dislike of Protestant clergymen. It would not make Ireland easier to govern. Above all, the Romanists would not be satisfied with anything less than absolute supremacy. Fifth, disestablishment would do immense harm. It would seriously damage one of the best Protestant churches in the world. It would disgust, annoy, and irritate the best and most loyal part of the Irish population and please the worst part.[90] Finally, it would lead to the disestablishment of the Church of England. The Irish church was a stepping-stone toward the Dissenters' grand object—the disestablishment of the Church of England.[91]

---

87. See J. C. Ryle, *A Word for the Irish Church* (London: William Hunt, 1868); J. C. Ryle, *Strike: But Hear! A Defense of Those Clergymen Who Opposed Mr. Gladstone at the Last Parliamentary Election* (London: William Hunt, 1868); and Ryle, *We Must Unite!*

88. Ryle wrote, "If the word 'disestablishment' means anything, it means that in the future English rulers will not recognize religion at all in governing Ireland." Ryle, *Strike: But Hear!*, 5.

89. Ryle, *Strike: But Hear!*, 6–7.

90. Ryle, *Strike: But Hear!*, 8–9.

91. Ryle also responded to the primary arguments for Irish disestablishment. Supporters of disestablishment argued that the Irish church had failed and

In addition to defending the Irish in print, Ryle also attempted to rally the evangelical body to her defense. In January 1868 he summoned evangelical clergymen to united action at the Islington Clerical Meeting.[92] In June of the same year he urged the members of the Church Association to attend the upcoming Dublin Church Congress to show solidarity with the Irish church and speak in her defense.[93] In July he scolded the party for failing to do its duty.[94]

---

therefore ought to be disestablished. This assertion, according to Ryle, was simply untrue. The Irish church had done "great things" in spite of suffering "injustice, ill-treatment, snubbing, and discouragement." Its real fault, in the eyes of Roman Catholics, was not that it had done too little, but too much. Some things ought to be improved, but these defects in no way warranted its destruction. Second, supporters of disestablishment argued that the Irish church was a minority and therefore ought to be disestablished. Ryle countered by arguing that governments must look at truth as well as numbers. Furthermore, Christian governments ought to consider what is best for their subjects and not be swayed by public opinion. Moreover, majorities should be weighed as well as counted. The four million Irish Papists were, for the most part, "the most ignorant part of the nation, and are entirely under the thumb of the priest." The remaining million and a half Protestants, however, were the most "intelligent and independent part of the population." Third, supporters of Irish disestablishment believed it was a matter of justice for Ireland. For Ryle, disestablishment would actually be a tremendous injustice to Ireland. It would not do justice for tithe payers, who were mostly Protestant landlords. Nor would it do justice to the feelings of Roman Catholics who would not be satisfied until Protestantism was banished or proscribed. "Justice for Ireland" really meant injustice for Irish Protestantism. Ryle, *Strike: But Hear!*, 11–13.

92. Ryle, *We Must Unite!*, 7: "The union of Greeks to take Troy is nothing to the union of political parties against the Irish Church. Now what is the Evangelical body in England going to do? Shall we desert our sister because she is unpopular and small? Shall we turn our back on her, like Edom, in the day of her calamity, and leave her out in the cold? Shall we forget that her danger is ours? 'Today thine: to-morrow mine.' When a neighbor's house is on fire, our own is in peril. Are the Evangelical body ready to act together?"

93. *The Church Association Monthly Intelligencer*, June 1868: 73–74.

94. Ryle, *We Must Unite!*, 31–32:

But what are Evangelical Churchmen doing? Absolutely nothing at all! They present at this moment the most melancholy spectacle that English Church history has exhibited for three hundred years. They seem unable to discern the signs of the times,—unable to comprehend the increasing peril of their position,—unable to get together and agree on any bold, decided, thorough line of action,—unable to show a compact,

Despite his efforts to unite the party and defend the Irish establishment, the Irish Disestablishment Bill passed in 1869. Nevertheless, Ryle proved to be one of the Irish church's staunchest defenders.

As predicted, an assault on the establishment of the Church of England soon followed, and once again Ryle came to the defense of the establishment. During the height of the controversy (1870–1885), he published a number of works defending the Church of England and his attachment to it as an evangelical clergyman.[95] He spoke on various platforms in the Church's defense.[96] He attempted to unite all churchmen—not just evangelicals—to "earnestly contend" for the maintenance and preservation of the union of church and state,[97] and he encouraged them to supply the reading public with plain, cheap, and popular literature to refute the claims of the liberationists.

Ryle's defense of the establishment was essentially practical, pragmatic, and pastoral.[98] He wanted Englishmen to consider the

---

united front against their enemies. Men look at one another, and say, "Something ought to be done," and then go quietly home, and do nothing at all! With nineteen Evangelical men out of twenty the interests of the Church at large seems as nothing compared to those of their own parishes. And yet they call themselves Episcopalians!

See Post Script dated July 25, 1868.

95. See the following works by Ryle: *Church and Dissent*; *Church Reform: Being Seven Papers on the Subject* (London: William Hunt, 1870); *Yes or No! Is the Union of Church and State Worth Preserving?* (London: Church Defense Institution, 1871); *What Good Will It Do? A Question about the Disestablishment of the Church of England, Examined and Answered*, 3rd ed. (London: William Hunt, 1872); *Church and State* (London: William Hunt, 1877); *Churchmen and Dissenters* (London: William Hunt, 1880); *Principles for Churchmen: A Manual of Positive Statements on Doubtful or Disputed Points* (London: William Hunt, 1884); *Disestablishment Papers* (London: William Hunt, 1885); *I Am a Churchman! And Why?*; and *Thoughts on the Prayer Book*.

96. During the disestablishment crisis, Ryle regularly addressed the annual Church congress on this subject.

97. See the following by Ryle: *Yes or No!*; *Can a Greater Amount of Unity Be Obtained among Zealous and Pious Churchmen of Difference Schools of Thought?*

98. This should not be seen as a critique of Ryle. More principled arguments

practical consequences of disestablishing the English church. More specifically, he wanted them to consider what good disestablishment would do for Dissenters, the Church, tithe payers, the poor, Christian charity, and the state.[99]

Disestablishment would do Dissenters no good. It would not destroy the Church and clear the field of their "great rival," nor would it ruin the Church financially, based on the principles of the Irish Disestablishment Bill.[100] The Church in large towns would not be injured by it; they were already funded largely by pew rents, Easter offerings, and offertories. Churchmen would not convert en masse into Dissenters. Dissenters would not win more liberty than they presently enjoyed. Furthermore, the social disabilities under which Dissenting ministers were said to labor would not disappear.[101]

Disestablishment would do the Church little good and a great deal of harm. It would give the Church more liberty, make reform easier, force the laity to assume their rightful position, create a properly constituted convocation, increase the number of bishops and the divisions of dioceses, end the system of patronage, destroy all sinecure offices, and make worship more elastic. These gains must not be exaggerated, however, and the negative consequences to the Church must not be ignored. It would impoverish thousands of rural clergymen, whose income depended on the tithe, which would make it necessary to reduce their number by half. It would tax the Church so heavily to support those who remained that it would be unable to do much for home and foreign missions. In

---

were unable to save the Irish church. Gladstone's justification for Irish disestablishment was largely practical and pragmatic.

99. This argument is set forth in the following by Ryle: *What Good Will It Do?*; *Principles for Churchmen*; and *Disestablishment Papers*.

100. Pew rents and offertories would remain. The endowments of the last two centuries would remain in the Church's possession. The life interests of the bishops and clergy would remain as well. Ryle predicted that the life interests would be invested in a safe investment, if one could be found. The Church might have been crippled financially but was not ruined.

101. This was added in *Principles for Churchmen*, 319–20.

short, it would reduce the influence of Christianity and help only "the Pope, the infidel, and the devil."[102]

Disestablishment would do no good for the tithe payers. Ryle was convinced that there was much confusion on this point. Many people mistakenly believed that disestablishment would mean more money in their pocket. If the Church was disestablished, the clergy would no longer receive the tithe, but it was not at all clear what Parliament would do with this centuries-old tax. If they did away with this tax altogether, landlords would likely raise the rent because rent had been calculated based on the tithe for centuries. But Parliament may decide to use that tax for other purposes, such as the payment of the poor rate or the highway rate. In either case, tithe payers would not be better off. Moreover, the rural clergyman was often the largest rate payer in the parish. If disestablishment took place and the tithe was abolished, he would cease to pay any rates except on his house and garden, and others must make up for it. Furthermore, if he was impoverished by disestablishment, he would be unable to spend in the parish as he did before. In this case, tithe payers would be worse off than they were before.

Disestablishment would do great harm to the poor. This was one of the most serious objections for Ryle because Scripture commands Christians "to remember the poor," and thus all changes that injure the poor are, on the face of them, objectionable. Disestablishment would inflict "grievous damage," both temporally and spiritually, on the agricultural poor: "the very poor who of all classes in England are most ill-paid, and deserve most consideration."[103] In thousands of rural parishes, the parish clergyman was the chief relieving officer of the district. His home was often the place of "a large machinery of charity" to men's bodies. He was expected to take the lead in forming "clothing clubs, shoe clubs, boot clubs,

102. Ryle, *What Good Will It Do?*, 11.

103. Ryle, *Principles for Churchmen*, 328. It is curious that Ryle added this phrase in 1884 after moving to Liverpool. After seeing both urban and rural poverty, what made him conclude that the rural poor are more deserving?

coal clubs, soup clubs, blanket clubs, libraries, and a hundred other means of helping the poor."[104] Furthermore, he was expected to be the unpaid friend of everyone who needs a friend, whether in the way of money, advice, or sympathy. Disestablishment would bring this to an end. Stripped of more than half of his income, he would no longer be able to do what he once did for the poor of the parish, and he would be forced to minister to his flock alone. Disestablishment would also injure the poor spiritually. Stripped of its endowments, the Church would no longer be able to do what it once did to advance Christ's kingdom. Aggressive measures for the evangelization of mining and manufacturing populations, the building of new churches and schools, and the formation of new districts in poor neighborhoods would be either entirely stopped or significantly curtailed. Given the impact of disestablishment on rural clergy, the congregations in large towns would be forced to devote much of their resources to supporting them rather than beginning new works.[105] Moreover, the voluntary system, which disestablishment would force on the Church, had proven to be a "total and entire failure" among the Dissenters.[106] Ryle wrote, "With all their many privileges and advantages, they can neither pay their ministers sufficiently in rural districts, nor provide sufficient chapels for poor neighbourhoods. Above all, they cannot provide day schools for their own poor children, and are obliged to confess it!"[107] The impact of disestablishment on the poor would be disastrous.

---

104. Ryle, *What Good Will It Do?*, 15.

105. Ryle, *What Good Will It Do?*, 16: "To sustain her without extending, to keep her alive without increasing, to enable her to live without growth, would require the utmost exertions of her children. None would suffer so much from this state of things as the poor."

106. Ryle, *What Good Will It Do?*, 17. Ryle dwelled on this at length and quoted from prominent Dissenting ministers such as Dr. Parker and C. H. Spurgeon. He included a letter from Spurgeon to the Baptist churches in which Spurgeon chided them for insufficiently paying their ministers. See Ryle, *Principles for Churchmen*, 352–53.

107. Ryle, *What Good Will It Do?*, 17.

Disestablishment would not promote peace and charity among English Christians. It would not bring an end to jealousy, envy, rivalry, or party spirit among English Christians, nor would it turn them into a "great Evangelical Alliance and happy family."[108] Instead, it would make a breach that would never be repaired and would be the very "grave of unity." Christians who disagree about nonessentials can get along comfortably, as long as they are tolerant of each other and do not assault one another. When a person attempts to ruin the other person's church and deprive him of half his income, however, it is absurd to expect the two to remain friends. Disestablishment would destroy what little unity existed between churchmen and Dissenters, severely cripple the work of Bible Society and London City Mission, make future cooperation nearly impossible, and injure Church-chapel relations for generations to come.

Disestablishment would do immense harm to the state. The dissolution of the union of church and state involved "far more serious consequences than most of its advocates dream of."[109] According to Ryle, the Scriptures plainly teach that God rules everything in this world and that He deals with nations as they deal with Him.[110] Therefore it is the state's first duty to honor and recognize God, and governments that refuse to do so offend the King of kings, provoke His displeasure, and invite judgment.[111] Additionally, the nation's moral standard is the "grand secret" to its strength and prosperity, and there is no surer way to produce moral virtue than by

---

108. Ryle, *What Good Will It Do?*, 18.

109. Ryle, *What Good Will It Do?*, 21.

110. Ryle, *What Good Will It Do?*, 22: "God rules everything in this world, that He deals with nations as they deal with Him, that national prosperity and national decline are ordered by Him, that wars, pestilences, and famines are part of His providential government of the world, and that without His blessing no nation can prosper."

111. Ryle, *Yes or No!*, 3: "In short, if the day should ever come when the English government shall dissolve the Union of Church and State, for fear of seeming to favour one Church more than another...I should expect God's heaviest judgments to fall on this realm."

promoting "pure Scriptural Christianity." Moreover, the practical consequences of disestablishment for the state are monstrous and appalling.[112] If the government resolves to have nothing to do with religion, then the Succession Act must be repealed; a Papist might sit on the throne; the Parliament would proceed without prayer; the regiments, prisons, and workhouses would no longer have chaplains; and Sabbath observance would be threatened. In short, disestablishment would prove the ruin of England's greatness.[113]

Ryle's defense of the establishment drew constant and fierce criticism from high churchmen and Dissenters. The high church journal, *The Church Quarterly Review*, remarked, "When a man can make no better defense of the Church than that, it is plain that neither his knowledge of her principles nor his attachment to them can be very strong, and that he is never likely to win converts."[114] Enoch Mellor, a Dissenter, published a lengthy reply to *What Good Will It Do?* on behalf of the Liberation Society and embarked on a lecturing tour of large towns (Leeds, Bradford, Liverpool, and

---

112. Ryle, *Yes or No!*, 3: "My whole soul revolts at the thought of such a nation treating its subjects as if they were no better than civilized gorillas, without souls, in order to avoid the charge of sectarianism—punishing and imprisoning them at vast expense if they do wrong, and yet refusing to teach them to do right. That modern fashionable expression, "an unsectarian system," is a fine high-sounding phrase; but so far as I can see it is only another name for a godless and irreligious system, a system which must be offensive to the King of kings."

113. Ryle addressed himself specifically to those who made no profession of religion whatsoever. Though such men might not "care a jot whether the Church of England is disestablished or not," he urged them to consider the moral consequences of disestablishment. He asked: "Are you quite sure that it would be a good thing to have less religion in England than there is now? Of course, if the Church is disestablished and impoverished, there will be less. Now are you quite sure you will like this? Do you wish your wife, your children, your servants, your clerks, your tenants, your labourers, your partners in business, to have less religion and to become more godless than they are now? I should like that question to be answered." In short, it was in their best interest, personally and professionally, to support and defend the union of church and state. Ryle, *What Good Will It Do?*, 28.

114. *The Church Quarterly Review*, January 1885: 277.

Birmingham) to refute it in 1873.[115] Ryle probably received more criticism for defending the establishment than he did for attacking ritualism. Though it is impossible to assess how influential Ryle's defense was, the sheer amount of criticism seems to suggest that it was significant. Ultimately, the opponents of the Church were unable to disestablish it in Parliament, and Ryle's popular and practical defense of the establishment contributed to its preservation.

Ryle also opposed attempts to secularize education. Secular education was an affront to God and a rejection of Christianity by the nation. Moreover, religion and morality were inseparably connected. If scriptural religion is not a part of education, then the "grand secret of the nation's prosperity," the moral standard of the English people, would be lowered and the nation's greatness would come to an end.[116] He urged parents to steadfastly refuse to send their children to a school where the Bible was not read, and he hoped that in every parish and town in the kingdom all who did not want their children to receive religious instruction would be "ticketed and remembered by everybody else."[117] Despite these grave concerns, he did not play a significant role in the education controversy.

Ryle was more concerned about ritualist schools than secular ones. The Woodard Schools are a good case in point. These schools were founded by Reverend Nathaniel Woodard, an extremely high churchman, to provide excellent religious education for the middle classes at a moderate cost. Though evangelicals applauded Woodard's zeal and liked his educational model, they were outraged to learn that his religious instruction included employing ritualist tutors, practicing auricular confession, adopting high rituals in church services, and insulting Protestantism. So in 1868 the

---

115. See Enoch Mellor, *Disestablishment: What Good Will It Do? A Reply to Canon Ryle* (London: Elliot Stock, 1873).

116. Ryle, *What Good Will It Do?*, 23.

117. J. C. Ryle, "Address before the Yorkshire Church Association," *The Church Association Monthly Intelligencer* 4 (1870): 282.

Church Association proposed setting up their own middle-class schools on Protestant and evangelical principles and formed a central committee on which Ryle served to that end.[118]

Again, ritualism, and not the principle of establishment, was Ryle's primary concern for the universities. The opening of Keble College in 1870 at his alma mater concerned him more than the University Tests Act of 1871. In response to the threat of ritualism, rationalism, and the evangelical party's general neglect of higher education, he played a critical role in the founding of Wycliffe Hall, Oxford, 1877, and Ridley Hall, Cambridge, in 1881, and served on both of their original councils.[119]

Though Ryle's role in the education and university debates was limited, he threw himself wholly into the Burial Bill controversy. In 1875 a London committee of evangelical clergymen met with a number of leading Dissenting ministers to reach a compromise and settle the "burials difficulty." Ryle was disgusted by the settlement and called it a "signal and disastrous failure." Churchmen conceded everything and received nothing in return: "It was a general surrender along the whole line."[120] The worst part of the conference was its composition. The clergymen who participated in the meeting were all London ministers whose churchyards were closed, and thus they would be unaffected by changes in law. Tensions over burials ran highest in rural districts, and those clergymen who would be most affected by changes in the law were "shut out in the cold."[121] Therefore, Ryle published his views "as a country clergyman" in *Shall We Surrender: Thoughts for Churchmen about Mr. Morgan's Burial Bills.*

---

118. See *Church Association Papers: The Woodard Schools*, 2nd ed. (London: Church Association, 1868). See also *Church Association Monthly Intelligencer*, May 1868, February 1869, and September 1869.

119. See Reynolds, *Evangelicals at Oxford 1735–1871*; F. W. B. Bullock, *The History of Ridley Hall*, Cambridge, vol. 1 (Cambridge: Cambridge University Press, 1941); Hylson-Smith, *Evangelicals in the Church of England*, 182–85.

120. J. C. Ryle, *Shall We Surrender? Thoughts for Churchmen about Mr. Morgan's Burials Bill* (London: William Hunt, 1876), 3.

121. Ryle, *Shall We Surrender?*, 4.

The question at the heart of the debate was not whether Dissenters may be buried in churchyards but whether Dissenting ministers should be allowed to conduct religious services in the parochial graveyards of the Church of England. Ryle answered in the negative and offered five objections to Morgan's Burial Bill.

First, the bill was subversive to the first principles of a national or established church.[122] The law of the land allowed every English citizen to worship in the parish church and be buried in the parish churchyard, but it did not allow all citizens to dictate the kind of worship that would take place in their local parish church or what kind of services could be used during burials. Moreover, the law did not compel attendance at the parish church nor did it penalize those who went to the chapel. All that the law required was that the religious worship of the national church be conducted by appointed persons in a particular way, and those who attended the established church worship be baptized, married, and buried with the services that the national church provided. Dissenters were not prohibited from being buried in the churchyard beside their families. But Dissenting ministers should not be allowed to perform religious services in parish churches or churchyards, which would "dethrone the National Clergyman from his position, and deprive him of his official privileges."[123] Morgan's Burial Bill failed to recognize the rights and privileges of the clergy of the established church that had stood for centuries and placed clergymen on equal footing with all other sects and denominations. For this reason, Ryle believed that the Burial Bill was really "only one part of that great strategical movement which has for its object the disestablishment of the Church of England."[124]

Second, the proposed changes would be particularly unjust to churchmen. The passage of the Compulsory Church Rates

---

122. Ryle, *Shall We Surrender?*, 5–6.

123. Ryle, *Shall We Surrender?*, 5.

124. Ryle, *Shall We Surrender?*, 5.

Abolition Act of 1868 placed the entire burden of maintaining the churchyard on churchmen. In some parishes, especially wealthy town parishes, the extra expense was barely felt. In many country parishes, however, it was a source of "irritation and vexation." Ryle explained, "Fences, ditches, graveled paths, gates, drains, and surface vegetation cannot be kept in decent order without some little yearly expenditure of money, and that money, in most cases, comes out of the pockets of a few farmers and the parson, or else nothing is done."[125] Churchmen accept this new reality, but they question the justness of a bill that would allow Dissenting ministers, who no longer contribute anything to the upkeep of the churchyard, to perform their services in parish churchyards. In sum, "after getting rid of the Church-rates we contend that they have deprived themselves of any right to interfere with the management of our churchyards, or the performance of religious services within them."[126]

Third, the bill placed the parochial clergy in an unfair position.[127] Clergymen were permitted to use only one form of burial service for all persons they buried, "whether a communicant or a non-communicant, of an eminently godly person or a careless neglecter of the means of grace." Morgan's bill, however, would allow Dissenting ministers to use any form that they pleased in parish churchyards without any restrictions. In short, "he is to come when he pleases, do what he pleases, and say what he pleases, so long as he calls it a 'religious service'; while the clergyman is tied and bound to one single form, and must use it (with very rare exceptions) at every funeral where he officiates."[128] Furthermore, Morgan's proposed safeguard clause, which required all religious services to be conducted in a "decent and orderly manner," was too vague to be of any use. Who would decide what is decent and orderly?

---

125. Ryle, *Shall We Surrender?*, 6.
126. Ryle, *Shall We Surrender?*, 7.
127. Ryle, *Shall We Surrender?*, 7–8.
128. Ryle, *Shall We Surrender?*, 7.

Fourth, the bill was not restrictive enough.[129] The bill would not prevent a Roman Catholic priest or a Socinian minister from conducting religious services according to their own particular tenets in the parish churchyard. Nor would it prevent gravestones from being erected with Popish or Socinian inscriptions. Such actions would offend all conscientious churchmen who did not want the first principle of their creed contradicted in their own church. Ryle believed that Morgan should have amended his bill to allow only Trinitarian Protestants to perform religious services in parish churchyards.

Fifth, the bill would ultimately allow non-Episcopal religious services to be conducted in the parish churches.[130] Ryle anticipated a scenario in which Dissenters were permitted to conduct a funeral within the parish church due to inclement weather. This would establish a precedent that would ultimately "throw open" the church doors anytime a Dissenting minister claimed the right at funerals, and religious services would take place in parish churches that flatly contradicted the principles of the Church of England. The bill contained no clause that expressly forbade religious services at a funeral that were not episcopal to be conducted within the walls of the parish under any circumstance. This "most suspicious absence" led Ryle to conclude that the promoters of the bill "want to supersede the clergyman in the church as well as in the churchyard."[131]

In addition to offering objections, Ryle offered an alternative proposal. The simplest solution was to procure an act of Parliament that would empower parishes in which there was no burial ground except the churchyard to provide themselves with a public cemetery. For example, the ratepayers of a rural parish could vote to purchase land for a public cemetery. Such money could be borrowed and paid back in installments over time, and the annual

---

129. Ryle, *Shall We Surrender?*, 8–9.

130. Ryle, *Shall We Surrender?*, 9–10.

131. Ryle, *Shall We Surrender?*, 10.

payments could be met by the creation of a cemetery rate. In such a cemetery, a Dissenting minister or Roman Catholic priest could perform whatever service he wished without offending the conscience of any churchman. Furthermore, such a solution would make enlarging the parish churchyard, "which is often a very difficult business," unnecessary. Ryle said that he would "gladly consent" to such an arrangement for the sake of peace, even though he was the largest ratepayer in his parish and would feel the burden of the cemetery rate more than anyone.[132] If Morgan and his supporters refused to accept such an agreement, their real intentions would become clear. Ryle asked, "But would it not be more straightforward if Mr. Morgan would throw aside all disguise, and, like honest Mr. Miall, bring forward a Bill for *disestablishing and disendowing the Church of England*?"[133]

The publication of *Shall We Surrender?* caused a sensation. *The Church Union Gazette*, the monthly paper of the English Church Union, commended it as a "clear and true" defense of the Church and summoned all churchmen to unite around this cause.[134] *The Church Portrait Journal* said, "Its circulation was large, and its opinions were widely adopted, for its view of the Burials Bill introduced by Mr. Osborne Morgan and its opposition to that were just, its statements substantiated by facts, its arguments unanswerable."[135] Furthermore, it was mentioned and quoted in the parliamentary debates addressing this very issue in 1876 and 1880.[136]

Morgan's Burials Bill was defeated in 1875, and a similar bill was proposed and later withdrawn in 1877. But three years later the Burials Act of 1880 was passed, which virtually conceded all

---

132. Ryle, *Shall We Surrender?*, 15–16.

133. Ryle, *Shall We Surrender?*, 16.

134. "The Burials Question," *The Church Union Gazette*, January 8, 1878: 22.

135. "The Rev. Canon Ryle, M.A.," *The Church Portrait Journal*, December 1876: 18.

136. See *Parliamentary Debates, Official Report* (London: Cornelius Buck, 1876), 1:1336–38; *Parliamentary Debates*, 1880, 1:1039–41.

Morgan's demands. The bill was supported by Archbishop Tait and urban clergymen like Joseph Bardsley in hopes of strengthening the establishment and fostering brotherly relations between churchmen and Dissenters.[137] Though Ryle opposed its passage, as the newly appointed bishop of Liverpool, he urged the clergymen of his diocese to willingly obey it as the law of the land. His tone was remarkably conciliatory for one who so strenuously opposed the bill. He urged his clergy to "allow it to work as easily and pleasantly as possible, and to avoid all friction and collision on the occasion of funerals under the act."[138] He advised them to make no difficulties regarding the use of the parish bier and pall and tolling the church bells. He encouraged them to allow Nonconformists dying outside the parish to be buried in the churchyard if their friends so desired in order to promote peace and charity. He even offered suggestions about burying those who died unbaptized.[139] The only point he would not concede was to allow Nonconformist ministers to perform religious services within the walls of the parish church,

---

137. Marsh considered the Burials Act of 1880 to be Archbishop Tait's most successful political measure. See Marsh, *Victorian Church in Decline*, 256–63. See also Society for the Liberation of Religion from State Patronage and Control, *The Rev. Joseph Bardsley versus Canon Ryle: Extracts from Letters Addressed to the* "Record" *December 13th, 1875, in Reply to a Tract by Canon Ryle, Entitled,* "Shall We Surrender?" (London: Society for the Liberation of Religion from State Patronage and Control, 1875).

138. J. C. Ryle, *The Charges Delivered at His Primary Visitation* (London: William Hunt, 1881), 2:17. Bishop Ryle delivered two charges at his primary visitation. The first was delivered on October 19, 1881, in the Pro-Cathedral of St. Peter, Liverpool. The second was delivered on October 20, 1881, in the parish church of All Saints, Wigan. They were published together as J. C. Ryle, *The Charges Delivered at His Primary Visitation* but numbered separately. To avoid confusion, I will refer to them as 1 and 2.

139. He advised them to "meet the natural feelings of the friends of the deceased by using a service suited to the occasion." The prayer book office could not be legally used, but he pointed them to a form of service drawn up by "three eminent prelates." He also agreed to sanction the use of a form of the incumbent's own composition, though he recommended that he confine himself to collects taken from the prayer book and portions of Holy Scripture. Ryle, *Charges Delivered at His Primary Visitation*, 2:18.

which would inevitably create strife and confusion. Ryle may have been defeated, but he was not embittered by it.

In its inaugural issue, *The Church Portrait Journal* published a short, one-page biography of Ryle that highlighted some of his more noteworthy achievements. After briefly discussing his tracts, hymnals, historical works, and commentaries, the author noted:

> He has also, strongly opposed through the press, in many ways, and upon various occasions, the designs and labours of the Liberation Society. He has pointed out the calamitous results which would follow if the Church were Disestablished and Disendowed as advocated by that Society, and he has emphatically warned the promoters of Liberationism that their designs, if carried out, would, so far from promoting unison and cordiality between Churchmen and Dissenters, serve rather to hinder their accomplishment.[140]

Sadly, most of Ryle's later biographers mention this aspect of his ministry only in passing or ignore it altogether. This is unfortunate for a number of reasons.

First, Ryle devoted a considerable amount of time and energy to defending the establishment. He actively opposed the disestablishment movement in print for at least twenty-seven years (1858–1885), and he was particularly active from 1868 to 1876 when the establishment of the Church of England was most vulnerable. His works defending the establishment were widely circulated, vigorously opposed, and debated on the floor of the House of Commons and the House of Lords. Both friend and foe alike considered him to be one of the leading defenders of the Church of England. Therefore, any account of his life or thought that ignores his contributions to this important debate is simply incomplete.

Second, Ryle's defense of the establishment provides important insight into his churchmanship. Ryle's antiritualist writings explain

---

140. "The Rev. Canon Ryle, M.A.," *The Church Portrait Journal*, December 1876: 18.

and defend his conception of the Church of England as being a Protestant, Reformed, and evangelical church. His anti-disestablishment writings explain and defend his attachment to the Church of England's system of government and establishment as a Protestant, Reformed, and evangelical Christian. Both perspectives are needed to fully understand Ryle's churchmanship.

Third, Ryle's disestablishment writings provide insight into his attitude toward dissent. He respected orthodox Dissenters, especially the Methodists. He blamed the Church of England for creating the vast majority of dissent in the first place. He was thankful for the good work the Dissenters had done, and he was convinced that the most scriptural policy was to work with them whenever possible.[141] His attitude toward dissent cooled during the disestablishment controversy, but it warmed again during his episcopacy. Ryle was probably better at speaking about Dissenters than to them. When he spoke to churchmen about them, at Church congresses for example, he spoke with appreciation and admiration. When he addressed "honest Dissenters" in some of his anti-disestablishment writings, however, he sounded condescending and dismissive.[142] In any case, these works are essential for understanding Ryle's changing attitude toward dissent.

---

141. Ryle joined with Dissenters in supporting the British and Foreign Bible Societies and the London City Mission. He spoke with their ministers on various platforms. He entertained their leading members in his home. He even preached for successive weeks in a Presbyterian pulpit. For one of Ryle's earliest treatments of Dissent (1854), see *Bishop, the Pastor, and the Preacher*, 47–48.

142. Ryle advised "honest dissenters" to use their common sense and not be misled by the "gross misstatements" of the liberationists. He urged them to make the proper distinction between a system and the faults of those who worked it. He reminded them that many of their great forefathers, like Owen, Baxter, Flavel, Howe, and Henry, were strongly in favor of the connection between church and state, and he speculated that if they were to rise from their graves they would be "among the foremost opponents of the Liberation Society." Finally, he pointed out that the disestablishment would not remove a single Dissenting grievance, especially the social one, which was totally unconnected to the question of the Church's relationship to the state. Therefore, Ryle asked, "Why, then, cannot Dissenters keep quiet, and let the Church alone?" Ryle, *What Good Will It Do?*, 33.

Fourth, it reveals his concern for rural parishes. As a rural clergyman, Ryle was particularly concerned about the impact disestablishment or a change in the burial laws would have on rural parishes.[143] Disestablishment would impoverish rural clergy, force the Church to reduce their number by half, and bring an end to religious services in rural parishes all over England. It would severely injure the poor both materially and spiritually. Finally, it would inflame existing tensions between Church and chapel in rural districts and destroy what little peace and charity that remained between them. He was convinced that neither the town clergy nor the liberationist orators had any idea about the potential impact new legislation would have on rural parishes, and so he sounded the alarm as a country clergyman.

Fifth, it provides a rare glimpse into his political views. Ryle believed it was his duty as a clergyman to "preach and live the gospel" and not become entangled in political matters.[144] When he came to the defense of the Irish church, however, his opponents suggested that he did so only for political reasons. In reply to their accusations, he said, "Tory politics were not my reason. I am not a Tory, and never was: if I have any politics I am a Liberal. But I am not a politician: as a clergyman I have abstained on principle from voting at any election. This time I did vote on principle. My conscience told me that if I did not vote I should not be doing my duty to my God, my Church, and my country."[145]

---

143. Ryle described his parish as follows: "The parish of Stradbroke, of which I have now been Vicar for sixteen years, is an isolated open parish, in which there is not a single resident landlord, and the property is extremely divided. The circumstances of the parish are very peculiar. We are seven miles from a railway station, and in the whole hundred containing twenty-four parishes, of which Stradbroke is the centre, we have neither a turnpike, nor a yard of railway, nor a public conveyance, nor a manufactory, nor a lawyer." *Seventeenth Annual Meeting of the Church Congress Held at Croydon*, 111.

144. See Ryle's address to the Croydon Church Congress on the Agricultural Labourers' Union in *Seventeenth Annual Meeting of the Church Congress Held at Croydon*, 111–12.

145. Ryle, *Strike: But Hear*, 4.

This is the most revealing paragraph Ryle ever penned about his personal political views.

Finally, Ryle's participation in the disestablishment controversy helped establish his reputation as a national leader with an independent voice. Prior to this controversy, Ryle's extraparochial energies were focused almost exclusively on the evangelical party. But he opposed the disestablishment movement as a churchman and a clergyman, not as an evangelical. He attempted to unite all parties around this issue. He even criticized those within his party for failing to do their duty to their church on more than one occasion. In short, Ryle's defense of the establishment proved that he was not just a "party man," but a national figure with his own vision for the health and vitality of the Church. He set forth that agenda in his works on Church reform.

Reforming the Church

After 1868 it became glaringly obvious that the Church of England must be reformed if the establishment was to survive. After all, one of Gladstone's primary arguments for disestablishing the Irish church was its unpopularity and ineffectiveness. Although churchmen agreed on very little in the late 1860s and 1870s, nearly everyone agreed that some form of church reform was necessary to protect the Church of England from being disestablished.

Sir Robert Peel saw the need for church reform more than three decades earlier after the passage of the Great Reform Act of 1832. He formed the Ecclesiastical Commission in 1836 to address the Church's worst abuses: pluralism, nonresidency, and drastic variations in clerical incomes. These were addressed by three main acts of Parliament: the Established Church Act of 1836, the Pluralities Act of 1838, and the Chapter Act of 1840.[146] In addition, the commission helped create and endow new parishes in rapidly growing cities and two new sees in Ripon and Manchester. Furthermore,

---

146. For a description of these bills, see Chadwick, *Victorian Church*, 1:136–37.

by making grants for new church buildings conditional on the collection of local voluntary contributions, the Ecclesiastical Commission stimulated a degree of personal giving unparalleled since the Reformation: over 25.5 million pounds were spent on church building between 1840 and 1876.[147] Peel's commission strengthened the Church—some would even say saved it—and kept it relatively secure until 1868.

The results of the Religious Census of 1851 were not as unsettling as Edward Miall's proposal to disestablish the Church of England, but it did make churchmen uneasy.[148] It revealed that of the 7,261,032 who attended church on March 30, 1851, only a little more than half of the worshipers (3,773,474) attended services in the national church. The rest (3,177,208) attended one of the many Nonconformist chapels. Perhaps even more alarming was the number of nonattendants. Horace Mann estimated that there were over five million (5,288,294) English citizens who were capable of going to a religious service but chose not to do so.[149] Absenteeism was particularly prevalent in industrial towns among the working classes. Churchmen attempted to bring them in using a variety of new measures. New churches were built in urban areas where absenteeism abounded. The Church sponsored outdoor evangelistic services in large towns to reach working men. Money was raised to pay lay evangelists to go into the highways and byways to reach the lost as well.

Church reform became an imperative after the Irish church was severed from the state, and various proposals were put forth. These proposals can generally be grouped into three categories: theological, administrative, and organizational.

Each of the three major parties within the Church had their own agenda for theological reform. Broad churchmen, like

---

147. Marsh, *Victorian Church in Decline*, 4.

148. Horace Mann, *Census of Great Britain, 1851: Religious Worship in England and Wales* (London: E. Eyre and W. Spottiswoode, 1854).

149. Chadwick, *Victorian Church*, 1:365–66.

Matthew Arnold, wanted the Church to focus on the moral and ethical aspects of Christianity and not on its supernatural elements. High churchmen called the Church to return to its Roman Catholic roots and traditions. Evangelicals demanded more thorough and unmistakable Protestant teaching.

Archbishop Tait advocated modest administrative reforms that would appeal to the general public in the "age of improvement,"[150] and he succeeded in achieving a number of them. First, he revived the office of the suffragan bishop. Henry VIII originally created the office to assist diocesan bishops when necessary, and they were used widely in the sixteenth century. Due to the overall growth of the population in general and in urban dioceses in particular, they were needed once again. Their revival helped the Church, especially in large, overcrowded dioceses, run more efficiently. Second, with the help of Sir Richard Assheton Cross, Tait was able to increase the number of dioceses by six: St. Albans, Truro, Wakefield, Southwell, Newcastle-on-Tyne, and Liverpool. Like the revival of the suffragan bishop, these new dioceses helped alleviate some of the strain of population growth and urbanization placed on some dioceses and enabled the Church to minister more effectively. Third, Tait was the prime mover in the passage of the Public Worship Regulation Act of 1874.[151] Prior to its passage, a Protestant storm had been gathering over the excesses of ritualism and the Church's inability to curb them. In order to preserve the Church's internal cohesion and its union with the state, Tait proposed new legislation. The Public Worship Regulation Act did not fundamentally alter ritual law; it essentially created a simple and inexpensive process for securing obedience to existing laws governing public worship. Though it was presented by Disraeli as a bill to "put down

---

150. Marsh, *Victorian Church in Decline*, 95.

151. For an excellent discussion of the Public Worship Regulation Act of 1874, see March, *Victorian Church in Decline*, 158–92.

ritualism," which was nothing more than the "Mass in masquerade," it was remarkably moderate.[152]

The Church also enacted a series of organizational reforms that were designed to unify it by creating new, independent bodies for self-governance and self-expression in the event that disestablishment took place. These initiatives largely came from high churchmen who wanted to protect the Church from Erastian domination by the state. Evangelicals were initially distrustful of any attempts to free the Church from Parliament, which they regarded as a bulwark against popery. Over time, however, a group of influential leaders—Ryle, Garbett, and Hoare—convinced the party to abandon its isolationist stance and become actively involved in these new bodies.[153]

The revival of convocation was one such organizational reform. It was to express the mind of the Church at a time when it was not well represented by Parliament and the bishops of the House of Lords. Convocation was actually an ancient institution that dated back to the seventh century. It contained an upper house of bishops, which were appointed by the Crown, and a lower house of clergy, which was comprised of about forty elected clergymen and ex officio members. As a result of the Bangorian Controversy, it was prorogued by Royal Writ in 1717.[154] Evangelicals were the first to call for its revival, but they quickly changed their minds when it became obvious high churchmen wanted to use it for their own

---

152. Harold E. Gorst, *The Earl of Beaconsfield* (London: Blackie and Son, 1900), 161.

153. For an excellent survey of the evangelical party's response to new organizational reforms, see Bentley, "Transformation of the Evangelical Party," 195–235.

154. The Bangorian Controversy was a dispute that erupted in 1717 after Bishop Hoadly of Bangor argued that the Gospels afford no warrant for any form of church government. The backlash was fierce and immediate. In order to save Hoadly from synodical condemnation, King George I prorogued convocation in that year. It did not meet again, except formally, until 1852. See Thomas Lathbury, *A History of the Convocation of the Church of England from the Earliest Period to the Year 1742*, 2nd ed. (London: J. Leslie, 1853).

ends.[155] Despite evangelical opposition, the Convocation of Canterbury convened in 1852 to discuss church business, and York followed suit in 1861. By the 1870s convocation had become a fact of church life, and evangelicals could no longer afford to ignore it. They began to participate more actively, exerted an influence where they could, and called for convocation reform to make themselves more representative.

The creation of diocesan conferences was another organizational reform that took off in the late 1860s.[156] Like convocation, diocesan conferences were important organs for expressing the Church's opinion, but unlike convocation, laymen were permitted to participate. Their constitution and size varied from diocese to diocese and most met every year, although some met every two or three years. Many churchmen were suspicious, and none more so than evangelicals. *The Christian Observer* called on evangelicals to discountenance and resist diocesan conferences because they were illegal, unconstitutional, and "fatal to the Reformed Church of England."[157] On the one hand, Edward Garbett feared that the conferences would destroy all free and independent action on the part of clergymen.[158] Ryle, on the other hand, believed attendance was a duty and urged evangelicals to take an active part in the life of the Church. The first diocesan conference was called by the bishop of Ely, Harold Brown, in 1866, and by 1882 all but three dioceses had them. Once diocesan conferences became established institutions, evangelicals took an active part in them.

---

155. The *Christian Observer* notes, "The Convocation is the creature of circumstances; of circumstances which have passed away. It was not formed originally for ecclesiastical, but for secular, purposes; and the object for which it was formed no longer exists." "Notes on Convocation," *Christian Observer*, April 1866: 241–48.

156. For an excellent study of diocesan conferences, see Arthur Burns, *The Diocesan Revival in the Church of England: c. 1800–1870* (Oxford: Oxford University Press, 1999).

157. *Christian Observer*, December 1868: 899.

158. Edward Garbett, *Diocesan Synods* (London: William Hunt, 1868), 13.

Church congresses were part of the same organizational reform movement as the revival of convocation and diocesan conferences, but they were different in principle. Church congresses were purely voluntary and open to the public; they welcomed papers and discussion from clergy and laymen, and they met for discussion, not decision. They were modeled after the British Association, held annually in large towns, and presided over by the bishop of the diocese. The first was held in Cambridge in 1861, and the second was held in Oxford in 1862. Evangelicals were divided on the question of attendance. Older evangelicals believed participation in these voluntary assemblies necessarily involved doctrinal compromise.[159] Others, like Ryle, Garbett, and Hoare, saw them as an opportunity to expand evangelical influence, and they became regular Congress speakers. Anne Bentley notes that it was in this field that one of the bitterest battles between narrow and "neo" evangelicals was fought.[160] But by the Croydon Church Congress in 1877, evangelicals were firmly committed to attending the congresses, and they unanimously passed a resolution made by Ryle to continue to attend them.

The creation of the Lambeth Conference was another attempt at organizational reform. It consisted of a gathering of bishops under the archbishop of Canterbury and was held about every ten years. The original purpose of the conference was to discuss and determine doctrinal and legal questions of the highest moment, but it met with strenuous opposition and was abandoned. Instead, it became a means of building up the corporate identity of the

159. This is the position taken up by the *Christian Observer* in March 1865. It objected to the "voluntary gathering of men of opposite sentiments on essential matters, in order to discuss religious subjects which, however important in themselves, are yet subordinate to fundamental truth." It feared that such a union might lower the tone of piety, confuse the laity, and create a fusion of all religious differences into a "general mass of lax churchmanship and loose profession." "Words of Caution in Reference to the Position of the Evangelical Members of the Church of England at the Present Time," *Christian Observer*, March 1865: 210.

160. Bentley, "Transformation of the Evangelical Party," 221.

Anglican communion as a whole. The evangelical response was typical: internal division and opposition, which later gave way to acceptance and support. The first Lambeth Conference was held in 1867, and it was opposed by evangelicals like William Goode, the evangelical magazine *The Record*, and evangelical bishops like Jeune, Bickersteth, Baring, and Waldegrave, who refused to attend. Others, like Bishop Sumner of Winchester and McIlvaine of Illinois, attended in order to secure the Protestant character of the statement of faith and were satisfied. There was much less hostility to the second Lambeth Conference (1878) within the evangelical ranks, and the sympathies of the conference were clearly with the evangelical school. By the time the third Lambeth Conference met in 1888, it had become a permanent institution and enjoyed the support of the evangelical party.

Ryle did not attend either of the two Lambeth Conferences that took place during his episcopacy. He chose not to attend the third Lambeth Conference in 1888, which passed the famous Lambeth Quadrilateral. He claimed that "pressing diocesan engagements" prevented his attendance, but his absence was widely interpreted as a boycott—a view given credence by his public criticism of the Lambeth Encyclical.[161] He was unable to attend the fourth in 1897 due to illness. Attendance at these conferences was not a priority for Ryle, and he said very little about them in his diocesan charges and addresses. For that reason, I will not be discussing them any further.[162]

In 1854 (the year the results of the Religious Census were first published) Ryle began calling for a series of church reforms.[163] His

---

161. See "Monthly Notes," *Evangelical Christendom* 42 (1888): 300; and "The Bishop of Liverpool's Protest," *The Spectator*, August 25, 1888: 8–9.

162. For more information on the early Lambeth Conferences, see Randall T. Davidson, ed., *The Lambeth Conferences of 1867, 1878, and 1888, with the Official Reports and Resolutions, Together with the Sermons Preached at the Conferences* (London: Society for the Promotion of Christian Knowledge, 1889).

163. See the following by Ryle: "What Is Wanted?," in *Bishop, the Pastor, and the Preacher*, 26–55. See also "Closing Address," in *The Church: Its Duties, Claims,*

proposals were directed primarily at the evangelical party in general and its clergy in particular. He was convinced that a reformed and revived evangelical party would cure most of the ills plaguing the entire Church. Ryle was unsympathetic to merely mechanical or external reforms that would mend the fabric of the Church but not its heart. These included reforming cathedral bodies, reviving convocation, equalizing clerical incomes, building new churches, increasing the number of bishops, subdividing large parishes, and multiplying ministers—that is, many of the reforms the Ecclesiastical Commission and Archbishop Tait were attempting.[164] Ryle was equally unsympathetic with attempts at theological reform as proposed by broad churchmen like Frederic Denison Maurice in his *Theological Essays* or Catholic proposals by high churchmen.[165] These remedies were little better than quack medicine.[166] From 1854 to 1869 Ryle called on evangelicals to adopt a number of reforms. The most pressing need of the hour was more plain, thorough, and unmistakable evangelical teaching, coupled with a greater determination to rid the Church of false teaching. The standard of holiness among evangelical churchmen needed to be raised as well. They must return to the old paths of Bible reading, prayer, and evangelism. Evangelical ministers needed to give greater attention to preaching, prayer, communion with God, and maintaining union among themselves throughout the country. Evangelical laymen must be awakened to a sense of duty and responsibility and insist that their voices be heard in every movement affecting the

---

Perils, and Privileges. Being the Substance of the Addresses and Sermons Delivered at the Fifth Combined Clerical Meeting at Weston-Super-Mare (Weston-Super-Mare, U.K.: J. Whereat, 1858), 52–73. The latter was republished as a chapter in *Home Truths*, vol. 7 by Ryle's publisher, William Hunt, under the title "What Is Our Position?" See *Home Truths: Being Miscellaneous Addresses and Tracts by the Rev. J. C. Ryle, B.A*, vol. 7 (Ipswich: W. Hunt, 1859), 248–68.

164. Ryle, "What Is Wanted?," 27–29, 54–55.

165. Ryle, "What Is Wanted?," 27. See Fredrick Denison Maurice, *Theological Essays*, 2nd ed. (Cambridge: Macmillan, 1853).

166. Ryle, "What Is Wanted?," 27.

doctrine, discipline, or formularies of the Church. The character and conduct of the evangelical society meetings needed improvement. Young men seeking ordination needed to demonstrate greater faithfulness and truthfulness in giving testimonials. And a new theological college was needed to teach evangelical views of the Church, ministry, and sacraments.

The year 1870 was a turning point in Ryle's career as a Church reformer. He ceased to speak merely to his party and began addressing the Church at large. Convinced that the Church was in grave danger, he called on all churchmen to strengthen the establishment and repulse the attacks of the liberationists by reforming its abuses. The times demanded a series of "external reforms, re-arrangements, and re-adjustments," and he presented his proposals in *Church Reform: Being Seven Papers on the Subject.*[167]

The subject of the first reform paper is dioceses and bishops.[168] Ryle argued that the entire episcopal system needed complete reform. Dioceses needed to be divided and subdivided. There should be one bishop for each county, and large counties should be subdivided into three or four dioceses. Additionally, bishops would be more effective pastors if they had no seats in the House of Lords. Four or five could be elected to sit in the Lords by representation, which would save a significant amount of money and enable bishops to devote themselves entirely to their ministerial work. Furthermore, bishops had too much autocratic power. A bishop should not be able to act without consulting council made up of clergymen and laymen. The method of appointing bishops was also in need of reform. Ryle did not want popular elections, which would only create more divisions within dioceses. He wanted a system in which the dioceses presented three names to the Crown, leaving the final decision in its hands.

---

167. See Ryle, *Church Reform: Being Seven Papers on the Subject.* These papers were originally published as articles in a London newspaper.

168. J. C. Ryle, "Our Dioceses and Bishops," in *Church Reform: Being Seven Papers on the Subject* (London: William Hunt, 1870), 7–16.

The subject of the second reform paper is convocation.[169] Ryle made it clear from the outset that he did not support its revival, and he faulted Archbishop Sumner for waking it from its useful sleep. By 1870 convocation had become a great fact, and its suppression was highly unlikely; therefore, he called for a series of sweeping reforms to remedy its defects. The Convocations of York and Canterbury should be fused to form one body and represent the whole Church. Following the lead of the disestablished Church of Ireland, there should be no ex officio members. Each diocese, when properly reduced in size, should send three clerical representatives chosen by the clergy and an equal number of laymen as representatives. Bishops, clergy, and laymen should sit together in one house and discuss all subjects together, including Church doctrine and discipline. Without sweeping reform, convocation would never secure the confidence or respect of English churchmen and would continue to be held up to scorn in works like *The Comedy of Convocation in the English Church.*[170]

Ryle returned to the subject of convocation reform in addresses delivered at the Leeds and Brighton Church Congresses. The reforms he proposed in these addresses were similar to the ones made in the second *Church Reform* paper: fuse the two houses of Canterbury and York into one, include more parochial clergy, exclude ex officio members, change the method of electing proctors, ensure that minorities are represented, and include the laity. New developments made this subject even more pressing. Edward Miall was campaigning in Parliament to disestablish the Church of England, and by this date he had the support of at least one hundred MPs. More importantly, convocation was now doing real business. The Lectionary Bill was referred to convocation by Parliament. The queen issued convocation a letter of business to consider the Report

---

169. J. C. Ryle, "Convocation," in *Church Reform: Being Seven Papers on the Subject* (London: William Hunt, 1870), 1–16.

170. Arthur Featherstone Marshall, *The Comedy of Convocation in the English Church in Two Scenes* (New York: Catholic Publication Society, 1868).

of the Ritual Commission and to endorse the Shortened Services Bill. As long as convocation remained nothing more than a clerical debating society, convocation reform could be safely left alone. Now that it had real power and influence, however, it must be reformed to become truly representative of the Church as a whole.[171]

In 1872 Ryle discussed this subject with a very different body— the Church Association. At the annual conference of the Church Association, Ryle pleaded with evangelical churchmen to take the issue of convocation reform seriously. Their policy of "standing by and letting [it] alone" was a disaster.[172] By standing aloof from convocation, they lost the ability to influence its proceedings, and now that convocation was doing real business, evangelicals had to change their tactics, awaken to their sense of duty, and interfere. He acknowledged that evangelicals naturally preferred spiritual work and working with congenial souls for foreign and home missions, but they should not leave the question of convocation to be handled by high and broad churchmen alone. He was convinced that if Romaine and Venn, Grimshaw and Simeon, and Bickersteth and Marsh and Stowell would have had the opportunity, they would have "come forward boldly on all occasions, and asserted the right and duty of Evangelical Churchmen to take part in any question of Church organization."[173] In short, the Church of England expects all her children to do their duty, including her evangelical sons.

The subject of the third reform paper is cathedral reform.[174] The cathedral establishments were the weakest and most vulnerable part of the Church of England. The reason for their weakness

---

171. See "Convocation Reform," in the *Authorized Report of the Church Congress Held at Leeds* (London: John Hodges, 1872): 209–17; and "Address on Convocation of the Church of England," in *Authorized Report of the Church Congress Held at Brighton* (London: William Wells Gardner, 1874): 204–8.

172. J. C. Ryle, *Convocation Reform! Being Thoughts and Suggestions on the Subject* (London: William Hunt, 1872), 2.

173. Ryle, *Convocation Reform*, 17.

174. J. C. Ryle, "Cathedral Reform," in *Church Reform: Being Seven Papers on the Subject* (London: William Hunt, 1870), 1–16.

was simple: the theory of cathedral establishments was totally inconsistent with its present practice. Ryle pointed out a number of obvious failings. Deans were typically selected for political, as opposed to spiritual, reasons. Canons generally regarded their three-month residency as a vacation, not a time to "labour and toil."[175] As a result, cathedrals simply failed to supply the Church with a constant succession of able theological writers. The relations between the bishop of a diocese and the cathedral were often inharmonious. The Christian worship of a cathedral was rarely a model for the diocese. Cathedral establishments provided little benefit to the dioceses or cathedral towns but were enormously expensive, which often generated more dislike of the establishment. Therefore, Ryle proposed three reforms. First, the offices of deans and canons should be suppressed as they became vacant. Second, every bishop who had a cathedral in his diocese ought to be the dean so he could exhibit to his clergy a real pattern of prayer, praise, and preaching. Finally, instead of the present system of canons, each bishop, when he became dean, should appoint two chaplains to carry on the worship of the cathedral, and two minor chaplains should be appointed to help them. Furthermore, to ensure the proper superintendence of the whole body, the bishop should be given the deanery house for a residence, and his episcopal palace should be sold. The savings generated by these reforms would be considerable, and that money should be used to increase the small church livings in the cathedral city, set up a fund for pensioning off aged and superannuated ministers of small livings, and applied to meet the expenses of increasing the episcopate.

The subject of the fourth reform paper is the public worship and religious services of the Church of England.[176] The object of the Church's religious services is to edify the faithful, inform the

---

175. Ryle, "Cathedral Reform," 5.

176. J. C. Ryle, "The Public Worship and Religious Services of the Church of England," in *Church Reform: Being Seven Papers on the Subject* (London: William Hunt, 1870), 1–16.

ignorant, and awaken the careless. But at the present the Church's services suited only a small minority, and thus the services must be reformed. By calling for reform, Ryle insisted that he did not believe the prayer book to be unsound or popish in any respect. Rightly interpreted, it was "sound, Protestant, and Evangelical."[177] Nor did he wish to see the liturgy replaced with extemporaneous prayers, supplemented with other works, or altered in any respect. He wanted churchmen to consider two major reforms. First, he wanted the liturgical services to be divided, shortened, and simplified in order to win the affections of the people,[178] and the administration of the Lord's Supper must not remain in the "vague, uncertain, disputable, debatable position" that it presently occupied.[179] Second, religious services in unlicensed or unconsecrated places should not merely be tolerated; they ought to be "adopted, cherished, held up to honour, commended, recommended, and urged upon the clergy of every large parish throughout the district."[180]

---

177. Ryle, "Public Worship and Religious Services," 2.

178. He offered a number of suggestions. The morning service, afternoon service, and especially the baptismal service were too long. Liberty should be given to officiating ministers to shorten the services by omitting or replacing certain parts, under the supervision of the bishop and his council. He noted that these principles—omission and replacement with other parts of the prayer book—could easily apply to other services such as the marriage service, burial service, and the service for the churching of women. See Ryle, "Public Worship and Religious Services," 5–9.

179. Ryle made the following suggestions. It should be administered no less than once a month. The celebrant's dress must strictly conform to the direction of the rubrics. Any gestures or postures that gave the appearance of adoring the elements must be forbidden. Every minister should have the liberty to administer the elements to the whole rail at once and use the words of administration in the plural number. Every minister must have the full liberty to celebrate the Lord's Supper in the evening at his discretion. Ryle, "Public Worship and Religious Services," 9.

180. Ryle believed that the "semi-heathen" masses of working-class people in large urban parishes could not be expected to appreciate the Church's elaborate liturgy. They needed services with the simplest kind of worship: a hymn, a chapter, an extempore prayer, and an extempore sermon. If the Church was not prepared to adapt its services to their capacity, "we may say 'good-bye' to the idea of ever

The subject of the fifth reform paper is the ministerial office as it exists in the Church of England.[181] The Church was failing to enlist the caliber of men it needed into its clerical ranks, and the parochial system was failing to meet the demands of the times,[182] so Ryle called for a series of sweeping reforms to make the pastoral ministry of the Church more effective. A "vertical extension of the ministry" was needed to make it easier for qualified young men to enter the Church's ministry.[183] The canonical age for entering the ministry was twenty-three. This forced many university graduates to wait two to three years before taking orders. As a result, the Church lost many young men to secular professions or to dissent. The Church lost other qualified young men to the language requirement: knowledge of Latin and Greek was a prerequisite for taking orders. The solution was the revival of the office of subdeacon. It should be opened to anyone over twenty who could satisfy a bishop that he had received a good education, knew his Bible, had a right heart and good character, and was "apt to teach" (1 Tim. 3:2). The subdeacon would assist the incumbent by reading prayers, visiting house to house, and conducting nonliturgical services in unconsecrated places. He should be paid no less than seventy pounds per year and be allowed to resign his calling and take up a secular profession at any time.

There should be a lateral extension of the ministry, as well as a vertical, to reach the masses.[184] The parochial system, when properly worked, could do a tremendous amount of spiritual good, but when it was worked badly or not at all, the system became "a most

---

reaching the working classes in England." Ryle, "Public Worship and Religious Services," 10–11.

181. J. C. Ryle, "The Ministerial Office, as It Exists in the Church of England," in *Church Reform: Being Seven Papers on the Subject* (London: William Hunt, 1870), 1–16.

182. Ryle, "Ministerial Office," 2.

183. Ryle, "Ministerial Office," 3.

184. Ryle, "Ministerial Office," 9–17.

damaging institution, a curse and not a blessing."[185] In many large, industrial, urban parishes, the clergyman did little or nothing for the souls of his parishioners. The Church's hands were legally tied. As a result, the work of God stood still. To remedy this, Ryle called for the creation of a new class of ministers called evangelists. These evangelists could be either clergymen or laymen. They were to be selected by a bishop based on their "peculiar powers of preaching" and commissioned to preach anywhere in the diocese without being tied to any particular parish. They should be directed by the bishop and his council to preach where the need was greatest, and their main purpose would be to "proclaim Christ's Gospel, to arouse the careless, to arrest the attention of the indifferent, to inform the ignorant, to gather together scattered believers, and to show them how to keep their souls in the right way."[186] In short, they should be nineteenth-century Grimshaws and Berridges.

Other ministerial reforms were needed as well. "A great reform" in the preaching of the Church of England was needed.[187] Partly from a lack of adequate training and partly from a misguided emphasis on ceremony, the pulpits of the Church were below the requirement of the times. Universities should provide instruction in sacred rhetoric, and bishops should lay more stress on sermon composition in their examination for orders. Additionally, more effective safeguards must be put in place to keep unfit men from entering the ministry. The remedy was greater faithfulness and truthfulness in giving testimonials for candidates for orders. Furthermore, the rule of making orders indelible ought to be abolished.

The sixth reform paper addressed the most important subject of the series—the position of the laity.[188] In the apostolic era,

---

185. Ryle, "Ministerial Office," 10.

186. Ryle, "Ministerial Office," 13.

187. Ryle, "Ministerial Office," 17.

188. J. C. Ryle, "The Position of the Laity," in *Church Reform: Being Seven Papers on the Subject* (London: William Hunt, 1870), 1–20. At the conclusion of the paper Ryle wrote, "I lay down my pen with a deep feeling that I have only touched the

the clergy and the laity were united and worked together. In 1870, however, the position of the laity in the Church of England was falling short of the New Testament standard. In terms of the actual working machinery of the Church, the laity had almost no position at all. Lay churchmen had no voice in bishops' conclave, convocation, ruridecanal synods, or filling vacant livings. Furthermore, churchwardens and the House of Commons did not adequately represent the laity. Churchwardens, as a rule, were appointed with little regard for spiritual qualifications, and almost nothing was expected of them except handling secular or financial business. The House of Commons in 1870 was no longer an assembly made up exclusively of churchmen. Moreover, it rarely handled religious questions—or handled them well when it did. The cause of the laity's substandard position was, in a word, "Popery,"[189] and the consequences of this unreformed system were clericalism on the part of the clergy, and apathy and indifference on the part of laymen. Major reform was needed.

As a rule, nothing ought to be done in the Church without the laity.[190] No conclave or synod of bishops, convocation, or ruridecanal synod should be convened without the presence and assistance of the laity. No diocese ought to be governed by a bishop without the aid of a lay council. No parochial clergyman ought to attempt to manage his parish without constantly consulting the laity. No appointment to a living or cure of souls ought ever to be made without allowing the laity a voice in the matter. And no system of ecclesiastical discipline ought to be sanctioned that did not give the laity a principal place.

---

surface of my subject. In the whole field of 'Church Reform' I know no point of such real importance as that which I have tried to handle in this paper" (20).

189. Ryle, "Position of the Laity," 6.

190. He wrote, "I plead that the laity ought to have a party, and voice, and hand, and vote in everything that the Church says and does, except ordaining and ministering in the congregation." Ryle, "Position of the Laity," 9.

The seventh and final paper summarizes the previous reform proposals and offers some "practical conclusion" about what should be done.[191] The impetus for reform would not come from the bishops, convocation, the parochial clergy as a body, or the House of Commons—it must come from the individual efforts of Church reformers throughout the land.[192] Individual reformers must begin by attempting to inform the public mind and direct public opinion with "the press and the platform, the pen and the tongue."[193] This work must be carried out by the voluntary efforts of reformers in their own neighborhoods, not by creating a new and expensive society. If reform came, it would come slowly, and thus individual reformers must "work on patiently" and not despise "bit-by-bit reforms." Ryle encouraged friends of reform to begin with the laity, believing that getting them to assume their rightful position within the Church was "half the battle."[194]

Ryle briefly discussed diocesan conferences (or synods, as he liked to call them) in the sixth Church reform paper.[195] At this time he doubted their usefulness. Dioceses were simply too large and unwieldy. If diocesan conferences were collective, meaning they included all the clergy of a diocese and an equal number of

---

191. J. C. Ryle, "Practical Conclusions," in *Church Reform: Being Seven Papers on the Subject* (London: William Hunt, 1870), 1–20.

192. Ryle pointed out that the bishops, as a body, were not united, were unwilling to undermine their own dignity and importance, and, with rare exceptions, never initiated popular reform movements. Convocation was an "anomalous assembly," unable to act without royal license, and the House of Commons would never tolerate a legislative rival. The majority of the parochial clergy disliked anything new and would not like bishops, much less a lay council, interfering with their work. The House of Commons was a heterogeneous body that disliked religious questions, and unless the public made Church reform the great question of the day, they would not initiate it. Ryle, "Practical Conclusions," 14.

193. Ryle, "Practical Conclusions," 15.

194. Ryle, "Practical Conclusions," 16–17.

195. Ryle made similar comments at the autumnal conference of the Church Association in October 1869. See *The Church Association Monthly Intelligencer* 3 (1869): 267–68.

laymen, they would be so enormous nothing could be done. If they were elective, meaning they were made up of representatives from each rural deanery, then they would create division and strife.[196] A rightly constituted diocesan conference should comprehend all the clergy of the diocese and at least one or two laymen from each parish.[197] But until there was a properly constituted synodical body for the whole Church, and until dioceses were properly reduced in size (one for each county), diocesan conferences would do little good and much harm.

In the same year Ryle published *Church Reform*, he read a paper on the subject of diocesan conferences to the annual meeting of the Home Counties Clerical and Lay Association titled "A Churchman's Duty about Diocesan Conferences: Being Hints and Thoughts about Them."[198] In this paper, he pointed out that diocesan conferences had become "a great fact," and thus it was "impossible," "childish," and "unwise" to ignore them.[199] There was nothing wicked or unreasonable about them in theory. They tended to diminish the autocratic power of bishops, lessen their isolation, and encourage them to take counsel with their clergy and laity. They may not be evangelistic institutions or directly edifying, but that did not justify their neglect. He wrote, "To affect to despise ecclesiastical machinery because it is only *machinery* is wild work, and unworthy of any but a fanatic."[200] Evangelical churchmen must do their duty and attempt to make them as useful as possible. He encouraged them to take three lines of action.

The first issue was the constitution of diocesan conferences. He took for granted that the laity would be included in these

---

196. Ryle, "Position of the Laity," 19. Ryle first voiced these concerns in May 1868 at the spring conference of the Church Association.

197. Ryle, "Position of the Laity," 20.

198. See J. C. Ryle, *A Churchman's Duty about Diocesan Conferences: Being Hints and Thoughts about Them* (London: William Hunt, 1871).

199. Ryle, *Churchman's Duty about Diocesan Conferences*, 3.

200. Ryle, *Churchman's Duty about Diocesan Conferences*, 4.

conferences. The major question was whether these conferences should be elective or collective bodies.[201] Ryle had four "very grave" practical objections to elective conferences.[202] First, they were unlikely to interest the diocese because at least three-fourths of the parishes would have no place or voice in its proceedings. Second, elective conferences would almost certainly promote more party spirit and division. Third, an elective conference in the southern part of England would probably exclude almost every evangelical clergyman since they formed only a small minority. Finally, elective conferences would lack popular representation among the laity. He speculated that in most rural deaneries, the nobility, gentry, or magistrates would be elected, thus making the conferences purely aristocratic. The middle classes would be virtually excluded and driven that much closer to dissent. The only objection he raised to collective conferences was their size and unwieldiness, but even this was not insuperable. He noted that the diocese of Norwich overcame this difficulty by splitting up the conference into five sections, each held on different days at different locations, and each discussed the same subject with the bishop presiding.

The second issue Ryle addressed was the extent of the action and operation of diocesan conferences. In order to preserve dioceses from strife and confusion, evangelicals would have to labor to confine diocesan conferences to their proper work, which was "consultation, deliberation, expression of opinion, discussion, com-

---

201. An elective diocesan conference is formed by each rural deanery or hundred or district in a county electing two or three clergymen and two or three laymen to act as its representatives. These representatives, together with the bishop and certain ex officio clerical and lay members, compose the diocesan conference. A collective diocesan conference consists of all the clergy of every parish in the diocese, together with all the churchwardens and one or two lay representatives chosen by the churchmen of the parish. These clergymen and laymen, together with the bishop and certain ex officio clerical and lay members, compose the conference.

202. Ryle, *Churchman's Duty about Diocesan Conferences*, 6. He also pointed out that ancient diocesan synods always included the whole of the clergy and as many as seven laymen from each parish.

parison of views, and not action."[203] In short, they were to be like Church congresses on a diocesan level. But the moment they attempted to act without authority, Ryle anticipated that free English citizens would assert their independence, entrench themselves behind their legal rights, and refuse to comply.[204] Diocesan conferences may lead to united action after the fact, but they should never attempt to initiate it.

The third issue was that of duty. What was the duty of churchmen regarding diocesan conferences? Ryle offered three remarks. First, no churchman should absent himself from a diocesan conference as long as its business was conducted fairly and impartially. Second, all who attended should strive to do their duty and give the right tone to the proceedings.[205] Third, the tendency to a "narrow-minded, isolated line of action" must be avoided. Ryle wrote:

> To shut ourselves up in a corner,—to avoid the company of everyone who disagrees with us,—to allow the affairs of the Church to be managed by unsound men, and the help to be left in untrustworthy hands,—all this may seem to some very spiritual and very right. I cannot agree with them. If we want Diocesan Conferences to be really useful to the Church of England, we must come forward and labour incessantly to make them what they ought to be.[206]

In sum, it was the duty of every Protestant churchman in the present day to come forward on every opportunity to speak boldly and

---

203. Ryle, *Churchman's Duty about Diocesan Conferences*, 11.

204. Ryle, *Churchman's Duty about Diocesan Conferences*, 12.

205. Ryle explained, "Let the Churchman who goes to a Diocesan Conference go for business, and speak to the point, if he speaks at all. Let him express his own views courteously, keep his temper, and respect those who disagree with him. But let him stand up boldly for truth, protest courageously against error, and testify against everything that is wrong." Ryle, *Churchman's Duty about Diocesan Conferences*, 14.

206. Ryle, *Churchman's Duty about Diocesan Conferences*, 15.

courteously for Christ's truth and to contend earnestly for the faith and the real doctrine of the Church of England.

At the 1874 Brighton Church Congress, Ryle participated in the discussion of "Diocesan Synods."[207] His address, in many respects, was a distillation of "Churchman's Duty about Diocesan Conferences," though slightly more positive. The triple threat of popery, infidelity, and liberationism made church organization more important than ever, and diocesan conferences had a critical role to play.[208] Once again Ryle advocated the collective model, despite the challenges posed by large, undivided parishes. And once again he held up the Norwich pattern as a model. The elective model, on the other hand, was unpopular, exclusive, and unrepresentative.

In 1879 Ryle published a new treatise on diocesan conferences titled *Our Diocesan Conference: What Good Is It Likely to Do? And What Dangers Must It Try to Avoid?*[209] By 1879 diocesan conferences were more firmly established than they were in 1870. They existed in at least twenty dioceses, and those without them were the exception rather than the rule. Once again he wrote to encourage evangelicals to support them and participate, but his position on them had changed significantly. He no longer supported the collective model. Norwich attempted a collective conference, but it "failed to excite interest, and proved too unwieldy to work."[210] A new elective conference had been formed, and he wrote to commend it.

The subject of the paper is the advantages and dangers of the newly formed Norwich Diocesan Conference. Ryle argued that East Anglian churchmen could expect four blessings from the new conference. First, it would lead to greater unity. It would draw together the clergy and the laity, churchmen of various schools of thought, and churchmen of different ranks of society. Apparently Ryle no

---

207. See *Authorized Report of Church Congress Held at Brighton*, 277–78.

208. *Authorized Report of Church Congress Held at Brighton*, 277.

209. See J. C. Ryle, *Our Diocesan Conference: What Good Is It Likely to Do? And What Dangers Must It Try to Avoid?* (London: William Hunt, 1879).

210. Ryle, *Our Diocesan Conference*, 4.

longer feared that the elective system would exclude minorities as well as the middle classes and increase divisions, but he offered no explanation as to why. Perhaps he simply hoped this would not be the case.[211] Second, he expected the new conference to increase the strength of the Church of England in the eastern counties and organize them into an army. A third advantage that may be expected was the collection of valuable information about matters affecting the diocese. Ryle stated that over the last thirty-seven years of ministry, he attempted many "foolish experiments" and experienced many "humbling failures" from the sheer want of knowledge about the right way to work.[212] Valuable information about important practical subjects could be collected, different opinions from qualified persons could be solicited, and the experience of others could be shared.[213] Finally, the conference could elicit the opinions of the diocese about public measures that may be introduced to Parliament or convocation. Neither the unreformed convocation nor the reformed House of Commons represented the rural dioceses of England. In the place of these unrepresentative bodies, diocesan conferences had the potential to truly be the "mouthpiece" and

---

211. Ryle said, "I cannot help *hoping* that an order of men will be brought forward, and gradually induced to take an active interest in Church affairs, who have hitherto been kept too much in the back ground, and left out in the cold." Ryle, *Our Diocesan Conference*, 6. Italics added.

212. Ryle, *Our Diocesan Conference*, 11. This is a rare statement.

213. The important practical subjects Ryle mentioned included drunkenness; Sabbath breaking; the breach of the seventh commandment; the condition of farm servants; rural Sunday schools; the real causes of Dissent; home missions; reading rooms; penny readings; provident clubs; servant girls' friendly society; funeral reform; prayer meetings; shortened services; lay preaching; book hawking; recreations; harvest festivals; the special spiritual wants of watering places; the better use of provincial newspapers; village hospitals; medical clubs; Church patronage; strikes; parochial councils; laborers' unions; East Anglian forms of infidelity; the actual state of religious education in the diocese; the collection of funds for small livings or repairing and enlarging churches; young men's societies; the dwellings of the poor; the religious education of the middle classes; the spiritual wants of sailors, fishermen, and railway servants; parochial choirs; and the rights and duties of the laity.

"living voice" of the Church in a given diocese.[214] As long as the conference focused on practical business and did not overstep its authority, it would help make "our dear old Reformed Church of England in the Eastern counties fair as the moon, clear as the sun, and terrible as an army with banners."[215]

After being appointed bishop of the newly formed diocese of Liverpool, Ryle had the opportunity to build its diocesan conference from the ground up. Interestingly, he abandoned the elective model he championed in 1879 and formed a collective conference because it was better suited to the wants of his new diocese, which had only 180 incumbents and 120 curates. The first Liverpool Diocesan Conference took place in November 1881, and Ryle's address, "First Words," was published later that year.

Ryle opened "First Words" by explaining the utility and desirableness of diocesan conferences in general, utilizing the arguments (and the very words) of the previous treatises. Diocesan conferences were a great fact in almost every diocese in England and Wales. Liverpool would be "behind the times" if they did not have one.[216] They were reasonable, wise, and right. They promoted unity and drew together the clergy and laity, as well as churchmen of different schools of thought. They promoted diocesan organization, which in turn promoted strength. Furthermore, they provided a valuable forum to elicit opinions of the diocese about public measures and legislation affecting the Church of England. The second and third sections covered familiar territory as well. Ryle explained the two different kinds of conferences (collective and elective), presented his objections to the elective model, and justified the adoption of the collective system. Then he discussed the action and operation of diocesan conferences. If they were to be of any value, they must focus on practical questions and business and avoid even the

---

214. Ryle, *Our Diocesan Conference*, 15.

215. Ryle, *Our Diocesan Conference*, 19.

216. J. C. Ryle, *First Words: An Opening Address Delivered at the First Liverpool Diocesan Conference* (London: William Hunt, 1881), 4.

appearance of dictating to the diocese; also, churchmen must not adopt a narrow-minded, isolated line of action with respect to them.

The only new material is found in the final section of the address. He discussed practical business that demanded immediate attention, such as the constitution, rules, and regulations of the diocesan conference; the financial position of diocesan institutions; the results of a recent religious census that appeared in the *Liverpool Daily Post*; the desirableness of creating a small parliamentary committee of vigilance; and the question of sending delegates to the new Central Council of Diocesan Conferences. For the most part, "practical business" formed the substance of his other diocesan conference addresses.[217]

Of the three major organizational reform movements (convocation, diocesan conferences, and Church congresses), Ryle was most active in the annual Church congresses. At some point, he held virtually every position except president in Church congresses.[218] He regularly participated in discussions on a wide variety of subjects. He delivered numerous papers and addresses. He was appointed to the executive committee of the Plymouth Church Congress (1876) and the consultative committee of the Church congresses of Croydon (1877) and Swansea (1879). He was the chairman of a Church reform meeting in 1886. As the bishop of Liverpool, he was a vice president of congresses from 1880 until 1899. In short, Ryle was one of the first and most active evangelical

---

217. See the following by Ryle: *Our Position and Dangers* (London: William Hunt, 1885); *The Outlook* (London: William Hunt, 1886); "Our Diocese, Our Church, Our Times [1889]," in *Charges and Addresses* (Edinburgh: Banner of Truth, 1978), 185–202; *Thoughts for the Times* (London: William Hunt, 1892); *The Present Crisis: Some Words about the Privy Council Judgment and Old Testament Criticism* (London: William Hunt, 1892); *Watchman, What of the Night?* (London: William Hunt, 1894); *What Is Wanted?* (London: William Hunt, 1895); *About Our Church in 1896* (London: William Hunt, 1896); *Thoughts for Thinkers* (Liverpool: J. A. Thompson, 1897); *The Present Distress* (London: Chas. J. Thynne, 1898).

218. The president of the congress was the bishop of the diocese in which the congress was held. Liverpool hosted a Church congress in 1869.

participants in the Church congresses, and he went on to become one of the most popular regular speakers.

At the Dublin Church Congress in 1868, the dean of Chester remarked that Ryle was "eminently in his place" on the platform of Church congresses. He added, "I never saw a man more entirely in his place in my life."[219] Once again 1870 proved to be a watershed year. At the annual Church congress, the historian Eugene Stock argued that Ryle "laid the foundation at Southampton of the remarkable popularity he enjoyed for many years as a Congress speaker, his *bonhomie* making his hard hitting agreeable even to those whom he vigorously but good-humouredly (may I say?) pommelled."[220] He was especially impressed by one particular debate:

> But the most interesting of the debates was one on Home Reunion. Mr. Ryle had lately been making the flesh of older-fashioned Evangelicals creep by his letters in the *Record* advocating radical reforms in the Church; and these, in his paper on this occasion, he summarized in his usual incisive language, almost every sentence being loudly applauded by "High," "Low," and "Broad" alike. "Repeal the Act of Uniformity," he exclaimed amid tremendous cheering; "Shorten the services"; "Use the laity"; "Treat Dissenters kindly." The Church of England, he complained, had adopted Talleyrand's motto: "*Surtout, point de zele.*" "Over and over again she has poured cold water on zeal, jumped on it, kicked it, heaped wet blankets on it, shut the door in its face." The great audience screamed with delight; and when he ventured to think things would have been different if John Wesley had been made Archbishop of Canterbury the shouts of applause seemed as if they would never stop. When he said "Join the Bible Society" there was a cry of "No"; upon which, reminding them that Dissenters had just been asked to assist Churchmen in

---

219. *Authorized Report of the Church Congress Held at Dublin* (Dublin: Hodges, Smith, Foster, 1868), 313.

220. Eugene Stock, *My Recollections* (London: James Nisbet, 1909), 88.

making a Revised Version—for it was planned in that very year, on Bishop Wilberforce's motion, too—he exclaimed: "If we may unite to revise our Bible, why not also to print and circulate it?" At which rejoinder the cheering broke out again. I do not remember a more successful speech at any subsequent Congress.[221]

Ryle went on to become one of the most popular Congress speakers among all parties for several years.[222]

He attended his first Church congress in 1865 (Norwich) at the request of his bishop, but as early as 1868 he was urging his fellow evangelicals to participate in the upcoming congress in Dublin. Some, like Edward Hoare, supported the proposal. Others, like Daniel Wilson, strongly opposed it. Still others, like Rev. W. Richardson, predictably advocated organizing a rival evangelical conference.[223] Ryle raised the issue again at the Islington Clerical Meeting in 1872 and was dubbed a "Neo-Evangelical" and "Congressing-going Evangelical" by The Rock.[224] In 1878 he raised the question of attendance once again in Shall We Go?[225]

Like convocation and diocesan conferences, Church congresses were now established institutions. Ryle summed up the choice facing evangelicals: "Shall we throw ourselves manfully into them, and try to turn them to good account? Or shall we keep away, and leave them entirely in non-Evangelical hands?"[226] He advocated

---

221. Stock, My Recollections, 90–91. He also noted that at the Croydon Church Congress (1877), "the popularity of Ryle as a Congress speaker was especially manifest." Stock, My Recollections, 96.

222. Stock, History of the Church Missionary Society, 2:358.

223. The Church Association Monthly Intelligencer 2 (March 1868–February 1869): 73–75.

224. See George Balliene, A History of the Evangelical Party, 272.

225. J. C. Ryle, Shall We Go? Being Thoughts about Church Congresses, and Our Duty with Regard to Them, from the Stand-Point of an Evangelical Churchman (London: William Hunt, 1878).

226. Ryle, Shall We Go?, 3–4.

attendance and participation[227] and offered four reasons for taking this position. First, congresses gave evangelicals an opportunity to show the public what they thought about the chief ecclesiastical questions of the day. Second, they gave them an opportunity to answer erroneous statements and defend God's truth. Third, they gave them an opportunity to dispel misconceptions and false caricatures about the evangelical body. Finally, congresses gave evangelicals an opportunity to influence thousands of undecided and uncommitted churchmen who regularly attended.

Ryle acknowledged that some of his brethren regarded a "Congress-going [Evangelical]" as little better than "a renegade, a traitor, and an apostate."[228] He answered some of their chief objections to attendance. Some suggested that congresses were not fairly conducted and that evangelical participants were intentionally marginalized. This charge, according to Ryle, was baseless. Speaking from personal experience, Ryle noted that for the past seven years there had been an "honest effort made to conduce the meetings justly and impartially."[229] Others objected to the presence of unsound men being allowed to read papers and speak at congresses. Ryle admitted that this had occurred on some occasion and caused great annoyance, but each year fewer and fewer of these mistakes were made. Furthermore, mixed congress audiences had proven to be hostile to heresy. Still others objected that congresses give occasion for "semi-Popish trumpery"—that is, vestments, crucifixes, ornaments, and ritualistic preachers being brought into a town. Ryle pointed out that English capitalists seized every opportunity to "push their goods" on large crowds. Therefore, it should come as no surprise that enterprising ritualists would do the same

---

227. Ryle, *Shall We Go?*, 9: "So long as Church Congresses are fairly, honourably, and impartially conducted and arranged, so long I advise Evangelical Church to attend them."

228. Ryle, *Shall We Go?*, 17.

229. Ryle, *Shall We Go?*, 17.

with congresses.[230] Moreover, no ritualist could address a congregation he had not been invited to address. In short, if the town clergy refused to give them a platform, they would have no voice. Still others objected that congresses only discussed secondary matters, and the burning questions of the day were excluded from the program. Ryle denied that this was the case. He pointed out, for example, that at the previous congress (Croydon) skepticism, trade unions, the union of church and state, and Nonconformity were all discussed.

Ryle concluded his appeal by offering two cautions. The first was the danger of "narrow-mindedness in our judgment both of rivals and friends."[231] This took the form of denying that any truth was preached or good was done except by evangelicals. It was also evident in the disposition of some evangelicals to condemn the conduct of their other brethren if they happened to do things which they did not do themselves. The second danger was to carry the policy of abstention from ecclesiastical movements too far. Ryle said:

> To speak plainly, we must come forward boldly on all occasions, and assert our right to take part in every movement that concerns our Zion. We must give up the old-fashioned policy of confining our attention to direct Evangelistic work in our parishes and districts, and leaving the machinery and organization of the Church to others. We must put in an appearance on every occasion, whether at conferences, Congresses, synods, or Convocation-elections, and not be afraid to speak out. We must boldly assert that we are as good and

---

230. Ryle replied rather humorously by noting, "Well, I reply, you will never alter the peculiar character of Englishmen. Wherever there is a crowd, advertising tradesmen and showmen will seize the opportunity of pushing their goods. On Margate sands Punch and Judy will turn up. At Cattle-shows dwarfs, giants, and fat-women are sure to be exhibited. At the largest railway stations you are surrounded with huge pictures, puffing Thorley's Cattle Food, or Coleman's Mustard, or Mrs. Allen's Hair Restorer. It is foolish to suppose that such huge gatherings as Congresses will not be utilized in the same way." Ryle, *Shall We Go?*, 18–19.

231. Ryle, *Shall We Go?*, 21.

sound and loyal Churchmen as any in the land, and, as such, demand everywhere a footing and a hearing.[232]

In short, evangelicals had no reasons to be ashamed of their distinctive doctrinal system, strategy for Church work, or their plans and views. Congresses, like convocation and diocesan conferences, continued to meet and influence the public. Therefore, evangelicals must participate because it was the best course "for the cause of Christ's Gospel, for the souls of our fellow-countrymen, [and] for the interests of the Church of England."[233]

Rev. Samuel A. Walker replied to *Shall We Go?* with his own pamphlet appropriately titled *No!*[234] After reading Walker's reply, one caustic reviewer remarked that the only excuse for attendance now was either "sacerdotal blindness" or "ecclesiastical imbecility of mind, judicially inflicted from Heaven."[235] These views, however, were becoming increasingly rare. At the Croydon Church Congress, a meeting of evangelicals unanimously adopted a resolution made by Ryle that evangelical churchmen should continue to attend the congresses.[236] That is precisely what they did. By 1880, a correspondent to the *Record* noted that evangelical attendance was no longer a question: it was a fact. Evangelicals went.[237]

Two questions deserve attention: What did Ryle accomplish as a Church reformer, and what does his reforming work reveal about him? In terms of actual policy changes, Ryle's Church reform proposals accomplished very little. Six new dioceses were created, but that is hardly one per county. A Public Worship Regulation Act was passed in 1874, and Ryle supported its passage, but it was far more moderate than the proposals outlined in the fourth *Church*

---

232. Ryle, *Shall We Go?*, 27.

233. Ryle, *Shall We Go?*, 32.

234. See Samuel A. Walker, *No! An Answer to Canon Ryle's Tract* "Shall We Go?" *Being Thoughts about Church Congresses, etc.* (London: Elliot Stock, 1878).

235. *Magazine of the Free Church of England* 11 (1878): 215.

236. See *Evangelical Christendom* 31 (1877): 223–24.

237. Bentley, "Transformation of the Evangelical Party," 226.

Reform paper. In 1885 a House of Laymen was created to sit with convocation, but they were not to be consulted on matters of faith and doctrine. Undoubtedly, Ryle would have liked to see more sweeping and thorough reforms, but he knew his reforms were too revolutionary to be adopted entirely. But he regarded *any* reform to be a step in the right direction and a cause for rejoicing.[238]

In terms of the actual purpose of the papers themselves, they were wildly successful. The object of the series was to "set men thinking" about Church reform, and Ryle certainly did that.[239] In the seventh paper he noted, "As I expected, my papers have brought down on me a legion of correspondents. Some are favourable and some are unfavorable; some are complimentary and some are not; some bid me 'go ahead,' and some bid me 'turn astern.' I am quite unable to reply to them all."[240] The series as a whole gave rise to numerous published responses from friend and foe alike. Ryle received an unexpected endorsement from the ritualist (and author of *Innovations*) Richard Frederick Littledale, who said, "I am in virtual agreement with Mr. J. C. Ryle on almost all the heads of his project of Church Reform, albeit I need hardly tell you that we belong to very different schools of theological teaching."[241] A more Protestant churchman, Charles Henry Davis, argued Ryle's proposals were too late and too radical and would ultimately lead to the disestablishment or the eventual destruction of the national church.[242]

---

238. Ryle concluded *Church Reform* on this note: "Our business is to work on patiently, and if we cannot get all that we want, to get all that we can. Let us not despise bit-by-bit reforms. Let us accept them with thankfulness, as installments, so long as we find principles are admitted, and the train is set in motion. Better a thousand times creep slowly forward, than not move at all." Ryle, "Practical Conclusions," 16–17.

239. Ryle, "Our Dioceses and Bishops," 7.

240. Ryle, "Practical Conclusions," 4.

241. Littledale, *Church Reform*, 2.

242. [Charles Henry Davis], *Suggestive Sketch of an Irish Church Constitution and Canons, with an Adaptation to the English Church of the Future, whether Established or Disestablished, and Some Remarks on the Rev. J. C. Ryle's Church Reform Scheme* (Dublin, 1870), 24.

The *Christian Ambassador*, a Primitive Methodist publication edited by C. C. McKechnie, reviewed the series and commended some of his reforms but argued that "no system of reform which leaves the Church connected to the State will effectually amend and permanently secure the Church of England."[243] An anonymous lay churchman, who was critical of the sectarian leaning of some of Ryle's proposals, offered a generally constructive critique in *Mission Life* and suggested several additions.[244] Ryle's Church reform proposals continued to "set men thinking" for the next two decades.[245]

Without question, Ryle's greatest achievement as a Church reformer was to convince the evangelical body to abandon their policy of principled isolation and take an active role in convocation, diocesan conferences, and Church congresses. Ryle's writings and personal example were instrumental in this respect. In 1870 few evangelicals took part in these new organizational institutions; most were suspicious and stood aloof. By 1880 the opposite was true, thanks in large part to the work of the "three Canons": Ryle, Hoare, and Garbett. It is not overstating the case to say that no single evangelical churchman did more to encourage evangelical participation in these important new organizations than J. C. Ryle.

It must also be mentioned that as a result of his work as a party unifier, Church reformer, establishment defender, and congress speaker, Ryle achieved the status of a party spokesman and national leader. For example, at the Brighton Church Congress, the Venerable Archdeacon Emery said that "we look on him as one of the leaders of a great party in our Church."[246] Kenneth Hylson-Smith argues that by 1880 Ryle had become the most trusted of

---

243. A. C., "Church Reform," *The Christian Ambassador* 11 (1873): 43.

244. See A Layman [pseud.], "A Layman's View of Church Reform: Being Notes on *Church Reform Papers* by the Rev. J. C. Ryle," *Mission Life* 3 (1872): 305–10.

245. For example, Ryle's church reform proposals were included in Albert Grey and Rev. Canon Fremantle, *Church Reform* (London: Swan Sonnenschein, Lowrey, 1888), 216.

246. *Authorized Report of the Church Congress Held at Brighton*, 278.

all the evangelical clergy and the first undisputed leader in their ranks since Charles Simeon.[247] Ryle's rise from rural parish ministry to the bishopric of one of the largest cities in England will be discussed in the next chapter, but it should be noted at the close of this chapter that his work on behalf of his party and the Church as a whole formed an essential part of this journey and made him a viable candidate for the newly formed bishopric of Liverpool.

What does Ryle's work as a reformer reveal about Ryle himself? At the very least, it reveals that he came to regard Church organization as increasingly important. In 1854 Ryle was skeptical of the external and mechanical reforms, but by 1870 he was championing them and summoning evangelical churchmen to support them. So why the reversal? Ryle became convinced that the evangelical party must change with the times:

> The times are changed. The tactics and line of action which our Evangelical forefathers adopted were well suited to their days. Fifty years ago Congresses, and convocation, and diocesan conferences, and ruri-decanal synods, and special missions, were things unknown. The weapons of Scott, and Cecil, and Simeon, were good and true "Jerusalem blades." We shall never improve them. But these worthy men knew no more of some of the questions we have to face than of electric telegraphs, ironclads, breechloaders, guncotton, and torpedoes. The condition of the Church of England is completely altered as to outward machinery and organization, and we must not shut our eyes to the fact. In altered times we must alter our tactics.[248]

Perhaps Ryle's study of John Wesley helped him see the potential value of church organization. In the years before Ryle began championing the cause of Church reform and evangelical participation in new church organization, he had been studying the

---

247. Hylson-Smith, *Evangelicals in the Church of England*, 162–63.
248. Ryle, *Shall We Go?*, 26.

leaders of the evangelical revival in general and John Wesley in particular. In *Christian Leaders of the Last Century*, published a year before *Church Reform*, Ryle singled out Wesley's organizational genius for high praise.[249] In the same year, at the autumn conference of the Church Association, he praised the Methodists for having "a most complete and perfect organization."[250] At the Southampton Church Congress (1870) he told the audience, "I often think, if John Wesley had been Archbishop of Canterbury for a few years, he would have bequeathed to the Church some very useful schemes and planned some admirable machinery."[251] It is noteworthy that Ryle frequently spoke about John Wesley's and the Methodists' organizational prowess in the years he began advocating for Church reform and evangelical participation in new Church machinery. Perhaps Wesley convinced Ryle that Church organization and Church machinery could, if rightly used, become spiritual engines to achieve spiritual ends.

Ryle's change of mind with respect to external Church reform and organization reveals an often overlooked fact about the man: he was adaptable, open to change, and willing to adopt new, progressive measures to achieve traditional evangelical ends. Perhaps the best example of this openness is his attitude toward diocesan conferences. He initially seemed to doubt their usefulness, and he did not single them out for reformation or improvement in his

---

249. Ryle, *Christian Leaders of the Last Century*, 79:

> To unite his people as one body—to give every one something to do—to make each one consider his neighbour and seek his edification—to call forth latent talent and utilize it in some direction—to keep "all at it and always at it" (to adopt his quaint saying),—these were his aims and objects. The machinery he called into existence was admirably well adapted to carry out his purposes. His preachers, lay-preachers, class-leaders, band-leaders, circuits, classes, bands, love-feasts, and watch-nights, made up a spiritual engine which stands to this day, and in its own way can hardly be improved.

250. *The Church Association Monthly Intelligencer*, November 1869: 267.

251. J. C. Ryle, "Paper on Christian Unity with Nonconformity," in *Authorized Report of the Church Congress Held at Southampton* (London: Rivingtons, 1870), 358.

Church Reform (1870). Once he became convinced they were an established fact, he advocated the collective model and encouraged evangelicals to participate in *A Churchman's Duty about Diocesan Conferences* (1871). He later changed his mind and reversed his position on the collective model and advocated an electively constituted model in *Our Diocesan Conference* (1879). Then, as bishop of Liverpool, he adopted the collective model for the new diocese because it was better suited to Liverpool's needs.

Ryle was constantly evaluating methods and organizations by their practical usefulness and pastoral effectiveness.[252] The Church was not reaching the masses, so it must be reformed. Diocesan conferences were more likely to do harm than good, and so their constitution and aims must be altered. Church congresses were important influential meetings; therefore evangelicals must attend and speak up. Ryle's various reforming proposals and his changing attitude toward organization machinery should be seen as a practical outworking of his pastoral concern for the nation at large.

Ryle's career as a Church reformer also reveals the importance Ryle attached to lay participation in the life of the church. Nearly every *Church Reform* paper called for the creation of some new avenue for laymen to participate in church life. Bishops should have an advisory lay council. Laymen must be allowed to participate in convocation. The sixth reform paper is devoted exclusively to the position of the laity. He concluded the series by calling individual reformers to begin by "pressing everywhere and in every way the rights and duty of the laity.... They are a beginning; and that is half the battle."[253] The same is true regarding diocesan conferences. He initially opposed the elective model because they would lack popular support and representation of the laity. He later gave it his support because the collective model failed to excite their interest, and he hoped the elective system would be more successful in this

---

252. For example, Ryle said, "Usefulness is the only test. Everything is to be tried on its own merits." Ryle, "Public Worship," 14.

253. Ryle, "Practical Conclusions," 17.

respect. He did not campaign for lay representation in Church congress, as laymen were already included. He did, however, regularly address congresses on issues related to lay churchmen, such as rural populations, trade unions, intemperance, and lay preaching. Also, he addressed the working men's meeting frequently.

The strength of the evangelical party was the laity, and Ryle believed that the average English citizen was Protestant at heart and had a patriotic aversion to Roman Catholicism. So it is not surprising that Ryle would want to see the laity get more involved in the life of the Church. More lay involvement would possibly limit the influence of the ritualists. It may be surprising that a minister as independent and to some degree authoritative as Ryle would advocate as much lay involvement as he did, especially in light of the trouble one influential layman, Mr. Tollemache, gave him. Perhaps he experienced little conflict in Stradbroke. Perhaps it was a deeply held conviction. Perhaps it was both. In any case, Ryle championed the cause of the laity and repeatedly urged them to take their place in the Church.

Finally, Ryle's Church-reforming career illustrates the importance he attached to independent action. As previously mentioned, Ryle believed that Church reform would only come from the individual efforts of Church reformers. Every Church reformer must "put his own shoulder to the wheel" and "set to work in his own neighborhood." Ryle said, "Give me in every county the 'one man' system! I doubt whether Noah's ark would ever have been built, if it had been left to some modern committees."[254] Even more important was his personal example. Ryle was one of the earliest evangelical supporters of Church reform and new Church machinery. For a time, he virtually stood alone. Despite a good deal of criticism, he maintained his ground and gradually persuaded his party to abandon their isolationist stance and participate in Church organization.

---

254. Ryle, "Practical Conclusions," 14–15.

Conclusion

J. C. Ryle's work as a party unifier, Church defender, and Church reformer solidified his position as the leader of the evangelical party. It also extended his influence beyond traditional party lines, brought him closer to churchmen of other schools of thought, and made him a nationally recognized Church leader.

Ryle's work within his parish and beyond began to receive ecclesiastical recognition as early as 1869. In that year he became the rural dean of Hoxne. This gave him a degree of pastoral oversight over the deanery, which consisted of twenty-five adjacent parishes.[255] In 1872 he was appointed an honorary canon of Norwich Cathedral in recognition of his dedicated service to the diocese. Canon Ryle continued to preach, lecture, visit, and write. In March 1880, after much soul-searching, he accepted the offer to become the dean of Salisbury, but within a month a new offer presented itself. On April 16, he received a telegram summoning him to London to meet the prime minister. He was met at the station by Lord Sandon, MP for Liverpool, and was asked to accept the bishopric of Liverpool.

---

255. Bishop Pelham required his rural deans to meet with his clergy twice a year during Lent and Michaelmas. He also had to submit yearly reports on each parish to the archdeacon for the bishop.

6

Bishop

No aspect of J. C. Ryle's life and ministry has received more attention than his episcopacy. Ian Farley has produced an excellent study of Ryle's episcopacy.[1] Alastair Wilcox has analyzed the Anglican Church's mission to Liverpool's poor.[2] Many of Ryle's biographers devote considerable space to it in their works, and more is needed.[3] The scope of a single chapter on Ryle's episcopacy must necessarily be narrow. The focus of this final chapter will be on Ryle's diocesan strategy and his response to the most pressing churchwide issues of the day. As a result, many important but secondary matters, such as his fund-raising on behalf of diocesan institutions and voluntary societies, his social concern, and his interest in elementary education, will not be included.

After setting the historical and ecclesial context and briefly discussing Ryle's appointment, I will evaluate his diocesan strategy by using a number of metrics. When the challenges of the city and the diocese are taken into consideration, and when factors besides religious census data are taken into account, Ryle's diocesan strategy

---

1. See Ian D. Farley, *J. C. Ryle, First Bishop of Liverpool: A Study in Mission among the Masses* (Waynesboro, Ga.: Paternoster, 2000).

2. Alastair Wilcox, *The Church and the Slums: The Victorian Anglican Church and Its Mission to Liverpool's Poor* (Newcastle-upon-Tyne, U.K.: Cambridge Scholars Publishing, 2014).

3. A study comparing Ryle's episcopacy with another newly formed, urban, late Victorian diocese would be a useful contribution, as would a number of biographical studies on prominent clergymen.

appears to be sound, even effective. After this, Ryle's response to the most pressing churchwide issues of the day—new assaults on the establishment, the ongoing decay of doctrinal Christianity, and the progress of ritualism—will be considered. Ryle's office gave him a new platform to combat old enemies. He was able to rally the diocese in defense of the establishment, but slowing the spread of doctrinal indifference and ritualism proved to be much more difficult and much more personal.

The Second City of the Empire

In 1880 Liverpool was regarded as the second city of the British Empire due to the enormous wealth generated by its seafaring commerce. The foundation of modern Liverpool's economic growth and prosperity was laid between 1760 and 1835.[4] A confluence of events contributed to its remarkable development and expansion. One such factor was a population boom, due in large part to urbanization and immigration. In 1760 fewer than 30,000 people lived in the borough of Liverpool, but by 1831 the population had risen to 165,000, with 40,000 more living in nearby suburbs. Liverpool's shipping industry expanded significantly during this period as well. In 1751, Liverpool owned 220 ships of 19,175 tons, which employed 3,319 men. Fifty years later, the number of ships and men quadrupled (821 ships and 12,315 men), and the tonnage increased sixfold (129,470 tons). The growth of Liverpool's docks tells the same story. There were only eight acres of docks in 1751, but by 1835 there were seventy-two acres. Perhaps the most telling statistic is the total tonnage of British and foreign shipping that entered or departed from Liverpool. In 1751 the total tonnage amounted to 65,406, but by 1835 that number had risen to 1,768,426. Liverpool also benefited from the Napoleonic Wars. The defeat of the French left England unrivaled as a

---

4. I am indebted to Ramsay Muir's *History of Liverpool* for much of the content of this introductory section. See Ramsay Muir, *A History of Liverpool*, 2nd ed. (London: Liverpool University Press, 1907).

seafaring power, which in turn gave her a virtual monopoly on sea-faring trade. With their foreign rivals defeated, Liverpool merchants had greater access to lands beyond the Atlantic than ever before. But the real secret to Liverpool's progress was the engineering and tech-nological advances associated with the Industrial Revolution.[5]

Liverpool's economic power and prosperity continued to expand during the Victorian era. During the first half of Victoria's reign, England was unrivaled as the supreme industrial, commer-cial, and colonial power in the world. The European continent was plagued by political unrest and revolution. The United States was focused on westward expansion and civil war. The widespread adoption of free trade principles magnified England and Liver-pool's prosperity amazingly as well.[6] Even after other nations began to compete with Britain and impose tariffs to protect their native goods, England and Liverpool continued to thrive. By the end of the Victorian era, the total tonnage of Liverpool shipping rose from 1,768,426 tons in 1835 to 5,728,504 in 1870 and then again to 15,996,387 in 1905. Liverpool conducted one-third of the export trade and one-fourth of the import trade of the entire United Kingdom. The city owned one-third of the total shipping of the United Kingdom and one-seventh of the total registered shipping of the world. In short, during the Victorian era, England became the workshop of the world, and Liverpool, its distribution center.

---

5. Muir explained,

> The invention of machinery for the textile industries; the use of coal for the smelting of iron; the application of steam to machines; the concentration of most of the great English industries within a radius of a hundred miles from the Mersey; the opening of the markets of India and Spanish America; the vast and rapid growth of America; the concentration of its principal trade in the great port of New York; the opening up of the whole of England, as never before, by means first of roads and canals, and later of railways: these are the secrets of the majestic progress of Liverpool.

Muir, *History of Liverpool*, 260–61.

6. Muir, *History of Liverpool*, 296.

The population of Liverpool continued to rise as the city became even more prosperous in the Victorian era. The Irish population of Liverpool exploded as a result of the Irish Potato Famine. It is estimated that 90,000 people fled to the city in the first three months of 1846, followed by another 300,000 in the following months. Though many Irish emigrated to America, enough remained to exacerbate the perennial problem of overcrowding. A large Welsh population grew up as well. By 1835 the population of Liverpool was approaching 200,000. In 1851 the population rose to 376,065. In 1881 it had risen again to 552,508. When Ryle became the first bishop of the newly formed diocese of Liverpool, he had charge of well over a million souls in the second most densely populated diocese in England.

Many of the inhabitants of Liverpool did not share in its growing wealth and prosperity. As Liverpool was becoming the second city, another city, "Squalid Liverpool," was growing alongside it. As the population grew, the wealthy abandoned the city center for the suburbs southeast of the city, and the middle class soon followed. The swelling population of workers filled their place, forming a semicircular ring around the city that separated the city center from the fashionable suburbs. Housing in this part of the city consisted of vast tracts of densely populated terraced housing, which lacked proper ventilation, light, sanitation, and access to clean water. Furthermore, they were so cheaply built that a windstorm blew many of them down in 1823.[7] Those who lived in inhabited cellars were even worse off. In 1790, 6,780 people lived in 1,728 inhabited cellars. By 1837 there were more than 32,000 living in 7,862 cellars within the borough limits. Due to these unsanitary conditions, epidemics were not uncommon. For example, in 1849 cholera killed 3,571 people, and a lethal outbreak of smallpox occurred in 1870. Not surprisingly, the average life expectancy was extremely low. In 1847, the life expectancy in some of the worst parts of the city was twenty years and five months. But in Ulverstone, a town in the same county,

---

7. Muir, *History of Liverpool*, 272.

it was forty-one years and eight months.[8] After the passage of the Municipal Reform Act (1835), the town council began in earnest to relieve some of the misery of Squalid Liverpool. As late as 1869, however, Abraham Hume, who ministered in one of the worst parts of the city (Vauxhall), remarked, "A greater amount of attention to health, on the part of the special committee of the Town Council, has much improved the sanitary condition of it; but even in the most favourable condition, the circumstances of a large portion of the population are such as might well appall the stoutest heart."[9]

In addition to unsafe and unsanitary housing, intemperance was a chronic problem. In 1795, an observer noted that one in seven houses was a liquor shop, large quantities of rum from the West Indies could be purchased for very little money, and there were as many as thirty-seven ale breweries supported by drinking habits of the lower classes.[10] Between 1831 and 1841, the number of licensed public houses rose from 1,752 to 2,274. In 1861 to 1863, the licensing board attempted a free-trade experiment: it granted licenses to every applicant, hoping that competition would reduce the overall number of liquor shops. The experiment proved to be a total disaster, and the problem of intemperance was only exacerbated.[11] By 1884 the number of drinking houses had risen again to 2,402. In 1892 it was estimated that Liverpudlians spent ten thousand pounds a day on drink.[12]

Crime, as well as drunkenness, flourished in Liverpool.[13] Riots and open fights were commonplace. According to the head

---

8. Abraham Hume, *Condition of Liverpool: Religious and Social, Including Notices of the State of Education, Morals, Pauperism, and Crime* (Liverpool: T. Brackell, 1858), 26.

9. Abraham Hume, *State and Prospects of the Church in Liverpool* (Liverpool: Adam Holden, 1869), 29.

10. Muir, *History of Liverpool*, 273.

11. Muir, *History of Liverpool*, 323.

12. Farley, *J. C. Ryle, First Bishop of Liverpool*, 146.

13. See Malcolm Archibald, *Liverpool Gangs, Vice, and Packet Rats: 19th Century Crime and Punishment* (New York: Black and White Publishing, 2015); Mick

constable and superintendent, there were 115 streets in the city that were known to be the "residences and places of resort for known thieves, and reputed bad character."[14] The "social evil" (prostitution) was rampant. In 1869, Abraham Hume reported that Liverpool contained 847 "houses for immoral purposes" on 208 streets. Ninety-nine streets contained two or more, and one contained thirty-seven. The number of violent deaths was also staggering. For example, in 1857 there were 609 inquests held at the coroner's court for the borough: 108 were dock-related injuries, 4 were connected with the prison, and the rest (493) were assumed to involve foul play.[15] At the beginning of the century, the police force was woefully inadequate. For example, in 1821 there were only twenty-one police officers for a city with more than one hundred thousand residents. Those criminals who were arrested were sent to some of the most barbarous prisons in the empire. The prison reformer John Howard described them in detail in the infamous work *State of the Prisons in England and Wales*.[16]

Education for the children residing in Squalid Liverpool was either inadequate or nonexistent. In 1857 it was determined that the denominational schools in Liverpool were educating 44,767 students, which was only 55 percent of school-aged children.[17] This figure is even more discouraging than it appears on the surface when other factors are taken into consideration. There were an abundance of schools in areas where they were least needed, but there was a dearth of them in the areas that needed them most. When there were schools in poor districts, they were often poorly attended due to the apathy of parents or the need for children to work. Prior to

Macilwee, *The Liverpool Underworld: Crime in the City 1750–1900* (Liverpool: Liverpool University Press, 2011).

14. Hume, *State and Prospects of the Church in Liverpool*, 26.

15. Hume, *Condition of Liverpool*, 26.

16. See John Howard, *The State of the Prisons in England and Wales*, 4th ed. (London: J. Johnson, C. Dilly, and T. Cadwell, 1792), 436–37.

17. Hume, *State and Prospects of the Church in Liverpool*, 32–33.

the Education Act of 1870, most schools in Liverpool were wholly supported by the district. The school fee disproportionally impacted poor districts, and many parents were unwilling or unable to pay it. This placed the burden of the school on the clergyman of the district, who was often responsible for around ten thousand souls and was underpaid. Surveys of Sunday school education tell a similar story.[18] Sunday school education was plentiful in areas where it was needed the least, and it was wanting in areas that needed it most.

The Liverpool historian Ramsay Muir provides an apt summary of Squalid Liverpool: "All the new towns of the north which had been created by the industrial revolution were hideous enough; but it is hard to believe that any of them can have been more dreadful than Liverpool."[19]

Challenges Facing the Diocese

The challenges Ryle faced as the chief pastor of the new diocese of Liverpool were formidable to say the least. In terms of geography, the new diocese was the second smallest in Great Britain after London. However, in terms of population, it was one of the largest. According to the census of 1881, the population of the diocese was nearly 1,100,000: 650,000 in Liverpool and its suburbs; 250,000 in Wigan and its suburbs; and 200,000 outside these two towns. Liverpool was the second most densely populated diocese after London.

The composition of the population provided its own unique challenges. Tremendous wealth and abject poverty could be found within blocks of each other. The influx of immigrants for dock work created a remarkably diverse and, in some ways, segregated population.[20] Ministering to seafarers also presented its own unique set of challenges. Roman Catholicism was particularly strong

---

18. Hume, *Condition of Liverpool*, 20.

19. Muir, *History of Liverpool*, 270.

20. More than two hundred thousand Irish, fifty thousand Welsh, and a large Scottish population made Liverpool their home, and they often formed their own distinct communities.

in Liverpool. A census of religious profession in 1881 revealed that 157,021 (28 percent) Liverpudlians professed to be Roman Catholics.[21] Furthermore, urban migration often completely changed the composition of a congregation on the average of two to three years, leaving the incumbent with the discouraging conviction that he was only "writing in water."[22]

One of the greatest challenges to the new diocese was lack of accommodation for religious services. As a national and territorial church, the Church of England was tasked with providing religious services for its citizens, but as the returns of Ryle's primary visitation articles indicated, the Church's provision of the means of grace to the new diocese was painfully inadequate. The research of religious statistician Abraham Hume sheds light on the problem of Church accommodation.[23]

Table 2. Church of England Church accommodation
in Liverpool 1650–1851

Date	Population	Number of churches	Accommodation	Percentage seating provided for population
1650	Less than 1,000	1	700	70
1725	11,800	2	1,987	17
1765	29,000	4	4,204	15
1785	52,947	10	10,909	21
1801	77,653	14	15,923	20.5
1821	118,972	19	23,533	20
1841	236,688	34	44,452	19
1851	376,065	45	55,216	15

21. R. B. Walker, "Religious Changes in Liverpool in the Nineteenth Century," *Journal of Ecclesiastical History* 19 (1968): 195–211.

22. Abraham Hume, "The Church's Work in Large Towns," in *Authorized Report of the Church Congress Held at Liverpool* (Liverpool: Adam Holden, 1869), 357.

23. Hume, *Condition of Liverpool*, 7–10.

It should be noted that only a small portion of the added seats were free. For example, in the years between 1801 and 1821, six new churches were built (and one was demolished), creating 7,610 additional seats, but of these seats only 853 (11 percent) were free. From 1821 to 1841, fifteen new churches were built, creating 20,919 more seats, but of these only 6,683 (32 percent) were free. And from 1841 to 1851 eleven new churches were built, creating 11,764 additional seats, but only 5,517 (47 percent) were free. In sum, the Church of England found it increasingly difficult to provide religious services for the growing population of nineteenth-century Liverpool, and it was slow to provide free seats for the poorest of its inhabitants.

Another serious challenge was the lack of pastoral oversight. In 1858 the population of the borough of Liverpool was estimated to be 458,799, but there were only forty-eight incumbents to minister to this population. Thus there was only one clergyman for every 9,558 souls if the districts were of equal size, which they were not. The wealthy district of St. Philip's, for example, had a gross population of only four hundred, while the impoverished district of St. Thomas Toxteth had over twenty-two thousand. There were seven districts with more than ten thousand people, two with more than eleven thousand, two with more than twelve thousand, and five with more than sixteen thousand. When the diocese of Liverpool was created in 1880, there only 180 incumbents and 120 curates for a diocese of more than 1,100,000. Compare this with the diocese of Norwich (Ryle's previous diocese), which had nearly four times as many clergymen (1,160) for nearly half the population (660,000). Ryle was not exaggerating in his first charge when he commented, "I venture boldly to say that there is not another diocese in all England in which the disproportion between the demands on the Church and the supply the Church has provided, is so startling and so serious."[24]

---

24. Ryle, *Charges Delivered at His Primary Visitation*, 1:8.

The problem of the lack of clergymen was only compounded by clerical poverty, urban migration, ministerial burnout, unclear (or nonexistent) parish boundaries, and "lame-duck" ministers. As table 2 demonstrates, most of the churches in the new diocese were relatively new in 1880 and thus had no endowments. Therefore, their incumbents were financially dependent on fees, pew rents, and offertories. The result was that many clergymen, especially those in the poorest and largest districts, were inadequately paid and were thus unable to provide for a family, the necessary expenses of worship, or the adequate maintenance of the district school. Hiring a curate to help was simply out of the question for many. Rev. A. J. Tomlin, for example, ministered in a parish of sixteen thousand souls but was paid only eighty pounds a year. In fact, endowments were so rare (or so meager, as in the case of Tomlin) that Ryle conjectured that disestablishment would have virtually no impact on the majority of his clergymen.[25] As a result, these positions were not coveted by the best ministerial candidates, and they often proved difficult to fill once becoming vacant.

Like poverty, urban migration proved to be a hindrance to parish ministry, especially in the worst districts. When wealthy and middle-class churchmen moved to the suburbs, their financial support disappeared, but their rented pews remained and went unrented, thus depriving the poor of a free seat and the minister of a source of income. Dissenting chapels, which helped shoulder some of the ministerial burden, frequently followed their middle-class members to the suburbs, leaving the parish minister virtually alone to tend vast spiritual deserts.[26]

---

25. Ryle, *Charges Delivered at His Primary Visitation*, 1:9.

26. Abraham Hume wrote on this subject extensively. See the following by Hume: *Condition of Liverpool*, 12–14; *State and Prospects of the Church in Liverpool*, 12–14; and especially *The Church of England the Home Missionary to the Poor, Especially in Our Large Towns* (London: Seeley, Jackson, and Halliday, 1862). In his testimony before the House of Lords, he instanced nineteen relocations by seven Dissenting chapels over a relatively short period of time. Charles Spurgeon also

Under these circumstances it is not surprising that ministerial burnout was a chronic problem in large, overgrown, and pauperized parishes. Hume, who ministered in one of these districts, observed, "Need we wonder that in many cases the Clergyman finds hope and heart fail him, not from the magnitude of the task, which he does not fear, but from the want of adequate means, which renders him in a great degree helpless."[27]

---

addressed this phenomenon in London in a sermon preached at the Metropolitan Tabernacle on May 26, 1861:

> The next piece of practical instruction is this—let us learn, my Brothers and Sisters, the wicked folly of those professed Christians who despise the poor. There is growing up, even in our Dissenting Churches, an evil which I greatly deplore—a despising of the poor! I frequently hear in conversation such remarks as this, "Oh, it is no use trying in such a place as this, you could never raise a self-supporting cause; there are none but poor living in the neighborhood." If there is a site to be chosen for a Chapel, it is said, "Well, there is such a lot of poor people round about, you would never be able to keep a minister. It is no use trying; they are all poor." You know that in the City of London itself, there is now scarcely a Dissenting place of worship! The reason for giving most of them up, and moving them into the suburbs is that all the respectable people live out of town, and of course, they are the people to look after! They will not stop in London—they will go out and take villas—and live in the suburbs! And therefore, the best thing is to take the endowment which belonged to the old Chapel, and go and build a new Chapel somewhere in the suburbs where it may be maintained. "No doubt," it is said, "the poor ought to be looked after, but we had better leave them to another order, an inferior order—the City Missionaries will do for them—send them a few street preachers." And as to the idea of raising a cause where they are all poor people, why there is hardly a minister that would attempt it!

Charles Spurgeon, "Even So, Father!" in *The New Park Street and Metropolitan Tabernacle Pulpit* (Pasadena, Tex.: Pilgrim Publications, 1969), 7:374–75.

27. Hume, "Church's Work in Large Towns," 358. For a sad testimony of ministerial burnout in slum parishes, see the letter of Reverend Carson, vicar of St. Bartholomew, to a local MP begging for a new appointment:

> I am thoroughly disheartened. My work is a failure. I get little or no support from so-called Christian people. I have but a faithful few and "few" must be written in large capitals. Of most of the streets and their occupants I have very little hope; but of Cherry Lane, Oriel Street, Migdall Street and Paul Street I have no hope whatsoever! As far as I can see it

Unclear or nonexistent parish boundaries, which resulted from
the piecemeal development of Liverpool, did little to promote
pastoral oversight. For example, in 1879 the incumbents of Holy
Trinity, St. Michael, St. Thomas, and St. Philip's were unaware of
the extent of their parish boundaries.[28] Finally, lame-duck ministers hindered the Church's ability to minister to the masses. Aged
or infirm clergymen in poor urban districts often found themselves unable to fully discharge their ministerial duties to their
large parishes but were too poor to retire or hire a curate to assist
them. Others simply gave up. For example, one minister made the
following confession before the Liverpool Clerical Society in 1863:
"Since, not having been fortunate enough to scrape acquaintance
with any dignitary in either Church or State—not being a 'cheese'
with an episcopal father-in-law to pour into me the good wine of
a rich living—I have been long compelled by the *dura necessitas*
of clerical poverty to give up the active exercise of my ministerial
functions, and for the last fifteen years have, like any mere layman,
lived by my wits, as a private schoolmaster."[29]

The Appointment

On April 16, 1880, a little more than a month after being appointed
dean of Salisbury, Ryle received a telegram from Lord Beaconsfield

---

is quite beyond any human being to benefit them at all! If relief is given
in clothes, they are pawned, and the money drunk. If groceries or bread
are distributed they are sold for a copper or so of drink. The streets are a
hell in themselves, and I am a broken-hearted man. Use what influence
you have to get me removed for a few years, if I may be spared to work
under brighter auspices, with less heart-rending worry than I have here.

Alistair Wilcox, *The Church and the Slums: The Victorian Anglican Church and
Its Mission to Liverpool's Poor* (Newcastle-upon-Tyne, U.K.: Cambridge Scholars
Publishing, 2014), 126.

28. Wilcox, *Church and the Slums*, 14.

29. [J. S. B.], *The Deficient Supply of Well-Qualified Clergymen for the Church
of England, at the Present Time: A Paper Read before the Liverpool Clerical Society*
(Birkenhead, U.K.: W. Osborne, 1863), 10.

summoning him to London to discuss an important matter. He was met by Lord Sandon, MP for Liverpool, who informed him that he was being asked to accept the bishopric of Liverpool. Disraeli's government lost the general election in February and was about to leave office. If Disraeli did not act quickly, Gladstone, a high churchman, would get to make the appointment. Believing it was the clear path of duty, Ryle accepted it almost immediately. He later commented that he would much rather wear out as bishop of Liverpool than rust out as dean of Salisbury.

The choice of Ryle remains something of a mystery. As Ian Farley points out, his appointment was not the result of political consideration, nor was it the result of ecclesiastical planning. Instead, it was simply a matter of personal preference.[30] Lord Sandon was probably chiefly responsible for Ryle's appointment. Algeron Turner, Disraeli's secretary, later remarked that the choice was between Dean Ryle and Canon Fleming. Disraeli favored Fleming, but Lord Sandon changed his mind.[31] Queen Victoria, who took an active interest in church patronage, was an antiritualist and thus made no objections. The chief promoters of the new diocese, Abraham Hume and John Torr, were low church in their sympathies and knew Ryle from his involvement in Church congresses and various evangelical societies, as well as from his writings. Ryle's appointment was rushed through with remarkable speed. On May 4 he became a doctor of divinity of Oxford. On June 11 his consecration took place at York Minster, and his charge was delivered by his friend Edward Garbett, canon of Winchester. On July 1 he was enthroned as the first bishop of Liverpool.

If Ryle's appointment was a mystery, his mission as the new bishop was not. Canon Garbett summarized it well in his consecration charge: "Here, if anywhere, must be tried the great experiment of our day. Can the innate powers of the Kingdom of Christ grapple

---

30. Farley, *J. C. Ryle, First Bishop of Liverpool*, 86–87.

31. Marcus L. Loane, *John Charles Ryle: 1816–1900* (London: Hodder and Stoughton, 1983), 82.

with such a state of things and recover to the Cross the alienated affections of mankind?... The life of the Church of England, the welfare of the nation, and the prospects of the Kingdom of Christ in our land...hang in the balance."[32]

In many respects, Ryle's appointment was a test case: Could the Church of England effectively minister to the masses in England's large, modern, urbanized, and industrialized towns? The eyes of the nation and the Church were on him.

Ryle's Diocesan Strategy

Ryle accepted the challenge and set forth his goals in his first charge as the new bishop. He told the diocese:

> If the Established Church of this country claims to be "the Church of the people," it is her bounden duty to see that no part of "the people" are left like sheep without a shepherd. If she claims to be a territorial, and not a congregational, Church, she should never rest till there is neither a street, nor a lane, nor a house, nor a garret, nor a cellar, nor a family, which is not regularly looked after, and provided with the offer of means of grace by her officials. Of course she cannot make people value religion, or care for the means she provides. But

---

32. Edward Garbett, *Liverpool Daily Post*, June 12, 1880, quoted in Farley, *J. C. Ryle, First Bishop of Liverpool*, 95. John Howard, the dean of Chester, echoed Garbett's challenge in Ryle's enthronement sermon based on Acts 5:20. He said:

> But the grand charter had gone forth—"To the poor the Gospel is preached." Under this charter every Christian bishop holds his office: he is bound by personal influence, by careful organization, to use his best endeavours to bring the ministrations of his clergy with the reach of the poorest of the poor.... The time for probation is over, and the time for active work, for systematic arrangements, for stimulating zeal, for correcting anomalies must now begin. Among you questions visibly present themselves for solution, more especially we cannot take our eyes from the large section of the population which are destitute of any adequate supply of churches and clergy.

John Howard, "The Enthronement of the Bishop of Liverpool," *Liverpool Echo*, July 2, 1880: 1.

her aim should be to produce such a state of things, that no one shall be able to say, "I am no man's parishioner. I am never visited or spoken to: no one cares for my soul."[33]

His top priority was to provide the means of grace and pastoral oversight to the masses of the new diocese through organized, systematic, and aggressive evangelism.[34] His two chief means of accomplishing this end were more living agents and more places of worship.

More Living Agents

The "first, foremost, and principal" want of the new diocese was more "living agents"—ordained ministers of the Word.[35] When the diocese was formed, the supply of ministers simply could not meet the demand of the population.[36] At most there should have been no more than five thousand souls for each incumbent, but in 1881 only 74 of 182 parishes were under this maximum. By 1884 Ryle was calling for large, overgrown urban parishes to be subdivided into districts of no more than thirty-five hundred people. In short, in order to reach the masses, more clergy were desperately needed.

Ryle was concerned for quality as well as quantity. In his quest for more living agents he had no intention of lowering ministerial standards. He said, "I cannot sympathize with those who press the Bishop to bring into the ministry men who know little or nothing

---

33. Ryle, *Charges Delivered at His Primary Visitation*, 1:7.

34. Ryle presented his diocesan strategy in his diocesan charges and addresses, as well as in other formats, such as Church congress papers, sermons, and treatises.

35. Ryle, *Charges Delivered at His Primary Visitation*, 1:13, 15.

36. Ryle compared the diocese to an undermanned ship in *Charges Delivered at His Primary Visitation*, 1:14–15: "How frightfully undermanned the Church of England is at present in Liverpool must be evident to any one of the slightest reflection!… In such a condition of things the Church of England cannot possibly do herself justice, and to expect her to be "the Church of the people" in Liverpool is simply absurd. You might as well send out of the Mersey a Cunard or White Star steamer, with a crew of only twenty men, all told,—officers, seamen, engineers, and stokers,—and expect her to cross the Atlantic and reach New York in safety."

of Latin, Greek, Church History, the story of the English Reformation, and Prayer-book, the Church Catechism, or Evidences of
Christianity."[37] In addition to being properly educated, they needed
to have the right mind-set for the work. A "right-minded" living
agent had four qualities.

First and foremost, right-minded living agents proclaimed the
right message. He explained:

> They must know what they have got to do. If they only go
> about telling men not to get drunk, not to fight, not to gam-
> ble, not to swear, not to break the Sabbath, they may just as
> well stay at home. If they want to do good, they must tell
> men to believe as well as repent. They must tell the story of
> the cross of Christ. They must magnify that grand article of
> the Apostles' creed, "I believe in the forgiveness of sin." They
> must make much of that doctrine which fits the empty heart
> of man just as the right key fits the lock, I mean the doctrine
> of free and full pardon of sin through faith in Christ.[38]

The message of free forgiveness through faith in Christ was the
strength of the apostles, the lever of the Reformation, the doctrine
that revived England in the eighteenth century, and the only hope
for the unreached masses of Liverpool. "Everything depends on
the message which your living agents proclaim," Ryle asserted.

Second, right-minded living agents use the right methods to
bring the right message to the masses. Ryle had two complemen-
tary methods in mind. The first was the "direct and lively preaching
of the gospel."[39] He was convinced that one of the reasons why the
working classes were absent from church was the unattractive man-

---

37. Ryle, *Charges Delivered at His Primary Visitation*, 2:19–20.

38. Ryle, *Charges Delivered at His Primary Visitation*, 2:12.

39. See J. C. Ryle, *Can They Be Brought In? Being Thoughts on the Absence from Church of the Working Classes* (London: William Hunt, 1883), 31–40. The substance of this work was originally a paper delivered at the Derby Church Congress (1882) on the subject of evangelistic work at home. It was enlarged and expanded in *Can They Be Brought In?* It was republished as a chapter titled "Can the Church Reach

ner in which the gospel was often presented. They would not come to hear monotone, dry, heavy, stiff, dull, cold, tame, orthodox, theological essays. They would, however, come to hear the "fiery liveliness" and "directness of style" that characterized the preaching of Spurgeon, Guthrie, Moody, Aitken, and General Booth.[40] The new diocese needed living agents who gave attention to the style and manner of their sermons as well as the substance. It is worth noting that *Simplicity in Preaching* was published in the same year Ryle read the substance of *Can They Be Brought In?* before the Derby Church Congress. Perhaps that work should be read as a how-to manual for living agents. The second method was systematic, house-to-house, pastoral visiting.[41] Ryle learned from his earliest days in the ministry that agricultural laborers and working men would come to church if the clergyman would come to their home and treat them in a brotherly, friendly, kind, and sympathizing way.[42] In sum, "give us the right preaching in every pulpit,

the Masses?," in *Principles for Churchmen*. These works contain the clearest presentation of Ryle's evangelistic strategy for the masses.

40. Ryle, *Can They Be Brought In?*, 33.

41. H. D. Rack argues that domestic visitation was the most characteristic device during the second quarter of the century for extending religious influences to adults outside the Church. He identifies a number of visiting systems that served as a model for churchmen: Thomas Chalmers in Glasgow, David Nasmith's Town and City Missions, and Joseph Tuckerman in Boston. See H. D. Rack, "Domestic Visitation: A Chapter in Early Nineteenth-Century Evangelism," *Journal of Ecclesiastical History* 24 (1973): 357–76.

Ryle admired the work of Thomas Chalmers, but Richard Baxter was the pastoral visitor par excellence. Ryle regarded Baxter as one of the most successful parish pastors who ever lived, and he attributed his success to his system of household visitation and private conference. See J. C. Ryle, *Baxter and His Times: A Lecture* (London: G. Barclay, 1853), 26–28.

Rev. Richard Hobson, vicar of St. Nathaniel's in Liverpool, was Ryle's favorite living example of a pastoral visitor. Hobson's autobiography, *What Hath God Wrought: An Autobiography* (London: Charles J. Thynne, 1909), provides an illuminating glimpse into his visitation strategy as well as the challenges a clergyman faced in squalid Liverpool. It has recently been republished (2003) by the Banner of Truth as *Richard Hobson of Liverpool: The Autobiography of a Faithful Pastor*.

42. Ryle, *Can They Be Brought In?*, 41–43.

accompanied by the right house-to-house visiting in every parish, and I believe the working classes will be found the best friends and members of the Church of England."[43]

Third, right-minded living agents must be rightly deployed. In some large parishes in the diocese there were clergymen who did little or nothing for their district, and the people were like "sheep without a shepherd."[44] Canonical law prevented bishops from doing anything more than waiting and praying. Ryle believed the time had come to "break the bonds which black tape has too long placed on us, and cast them aside"[45] by creating a new class of ministers called evangelists. The bishop, with the advice of a select council of presbyters and laymen, in conjunction with the incumbent, should be empowered to separate three to four thousand souls from a large parish and place them under the charge of an evangelist, whose main object would be to "proclaim Christ's gospel in its simplest form, to arouse the careless, to arrest the attention of the indifferent, to inform the ignorant, to gather scattered believers, and to show them how to keep their souls in the right way."[46] In short, they were to be ecclesiastically authorized and sanctioned William Grimshaws and John Berridges.[47]

---

43. Ryle, *Can They Be Brought In?*, 47.

44. Ryle, *Can They Be Brought In?*, 21.

45. Ryle, *Can They Be Brought In?*, 28.

46. Ryle, *Can They Be Brought In?*, 25.

47. Ryle made a similar proposal in 1870 in the fifth Church reform paper. Apparently, it was considered too radical to adopt at that time, and so, as a bishop, he called for its creation again in 1883 to reach his diocese. He expanded his argument for the office considerably in 1883. He argued that it is a scriptural office, or at the very least, it is not unscriptural. Furthermore, he pointed out that there is no direct scriptural warrant for rural deans and archdeacons, but those offices were acceptable to most churchmen. Moreover, during the English Reformation, certain preachers like Bradford, Knox, and Grindal were given a general commission to preach throughout England. Something similar had recently been attempted to great effect in the diocese of London and Rochester. Therefore, the charge of novelty could not be supported. The creation of the office would help and not harm the parochial system. It would show the unreached masses that the Church had not

The financial position of the clergy was related to deployment. Inadequate pay, debt, or the combination of the two could sideline even the most zealous living agent and impede parish work. At the very least, poor clergymen could not afford to hire curates. Additionally, clerical poverty kept many aged or infirm clergymen from retiring, and as a result, their parishes remained unevangelized. Ryle called for two reforms. The first was to raise the annual income of clergymen, especially those in densely populated districts. This would raise morale, keep clergymen from taking on second jobs, enable the diocese to attract better ministers, and provide additional resources that could be used to hire curates or paid Scripture readers. The second reform proposal was the creation of a pension fund to help aged, worn-out, and infirm clergymen retire. Such a fund would allow these men to retire and be replaced by new, zealous, right-minded living agents.

Fourth, right-minded living agents must utilize the laity and invite their help and assistance. More specifically, Ryle encouraged incumbents to organize their parishes into mini dioceses and systematically deploy lay helpers like a bishop would clergymen. He explained:

> Stir up every Christian man and woman in your congregation, who has a few hours to spare in the week, to give you some voluntary aid. Break up your huge parish into well-organized territorial districts, and give to each helper his own special district. Urge your helpers to get together people wherever they can, in a shed, or a cottage, or a barn, and to give them simplest and most elementary Christian instruction, plain, kindly talk about Christ, simple extempore prayer, and hearty, lively singing. Do this, and persevere in doing it, and I am sure you will not labour in vain. Do this, and persevere in doing it, and in process of time, the Mission-room, the Church, and the

---

forgotten about them. It would preserve them from joining the Dissenters. Their work would aid overworked clergymen and provoke the lazy to action.

regular parochial district will be the happy result, and, what is far better, a harvest of saved souls.[48]

Utilizing lay help was simply a practical necessity in Liverpool. Few clergymen had the time, the talent, or the resources to provide pastoral oversight to a parish of five thousand or more. If the masses were going to be reached, right-minded laymen must be recruited, trained, and deployed.

By the century's end, some churchmen, like Frederick Farrar, canon of Westminster, argued that the creation of brotherhoods was the solution to reaching the masses. These brotherhoods consisted of ordained men who took vows and formed a living community whose goal was to make Christ visible to the masses. The subject was discussed extensively at the Hull Church Congress.[49] Ryle spoke and voiced his opposition to this "new machine."[50] He doubted if there would be a sufficient supply of men for them since they were not paid positions, and he wondered if they could fit within the current parochial system without causing much strife and quarreling. He was uncomfortable with the multiplication of extrabiblical vows. His primary objection was that they were not needed. The Church needed more Richard Hobsons, not brotherhoods.

Richard Hobson was the living agent par excellence. Hobson was the vicar of St. Nathaniel's Windsor from 1868 to 1901, which was located in one of the poorest sections of Squalid Liverpool.[51] He began alone in a cellar with four people. Fourteen years later he had an average attendance of 700 on Sunday morning, 300 in the afternoon, and 950 in the evening. At his first Communion service held in St. Nathaniel's, he had only eight communicants,

---

48. Ryle, *Charges Delivered at His Primary Visitation*, 2:11.

49. See *The Official Report of the Church Congress Held at Hull* (London: Bemrose and Sons, 1890), 344–78.

50. J. C. Ryle, "A Paper on Brotherhoods," in *The Official Report of the Church Congress Held at Hull* (London: Bemrose and Sons, 1890), 351. This paper was later republished as *Brotherhoods* (London: William Hunt, 1890).

51. Hobson, *What Hath God Wrought*.

but fourteen years later there were eight hundred; all were working class and nearly half were men. There were six services in the
church each week, four in mission rooms, and two prayer meetings
every month. Furthermore, Hobson extensively utilized the laity.
In 1883, St. Nathaniel's had 82 voluntary Sunday school teachers
who taught 1,700 Sunday scholars, 120 church workers, and 18
Bible classes with 600 adults on the register. This poor congregation managed to raise eight hundred pounds a year for "the cause
of God," and there were eleven hundred pledged abstainers in the
district.[52] Ryle attributed Hobson's remarkable success among Liverpool's poorest to two factors: "He is a man who tries to preach
Christ in the pulpit, and to visit his people in a Christ-like, sympathizing way as a pastor, at the rate of seventy-five families a week."[53]

More Places of Worship

The second "chief want" of the diocese was a greater number of
places of worship.[54] Even if the masses were brought in by an army
of the right kind of living agents, the vast majority would have to
be turned away due to the lack of accommodation.[55] Prior to Ryle's
arrival, a committee appointed by the bishop of Chester declared
that at least twelve new churches were urgently required in Liverpool. Ryle estimated that at least one new church ought to be
built a year to keep pace with the city's rising population. Outside
the city there were other parts of the diocese that needed more
places of worship as well. Simply put, churchmen should not be
satisfied until there were more places of worship for the population
of the whole diocese.

In addition to building new churches, some older churches
near the docks needed to be torn down and rebuilt in other places
where they were more necessary. The growth of the docks, which

---

52. Ryle, *Can They Be Brought In?*, 46.
53. Ryle, *Can They Be Brought In?*, 46.
54. Ryle, *Charges Delivered at His Primary Visitation*, 1:15.
55. See table 1.

was accompanied by the construction of more warehouses, offices, and railway stations, consumed vast areas of residential housing. As a result, many of the large churches in that area were poorly attended, and the seats, which were so badly needed in other parts of the city, went unfilled. But only an act of Parliament could authorize their deconstruction and reconstruction elsewhere. So at the first diocesan conference Ryle urged the Diocesan Church Building Society to form a committee to help make this a reality.[56]

Ryle was concerned about the quality as well as the quantity of new churches. He wanted to see every pound stretched as far as possible. Economy, practical usefulness, comfort, and simplicity were paramount, and he warned against wasting money on external decoration or being victimized by architects who were anxious to display their talents. If the land was expensive, as it was in many parts of the city, the parish school should be located under the new church. If the neighborhood was "low in character and destitute of good houses," a parsonage should accompany it. In every instance Ryle recommended the construction of a large vestry for the use of confirmation and communicants' meetings.[57] He also warned about the paralyzing effects debt can have on a new minister during the first critical years of his ministry. Therefore, he encouraged patrons of new churches to carefully consider the income of their ministers. Ryle wrote, "A grand Gothic church, with a half-starved Incumbent in the pulpit, is a very sorrowful and unsatisfactory sight."[58]

In addition to new churches, Ryle strongly promoted the building of mission rooms, which he regarded as immensely valuable to an active clergyman. Ryle went as far as to say that in terms of usefulness, they were even more important than new churches.[59] A well-built mission room could accommodate between four and five hundred people and could be purchased at about a fourth of

---

56. Ryle, *First Words*, 26–27.

57. Ryle, *Charges Delivered at His Primary Visitation*, 1:17.

58. Ryle, *Outlook*, 8–9.

59. Ryle, *Charges Delivered at His Primary Visitation*, 1:16.

the cost of a new church. Mission rooms allowed a clergyman (or a qualified layman, like a Scripture reader) to provide a short, simple, and nonliturgical service for his parishioners. They often attracted the working classes, who were willing to attend a simple elementary service in a room but shied away from a large parish church. They were a valuable tool for reaching those who never attended any place of worship whatsoever. Furthermore, they often paved the way for churches to be built in the future. Blowick, Southport; All Saints', Hindley; and St. Nathaniel's, Liverpool, are all examples of mission rooms leading to new church buildings.[60]

The great question of the hour was, who would fund the needed construction? Ryle doubted that the ecclesiastical commissioners would do much. Some funds might be provided to support the clergyman of a new district in certain populations and, in some rare cases, an assistant curate, but he believed that the days of two hundred pounds-per-year endowments from the ecclesiastical commissioners for every new church with four thousand or more people had come to an end. The funds must come almost exclusively from the voluntary generosity of the laity.[61]

Ryle had high hopes that the support would come. In his first charge he urged the diocese to create a Twelve Churches Fund to pay for the churches the bishop of Chester's report recommended, and he hoped that the Diocesan Church Aid Society and the Diocesan Church Building Society would each receive an annual income of ten thousand pounds by voluntary subscription. The city raised

---

60. Ryle lauded the use of mission rooms throughout his episcopacy. See the following by Ryle: *A Charge to the Clergy of the Diocese of Liverpool, Delivered in St. Peter's Cathedral, on Tuesday, October 21, 1884, at His Second Visitation* (London: William Hunt, 1884), 16–17; *A Charge Delivered to the Clergy of the Diocese of Liverpool, at His Third Triennial Visitation, in St. Peter's Cathedral, on Thursday, October 27, 1887* (London: William Hunt, 1887), 22–23; *The Opening Address at the Diocesan Conference* (London: William Hunt, 1889), 8–10.

61. Ryle, *Charges Delivered at His Primary Visitation*, 1:18: "But for building new churches, and mission-rooms, and for any large increase of clergy, we must depend on the voluntary help of the laity."

nearly two hundred thousand pounds within five years to found its own bishopric and university, and he believed that it could raise another one hundred thousand pounds for church building if all the churchmen of the diocese "were alive to their responsibility, and made it a duty to give."[62] He urged the wealthy not to forget the spiritual wants of the great city that made them rich, and he reminded them of the spiritual blessings that flow from promoting "true religion" by building and endowing a church. Such offerings pleased the Lord and became a "fountain of blessing" to the city.[63] Additionally, there were temporal blessings for the rich to build a church. Promoting true religion by building and endowing a church was ultimately in their best financial interests. The secret to the nation's or the city's prosperity was the moral condition of its people. Ryle reasoned thus, "The more true religion, the better people! The more good people, the more prosperity!" Therefore the wealthy man who ignored religion and was indifferent to the spiritual condition of the city was guilty of an act of "suicidal folly."[64]

A Cathedral Fit for the Second City

Undoubtedly more living agents and more places of worship were Ryle's top diocesan priorities. In his first charge he listed a third and final "chief want" of the diocese: "a cathedral suited to the

---

62. Ryle, *Charges Delivered at His Primary Visitation*, 1:18.

63. J. C. Ryle, *Seest Thou These Great Buildings?* (London: William Hunt, 1889), 23:

> The weekly religious services inside a new church are only a small part of the benefit it confers on the district in which it is built. Placed in the hands of a clergyman with heart and head in the right place, it becomes an endless fountain of blessing. Sunday schools, district visiting, temperance agencies, home and foreign missions, Bible-classes, and a general increase of the tone of morality, an insensible check on sin in the parish, causing its wheels to drive heavily, a raised standard of brotherly feeling among all ranks,—all these and many other blessed results which I have not time to name, are sooner or later the result of a new church.

64. Ryle, *Charges Delivered at His Primary Visitation*, 1:21.

size and wealth of our Diocese, and to the importance of the second city in Great Britain."[65] Though he was often accused of being opposed to cathedrals, Ryle actually believed that they were excellent in theory. He explained,

> Let the principal town of every diocese have a magnificent church, which in architecture and arrangements shall as much surpass all other churches as a Bishop surpasses a presbyter in his official position!—Let the services of this church be a model to the whole diocese, and let the public prayer, and praise, and preaching be a standing pattern of the highest style of Christian worship!—Let the management of this church be confided to some grave, learned, and eminent clergyman called a Dean, assisted by three or four other clergymen called Canons!—Let these Canons be picked men, selected solely on account of their singular merits, and not for family or political reasons, and famous for deep theological learning, or great preaching power, or wisdom in counsel, or spirituality of life!—Let such a choice body as this Dean and Canons be in intimate and friendly connection with the Bishop, be his right hand and his right eye, his counselors, his helps, his sword, his arrows, and his bow!—Let the cathedral body, so constituted, be the heart, and mainspring, and centre of every good work in the diocese!—Let its members be well paid, well housed, and have no excuse for not residing in the Cathedral Close the greater part of each year!—Let the influence of the cathedral body, as a fountain of spirituality and holiness, be specially felt in the cathedral city!—Let its active usefulness be seen in the energetic management of every sort of diocesan machinery for spreading the Gospel at home and abroad!—Let Deans and Canons be known and read of all men as "burning and shining lights," the very cream and flower of Churchmen, and let the cathedral city in consequence become the ecclesiastical Athens of every

65. Ryle, *Charges Delivered at His Primary Visitation*, 1:22.

diocese, the stronghold of Church influence in the district, and the nursery of theological learning![66]

Liverpool presented a number of serious challenges to the construction of a cathedral. First, unlike other newly created dioceses, Liverpool did not have any existing church buildings that were fit to be cathedrals. Second, given the size, density, and property value of the land, purchasing a site for a cathedral would cost an enormous sum. Ryle estimated that it would cost a quarter of a million pounds before it was finished. Finally, it would be difficult to justify such a tremendous expenditure of money when the diocese's most pressing needs were more clergy and more places of worship. Ryle insisted that he had no objection to cathedrals, and if anyone came forward with a generous offer to build one for the new diocese he said that he would be "deeply grateful." But he insisted that his first and foremost business as chief pastor of the new diocese was to "provide for preaching the Gospel to souls now entirely neglected, whom no cathedral would touch."[67]

Evaluation

Ryle believed that accurate statistics were of the utmost importance in forming an estimate of the diocese's position. Many of his diocesan charges and addresses begin with a statistical summary of the diocese, which is followed by his assessment of the data. In order to evaluate Ryle's diocesan strategy, the data in these addresses, as well as other sources, will be consulted in order to form a just estimate of his diocesan strategy.

Ryle's top diocesan priority was more living agents—ordained ministers of the Word. Table 3 provides a summary of the total number of clergy for the diocese taken from his charges and addresses.

---

66. Ryle, *Charges Delivered at His Primary Visitation*, 1:22–24.
67. Ryle, *Charges Delivered at His Primary Visitation*, 1:25–26.

Table 3. The number of clergy for the diocese of Liverpool 1880–1897

	1880	1884	1887	1895	1897
Incumbents	180	187	200	205	205
Curates	120	170	194	213	220
Total	300	357	394	418	425

By the end of his episcopacy, Ryle added twenty-five incumbents and one hundred stipendiary curates, raising the clergy totals from 300 in 1880 to 425 by 1897. There were two other bright spots as well. First, the number of ordinations increased significantly. Between 1880 and 1887, Ryle ordained 217 deacons. In the seven years before the See was created, only 133 were ordained for the same districts.[68] Second, the clergy were assisted by a growing number of organized lay workers. These included the Scripture readers, Bible-women, and an active Society of Voluntary Lay Helpers. Despite the addition of new living agents and increased lay help, the population of the diocese grew by more than one hundred thousand during Ryle's episcopacy. The supply of new "living agents" and quality lay helpers simply could not keep up with demand. Ryle was never able to achieve the desired ratio of one incumbent for five thousand souls.

He was, however, able to create a pension fund and raise clerical incomes. In 1887, Mrs. Charles Turner donated twenty thousand pounds to establish a pension fund for the benefit of aged and invalid clergy. The fund, which became known as the Turner Pension Fund, continued to be well supported by the diocese after its founding, and its annual income exceeded its requirements. Ryle also oversaw the creation of a Clergy Sustentation Fund to annually supplement the poor incomes and endowments of the diocese, which he regarded as a "gratifying success." By 1897, the annual income of all parishes with a population of more than five thousand had been raised to a minimum of 275 pounds, and those with

---

68. Ryle, *Charge Delivered to the Clergy of the Diocese of Liverpool, at His Third Triennial Visitation*, 18.

less to an income of 235 pounds. He continued to urge the diocese to support the fund after its creation—which it did—and he hoped to see the minimum annual income raised to 300 pounds.

Though the diocese was often criticized for reasons that will be discussed below, with respect to its Turner Pension Fund and Clergy Sustentation Fund, it was regarded as a model. At the time of its founding, there were no other pension funds in existence except in York. Soon, other dioceses followed Liverpool's example. The diocese's Clergy Sustentation Fund proved to be even more popular. It became known simply as the Liverpool Plan, and the creation of a national fund based on the Liverpool Plan was discussed at Church congresses in 1893, 1895, and 1897.

Ryle's other top diocesan priority was building more places of worship. Table 4 provides a summary of new church building during his episcopacy.

Table 4. The total number of new churches built
for the diocese of Liverpool 1880–1900

1884	1885	1886	1887	1889	1890	1894	1895	1897	Total
9	12	15	20	26	27	36	37	42	44

In addition to these new churches, eighty-five new mission rooms were built, and a number of additions and expansions were made to existing churches to increase accommodation. By 1889 the Church provided 196,000 seats: 162,000 in churches and 34,000 in mission rooms. And of these 196,000 seats, 144,000 (73 percent) were free, and only 52,000 were rented.[69] Ryle constantly pointed to the progress of church building and mission room construction as an indication of life and health in his diocesan charges and addresses. Even though he admitted that more needed to be done, he exceeded his initial goal of one new church a year by twenty-four. In no aspect of his diocesan strategy was Ryle more

---

69. Ryle, *Opening Address at the Diocesan Conference*, 13–14.

successful than this. Ryle's successor, Francis Chavasse, declared that one of his greatest legacies was "a magnificent record of the building of Churches and Mission Rooms."[70]

How effective was Ryle's diocesan strategy of more men and more buildings? There are a number of sources of church attendance for mid to late Victorian Liverpool. There are two national religious censuses: the 1851 Religious Census and the Report from the Select Committee of the House of Lords on the Deficient Means of Spiritual Instruction and Places of Divine Worship of 1858. There were two local religious censuses taken in 1853 and 1855 by two prominent Nonconformists, Nathaniel Caine and John Calderwood, which were published in the pro-Liberal *Liverpool Mercury*. The *Liverpool Daily Post* conducted its own religious censuses in 1881, 1891, and 1902 as well.[71] A comparison of the returns of these various religious censuses may shed some light on the effectiveness of Ryle's diocesan strategy.

---

70. Francis James Chavasse, *Address Delivered at the Nineteenth Annual Meeting of the Liverpool Diocesan Conference* (Liverpool: Henstock and Foulkes, 1900), 14.

71. For the sake of space, the merits of these various religious censuses will not be discussed at length. Horace Mann's methodology has been criticized by some and defended by others since the publication of his findings in 1854. Nathaniel Caine and John Calderwood accused Mann of overestimating Church attendance while underestimating chapel attendance, and so they conducted their own censuses in 1853 and 1855. For more recent critiques of Mann, see K. S. Inglis, "Patterns of Religious Worship in 1851," *Journal of Ecclesiastical History* 2 (1960): 78–92; W. Pickering, "The Religious Census of 1851—A Useless Experiment?" *British Journal of Sociology* 18 (1967): 382–407; D. M. Thompson, "The 1851 Religious Census Problems and Possibilities," *Victorian Studies* 11 (1968): 263–80. For Mann's analysis, see "On the Statistical Position of the Religious Bodies in England and Wales," *Journal of the Statistical Society* 18 (1855): 141–59. The religious censuses conducted by the *Liverpool Daily Post* in 1881, 1891, and 1902 have generally been praised by historians for their methodological rigor. But they are not without their faults. For example, they counted attendance only on Sunday morning and evening services, which excluded Sunday afternoon services as well as midweek services. For two excellent surveys of the data, see Walker, "Religious Changes in Liverpool in the Nineteenth Century," 195–211; and Alastair Wilcox, "Church Attendance," in *The Church and the Slums: The Victorian Anglican Church and Its Mission to Liverpool's Poor* (Newcastle-upon-Tyne, U.K.: Cambridge Scholars Publishing, 2014), 40–75.

Table 5. The number of Anglican worshipers in the city of
Liverpool in comparison to the population based on the
1851 Religious Census and the *Liverpool Daily Post*

	1851	1881	1891	1902
Anglican worshipers	69,157	54,551	62,599	67,898
Population of Liverpool	376,065	552,508	617,032	704,134
Percentage of population	18.3	9.8	10.1	9.6

In a recent study on the Church of England's mission to Liverpool's poor, Alastair Wilcox challenges the accuracy of the religious censuses taken by Mann and the *Liverpool Daily Post*.[72] He believes that Mann's figures were inflated by the inclusion of children and clerical errors and prefers Caine and Calderwood's census of 1855, which suggested that attendance in parish churches was considerably lower than Mann's estimate. It is worth noting, however, that in 1853 the returns of Caine and Calderwood's first religious census yielded similar results to Mann's. At the very least this reveals that the clergymen were consistent in their accounting. Furthermore, he believes that the *Liverpool Daily Post* underestimated attendance at parish churches in 1881 and 1891 due to some critical omissions and discrepancies in counting children and mission services. Table 6 presents Wilcox's adjusted data.[73]

---

72. Wilcox, *Church and the Slums*, 42–57.

73. It should be noted that Wilcox utilizes the census data of 1851 in calculating the percentage of the population in 1855. This is a mistake. The population of the city of Liverpool grew from 376,065 in 1851 to 462,749 in 1861—an increase of 86,684. Thus, during that decade the population grew by an average of 8,668 people every year. This would place the population of the city around 410,738 in 1855, which would mean that the population of Anglican worshipers should be 10.9 percent instead of 11.9 percent.

Table 6. Alastair Wilcox's adjusted data on Anglican
worshipers as a percentage of Liverpool's population

	1851	1855	1881	1891	1902
Anglican worshipers	69,157	44,842	55,803	74,660	67,898
Population of Liverpool	376,065	376,065	552,508	617,032	704,134
Percentage of population	18.3	11.9	10.1	12.1	9.6

Interpreting the data from the various religious censuses is fraught with difficulties. The different counting methods regarding children, as well as afternoon and mission services, make meaningful comparison difficult. Denominational and political rivalries must not be discounted either.[74] Despite these difficulties, some trends can be discerned. First, in the decades between the Religious Census of 1851 and Ryle's appointment, worship attendance in parish churches was declining. If Mann was correct, that drop was drastic: the Church of England was losing worshipers both relative to the population and absolutely. If Caine and Calderwood were correct, the decline was more gradual or more plateau-like. Perhaps the truth is somewhere in the middle. Second, by the end of Ryle's first decade as bishop, the Church was reclaiming lost ground. If the unadjusted returns of the *Liverpool Daily Post* are correct, attendance in parish churches rose by more than eight thousand and grew relative to the population (.3 percent). If Wilcox is correct, however, that growth

---

74. The disestablishment movement was building momentum during the 1850s, and church attendance played an important role in discussions about the Church rates and the principle of establishment. When the returns of Caine and Calderwood's first census (1853) seemed to confirm Mann's findings, they suspected that incumbents inflated their numbers. So in their next census (1855), they sent their own census takers to estimate attendance, and they returned with significantly different numbers. Abraham Hume dismissed their findings and later conducted his own census of religious profession in 1881, which found that 53 percent of Liverpudlians considered themselves to be churchmen.

is even more remarkable: 18,857 and 2 percent.[75] This growth coincided with the building boom of Ryle's episcopacy. Twenty-eight of the forty-four (64 percent) new churches and sixty-one of the eighty-five (72 percent) new mission rooms that were built during Ryle's episcopacy were completed by 1891.

This growth also coincided with the largest increase of living agents. Of the 125 new clergymen added during Ryle's episcopacy, at least ninety-four (75 percent) were added during the first decade. Third, during the second decade of Ryle's episcopacy, attendance began to decline. If the unadjusted returns are correct, attendance rose by more than five thousand, but the Church was unable to keep up with the growth of the population. But if Wilcox is correct, attendance declined both relative to the population and absolutely. This decline also coincided with the slowing of church building and the appointment of new living agents. With the exception of 1893, when five new churches were built, only one new church was built each year after 1891. Mission room licensing slowed during the same period: only twenty-four were licensed after 1890.[76] The deployment of new living agents slowed as well: only five new incumbents and twenty-six new curates were added after 1887.

While it is impossible to prove causation, the data seems to suggest Ryle's strategy may have been sounder than some of his critics would allow. At the very least, it must be admitted that attendance at parish churches in Liverpool began to increase during Ryle's episcopacy and even kept pace with the explosive growth of the population for the first decade—the time when Ryle's diocesan strategy was being the most fully implemented. It is also noteworthy that during Ryle's episcopacy, attendance at parish

---

75. Wilcox attributes the spike in attendance to the inclusion of children and mission room services. This explanation is insufficient. As noted above, there were twenty-eight new churches and sixty-one new mission rooms in 1891. Moreover, many mission services were held during the week and thus would not have been included in these census returns.

76. Farley, *J. C. Ryle, First Bishop of Liverpool*, 112.

churches increased at a greater rate (24.4 percent) than the four largest Dissenting denominations (16.1 percent).[77] Even so, by the end of Ryle's episcopacy, fewer Liverpudlians attended a parish church than they did in 1851 according to Mann's calculations.

Was Ryle able to bring the working classes of Liverpool into the fold of the Church of England? Determining the level of working-class participation from the various religious censuses of Ryle's episcopacy is challenging at best. It was not unusual to find the middle classes worshiping in working-class parish churches. Determining the class percentages of a gathered congregation is a rather subjective endeavor, and clothing tended to be the typical class indicator. Furthermore, the working classes frequently attended mission services held on Sunday afternoon or during the week and thus were not counted by the various censuses that focused on Sunday morning and Sunday evening attendance. Thus, working-class attendance is often higher than the returns suggest.

Wilcox's research sheds some light on this question. He identified eight known working-class parishes and followed their attendance figures through the religious censuses of 1881, 1891, and 1902.

Table 7. Attendance at eight working-class parish churches 1881–1902

Parish	1881			1891			1902		
	a.m.	p.m.	total	a.m.	p.m.	total	a.m.	p.m.	total
All Souls	109	75	184	54	132	186	65	162	227
St. Alban	30	49	79	51	134	185	57	140	197
St. Bartholomew	81	115	196	67	73	140	171	350	521
St. Matthias	114	196	310	70	140	210	73	154	227
St. Nathaniel	879	1,196	2,075	827	962	1,789	320	885	1,205
St. Stephen	150	449	599	119	120	239	25	62	87
St. Anne	14	45	59	56	115	171	53	87	140
Holy Trinity	380	250	630	430	410	840	349	650	999

77. The four largest Dissenting denominations were the Presbyterians, Methodists, Congregationalists, and Baptists.

According to Wilcox's sample, attendance in half these working-class parish churches continually increased from 1881 to 1902, while only two experienced continual decline during the same period. One parish saw an increase in attendance in 1891 but then saw a decrease in 1902, while two parishes saw decreases in attendance in 1891 but then experienced increased attendance in 1902. The results of the censuses seem to suggest that in some parishes the Church of England was able to attract the working classes, while in others it was less successful. The censuses, however, do not tell the whole story.

There was a steady rise in confirmations during Ryle's episcopacy. In his first year he confirmed 4,719 young people; in 1896 he confirmed 8,300. Ryle typically confirmed seven to eight thousand children every year from 1890 onward. In total, he confirmed more than 133,000 children. There was also a rise in Sunday school attendance. In 1884 he estimated that there were roughly 40,000 children in Church Sunday schools. By 1887, that number rose to 69,776. By the end of his first decade as bishop, the number of Sunday school scholars topped 100,000. Reaching the young was a top priority. It was a good investment for the future, and it was a means to bring in the working classes. Ryle believed that working-class parents could often be reached through their children, which is why he regarded the Church's expanding ministry to children to be so important. He regarded the rise in the number of confirmations and Sunday school attendance to be one of the most positive developments of his episcopacy.

Ryle also encouraged the use of mission services to reach the masses.[78] In 1890 he told his clergy, "All well-conducted Missions have my entire approval."[79] He respected and supported the evan-

---

78. It should be remembered that Ryle himself was a pioneer in this respect and one of the founders of the special services for the working classes in 1857.

79. J. C. Ryle, *Thoughts about a Mission* (London: William Hunt, 1890), 1. According to Ryle, a successful mission should give people a new sense of the value of their soul and the importance of saving it. It promotes repentance, faith, and practical

gelist Edward Sunners.[80] Sunners was an uneducated, illiterate, combative drunkard who became converted through the influence of a Christian coworker. He joined a Wesleyan chapel, learned to read, and began conducting cottage services and well-attended open-air meetings. His main work was tract distribution, and Ryle happily kept his supplies full. Ryle knew him well and encouraged others to follow his example to promote the gospel. Ryle also supported Dwight L. Moody's mission of 1883, which conducted services in Liverpool from April 1 to 27. Though Ryle did not attend, he spoke highly of Moody, held up his direct and lively preaching as a model to his clergy, praised the soundness of his message, and said an opening prayer for Moody's mission in London in June of 1884.

Ryle helped plan a citywide mission in Liverpool that was held in 1894. He handpicked the planning committee and preached the opening and closing sermons of the mission. By all accounts the mission was remarkably successful. Seventy-three churches participated. There were special services for men, women, and children. Special choirs led the worship. Sunday attendance was particularly high. At the diocesan conference the following year, Ryle admitted that the mission "far surpassed [his] expectations" and that its success was a "cause of deep thankfulness."[81] One attendee, an assistant curate at the time, later recalled, "During the nine days that it lasted the church (Walton Parish Church) was well filled, sometimes crowded, every day; and a deep impression was made on the hearts and minds of many who attended. The same was the

---

holiness. It leads to more Bible reading, prayer, Sabbath keeping, and regular participation in the Lord's Supper. As a successful missioner himself, Ryle offered four hints to help promote successful missions. First, pray for the Spirit's blessing before the mission begins. Second, personally attend the services and encourage others to do so as well. Third, invite opponents to attend and hear the services for themselves. Finally, after the service is over, pray regularly for God's blessing upon it.

80. See Johnson Simpson, *Edward Sunners: The Liverpool Cabmen's Missionary, His Life and Work* (Liverpool: Adam Holden, 1886).

81. J. C. Ryle, *What Is Wanted? The Opening Address at the Fourteenth Liverpool Diocesan Conference, November 5, 1895* (London: William Hunt, 1895), 7.

case in other churches also, and there can be no doubt that the mission did much to forward the cause of religion in Liverpool and elsewhere."[82] More than thirty years after Ryle's death, the mission was still considered a significant spiritual event.[83]

Ryle's personal example is noteworthy as well. When he was not preaching, he attended St. Nathaniel's, an exclusively working-class parish church. He urged his clergy to promote sympathy between classes and sought to model this for them. The heart of his personal evangelistic strategy was constantly preaching the simple gospel message.[84] He preached throughout his episcopacy. For example, in 1887 he calculated that he had preached at least 650 times for his clergy in the past seven years. He continued to preach regularly (usually twice a week) up through his eighty-third birthday in 1899. His preaching often drew large working-class audiences. For example, in 1882, one evangelical magazine noted:

> In every part of his diocese this preaching prelate has pro-claimed the gospel message now for more than eighteen months, and especially in those portions where the lapsed masses reside, and where, alas! the churches are to a great extent deserted. It is a matter of common knowledge that in every case these very churches have been crowded—the church of two thousand seats, with its scanty fifty or one hundred of a regular congregation, being unequal to receive

---

82. J. B. Lancelot and J. W. Tyrer, "A History of the Diocese: 1880–1930," *Liverpool Diocesan Review* 5, no. 7 (1930): 243.

83. Farley, *J. C. Ryle, First Bishop of Liverpool*, 120.

84. J. C. Ryle, *The City: or, The Sight Which Stirred St. Paul* (London: William Hunt, 1882), 22:

> The grand subject of our teaching in every place ought to be Jesus Christ. However learned or however unlearned, however high-born or however humble our audience, Christ crucified—Christ—Christ—Christ—crucified, rising, interceding, redeeming, pardoning, receiving, saving—Christ must be the grand theme of our teaching. We shall never mend this Gospel. We shall never find any other subject which will do so much good. We must sow as St. Paul sowed, if we would reap as St. Paul reaped.

those who would enter—by the very people who, *as a rule*, never enter the sanctuary.[85]

He was regarded as one of the few preachers who could "attract, arrest, and retain great masses of the poor."[86] Herbert, Ryle's son, offered a noteworthy description of his father's funeral: "The grave-yard was crowded with poor people who had come in carts and vans and buses to pay the last honours to the old man—who certainly had won their love."[87]

What about the construction of a cathedral? The progress of the cathedral, or the lack thereof, can be traced in Ryle's charges in addresses. In 1884 Ryle referred to the subject as "thorny" and "troublesome."[88] A committee had been formed two years earlier, and they selected two potential sites for the cathedral—both cemeteries—after much heated debate, but beyond that, there was no progress. Two years later, at the annual diocesan conference (1886), Ryle informed his clergy that there was little to no progress to report with respect to the cathedral. The diocese was still waiting on construction plans in the form of a report from the Royal Society of Architects, but it was delayed. The question of funding continued to loom large. In his third triennial charge (1887), Ryle urged his clergy not to make an idol of a cathedral; more clergy and more buildings remained the greatest needs of the diocese. He noted that a cathedral would be an asset to the diocese, however, and he remarked that it looked doubtful if they would ever get one. In 1889 Ryle opened the diocesan conference with a discussion of the progress of the cathedral. He said that it was not dead, but it

85. Archdeacon John W. Bardsley, "The Non-Church-Going: How Can Our Churches Reach Them?," in *The Christian Monthly and Family Treasure for 1882* (London: T. Nelson and Sons, 1882), 139.

86. *Christian Monthly and Family Treasure for 1882*, 139.

87. Fitzgerald, *Memoir of Herbert Edward Ryle*, 135.

88. J. C. Ryle, *A Charge to the Clergy of the Diocese of Liverpool, Delivered in St. Peter's Cathedral, on Tuesday, October 21, 1884, at His Second Visitation* (London: William Hunt, 1884), 40.

was sitting "on the shelf and sleeps for the present."[89] He admitted that this was a humbling failure, and he was not surprised by the criticism from those who were not acquainted with the difficulties of the diocese.

In the place of a cathedral, he urged the diocese to build a diocesan church house that would be practically useful to the diocese. It should be large, commodious, and centrally located. It should house the diocesan registry and offices for the registrar, which would finally make the new diocese independent of Chester. It should contain offices for the bishop to conduct interviews and licensing, as well as two large rooms for committee meetings and consistory court. It should also serve as headquarters for diocesan institutions and societies. He wanted a large reading room to be included that would contain a diocesan theological library. He estimated that the cost of a church house would be twenty thousand pounds, which was only a fraction of what a cathedral would cost.[90]

At the diocesan conference of 1895, Ryle mentioned the cathedral only in passing. He mentioned the frequent criticisms of it, the desirability of it, but the lack of adequate funds. In 1897 Ryle urged the diocese to abandon plans for a cathedral. The diocese simply could not agree on a site and could not raise the money. Instead, he urged the diocese to build a more practical and useful building—a central church house to conduct diocesan business. Construction on what became the Victoria Church House began in 1897. Ryle believed it would strengthen the Church of England in the diocese, promote unity, bring the clergy together, and facilitate diocesan business.[91]

Clearly the cathedral project was a disaster, but how much blame should Ryle shoulder? Ian Farley argues that the failure of the cathedral project was largely out of his control.[92] It wasn't

---

89. Ryle, *Opening Address at the Diocesan Conference*, 4.
90. Ryle, *Opening Address at the Diocesan Conference*, 6–7.
91. Ryle, *Thoughts for Thinkers*, 7–9.
92. Farley, *J. C. Ryle, First Bishop of Liverpool*, 176–81.

until 1882 that the original Bishopric Committee decided that the founding of a cathedral was outside its scope and turned it over to the diocese. Once the diocese formed its own committee, it was plagued by delays. Site selection proved to be one of the biggest and most contentious challenges. Neither of the cemeteries that were the two major options happened to be a favorite with Ryle. The champions of each site contended vigorously for their cause. For example, T. W. Christie, a Liverpool doctor whose wife was buried on one of the proposed sites, accused Ryle of mutilating the body of Christ and taking the side with the devil if he consented to the St. James Cemetery site.[93] Even after the committee reached a decision, the debate continued, as many churchmen simply refused to accept the decision. Ryle's archdeacon and personal friend, Joseph Bardsley, led the opposition, which caused further delay. Ultimately the unpopular site had to be abandoned because it proved ill-suited for the erection of the proposed structure. Choosing a design was a lengthy and time-consuming process that was plagued by delays as well. And then there was the cost. It was estimated that it would cost five hundred thousand pounds, which was twice Ryle's initial estimate. Ryle gave one thousand pounds for the project, but by 1888 only fifteen thousand pounds had been raised.

Ryle was never against the cathedral, as some have suggested.[94] He championed its cause and took an active role in the various steps of the failed process. He remained hopeful that a wealthy merchant might make a princely gift and fund the entire project, but that gift never came. More men and more churches were undoubtedly higher diocesan priorities, but that certainly does not mean he was against the project altogether. It should be noted that Ryle was not the only bishop to find cathedral building a challenge in Liverpool.

---

93. Farley, *J. C. Ryle, First Bishop of Liverpool*, 179.

94. Even Peter Toon suggests that Ryle did not really want a cathedral. He writes, "Had Ryle really believed that it was right to erect a cathedral he would surely have raised the money and carried the committee with him." Toon and Smout, *John Charles Ryle*, 86.

The Liverpool Cathedral was finally completed in October 1978 during the episcopacy of David Sheppard, the sixth bishop of Liverpool.

In the final analysis, how effective was Ryle's diocesan strategy? Some of his contemporaries regarded it as a complete failure. In a speech before the House of Commons, W. E. Gladstone voiced his displeasure with the diocese, saying: "We have recently had a certain number of religious Censuses in the large towns, and it is impossible to go through these Censuses without a sentiment of pain. Some of them disclose a state of things that is disgraceful to the country. The religious Census of Liverpool, I do not hesitate to say, is a disgrace to Liverpool and to the country generally."[95]

The *Liverpool Review* was even more critical: "Dr. Ryle is simply about the most disastrous episcopal failure ever inflicted upon a long-suffering diocese.... He is nothing better than a political fossil, who has been very unwisely unearthed from his rural obscurity for no better purpose apparently than to make the episcopacy ridiculous."[96]

Such criticism was undoubtedly unfair. During Ryle's episcopacy, 125 new clergymen were added to the diocese's ministerial ranks; 44 new churches and 85 new mission rooms were built; the percentage of free seating rose to nearly 75 percent; confirmations, ordinations, and Sunday school attendance rose dramatically; a successful citywide mission was held in 1894; and the Victoria Church House was built. In 1895 Liverpool could boast that it was the only diocese in England that had a pension fund, sustentation fund, and mission room in every district.[97] Ryle was also concerned about an array of social issues facing the diocese.[98] It is worth

---

95. *Hansards's Parliamentary Debates* (London: Cornelius Buck, 1884), 292–360. For Ryle's response to Gladstone's comments, see *Charge to the Clergy of the Diocese of Liverpool*, 25–37.

96. *Liverpool Review*, November 21, 1885, as quoted in Farley, *J. C. Ryle, First Bishop of Liverpool*, 236.

97. *The Official Report of the Church Congress Held at Norwich* (London: Bemrose and Sons, 1895), 226.

98. See Farley, *J. C. Ryle, First Bishop of Liverpool*, 123–64.

noting, at least in passing, that the Liverpool historian Ramsay Muir described Ryle as a leader who was "never slack to encourage the labours of social progress."[99] He championed the cause of temperance, elementary education, and Sabbath observance in the diocese. All this was achieved as secularism began to change the religious landscape of Great Britain.

Recent evaluations of Ryle's episcopacy have been more favorable. Alastair Wilcox says that it is impossible to deny that, in terms of attracting a number of adherents through the provision of much-needed social ancillary services, the diocese was considerably stronger.[100] And R. B. Walker argues that by the end of Ryle's episcopacy, the diocese was stronger than ever before in its array of churches, clergy, and dedicated lay workers.[101] Though Wilcox and Walker are right, they probably do not go far enough. Though it is often unnoticed, Ryle's diocesan strategy actually worked when it was implemented. Church attendance rose in the first decade of his episcopacy when the majority of the new living agents were deployed and new places of worship were built. The failure of the cathedral project and the imprisonment of James Bell Cox (which will be discussed below) tend to overshadow this important fact. These failures also may have negatively impacted Ryle's ability to raise money, which may have contributed, in some degree, to the slowing of sending out new ministers and building new buildings. But the role Ryle played in both diocesan crises hardly amounts to mismanagement. When all relevant factors are taken into consideration, Ryle's diocesan strategy appears both sound and effective.

The Bishop and the Church

As a bishop of a national church, Ryle believed it was his duty to take an interest in Church affairs outside his own diocese.

---

99. Muir, *History of Liverpool*, 329.

100. Wilcox, *Church and the Slums*, 218.

101. Walker, "Religious Changes in Liverpool in the Nineteenth Century," 208.

Therefore, in nearly every diocesan address, he discussed matters affecting the entire Church as well as the diocese. Though he spoke on a wide variety of issues throughout his episcopacy, there were a number of churchwide issues that were of perennial concern. The most pressing were disestablishment, the growing dislike of dogmatic Christianity, the growing acceptance of Old Testament criticism, and the continued spread of ritualism.

Disestablishment

The establishment survived the assaults of Edward Miall and the Liberation Society in the early 1870s. In many respects the Church was stronger in 1880 than it was when the crisis began. Ryle did not believe the storm had passed, however. In his first charge as the new bishop of the diocese, he told the diocese that the chief external danger facing the Church of England came from the Liberation Society.[102] They may have been unsuccessful in the past, but they were undeterred. Churchmen should prepare for new assaults.

The first major new offensive came as a result of the passage of the Third Reform Act of 1884, which extended the franchise by almost two million to all men who paid an annual rent of ten pounds or owned land valued at the same amount. The liberationists, who disestablished the Irish church after the passage of the Second Reform Act, sought to achieve a similar victory in the general election of 1885 by making disestablishment part of the Liberal Party platform and a litmus test for all Liberal candidates. The year 1885 was an anxious one for churchmen, but the threat soon passed. Though many churchmen, including Ryle, believed Gladstone supported disestablishment, he did not. He pledged not to support English or Scottish disestablishment later in 1885.[103] Furthermore, his conversion to Irish home rule injured the cause of disestablishment in that year. It eclipsed all other issues, weakened

---

102. Ryle, *Charges Delivered at His Primary Visitation*, 1:30.

103. Bentley, "Transformation of the Evangelical Party in the Church of England," 45.

the Liberal Party, and destroyed much of the political power of Dissent.[104] Unlike in 1868, the Church was prepared and united to form strong defense as well.

The second and last assault on the establishment that took place during Ryle's episcopacy began in earnest in 1893. Gladstone's conversion to home rule in Ireland spurred nationalism in Wales and gave rise to a strenuous campaign to disestablish the Welsh church.[105] A tithe war erupted in 1888 and lasted until 1890. Many Welshmen refused to pay their tithe, and as a result, many clergymen were nearly starved. The Tithe Act of 1891, which transferred the payment of the tithe from the tenant to the landlord, eased tension temporarily, but new attempts at disestablishment soon followed. The first was the introduction of the Welsh Suspensory Bill to the House of Commons in February 1893. It would suspend any further appointments to the Church of England in Wales, and when there were vacancies, the property and finances previously allocated for those offices would be devoted to Welsh national purposes. An even more straightforward bill, the Welsh Disestablishment Bill, was introduced in the following year. This bill would disestablish the Church in Wales, as the Irish Church Act of 1869 disestablished the Church in Ireland, but it would go even further by disendowing it and confiscating its property. The radical nature of the bill aroused intense opposition from churchmen of all schools of thought, and conservatives returned a large majority in the general election of 1895.

Ryle's response to these two disestablishment crises was predictable. He urged his clergy to unite and fight to the bitter end. He called on them to petition Parliament, circulate cheap literature, use every available means to answer objections, pursue Church reform, and oppose the efforts of Romanizers to deprotestantize the Church. He offered few new arguments for the establishment,

---

104. Chadwick, *Victorian Church*, 2:437.
105. Chadwick, *Victorian Church*, 2:436.

though he published a number of works on the subject and addressed it regularly in his diocesan charges and addresses.[106] Most of these consisted of repurposed old material published under new titles.[107] For example, the *Disestablishment Papers*, which Ryle sent to every incumbent prior to the diocesan conference of 1885, were essentially *What Good Will It Do?* broken up into ten short tracts. His primary concern, as before, was the negative practical consequences that would flow from disestablishment. The only novel feature of Ryle's episcopal campaign against the disestablishment movement was the new platform his office provided. Unsurprisingly, he took full advantage of it, and the diocese seemed to follow his lead. For example, in 1896, after the attempt to disestablish the Welsh church failed, he remarked, "The enemies of the Church entirely miscalculated their own strength, and the defenders were no less surprised by the amount of support which they received in almost every quarter, from north to south and from east to west, and nowhere more than in Lancashire."[108]

Decay of Doctrinal Religion

While disestablishment was a source of trouble during Ryle's episcopacy, growing opposition to doctrinal, or dogmatic, Christianity concerned him as well. Following this subject in his diocesan charges and addresses is quite revealing. He discussed this decline in 1881,

---

106. See the following by Ryle: *Churchmen and Dissenters*; "Church and Dissent," and "Disestablishment," in *Principles for Churchmen*; *Disestablishment Papers*; *I Am a Churchman! And Why?*; and *Thoughts on the Prayer Book and on Church and Dissent*. Also, see his charges and addresses in the following years: 1881, 1884–1885, 1893–1896, and 1898. These can be found in J. C. Ryle, *Charges and Addresses* (Edinburgh: Banner of Truth, 1978).

107. There is one possible exception. In his last published diocesan address, "The Present Distress" (1898), Ryle called for the creation of a qualified body of lectures to spread information about English Church history. He insisted that they be impartial and tell the story of the Church of England, warts and all. He believed a body of capable and honest lecturers might "spread much light, and dispel a vast amount of ignorance which now exists." Ryle, *Present Distress*, 8–10.

108. J. C. Ryle, *About Our Church in 1896* (London: William Hunt, 1896), 4.

1883, and then in nearly every address after 1886. A comparison of his early and later addresses is even more illuminating. For example, in the second charge of his primary visitation (1881), he told his clergy that he was not afraid of "revived infidelity" that scoffs at the Bible and denies the existence of God and the reality of judgment. But by the Liverpool Diocesan Conference of 1894, he sorrowfully acknowledged that "infidelity abounds" and that "many openly sneer at the Bible as an old-fashioned, defective book, and give God no place in their thoughts."[109] Ryle was not being excessively pessimistic in 1894. Secularism made significant progress in the 1880s. It was during this decade that the conflict between Christianity and reason reached its climax, an atheist (Charles Bradlaugh) was allowed to sit in Parliament, and the Church began to decline absolutely.[110] It was followed by the "naughty nineties," which were characterized by a relaxing of moral values and religious indifference.

The substance of Ryle's response to this "downgrade in theology" differed little from his earlier works. Most of the arguments he made in his charges and addresses can be found in *Dogma* (1878), but at least three new emphases can be detected. First, there was a new sense of urgency that coincided with the progress of the downgrade. He spoke of it as "a great danger" and "a black cloud," and he described the Church's condition as "perilous" as a result of it. The titles of his addresses that speak to this issue are even more ominous: *Are We in Danger?* (1888), *The Present Crisis* (1892), *Buy a Sword!* (1893), *Watchman, What of the Night?* (1894), and *The Present Distress* (1898). Second, there was a decidedly clerical emphasis. This is hardly surprising coming from a bishop, but it is noteworthy nonetheless. For example, in this third triennial charge of 1887, he warned of "low, meager, defective, and

109. Cf. Ryle, *Charges Delivered at His Primary Visitation*, 2:31; with Ryle, *Watchman, What of the Night?*, 19.

110. See Chadwick, *Victorian Church*, 2:112–50, especially 232–33. Here Chadwick argues that 1886 represented a turning point, which coincides with Ryle's increased concern about the decay of doctrinal Christianity.

imperfect statement of Bible truth in the pulpit" and addressed its causes and consequences.[111] Third, he regularly raised the issue of Church comprehensiveness and toleration. Ryle repeatedly insisted that neither he nor the evangelical school had any desire to narrow the established limits of comprehension (the Thirty-Nine Articles, creeds, and prayer book) or drive out all other schools of thought from the Church's pale. Comprehension and toleration, however, must have its limits. A clergyman who denied the Trinity, the deity of Christ, the person and work of the Spirit, the inspiration and authority of Scripture, or justification by faith had "no right to occupy our pulpits and reading desks."[112]

Perhaps the best example of Ryle's response to the theological downgrade of the 1880s and 1890s is *Hold Fast*, which was his charge to the diocese at his fourth triennial visitation in 1890.[113] In this address he said nothing about the condition of the diocese, which was how he typically opened visitation charges and diocesan conference addresses. Instead, he wanted to address his clergy about the "dangerous character" of the times in which they lived. The political, social, and ecclesiastical horizon looked black, and worst of all was the religious climate.[114] Ryle charged his clergy to "hold fast" to Christian doctrine, and he listed and discussed a number of its cardinal points. First, he charged them to hold fast the great principle that Christianity is entirely true and the only religion that God has revealed to humanity. It is somewhat telling that he felt compelled to make this point at all. Second, he charged them to hold fast to the authority, supremacy, and divine

---

111. Ryle, *Charge Delivered to the Clergy of the Diocese of Liverpool at His Third Triennial Visitation*, 57–66.

112. Ryle, *About Our Church in 1896*, 39.

113. See J. C. Ryle, *Hold Fast* (London: William Hunt, 1890).

114. Ryle, *Hold Fast*, 4: "The air seems filled with vague agnosticism and unbelief. Faith languishes and dwindles everywhere, and looks ready to die. The immense majority of men, from the highest to the lowest, appear to think that nothing is certain in religion, and that it does not signify much what you believe.... All the foundations of faith are out of course."

inspiration of the whole Bible. Third, he charged them to hold fast to the old doctrine of the sinfulness of sin and the corruption of human nature. Fourth, he charged them to hold fast to the great foundational principle of Scripture and our Church, that forgiveness of sins is given to people only through the atoning death of Jesus Christ on the cross. Fifth, he charged them to hold fast sound and scriptural views of the Holy Ghost. Sixth, he charged them to hold fast to the old doctrine of the Church about the two sacraments. Seventh, he charged them to hold fast to the old doctrine of the Church of England about the sanctity and right observance of the Sabbath day. Finally, he urged them to hold fast to the teaching of Scripture and the prayer book about the state of humanity after death. In conclusion, Ryle acknowledged that some would regard his prescription as being "some mere dry statement of fossilized theological points, unworthy of the nineteenth century." But, he said, "The dark days of sorrow, the sick-bed, the death-bed, and above all the day of judgment, will teach us all in a few years whether the old-fashioned theology which men are so fond of decrying in 1890, is a thing to be despised."[115]

Herbert Edward Ryle and Old Testament Criticism

The growth and gradual acceptance of Old Testament criticism was one of the most concerning churchwide issues of Ryle's episcopacy. In 1889 a group of influential high and broad churchmen joined hands and published *Lux Mundi*, which was an "attempt to put the Catholic faith into its right relation to modern intellectual and moral problems."[116] A small controversy erupted in the following years, but it paled in comparison to *Essays and Reviews*. In the year before its publication, however, one of Ryle's examining chaplains had to step down from his position for embracing Old Testament criticism. It was his second and favorite son, Herbert Edward Ryle.

---

115. Ryle, *Hold Fast*, 29.
116. Gore, Lux Mundi: *A Series of Studies in the Religion on the Incarnation*, vii.

Herbert was born in 1856 while his father ministered in Helm-ingham.[117] His mother died three years later, and he was raised by his stepmother, Henrietta Clowes. Like his father, he attended Eton College, beginning in 1868, and from there proceeded to King's College, Cambridge, in 1875. During his time at King's, he adopted critical views of the Old Testament. As a result of a sporting injury, he was forced to take an aegrotat degree in 1879, but in the following years (1879–1881) he won every distinction open to students of theology, including first-class honors in the theological tripos in 1881. He was elected a fellow of King's in 1881 and became intimate friends of Brooke Foss Westcott and Fenton John Anthony Hort. Herbert also served as an examining chaplain to his father from 1883 to 1887, until it became obvious that their differences over Old Testament criticism proved too great for them to work together in this capacity. In 1887 he was appointed to the prestigious Hulsean Professorship of Divinity at Cambridge, which allowed him to fulfill his life's calling, which was "to commend to successive generations of theological students at Cambridge the methods and the more assured results of what is known as the High Criticism of the Old Testament."[118] Through his teaching and publishing,[119] as well as his

117. For a biography of Hebert Edward Ryle, see Fitzgerald, *Memoir of Herbert Edward Ryle.*

118. Fitzgerald, *Memoir of Herbert Edward Ryle,* 45, 77.

119. See Herbert Edward Ryle, *Psalms of the Pharisees, Commonly Called the Psalms of Solomon* (Cambridge: Cambridge University Press, 1891); *The Canon of the Old Testament: An Essay on the Gradual Growth and Formation of the Hebrew Canon of Scripture* (London: Macmillan, 1892); *The Early Narratives of Genesis: A Brief Introduction to the Study of Genesis I–XI* (London: Macmillan, 1892); *The Books of Ezra and Nehemiah* (London: C. J. Clay and Sons, 1893); *Philo and Holy Scripture* (London: Macmillan, 1895); *On Holy Scripture and Criticism: Addresses and Sermons* (London: Macmillan, 1904); *On the Church of England: Addresses and Sermons* (London: Macmillan, 1904); *The Book of Genesis* (Cambridge: Cambridge University Press, 1914). Herbert also gave a number of addresses on Old Testament criticism at various Church congresses. See the official report of the Church congresses held at Rhyl (1891); Exeter (1894); London (1899); and Newcastle-upon-Tyne (1900).

connection to his father,[120] Herbert became an influential church-man. By 1898 he was regarded as one of the leaders of the liberal evangelicals, or moderate party, in the Church of England.

Herbert's views on the Old Testament and the value of criti-cism stand in stark contrast to his father's. He believed that modern advances in the study of Semitic languages, the history of the ancient Near East, and comparative religion had rendered traditional views of the Old Testament and the doctrine of ple-nary verbal inspiration untenable.[121] Modern people expect "juster statements of truth respecting the books of the Old Testament from modern study."[122] These "juster statements" included the acknowledgment of three conclusions, which Herbert argued were universally recognized by the best critical scholars of the Old Tes-tament. First, the narrative books of the Old Testament, along with a number of prophetical books, were not written by a single author but developed gradually over time as an editor or editors compiled material from multiple sources in order to meet the spiritual needs of the nation of Israel at a given point in time. Second, in terms of their origin and character, the books of the Old Testament were "merely human." They were no different from other books written in the same era. They often borrowed material wholesale from a variety of sources, and they were not elevated in either historical accuracy or in scientific conception above the intellectual stan-dards of their day.[123] Third, there was no ground for believing that the books of the Old Testament were regarded as sacred from the time of their composition nor for supposing that they were written

---

120. Herbert's biographer noted that his name and connection to his father, who was trusted and respected in evangelical circles, "won for him a hearing which might have been denied to others." He specifically mentioned Samuel Rolles Driver as an example. See Fitzgerald, *Memoir of Herbert Edward Ryle*, 92.

121. Herbert referred to his father's position as a "mockery of interpretation" and compared it to second-century Gnosticism and medieval Roman Catholicism.

122. Herbert Edward Ryle, *On Holy Scripture and Criticism*, 19.

123. Herbert Edward Ryle, *On Holy Scripture and Criticism*, 24.

for the purpose of contributing to form an authoritative canon.[124] In short, the canon of the Old Testament Scriptures developed gradually over time to meet the spiritual needs of Israel.

Herbert acknowledged that the result of modern criticism had shaken the faith of many people, but he argued that this did not need to be the case. Literary criticism of the Old Testament never touched its eternal, spiritual message, which must be discerned by the eyes of faith. The Old Testament is not identical to the word of God, but it contains and embodies it, and through it God speaks to people's hearts. Far from shaking faith, criticism should actually assure it, and he pointed out a number of gains as well as losses. First, criticism had clarified the Church's teaching on the inspiration of Scripture. Inspiration does not consist of an imaginary, supernatural method of communication but "in that spiritual force" that makes Scripture "God's word to men's hearts."[125] Second, criticism would strengthen apologetics. The old method of attacking the truthfulness of Christianity—that is, pointing out contradictions, flaws, and errors of a supposedly inspired Bible—is neutralized when imperfections are admitted and inspiration is redefined. Third, criticism had recovered the primary focus of the Old Testament—the religious instruction and discipline of the nation of Israel. Fourth, criticism had revealed the essential value of the Prophets. When seen in their proper historical, political, and social light, they cease to be "mysterious oracles" but "burn anew with living fire," which shed light on modern political and social issues.[126] Finally, criticism had rendered a universal service by its systematic treatment of Old Testament theology. It had enabled people to discern through the successive periods of Old Testament literature how the Spirit of God had brought about a continuous evolution of spiritual thought that culminated with the manifestation of our divine Lord.[127]

---

124. Herbert Edward Ryle, *On Holy Scripture and Criticism*, 27.

125. Herbert Edward Ryle, *On Holy Scripture and Criticism*, 34.

126. Herbert Edward Ryle, *On Holy Scripture and Criticism*, 39–40.

127. Herbert Edward Ryle, *On Holy Scripture and Criticism*, 40–41.

Herbert was not unaware of objections to his position, and he occasionally addressed them in his writings. Though he never mentioned his father by name, the objections he discussed are the same ones his father raised in his works against Old Testament criticism.[128] The two most important will be discussed. The first objection is that modern criticism undermines the doctrine of inspiration. Or put another way, How can the presence of errors, inaccuracies, and imperfections be compatible with divine inspiration? Herbert acknowledged that if inspiration implies perfection, then modern criticism does, in fact, injure the doctrine of inspiration. He denied, however, that the Scriptures or the Church have ever defined inspiration in those terms. The gift of inspiration did not result in a mechanical deification of earthly powers, nor did it raise the function of authorship beyond the limits of human frailty in matters of science, history, and, in some cases, morality.[129] Therefore, the doctrine of inspiration must be shaped or modified based on the findings of modern scholarship.

A second and perhaps more forceful objection centered on the person of Christ. How can Christ's use of the Old Testament be reconciled with His full divinity, specifically the divine attributes of omniscience, perfection, and veracity? Herbert proposed a number of solutions. First, a distinction must be made between the final compilation of the Pentateuch and the ultimate source from which it came. Moses may have been the ultimate source of the various components that eventually became the Pentateuch, and thus Christ was not inaccurate when He attributed various quotations of it to Moses. Second, the name Moses became synonymous with the Law in the same way the name David came to represent the Psalter. Therefore, Jesus was simply using the generally accepted taxonomy of His day to discuss the spiritual teaching of the

---

128. Herbert Edward Ryle, *On Holy Scripture and Criticism*, 81: "I ought, perhaps, before closing, to notice two objections which from experience I know to be constantly raised." Perhaps this is a reference to his father.

129. Herbert Edward Ryle, *On Holy Scripture and Criticism*, 122.

Pentateuch. Third, Herbert argued that in the incarnation Christ "took upon Himself all the limitations of our manhood, both in body and mind."[130] Therefore Christ, as a man, was not infallible, and His use of the Old Testament is not a valid objection to the conclusions of critical scholarship.

In the memoir of Herbert, the author noted that the relationship between father and son did not suffer as a result of this disagreement. He wrote, "But widely as father and son differed on questions of Old Testament scholarship, those differences were never permitted in the least degree to cloud the perfect trust and affection that subsisted between them.... Each had too high a regard for the other's sincerity to feel any diminution of sympathy or confidence. They agreed to differ in silence on points as to which they knew that nothing was to be gained by mutual discussion."[131]

It is to be hoped that this really was the case, but Fitzgerald may have been too optimistic. John Charles believed that modern criticism attacked the very foundation of the faith, and he had a particular aversion to Herbert's view of kenosis. He repeatedly stated, "My soul revolts from the very idea of a fallible Saviour, Redeemer, Priest, and Judge!"[132] At the very least, he did not remain silent publicly. After Herbert resigned his position as examining chaplain, John Charles spoke out against Old Testament criticism with renewed vigor. He wrote an introduction to C. H. Waller's *The Authoritative Inspiration of Scripture* in 1887. He discussed the dangers of criticism regularly in his charges and addresses between 1887 and 1894. In 1891 he updated and expanded *Biblical Inspiration* and published it as *Is All Scripture Inspired? An Attempt to Answer the Question.* Though the publication of *Lux Mundi* occurred during this time, John Charles was probably more

---

130. Herbert Edward Ryle, *On Holy Scripture and Criticism*, 122.

131. Fitzgerald, *Memoir of Herbert Edward Ryle*, 132.

132. J. C. Ryle, *The Bishop of Liverpool's Address at the Diocesan Conference, 1892* (London: William Hunt, 1892), 33. See also J. C. Ryle, *Stand Firm!* (London: William Hunt, 1893), 18.

concerned with Herbert Edward than with Charles Gore. After all, the spike in John Charles's publishing activities seems to coincide with Herbert's publishing activities, not Gore's.

Neither father nor son mentioned the other by name in their writings, but each could not be far from the other's mind. They regularly raised each other's objections and attempted to answer them. This controversy was undoubtedly both personal and painful to John Charles, although he never spoke about it. From his perspective, his son had embraced serious theological error and, based on his own arguments about Church comprehensiveness, was unfit to teach in the Church of England. There were other important theological differences between father and son, but they all stemmed from this one issue.[133] Herbert's rejections of his father's view of Scripture must have been a painful loss and a heavy cross to bear during John Charles's episcopacy.

James Bell Cox and Ritualism

No single churchwide issue concerned Ryle more than the continued growth and spread of ritualism. He identified it as the "chief internal danger of the Church" in his first charge to the diocese,[134] and it remained so throughout his episcopacy. Like Ryle's conflict with Old Testament critics, his conflict with ritualists became much more personal during his ministry in Liverpool, due in large part to the incumbent of St. Margaret's, Price's Road, James Bell Cox.

---

133. Both father and son stressed the importance of experimental religion and had a deep appreciation for the Protestant Reformation. Cf. J. C. Ryle, *Is It Real?* with Herbert Edward Ryle, "Experimental Religion in Connection with Its Doctrinal Character and True Foundation as Set Forth in Holy Scripture," in *The Official Report of the Church Congress Held at London* (London: Bemrose and Sons, 1899), 313–17. Cf. any number of J. C. Ryle's works on the Reformation with Herbert Edward Ryle's discussion of the Reformation in England in *The Official Report of the Church Congress Held at Newcastle-upon-Tyne* (London: Bemrose and Sons, 1900), 136–37.

134. See Ryle, *Charges Delivered at His Primary Visitation*, 1:34.

St. Margaret's was a source of controversy from its opening in 1863. Charles Parnell was its first minister and an advanced ritualist. He introduced many of the most controversial aspects of ritualistic worship to St. Margaret's, including the use of the cope, chasuble, ceremonial vestments, processions, incense, crosses, and lighted candles on the Communion table; mixing water with sacramental wine; adopting the eastward position; elevating the host; and making the sign of the cross. In 1863 he, along with Rev. H. S. Bramah, published a tract calling for the establishment of a sisterhood to help meet the spiritual needs of the women of their district. Within two years they had established two. In 1864 the two inaugurated a parochial mission in Liverpool and asked A. H. Mackonochie, who was perhaps the most famous ritualist clergyman in England, to lead it. Like Mackonochie, Parnell was eventually prosecuted for illegal ritual practices in 1876 but resigned before a judgment was reached.[135] James Bell Cox, his curate, became the incumbent and continued to conduct ritualistic worship services precisely as they had been done under Parnell.

Within three weeks of his arrival, Bishop Ryle collided with James Bell Cox. Ryle read an article in the *Liverpool Courier* describing the evening worship of St. Margaret's and noticed that St. Margaret's used four rituals in worship that the queen's courts had declared illegal—lighted candles, cope, biretta, and incense—so he wrote to Cox on July 26 and asked him for a friendly meeting. Ryle asked Cox to discontinue his use of these rituals since they had been declared illegal and were not essential to the right administration of the Lord's Supper. Cox refused on the following grounds. First, he did not recognize the spiritual authority of the queen's court of law in ecclesiastical matters. Second, he believed he owed his bishop only canonical obedience—that is, only when he acted within his spiritual authority as a bishop. A bishop could not claim

---

135. For the offenses Parnell was officially charged with, see *The Church Association Monthly Intelligencer* 8 (1874): 166–69.

this authority when he was attempting to enforce the decisions of secular courts. Third, canonical obedience was due only when a bishop acted within his legitimate discretion. Cox believed Ryle was exceeding his authority by asking him to contradict the ornaments rubric of the first prayer book (1549).

Ryle urged him to reconsider. He acknowledged that the Judicial Committee of the Privy Council may not be the best court for settling ecclesiastical questions, but it was the law of the land. He pointed out that he recently consecrated a church for the ritualists, St. John the Evangelist, Walton, in the face of much Protestant opposition because he was bound to respect the law, even if he disagreed with it. He also reminded Cox that order was essential to the health and prosperity of both church and state. Cox remained recalcitrant. Ryle refused to prosecute him, although he was encouraged to do so. He did, however, refuse to license another curate for St. Margaret's until they complied, lest he formally and officially sanction lawlessness. In response, to embarrass the bishop, Cox published their private correspondence along with an introductory address.[136]

Ryle may have been unwilling to prosecute Cox, but Dr. James Hakes, a member of St. Brides, a neighboring parish, was not. He filed a formal complaint on January 29, 1885, charging Cox with eleven ritual violations.[137] Ryle urged Cox to give up the disputed ritual practices for the sake of the peace of the diocese, as did other clergymen, but he refused. Ryle was then confronted with one of

---

136. See James Bell Cox, *Correspondence between the Right Rev. the Lord Bishop of Liverpool and the Rev. J. Bell Cox, Incumbent of St. Margaret's, Prince's Road, Liverpool* (Liverpool: M. Hynes, 1880).

137. Hakes alleged that Cox used lighted candles on the altar, elevated the host, mixed water with sacramental wine, prostrated himself before the altar while officiating the Communion service, bowed to the crucifix on the altar, used the sign of the cross while giving the elements, wore illegal vestments, sang the Agnus Dei after the prayer of consecration, read the epistle and gospel with his back to the congregation, could not be seen while breaking the bread, and washed the Communion cup ceremonially.

the most difficult decisions of his episcopacy—would he use the bishop's veto to bring the prosecution to an end?

Ryle had always been an outspoken critic of the episcopal veto. It gave bishops too much power. It undermined one of the first principles of the English constitution by depriving a citizen of justice under the law. Furthermore, it was arbitrary. Some bishops used it while others did not. He was also strongly opposed to imprisonment for contumacy, which he regarded as a relic of barbarism. Instead of imprisonment, he advocated suspension, and then deprivation. The case placed Ryle in an unenviable position. If he used the veto, Cox would go unpunished, illegal ritualistic practices would go unchecked, and Dr. Hakes would be deprived of justice. If he refused, the prosecution would continue, Cox could potentially be imprisoned, and he would be branded a persecutor. In the end, it all came down to the law for Ryle. The queen's courts declared certain ritual practices illegal, and thus it was a matter of Royal Supremacy, which is affirmed in article thirty-seven of the Thirty-Nine Articles of religion. The Clergy Discipline Act as well as the Public Worship Act had not been canceled, abrogated, or repealed, and the Miles Platting case, which led to the imprisonment of Rev. S. F. Green, ruled that the decisions of the queen's courts in matters of ritual were legally binding. So after conferring with the archbishops of York and Canterbury, as well as his diocesan chancellor, a former Royal Commissioner on the ecclesiastical courts, he forwarded the case on to the chancery court of the archbishop of York.[138]

---

138. Edward White Benson, the archbishop of Canterbury, said the following about his discussion with Ryle about letting the prosecution of Cox go forward: "Interview with Bishop of Liverpool as to his permitting the threatened ritual prosecution of Mr. B. He was very earnest and oppressed about it, seems to have tried honestly his best to avoid it. But these people like B who are so excellent in theory of obedience, never obey a Bishop even when he speaks of his own authority. The Bishop had behaved magnanimously in consecrating a church for them. Without any sense of honour the man immediately adopts all manner of illegal practice." Christopher Arthur Benson, *The Life of Edward White Benson, Sometime Archbishop of Canterbury* (London: Macmillan, 1900), 2:243.

Cox refused to appear for his trial in April 1885. He was ordered by the court to stop using the ritual practices in question in September, but he continued to do so. He was suspended for six months starting on January 3, 1886, but he continued his ministrations. He was arrested on May 5, 1887, placed in the Walton Gaol, and remained imprisoned until May 21. Cox's imprisonment created a storm of controversy. Support for Cox poured in from all over the nation. The English Church Union assumed the cost of his defense and launched a nationwide campaign to discredit Ryle and Hakes. Few people came to their defense. Hakes eventually became critical of Ryle's handling of the matter after he appointed A. Paine, one of Cox's ritualistic curates, to take over at St. Margaret's during Cox's suspension. As predicted, Cox was regarded as a hero and a martyr; Ryle, for his refusal to use the veto, was regarded as a persecutor and a villain.

The James Bell Cox prosecution did nothing to stop the spread of ritualism; if anything, it gave it more momentum. It was given another boost by the prosecution of Edward King, the popular and saintly bishop of Lincoln. In 1888 the Church Association initiated legal proceedings against him for a series of ritual offenses.[139] Archbishop Benson's ruling confirmed that making the sign of the cross during the absolution and benediction was illegal, as was mixing the water with wine *during* (but not before) the Communion service. However, the eastward position, the use of lighted candles, the singing of the Agnus Dei after the consecration of the elements, and the ceremony of ablution were given official sanction, which overturned a number of previous judgments that were made in the Church Association's favor, such as the Mackonochie, Purchas, and

---

139. King had practiced the following: using lighted candles on the Communion table, mixing water with wine and administering it to communicants, adopting the eastward position during the prayer of consecration, performing certain "manual acts" during the prayer of consecration that could not be seen, allowing the Agnus Dei to be sung after consecration, making the sign of the cross at absolution and benediction, and taking part in the ceremony of ablution.

Ridsdale judgments. The Church Association appealed the ruling to the Judicial Committee of the Privy Council in 1892, but the archbishop's judgment was upheld with one minor exception. It was a major victory for ritualism and a rout for the Church Association and the evangelical party. Owen Chadwick argues that evangelicals were more damaged by the Lincoln judgment than by any other circumstance in the entire ritualist controversy, including imprisonments.[140]

Ryle was extremely disappointed by the Lincoln judgment. After the Church Association's appeal failed to secure a different verdict, he said to the diocesan conference: "As a law-abiding Englishman and a believer in Royal Supremacy, I submit to it, though I cannot approve or admire it."[141] He believed it killed ecclesiastical discipline and was the harbinger of anarchy, chaos, and confusion. He expected it to only increase and deepen divisions within the Church. He feared that it could lead to disestablishment and that the battle of the Protestant Reformation would have to be fought all over again.

One way to observe the growth of ritualism is to note the changing tone of Ryle's charges and addresses in the 1890s. They became increasingly pessimistic, especially after the Lincoln judgment. By the end of his episcopacy, Ryle was urging ritualists to be satisfied with their victories and evangelicals not to secede. In his final public address, he said he had "great faith in our Church's tenacity of life." She survived the persecution of Bloody Mary, the overthrow of the episcopacy and liturgy during the days of the Commonwealth, the Great Ejection of 1662, the secession of the nonjurors when William III came to the throne, the loss of the Methodists in the eighteenth

---

140. Chadwick, *Victorian Church*, 2:354.

141. Ryle, *Bishop of Liverpool's Address at the Diocesan Conference*, 9. He doubted the soundness of the judgment's reasoning, interpretation, and conclusions. More specifically, he found it incredible that practices repudiated by the second prayer book of Edward VI, Queen Elizabeth, and Charles II would be declared legal by the Privy Council in 1892.

century, and the departures of Manning, Newman, Oakley, Faber, and the Wilberforces to Rome. But he feared that extreme ritualism and the division it created endangered the life of the Church in a way comparable to or even more serious than the previous crises.[142]

Evaluation

Ryle's response to what he deemed the most pressing churchwide issues of the day is even more difficult to evaluate than his diocesan strategy. English bishops were no more able to stop the spread of ideas and theological movements than they were to compel attendance. That does not mean, however, that some evaluation is not possible. Ryle's episcopal response to the disestablishment movement was a success. He used his new platform to defend the establishment. He republished a number of popular works under new titles for distribution. And, perhaps more importantly, he was able to unite the diocese in opposition in 1885 and 1895. The response of the diocese surprised both friends and foes alike, and the establishment survived another series of attacks.

Slowing the growth of antidogmatic Christianity, Old Testament criticism, and ritualism proved much more difficult. Each of these theological movements continued to make progress throughout the late Victorian era. Bishop Ryle opposed them throughout his episcopacy. His responses became increasingly pessimistic as these movements progressed. In his mind, the Reformed Church of England was being deprotestantized and de-evangelicalized right before his very eyes. Ecclesiastical discipline was dead. The Thirty-Nine Articles were ignored. Church comprehensiveness knew no doctrinal bounds. Bishop Ryle feared for the life of the Church. But these responses underscore the evangelical character of his episcopacy. His theological vision for the diocese, like his diocesan strategy for reaching it, was thoroughly and unashamedly evangelical.

---

142. Ryle, *Present Distress*, 21–22.

Farewell to the Diocese

J. C. Ryle's last work was published on February 1, 1900. It was his farewell to the diocese.[143] In September 1899 Herbert discovered that his father was losing his balance and suffering from hearing and memory loss. He encouraged his father to resign, and the bishop gratefully accepted his advice. His farewell address, published just a few months before his death, provides an excellent summary of his priorities as an evangelical bishop.

He charged his clergy not to neglect their preaching and pastoral work. Their people want "life, and light, and fire, and love in the pulpit as well as in the parish," and he urged them to "let them have plenty of it."[144] Lively, Christ-exalting ministers would always have a church-going people. He also encouraged them to beware of division and to be at peace with each other.

He charged the laymen of the diocese to cling to the Church of England and her Bible, articles, and prayer book. He urged them to support all charitable institutions, consider the poor, support missions at home and abroad, and help the underpaid clergy. He concluded with a final exhortation: "Never forget that the principles of the Protestant Reformation made this country what she is, and let nothing ever tempt you to forsake them."[145]

Ryle's resignation took effect on March 1, and he, along with his daughter Isabella, moved from Liverpool to Lowestoft. He died shortly thereafter of a stroke on June 10. His body was taken back to Liverpool, and he was buried at All Saints Childwall beside Henrietta, who died in 1889. Ryle had two verses inscribed on his gravestone. The first was Ephesians 2:8—a favorite among

---

143. Ryle's farewell address can be found in a number of places. I will be quoting it from the fourth and revised edition of J. C. Ryle, *Principles for Churchmen: A Manual of Positive Statements on Some Subjects of Controversy* (London: Chas. J. Thynne, 1900).

144. J. C. Ryle, "Bishop Ryle's Farewell to His Diocese," in *Principles for Churchmen: A Manual of Positive Statements on Some Subjects of Controversy* (London: Chas. J. Thynne, 1900), vi.

145. Ryle, "Bishop Ryle's Farewell to His Diocese," vi.

evangelicals. Ryle was converted after hearing it read aloud in the autumn of 1837, and it provides an excellent summary of the central message of his ministry: salvation by grace through faith in Christ. The second text was 2 Timothy 4:7, which in many ways provides an excellent summary of Ryle's view of ministry and the Christian life. The Christian pilgrimage is a good fight of faith.

7

Who Was J. C. Ryle?

One of Henrietta Ryle's many talents was photography, and several photographs of her husband have survived. Most of them were taken in the 1880s when Ryle was an older man. In these black-and-white photos, he is dressed in simple clerical garb, his beard is long and white, and he looks serious, if not stern. In many respects these pictures provide a good illustration of popular caricatures of Ryle that persist to this day. He was regarded as a one-dimensional, old-fashioned, serious, even combative evangelical. J. C. Ryle was far more complex and dynamic than is generally appreciated, however, and this complexity and dynamism is best expressed in terms of a series of tensions.

First, Ryle was both traditional and progressive. Ryle's traditionalism was most evident in his theological convictions. Theologically, Ryle was a man of the sixteenth, seventeenth, and eighteenth centuries. He was a thorough Protestant, moderate Calvinist, self-professed "lover of Puritan theology," and an evangelical. His Calvinism and Puritanism were especially out of step with the thinking of most churchmen of his day, as both were associated with regicide.[1] Furthermore, he showed no interest in the

---

1. The *Christian Observer*, which was generally favorable to Ryle, criticized his approval of the Puritans. In its review of *Bishops and Clergy of Other Days* they said, "With regard to the Puritans, we, perhaps, should not join the Author in claiming for them as much attention in the present day, as for the Reformers. The latter, not the Puritans, are our standard; and it is to their principles that an evil and perverse generation has to be recalled." *Christian Observer*, January 1869: 54.

new theological movements of his day. He lived and died in the old-fashioned faith of centuries past. Despite this traditionalism, Ryle was progressive in certain respects. His progressivism can be seen in his stance toward new organizational reforms, such as convocation, diocesan conferences, and Church congresses; new missions initiatives such as the special services for the working classes, working men's meetings, and city missions; and in his use and selection of hymns. Ryle's traditionalism has been well documented; his progressivism has not.

Second, Ryle was both principled and pragmatic. Both friend and foe recognized Ryle as a principled clergyman, but the way he handled difficult political and ecclesial challenges as a bishop underscores this aspect of his character. Though Ryle was an outspoken opponent of ritualism, he consecrated churches for ritualists because it was his duty to do so. He opposed the Burials Act of 1880, but after it passed he urged his clergymen to obey it willingly and make it work smoothly because it was the law of the land. He consented to the prosecution of James Bell Cox, even though he knew it would create a firestorm of criticism because he had sworn to uphold Royal Supremacy and it was a matter of constitutional law. However, as his *Church Reform Papers* demonstrate, Ryle could be pragmatic when it came to Church organization. To increase the pastoral effectiveness of the Church of England, Ryle was willing to reform the entire historical episcopal system, completely reorganize cathedral establishments, shorten liturgical services, revive the office of subdeacon, create a new office of ministers called evangelists, and include the laity in almost every level of church government. The question of practical usefulness was paramount. After asking the question, Is it biblical?, Ryle almost always asked, Will it do good to souls?

Third, J. C. Ryle was both a controversialist and a unifier. He took part in every major theological controversy within the Church in the second half of the nineteenth century. Ritualists and high churchmen, skeptics and broad churchmen, Dissenters and evangelical Anglicans were all critiqued by Ryle at some point during his ministry. According to the historian George W. E. Russell, Ryle was probably the most prolific and effective controversialist of the evangelical party in the nineteenth century.[2] Given this reputation, it is easy to see why Ryle's attempts to unify the evangelical party and the Church as a whole are often overlooked. Yet he labored for these ends most of his ministerial career, and his appeals for party and Church unity should be read as well as his polemics. Ryle's final exhortation to his clergy in his farewell address is worth noting. He urged them to "cultivate and study the habit of being at peace with all your brother ministers. Beware of divisions. One thing the children of the world can always understand if they do not understand doctrine. That thing is angry quarrelling and controversy. Be at peace among yourselves."[3]

Fourth, Ryle was both a popular preacher and a diligent pastor. From his earliest days in the ministry, Ryle's preaching drew large crowds. He filled his churches in New Forest and Winchester. The Religious Census returns indicate that benches had to be placed in the aisles of the parish church in Helmingham to accommodate the crowds. All Saints in Stradbroke had to be enlarged to keep pace with the Sunday attendance. The preaching prelate filled large slum churches in the diocese of Liverpool. Ryle's sermons remain popular today. Unlike many pulpit celebrities of Victorian England, however, Ryle was a diligent pastor. He delivered weekly lectures. For at least the first twenty years of his ministry, he visited every home in his parish once a month. He began a writing ministry in Helmingham to supplement his regular pastoral work. In Stradbroke, Ryle hired a curate to help him provide pastoral oversight as he became more involved in Church and party matters, but pastoral concern remained central to his work as a controversialist, Church defender, and Church reformer. The primary goal of his diocesan strategy in Liverpool

---

2. Russell, *Short History of the Evangelical Movement*, 119.

3. Ryle, "Bishop Ryle's Farewell to His Diocese," vi.

was to provide pastoral oversight to 1.2 million souls. Ryle was not the greatest preacher of Victorian England nor was he its greatest parish pastor, but it is difficult to name another parish clergyman who did both as well as he did.

Fifth, Ryle was both versatile and narrowly focused. He was a popular preacher, platform speaker, and Church congress debater. He served as a parish priest, rural dean of Hoxne, canon of Norwich Cathedral, and bishop of Liverpool. Perhaps the variety and popularity of his works are the greatest testament to his versatility. He wrote tracts, commentaries, hymnbooks, church histories, biographies, theological treatises, controversial works, book reviews, and a manual on preaching. Despite this versatility, the purpose of nearly all Ryle's pastoral labors can be narrowed down to two primary objects: to do good to souls (promote repentance, faith, and personal holiness) and to reform the Church of England (make it pastorally effective). Nearly every sermon, address, or lecture Ryle gave and nearly every work he ever published falls into one of these two categories. He used a wide variety of different means to achieve these two pastoral ends.

Finally, Ryle is both well known and unknown. Clarity and simplicity were distinguishing characteristics of Ryle as a communicator. His religious opinions may not have been widely embraced, but they were widely known. The personal side of Ryle, however, remains shrouded in mystery. Though he wrote a short autobiography of himself for his children that covered his life from 1816 to 1860, it is more didactic than revealing, and he does not discuss his inner spiritual life in detail. He rarely discussed his personal feelings or spiritual struggles in his writings, and when he did, the audience may not have known that he was speaking from personal experience.[4] This personal reserve, combined with

---

4. For example, in *Christian Leaders of the Last Century*, Ryle discussed Henry Venn's departure from Huddersfield after the death of his wife. Ryle said,

> People who have not been placed in similar circumstances, may probably not understand all this. Those who have had this cross to carry,

his entire devotion to his work, earned him a reputation for being unsociable, distant, and unfriendly. His work as a controversialist reinforced it. Others, however, tell a different story. Archdeacon S. R. James recalled a visit he made to the Stradbroke vicarage as a young man. He was initially intimidated by Ryle's "gigantic figure and stentorian voice" but discovered that he was "very kind and hearty" and quickly made him feel at home. Henry Lakin, "a notorious publican" living in Stapenhill, became concerned about his soul after hearing the preaching of a zealous colporteur. Even though he never met Ryle, he knew him from his tracts and wrote to him for advice. Ryle penned an encouraging reply and sent him a Bible and a number of tracts, which led to his eventual conversion. Perhaps the best insight into the unknown Ryle comes from his son, Herbert Edward, and Richard Hobson, vicar of St. Nathaniel's in Liverpool. Herbert said of his father, "In the country life of Suffolk he was everything to us—taught us games, natural history, astronomy, and insisted on our never being idle, and carefully fostered our love of books. To us boys he was extraordinarily indulgent. And he was tolerant to a degree little known or recognized. The High Church writers deliberately sought to destroy his position by detraction."[5]

Richard Hobson's recollections of J. C. Ryle are even more revealing. In his autobiography, *What Hath God Wrought*, readers

---

can testify that there is no position in this world so trying to body and soul as that of the minister who is left a widower, with a young family and a large congregation. There are anxieties in such cases which no one knows but he who has gone through them; anxieties which can crush the strongest spirit, and wear out the strongest constitution. This, I strongly suspect, was one chief secret of Venn's removal from Huddersfield. He left it, no doubt, because he felt himself too ill to do any more work there. But the true cause probably of his breaking down was the load of care entailed on him by the death of his wife. It was just one of those secret blows from which a man's bodily health never recovers.

Ryle, *Christian Leaders of the Last Century*, 279–80.

5. Fitzgerald, *Memoir of Herbert Edward Ryle*, 134.

can find Bishop Ryle laughing, joking, entertaining, and even crying. Hobson described his bishop as "bold as a lion for the truth,
he was yet tender, even to those who could not see anything good
in him, or in his work as a Bishop."[6] His boldness has been recognized; his tenderness, unfortunately, has not.

---

6. Richard Hobson, *What Hath God Wrought*, 293.

APPENDIX 1

Victorian Periodicals

The following is a list Victorian periodicals I consulted during the course of my research.

The British and Foreign Evangelical Review
The British Quarterly Review
The Bulwark or Reformation Journal
The Christian Advocate
The Christian Monthly and Family Treasury
The Christian Observer
Christian Work: The News of the Churches
The Chronicle of Convocation: Being a Record of the
*   Proceedings of the Convocation of Canterbury*
The Church Association Monthly Intelligencer
The Church Eclectic: A Magazine of Church Opinion,
*   Religious Literature, and Ecclesiastical Miscellany*
The Churchman
The Churchman's Penny Magazine, and Guide to
*   Christian Truth*
The Church Missionary Intelligencer
The Church of England Magazine
The Church of England Temperance Chronicle
The Church Portrait Journal
The Church Quarterly Review
The Church Union Gazette
The Congregational Magazine

Evangelical Christendom: A Monthly Chronicle of the
    Churches Conducted by Members of the
    Evangelical Alliance
The Gospel Magazine
The Irish Church Advocate
The Liberator: A Monthly Journal of the Society for the
    Liberation of Religion from State Patronage and Control
The Literary Churchman
The Magazine of the Free Church of England
Nonconformist and Independent
The Record
The Reformed Church Review
The Rock, a Church of England Family Newspaper
The Sword and the Trowel

J. C. Ryle's Church Congress Participation

As mentioned in chapter 5, J. C. Ryle was an active participant in Church congresses. The following list outlines his involvement in these annual assemblies. It should be noted that as a bishop, Ryle was automatically made a vice president of each Church congress from his appointment in 1880 until his death in 1900. I note this in 1880, but I do not make note of it after this date. It should also be noted that Ryle's specific contributions are listed in the order that they appear (chronologically) in the official report of each congress. It is hoped that this list will illustrate the level of Ryle's commitment to this new body, as well as the scope of the issues he addressed.

Norwich Church Congress (1865)
    Discussion of preaching and its adaption to the present time

Dublin Church Congress (1868)
    Discussion of the efficiency of our church services

Southampton Church Congress (1870)
    Discussion of Christian antiquity and Church ritual
    Paper on Christian unity with Nonconformists

Nottingham Church Congress (1871)
    Paper on the present duties of the church in relation to
        the state
    Discussion on the promotion of deeper unity within
        the Church
    Discussion on the deepening of the spiritual life

Leeds Church Congress (1872)
  Discussion on lay cooperation
  Paper on convocation reform

Brighton Church Congress (1874)
  Address on convocation reform
  Discussion of diocesan synods
  Discussion of the spiritual life

Plymouth Church Congress (1876)
  Canon Ryle on the executive committee

Croydon Church Congress (1877)
  Discussion on trade unions
  Discussion on mutual toleration
  Paper on church and state
  Discussion on Nonconformity
  Word of thanks at final meeting
  Canon Ryle on the consultative committee

Sheffield Church Congress (1878)
  Paper on comprehensiveness in the national church
  Discussion on intemperance
  Address to the meeting of workmen
  Discussion on candidates for holy orders
  Word of thanks at final meeting

Swansea Church Congress (1879)
  Discussion of dissent and home reunion
  Discussion on ecclesiastical courts
  Paper on internal unity
  Speech to the working men's meeting
  Member of consultative committee

Leicester Church Congress (1880)
  Bishop Ryle, vice president (1880–1900)
  Discussion of reform in foreign churches

Address on Church and dissent
Address to working men

Newcastle-upon-Tyne Church Congress (1881)
Discussion on ecclesiastical courts

Derby Church Congress (1882)
Paper on evangelistic work at home
Address to working men

Wakefield Church Congress (1886)
Paper on the Church in relation to rural populations
Chairman of Church reform (no. 3): the clergy

Hull Church Congress (1890)
Discussion of foreign missions
Address on brotherhoods

Bibliography

Primary Works

A. C. "Church Reform." *The Christian Ambassador* 11 (1873): 40–52.

Aitken, Robert. *Pamphlets on Church Reform*. London: Charles Higham, 1880.

Arnold, A. J., ed. *Jubilee of the Evangelical Alliance: Proceedings of the Tenth International Conference Held in London, June–July, 1896*. London: J. F. Shaw, 1897.

Baker, Henry Williams, and Louis Coutier Biggs, eds. *Hymns Ancient and Modern, for Use in the Services of the Church*. London: Novello, 1867.

Bardsley, John W. "The Non-Church-Going: How Can Our Churches Reach Them?" In *The Christian Monthly and Family Treasure for 1882*, 138–40. London: T. Nelson and Sons, 1882.

Bardsley, Joseph. *Bicentenarians in Perplexity: Being an Examination of the Contradictory Reasons Assigned by Dissenters for the Commemoration of the Ejectment of Certain Ministers from the Church of England in 1662. With a Reply to the Charges of Dishonesty and Perjury Made against the Clergy of the Church of England*. London: Wertheim, 1862.

———. *The Irish Church: Should It Be Dis-Established? A Few Plain Reasons Why It Should Not*. London: William Hunt, 1868.

———. *The Nonconformist Commemoration of St. Bartholomew's Day, 1662*. Cambridge: Deighton and Bell, 1862.

———. *Weighed in the Balances: The Rev. C. H. Spurgeon Self-Condemned; or, His Questions to the Clergy on the Prayer-Book, Considered; with Some Additional Questions Addressed to Himself*. London: William Macintosh, 1864.

Beeman, Thomas O. *Ritualism: Doctrine Not Dress. Notes of Lectures on Ritualism, the Development of Tractarianism.* Cranbrook, Kent: George Waters and Sons, 1868.

Benham, W. "Address on Nonconformity." In *The Official Report of the Seventeenth Annual Meeting of the Church Congress, Held at Croydon,* 498–99. Croydon: Jesse W. Ward, 1877.

Benson, Christopher Arthur. *The Life of Edward White Benson, Sometime Archbishop of Canterbury.* 2 vols. London: Macmillan, 1900.

Benson, Edward White. *The Anglican Pulpit Today: Forty Short Biographies and Forty Sermons of Distinguished Preachers of the Church of England.* London: Hodder and Stoughton, 1886.

Benson, Louis F. *The English Hymn: Its Development and Use in Worship.* New York: Hodder and Stoughton, 1915.

Bickersteth, Edward. *The Christian Student.* London: R. B. Seeley and W. Burnside, 1829.

———. *Five Letters on Christian Union.* London: Seeley, Burnside, and Seeley, 1845.

———. *A Practical Guide to the Prophecies: With Reference to Their Interpretation and Fulfillment, and to Personal Edification.* 4th ed. London: R. B. Seeley and W. Burnside, 1835.

———. *A Treatise on Baptism: Designed as a Help to the Due Improvement of That Holy Sacrament as Administered in the Church of England.* London: R. B. Seeley and W. Burnside, 1840.

Bickersteth, Henry Edward, ed. *The Hymnal Companion to the Book of Common Prayer.* Annotated ed. London: Sampson Low, Son, and Marston, 1870.

Bird, Claude Smith. *Sketches from the Life of the Rev. Charles Smith Bird.* London: James Nisbet, 1864.

"The Bishop of Liverpool's Protest." *The Spectator,* August 25, 1888.

Blakeney, R. P. *The Book of Common Prayer in Its History and Interpretation with Special Reference to Points Disputed in the Present Day.* London: James Miller, 1865.

Boardman, William Edwin. *The Higher Christian Life.* Boston: Henry Hoyt, 1859.

Bridges, Charles. *The Christian Ministry: An Inquiry into the Causes of Its Inefficiency; With an Especial Reference to the Ministry of the Establishment.* 3rd ed. London: R. B. Seeley and W. Burnside, 1830.

British Anti-State Church Association. *Proceedings of the First Anti-State Church Association Conference*. London: British Anti-State Church Association, 1846.

———. *Tracts of the British Anti-State Church Association*. London: British Anti-State Church Association, 1846.

Broadus, John A. *Lectures on the History of Preaching*. New York: A. C. Armstrong and Son, 1901.

Brown, John. *Dissent and the Church: The Substance of Three Letters to the Rev. J. C. Ryle in Reply to His Tract Entitled* "Church and Dissent." London: James Clarke, 1870.

Bullock, Charles. "The Very Rev. J. C. Ryle, M.A. Dean of Salisbury." In *Home Words for Heart and Hearth*, 99–102. London: Hand and Heart, 1880.

Butler, Joseph. *The Analogy of Religion, Natural and Revealed, to the Constitution and Course of Nature*. 2nd ed. Cambridge: Hilliard and Brown, 1830.

Chalmers, Thomas. *Essays on Christian Union*. London: Hamilton, Adams, 1845.

———. *On the Power, Wisdom and Goodness of God, As Manifested in the Adaptation of External Nature to the Moral and Intellectual Constitution of Man*. London: W. Pickering, 2012.

———. *Series of the Discourses on the Christian Revelation Viewed in Connection with Modern Astronomy*. Edinburgh: John Smith and Son, 1818.

Chavasse, Francis James. *Address Delivered at the Nineteenth Annual Meeting of the Liverpool Diocesan Conference*. Liverpool: Henstock and Foulkes, 1900.

Childe, C. F. *The Unsafe Anchor: Eternal Hope a False Hope, Being Strictures on Canon Farrar's Westminster Abbey Sermons*. London: William Hunt, 1878.

Church Association. *Church Association Papers: The Woodard Schools*. 2nd ed. London: Church Association, 1868.

———. *Church Association Tracts*. 5 vols. London: Church Association, 1865–?.

The Church Defense Institution. *The Church Defense Handy Volume Containing the Leaflets of the Institution Together with Papers, Speeches, and Statistics by Bishops, Eminent Statesmen, Members of Parliament, and Others*. 12th ed. London: Church Defense Institution, 1895.

———. *The Church Defense Smaller Handy Volume Containing the Leaflets of the Institution.* London: Church Defense Institution, 1885.

A Churchman [pseud.]. *The Church, Church Rates, and Dissenters.* London: J. and C. Mozley, 1860.

Church-Rates Vindicated: Together with Some Remarks on the Position and Prospects of the Present Ministry. London: Whitaker, 1858.

Clarke, J. E. "Mr. Ryle on the Reform of Convocation." *Church Bells* 74 (1872): 304–5.

A Clergyman of the Diocese of Exeter [pseud.]. *A Letter to the Rev. J. C. Ryle, A.B., in Reply to His Lecture on* "Baxter and His Times," *Delivered before the Young Men's Christian Association.* London: Rivingtons, 1853.

Close, Francis. *The Restoration of Churches Is the Restoration of Popery.* London: Hatchard and Son, 1844.

Colenso, John William. *The Pentateuch and Book of Joshua Critically Examined.* London: Longmans, Robert, and Green, 1862.

———. *St. Paul's Epistle to the Romans: Newly Translated and Explained from a Missionary Point of View.* Cambridge: Macmillan, 1861.

Collins, William Lucas. *Etoniana, Ancient and Modern.* London: William Blackwood and Sons, 1865.

Conference on Missions Held in 1860 at Liverpool: Including the Papers Read, the Deliberations, and the Conclusions Reached; with a Comprehensive Index Shewing the Various Matters Brought Under Review. Rev. ed. London: James Nisbet, 1860.

The Confraternity of the Blessed Sacrament. *The Manual of the Confraternity of the Blessed Sacrament of the Body and Blood of Christ.* 5th ed. London: John Masters, 1873.

Cox, James Bell. *Correspondence between the Right Rev. the Lord Bishop of Liverpool and the Rev. J. Bell Cox, Incumbent of St. Margaret's, Prince's Road, Liverpool.* Liverpool: M. Hynes, 1880.

Cross, Richard Assheton. "Church Rates: What Scheme Is Now Practicable?" In *Report of the Proceedings of the Church Congress Held in the Hall of King's College, Cambridge,* 31–36. Cambridge: Deighton, Bell, 1862.

Curnock, Nehemiah, ed. *The Journal of the Rev. John Wesley, A.M. Sometime Fellow of Lincoln College, Oxford.* 8 vols. London: Charles H. Kelly, 1909–1916.

Cust, Lionel. *A History of Eton College*. New York: Charles Scribner's Sons, 1899.

Dale, R. W. *Nine Lectures on Preaching*. London: Hodder and Stoughton, 1877.

Davidson, Randall T., ed. *The Lambeth Conferences of 1867, 1878, and 1888, with the Official Reports and Resolutions, Together with the Sermons Preached at the Conferences*. London: Society for the Promotion of Christian Knowledge, 1889.

[Davis, Charles Henry]. *Suggestive Sketch of an Irish Church Constitution and Canons, with an Adaptation to the English Church of the Future, whether Established or Disestablished, and some Remarks on the Rev. J. C. Ryle's Church Reform Scheme*. Dublin, 1870.

[Davis, George Jennings?]. *Papers on Preaching and Public Speaking, by a Wykehmaist*. London: Bell and Daldy, 1861.

Denison, George Anthony. *The Real Presence*. London: Joseph Masters, 1853.

Driver, S. R. *An Introduction to the Literature of the Old Testament*. New York: Charles Scribner's Sons, 1891.

Earles, John. *Streets and Houses of Old Macclesfield*. Macclesfield: Robert Brown, 1915.

Edwards, Alfred George. *A Handbook on Welsh Church Defense*. 2nd ed. London: Church Defense Institution, 1894.

Elliott, Charles. *Delineation of Roman Catholicism Drawn from Authentic and Acknowledged Standards of the Church of Rome*. 2 vols. New York: G. Lane and P. P. Sandford, 1842.

Elliott, Charlotte. *Hours of Sorrow Cheered and Comforted: Thoughts in Verse, Chiefly Adapted to Seasons of Sickness, Depression, and Bereavement*. London: James Nisbet, 1836.

———. *The Invalid's Hymn-Book*. Dublin: John Robertson, 1834.

Essays and Reviews. London: John W. Parker and Son, 1860.

The Eton System of Education Vindicated. London: J. G. and F. Rivington, 1834.

Faber, George Stanley. *The Difficulties of Infidelity*. Philadelphia: Thomas Kite, 1829.

Farrar, Frederic W. *Eternal Hope: Five Sermons Preached in Westminster Abbey*. New York: E. P. Dutton, 1878.

Finlayson, A. R. M. "Address on the Church and the Printing Press." In *The Official Report of the Church Congress Held at Portsmouth*, 372–74. London: Bemrose and Sons, 1885.

Finney, Charles G. *Views of Sanctification*. Oberlin, Ohio: James Steele, 1840.

Fitzgerald, Maurice H. *A Memoir of Herbert Edward Ryle: K.C.V.O., D.D., Sometime Bishop of Winchester and Dean of Westminster*. London: Macmillan, 1928.

Froude, J. A. *History of England from the Fall of Wolsey to the Death of Elizabeth*. 2nd ed. Vol. 3. London: John W. Parker and Son, 1858.

Froude, Richard Hurrell. *Remains*. 2 vols. London: J. G. and F. Rivington, 1838.

Furse, C. W. "The Moral State of Society." In the *Authorized Report of the Church Congress Held at Nottingham*, 414–15. London: W. Wells Gardner, 1871.

Garbett, Edward. *Diocesan Synods*. London: William Hunt, 1868.

———, ed. *Evangelical Principles: A Series of Doctrinal Papers Explanatory of the Positive Principles of Evangelical Churchmanship*. London: William Hunt, 1875.

Garratt, Evelyn R. *The Life and Personal Recollections of Samuel Garratt*. London: James Nisbet, 1908.

Gidney, W. T. *The History of the London Society for Promoting Christianity amongst the Jews: 1809 to 1908*. London: London Society for Promoting Christianity amongst the Jews, 1908.

Girdlestone, Robert Baker. Dies Irae: *The Final Judgment and Future Prospects of Mankind*. London: Hatchards, 1877.

Gladstone, William Ewart. *The State in Its Relations with the Church*. 3rd ed. London: John Murray, 1839.

———. *The Vatican Decrees and Their Bearing on Civil Allegiance*. Leipzig: Bernhard Tauchnitz, 1875.

Goode, William. *The Nature of Christ's Presence in the Eucharist*. 2 vols. London: T. Hatchard, 1856.

———. *Remarks on the Approaching Lambeth Conference and Its Proposed "Amendments."* London: Hatchard, 1867.

Gore, Charles, ed. Lux Mundi: *A Series of Studies in the Religion on the Incarnation*. 4th ed. London: John Murray, 1890.

Gorst, Harold E. *The Earl of Beaconsfield*. London: Blackie and Son, 1900.

Goulburn, E. M., C. A. Heurtley, A. W. Haddan, W. J. Irons, H. J. Rose, G. Rorison, and Christopher Wordsworth. *Replies to "Essays and Reviews."* London: John Henry and James Parker, 1862.

A Graduate of Oxford [pseud.]. *The Student's Guide to a Course of Reading Necessary for Obtaining University Honours by a Graduate of Oxford.* Oxford: Henry Slatter, 1837.

Grey, Albert, and Rev. Canon Fremantle. *Church Reform*. London: Swan Sonnenschein, Lowrey, 1888.

Grindon, Leo H. "The Rise and Fall of Daintry, Ryle, and Co." In *Manchester Banks and Bankers: Historical, Biographical, and Anecdotal*, 111–17. 2nd ed. Manchester: Palmer and Howe, 1878.

Hansards's Parliamentary Debates. London: Cornelius Buck, 1884.

Hedge, Fredrick Henry, ed. *Recent Inquiries in Theology by Eminent English Churchmen Being Essays and Reviews*. Boston: Walker, Wise, 1860.

Henry, Matthew. *An Exposition of the Old and New Testaments*. 1st American ed. Vol. 1. Philadelphia: Haswell, Barrington, and Haswell, 1838.

Hobson, Richard. "Funeral Sermon Preached by Canon Hobson in Liverpool Cathedral on the Late Bishop Ryle." In *What Hath God Wrought: An Autobiography*, 343–46. London: Charles J. Thynne, 1909.

———. *What Hath God Wrought: An Autobiography*. London: Charles J. Thynne, 1909.

Holland, Spencer L., and William Stubbs. *A Summary of the Ecclesiastical Courts Commission's Report and of Dr. Stubbs' Historical Reports: Together with a Review of the Evidence before the Commission*. Oxford: Parker, 1884.

Hook, Walter Farquhar. *A Church Dictionary*. 6th ed. Philadelphia: E. H. Butler, 1854.

Hooker, Richard. *The Works of Mr. Richard Hooker*. New ed. 3 vols. London: J. Bumpus, 1821.

Horbery, Matthew. *Enquiry into the Scripture Doctrine of the Duration of Future Punishments*. London: James Fletcher, 1744.

Howard, John. "The Enthronement of the Bishop of Liverpool." *Liverpool Echo*, July 2, 1880.

Howard, John. *The State of the Prisons in England and Wales*. 4th ed. London: J. Johnson, C. Dilly, and T. Cadwell, 1792.

Hume, Abraham. *The Church of England the Home Missionary to the Poor, Especially in Our Large Towns*. London: Seeley, Jackson, and Halliday, 1862.

———. "The Church's Work in Large Towns." In *Authorized Report of the Church Congress Held at Liverpool*, 356–63. Liverpool: Adam Holden, 1869.

———. *Condition of Liverpool: Religious and Social, Including Notices of the State of Education, Morals, Pauperism, and Crime*. Liverpool: T. Brackell, 1858.

———. *A Detailed Account of How Liverpool Became a Diocese: Read Before the Clerical Society of Liverpool, 6th December, 1880*. London: Rivingtons, 1881.

———. *Evening Classes for Adults*. Liverpool: Liverpool Standard Office, 1854.

———. *Facts and Suggestions Connected with Primary Education with Illustrations from the Borough of Liverpool*. Liverpool: T. Brakell, 1870.

———. *The Growth of the Episcopate in England and Wales during Seventeen Centuries*. Liverpool: Liverpool Clerical Society, 1880.

———. *Missions at Home: A Clergyman's Account of a Portion of the Town of Liverpool*. Liverpool: J. F. Rivington, 1850.

———. *State and Prospects of the Church in Liverpool*. Liverpool: Adam Holden, 1869.

Hymn-book for the Society for Promoting Christian Knowledge. London: SPCK, 1863.

Ingham, Richard. *Church Establishments Considered: Especially in Reference to the Church of England*. London: Elliot Stock, 1875.

"Is There Not a Cause? A Word to Evangelical Protestants in the National Churches of England and Ireland, on the Necessity Which Exists for the Evangelical Protestant Union." *The Irish Church Advocate*, May 1879.

James, John Angell. *The Christian Professor*. London: Hamilton, Adams, 1838.

Jones, William. *The Jubilee Memorial of the Religious Tract Society: Containing a Record of Its Origin, Proceedings, and Results AD 1799 to AD 1849*. London: Religious Tract Society, 1850.

[J. S. B.]. *The Deficient Supply of Well-Qualified Clergymen for the Church of England, at the Present Time: A Paper Read before the Liverpool Clerical Society.* Birkenhead, U.K.: W. Osborne, 1863.

Jullian, John. *A Dictionary of Hymnology.* London: John Murray, 1892.

Keble, John. *Catholic Subscription to the XXXIX Articles Considered in Reference to Tract XC.* Oxford: Rivingtons, 1841.

———. *The Christian Year: Thoughts in Verse for Sundays and Holidays throughout the Year.* 2nd ed. Oxford: W. Baxter, 1827.

———. *The Primitive Tradition Recognized in Holy Scripture.* London: J. G. and F. Rivington, 1837.

Kemble, Charles. *A Selection of Psalms and Hymns, Arranged for the Public Services of the Church of England.* London: David Batten, 1853.

Knox-Little, W. J. "Addresses." In *The Official Report of the Nineteenth Annual Church Congress Held at Swansea,* 396–99. London: John Hodges, 1879.

Lathbury, Thomas. *A History of the Convocation of the Church of England from the Earliest Period to the Year 1742.* 2nd ed. London: J. Leslie, 1853.

A Layman [pseud]. "A Layman's View of Church Reform: Being Notes on *Church Reform Papers* by the Rev. J. C. Ryle." *Mission Life* 3 (1872): 305–10.

Lectures Delivered before the Church of England Young Men's Society for Aiding Missions at Home and Abroad. London: Seeleys, 1852, 1854.

Leland, John. *A View of the Principal Deistical Writers That Have Appeared in England in the Last and Present Century with Observations upon Them, and Some Account of the Answers That Have Been Published against Them.* London: B. Dod, 1754.

Leslie, Charles. *A Short and Easy Method with the Deists.* London: F. and C. Rivington, 1801.

Liddon, Henry Parry. *The Divinity of Our Lord and Saviour Jesus Christ.* New ed. London: Rivingtons, 1868.

Lightfoot, J. B. *St. Paul's Epistle to the Philippians: A Revised Text with Introduction, Notes, and Dissertations.* London: Macmillan, 1868.

Littledale, Richard Frederick. *Church Reform.* London: G. J. Palmer, 1870.

————. *Innovations: A Lecture.* London: Simpkins and Marshall, 1868.

Lyte, H. C. Maxwell. *A History of Eton College 1440–1875.* London: Macmillan, 1877.

Mann, Horace. *Census of Great Britain, 1851: Religious Worship in England and Wales.* London: E. Eyre and W. Spottiswoode, 1854.

————. "On the Statistical Position of the Religious Bodies in England and Wales." *Journal of the Statistical Society* 18 (1855): 141–59.

Manning, Henry Edward. *The Eternal Priesthood.* 4th ed. London: Burns and Oates, 1884.

————. *The Rule of Faith.* London: J. G. and F. Rivington, 1838.

Mansel, Henry Longueville. *An Examination of the Rev. F. D. Maurice's Strictures on the Bampton Lectures of 1858.* London: John Murray, 1859.

Marshall, Arthur Featherstone. *The Comedy of Convocation in the English Church in Two Scenes.* New York: Catholic Publication Society, 1868.

Massie, James William. *The Evangelical Alliance: Its Origin and Development.* London: John Snow, 1847.

Maurice, Fredrick Denison. *Theological Essays.* 2nd ed. Cambridge: Macmillan, 1853.

McIlvaine, Charles Pettit. *The Evidences of Christianity: In Their External, or Historical, Division: Exhibited in a Course of Lectures.* London: Seeleys, 1851.

M'Clellan, John Brown. *Church Rates.* London: William Macintosh, 1868.

Mearns, Andrew. *The Statistics of Attendance at Public Worship: As Published in England, Wales, and Scotland, by the Local Press between October 1881 and February 1882.* London: Hodder and Stoughton, 1882.

Mellor, Enoch. *Disestablishment: What Good Will It Do? A Reply to Canon Ryle.* London: Elliot Stock, 1873.

Members of the University of Oxford. *Tracts for the Times.* 6 vols. 1840–1842. Reprint, New York: AMS Press, 1969.

Mercer, William, ed. *Church Psalter and Hymn Book.* London: James Nisbet, 1863.

Miall, Edward. *The British Churches in Relation to the British People.* London: Arthur Hall, Virtue, 1849.

————. *The Nonconformist's Sketch Book: A Series of Views, Classified in Four Groups, of a State Church and Its Attendant Evils.* London: Nonconformists Office, 1842.

Milner, Isaac, and Joseph Miler. *The History of the Church of Christ.* London: R. B. Seeley and W. Burnside, 1836.

M'Neile, Hugh. *The Collected Works of the Very Rev. Dean M'Neile, D.D.* 4 vols. London: Christian Book Society, 1877–1880?.

"Monthly Notes." *Evangelical Christendom* 42, [1888].

Moody, William R. *The Life of Dwight L. Moody.* New York: Fleming H. Revell, 1900.

[More, Hannah?]. *Cheap Repository Tracts: Entertaining, Moral, and Religious.* New ed. London: Law and Gilbert, 1807.

Moule, H. C. G. *Thoughts on Christian Sanctity.* London: Seeley, 1886.

Mozley, J. B. *Eight Lectures on Miracles.* Oxford: Rivingtons, Waterloo Place, 1865.

Newman, John Henry. *Lectures on the Prophetical Office of the Church.* London: J. G. and F. Rivington, 1838.

————. "Tears of Christ and the Grave of Lazarus." In vol. 3 of *Parochial and Plain Sermons*, 128–38. London: Rivingtons, 1877.

————. *Tract XC on Certain Passages in the XXXIX Articles.* Oxford: Rivingtons, 1841.

Newton, John. *Cardiphonia, or, the Utterance of the Heart in the Course of Real Correspondence.* Edinburgh: Waugh and Innes, 1824.

Orchard, B. Guinness. *Liverpool's Legion of Honour.* Birkenhead, U.K.: published by the author, 1893.

Ormerod, George. *The History of the County of Palatine and the City of Chester.* 3 vols. London: George Routledge and Sons, 1882.

An Orthodox Christian [pseud.]. *What Is Wanted? An Answer to the Rev. J. C. Ryle, B.A.* London: Hope and Company, 1855.

Paley, William. *A View of the Evidences of Christianity: In Three Parts.* London: Baynes, 1817.

Parliamentary Debates, Official Report. London: Cornelius Buck and Son, 1816–1900.

Pearson, John. *An Exposition of the Creed.* London: R. Priestly, 1824.

Pennefather, William. *The Church of the First-born: A Few Thoughts on Christian Unity.* London: John F. Shaw, 1865.

The People's Charter; With the Address to the Radical Reformers of Great Britain and Ireland. London: Charles Fox, 1848.

Picton, James A. *City of Liverpool: Municipal Archives and Records from A.D. 1700 to the Passing of the Municipal Reform Act of 1835.* Liverpool: Gilbert G. Walmsley, 1886.

Plumptre, Edward Hayes, H. Allon, J. H. Rigg, S. Cox, T. R. Birks, David Gracey. *The Future: A Series of Papers on Cannon Farrar's Eternal Hope.* Detroit: Rose-Belford, 1878.

Porteus, Beilby. *A Summary of the Principal Evidences for the Truth and Divine Origin of the Christian Revelation.* London: T. Cadell, 1801.

The Priest in Absolution: A Manual for Such as Are Called unto the Higher Ministries in the English Church. London: Joseph Masters, 1866.

Purchas, John. *Directorium Anglicanum.* London: Joseph Masters, 1858.

Pusey, Edward Bouverie. *Advice for Those Who Exercise the Ministry of Reconciliation through Confession and Absolution: Being the Abbe Gaume's Manual for Confessors.* 2nd ed. Oxford: James Parker, 1878.

[Pycroft, James?]. *The Student's Guide to a Course of Reading Necessary for Obtaining University Honours by a Graduate of Oxford.* Oxford: Henry Slatter, 1837.

Read and Others v. the Lord Bishop of Lincoln, Judgment Nov. 21, 1890. London: Macmillan, 1890.

Record of the Convention for the Promotion of Scriptural Holiness Held at Brighton May 29th to June 7th, 1875. London: S. W. Patridge, 1875.

Report from the Select Committee of the House of Lords, Appointed to Inquire into the Deficiency of Means of Spiritual Instruction and Places of Divine Worship in the Metropolis, and in Other Populous Districts in England and Wales, Especially in the Mining and Manufacturing Districts; and to Consider the Fittest Means of Meeting the Difficulties of the Case; and to Report Thereon to the House; Together with the Proceedings of the Committee, Minutes of Evidence, and Appendix. London, 1858.

Roberts, G. Bayfield. *The History of the English Church Union 1859–1894.* London: Church Printing Company, 1895.

Roscoe, E. S. *A Report of the Proceedings in the Court of the Archbishop of Canterbury of the Case of Read and Others v. the Bishop of Lincoln.* London: William Clowes and Sons, 1891.

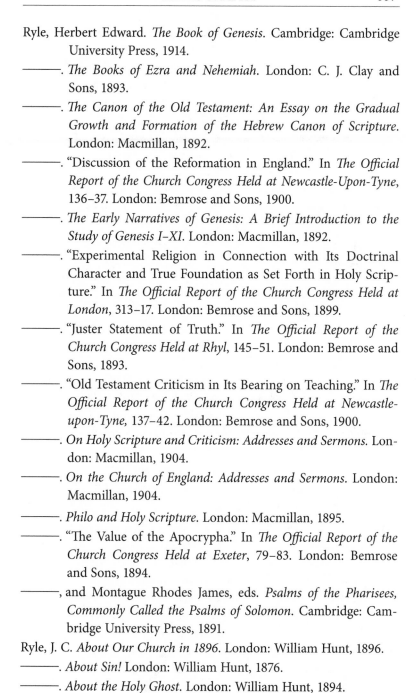

Ryle, Herbert Edward. *The Book of Genesis*. Cambridge: Cambridge University Press, 1914.

———. *The Books of Ezra and Nehemiah*. London: C. J. Clay and Sons, 1893.

———. *The Canon of the Old Testament: An Essay on the Gradual Growth and Formation of the Hebrew Canon of Scripture*. London: Macmillan, 1892.

———. "Discussion of the Reformation in England." In *The Official Report of the Church Congress Held at Newcastle-Upon-Tyne*, 136–37. London: Bemrose and Sons, 1900.

———. *The Early Narratives of Genesis: A Brief Introduction to the Study of Genesis I–XI*. London: Macmillan, 1892.

———. "Experimental Religion in Connection with Its Doctrinal Character and True Foundation as Set Forth in Holy Scripture." In *The Official Report of the Church Congress Held at London*, 313–17. London: Bemrose and Sons, 1899.

———. "Juster Statement of Truth." In *The Official Report of the Church Congress Held at Rhyl*, 145–51. London: Bemrose and Sons, 1893.

———. "Old Testament Criticism in Its Bearing on Teaching." In *The Official Report of the Church Congress Held at Newcastle-upon-Tyne*, 137–42. London: Bemrose and Sons, 1900.

———. *On Holy Scripture and Criticism: Addresses and Sermons*. London: Macmillan, 1904.

———. *On the Church of England: Addresses and Sermons*. London: Macmillan, 1904.

———. *Philo and Holy Scripture*. London: Macmillan, 1895.

———. "The Value of the Apocrypha." In *The Official Report of the Church Congress Held at Exeter*, 79–83. London: Bemrose and Sons, 1894.

———, and Montague Rhodes James, eds. *Psalms of the Pharisees, Commonly Called the Psalms of Solomon*. Cambridge: Cambridge University Press, 1891.

Ryle, J. C. *About Our Church in 1896*. London: William Hunt, 1896.

———. *About Sin!* London: William Hunt, 1876.

———. *About the Holy Ghost*. London: William Hunt, 1894.

———. *The Additional Hymn-Book: Being Three Hundred Hymns for Public Worship, Most of Them Not Found in the Collections Commonly Used*. London: William Hunt, 1875.

———. "Address before the Yorkshire Church Association." *The Church Association Monthly Intelligencer* 4 (1870): 281–82.

———. "Address on Convocation of the Church of England." In *Authorized Report of the Church Congress Held at Brighton*, 204–8. London: William Wells Gardner, 1874.

———. "Address on Nonconformity." In *The Official Report of the Seventeenth Annual Meeting of the Church Congress, Held at Croydon*, 497–98. Croydon: Jesse W. Ward, 1877.

———. *All in All*. London: William Hunt, 1853.

———. *Always to Pray*. London: William Hunt, 1888.

———. "The Anniversary Sermon of the British Society for Promoting the Religious Principles of the Reformation." *The British Protestant* 77 (1851): 117–34.

———. "The Anniversary Sermon of the Irish Church Mission." *The Banner of Truth in Ireland* 9 (1859): 66–77.

———. *Archbishop Laud and His Times: A Lecture*. London: Hatchards, 1869.

———. *Are We in Danger? A Question for Churchmen about Our Unhappy Divisions*. London: William Hunt, 1888.

———. *Are We Not in Perilous Times?* London: William Hunt, 1868.

———. *Are We Overcoming?* London: William Hunt, 1879.

———. *Are We Sanctified?* London: William Hunt, 1874.

———. *Are You an Heir?* London: William Hunt, 1852.

———. *Are You Converted?* London: William Hunt, 1864.

———. *Are You Fighting?* London: William Hunt, 1870.

———. *Are You Forgiven?* Ipswich: William Hunt, 1849.

———. *Are You Free?* London: William Hunt, 1866.

———. *Are You Happy?* London: William Hunt, 1856.

———. *Are You Holy?* London: William Hunt, 1852.

———. *Are You Looking?* London: William Hunt, 1870.

———. *Are You Ready?* Stirling: Drummond's Tract Depot, 1898.

———. *Are You Weary?* London: William Hunt, 1892.

———. *Assurance*. London: William Hunt, 1849.

———. *Baptism*. London: William Hunt, 1865.

———. *Baxter and His Times*. London: G. Barclay, 1853.

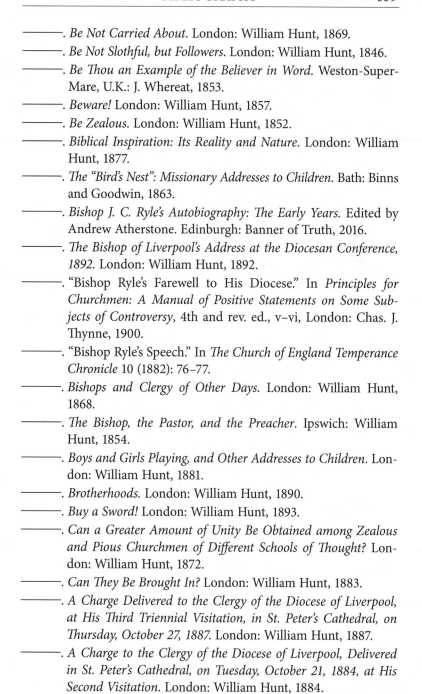

———. *Be Not Carried About.* London: William Hunt, 1869.

———. *Be Not Slothful, but Followers.* London: William Hunt, 1846.

———. *Be Thou an Example of the Believer in Word.* Weston-Super-Mare, U.K.: J. Whereat, 1853.

———. *Beware!* London: William Hunt, 1857.

———. *Be Zealous.* London: William Hunt, 1852.

———. *Biblical Inspiration: Its Reality and Nature.* London: William Hunt, 1877.

———. *The "Bird's Nest": Missionary Addresses to Children.* Bath: Binns and Goodwin, 1863.

———. *Bishop J. C. Ryle's Autobiography: The Early Years.* Edited by Andrew Atherstone. Edinburgh: Banner of Truth, 2016.

———. *The Bishop of Liverpool's Address at the Diocesan Conference, 1892.* London: William Hunt, 1892.

———. "Bishop Ryle's Farewell to His Diocese." In *Principles for Churchmen: A Manual of Positive Statements on Some Subjects of Controversy,* 4th and rev. ed., v–vi, London: Chas. J. Thynne, 1900.

———. "Bishop Ryle's Speech." In *The Church of England Temperance Chronicle* 10 (1882): 76–77.

———. *Bishops and Clergy of Other Days.* London: William Hunt, 1868.

———. *The Bishop, the Pastor, and the Preacher.* Ipswich: William Hunt, 1854.

———. *Boys and Girls Playing, and Other Addresses to Children.* London: William Hunt, 1881.

———. *Brotherhoods.* London: William Hunt, 1890.

———. *Buy a Sword!* London: William Hunt, 1893.

———. *Can a Greater Amount of Unity Be Obtained among Zealous and Pious Churchmen of Different Schools of Thought?* London: William Hunt, 1872.

———. *Can They Be Brought In?* London: William Hunt, 1883.

———. *A Charge Delivered to the Clergy of the Diocese of Liverpool, at His Third Triennial Visitation, in St. Peter's Cathedral, on Thursday, October 27, 1887.* London: William Hunt, 1887.

———. *A Charge to the Clergy of the Diocese of Liverpool, Delivered in St. Peter's Cathedral, on Tuesday, October 21, 1884, at His Second Visitation.* London: William Hunt, 1884.

———. *Charges and Addresses*. Edinburgh: Banner of Truth, 1978.

———. *The Charges Delivered at His Primary Visitation*. London: William Hunt, 1881.

———. *Christ and the Two Thieves*. London: William Hunt, 1849.

———. *The Christian Leaders of the Last Century; or, England a Hundred Years Ago*. London: T. Nelson and Sons, 1869.

———. *Christian Leaders of the Seventeenth Century*. Edited and introduced by Lee Gatiss. London: Church Society, 2015.

———. *The Christian Race and Other Sermons*. London: Hodder and Stoughton, 1900.

———. *Christ Is All*. London: William Hunt, 1877.

———. *Church and Dissent: or, Why Do I Prefer Church to Chapel?* London: William Hunt, 1870.

———. *Church and State*. London: William Hunt, 1877.

———. *The Church and the Rural Populations*. London: William Hunt, 1886.

———. "The Church Courts Commission." *The Contemporary Review* 45 (1884): 168–74.

———. *Church Discipline in 1887: A Few Thoughts on the Subject*. London: William Hunt, 1887.

———. *A Churchman's Duty about Diocesan Conferences: Being Hints and Thoughts about Them*. London: William Hunt, 1871.

———. *Churchmen and Dissenters*. London: William Hunt, 1880.

———. *The Church on the Rock!* London: William Hunt, 1860.

———. *Church Principles and Church Comprehensiveness*. London: William Hunt, 1879.

———. *Church Reform: Being Seven Papers on the Subject*. London: William Hunt, 1870.

———. *Church Reform: The Position of the Laity*. London: Church Association, n.d.

———. *The City; or, The Sight Which Stirred St. Paul*. London: William Hunt, 1882.

———. "Closing Address." In *The Church: Its Duties, Claims, Perils, and Privileges. Being the Substance of the Addresses and Sermons Delivered at the Fifth Combined Clerical Meeting at Weston-Super-Mare*, 52–73. Weston-Super-Mare, U.K.: J. Whereat, 1858.

———. *Come! A Christmas Invitation*. Ipswich: William Hunt, 1859.

————. *Come Out!* London: William Hunt, 1878.

————. *Comfort One Another.* Ipswich: Ipswich Journal, 1864.

————. *Coming Events and Present Duties.* London: William Hunt, 1867.

————. *Coming Events and Present Duties*, 2nd and enlarged ed. London: William Hunt, 1879.

————. *Consider Your Ways.* London: William Hunt, 1849.

————. *Convocation Reform!* London: William Hunt, 1872.

————. "Convocation Reform." In *Authorized Report of the Church Congress Held at Leeds*, 209–17. London: John Hodges, 1872.

————. *The Cross.* London: William Hunt, 1852.

————. "Daniel the Prophet." In *The Rule of Life and Conduct: Discourses Delivered before the Members of the Liverpool Young Men's Christian Association*, 1–17. Liverpool: Young Men's Christian Association, 1889.

————. *Disestablishment Papers.* London: William Hunt, 1885.

————. *The Distinctive Principles of the Church of England.* London: Church Association, 1878.

————. *Distinctive Vestments.* London: Church Association, n.d.

————. *Dogma.* London: William Hunt, 1878.

————. *Do You Believe?* London: William Hunt, 1860.

————. *Do You Confess?* London: William Hunt, 1858.

————. *Do You Love Christ?* London: Drummond's Tract Depot, 1896.

————. *Do You Pray?* London: William Hunt, 1852.

————. *Do You Want a Friend?* London: William Hunt, 1855.

————. *The Eastward Position* [no. 30]. London: Church Association, n.d.

————. *The Eastward Position* [no. 136]. London: Church Association, n.d.

————. "An Estimation of Manton." In *The Complete Works of Thomas Manton D.D.*, 2:ix–xix. London: James Nisbet, 1871.

————. *Evangelical Churchmen! A Statement and a Defense.* London: William Hunt, 1890.

————. *Evangelical Religion: What It Is, and What It Is Not.* London: William Hunt, 1867.

————. *An Example in Word.* London: William Hunt, 1853.

————. *Facts and Men: Being Pages from English Church History between 1553 and 1683.* London: William Hunt, 1882.

———. *Faith's Choice*. London: William Hunt, 1852.

———. "Farewell to the Diocese." In *Principles for Churchmen: A Manual of Positive Statements on Some Subjects of Controversy*, v–vi. London: Chas. J. Thynne, 1900.

———. *First of All*. London: William Hunt, 1880.

———. *First Words: An Opening Address Delivered at the First Liverpool Diocesan Conference*. London: William Hunt, 1881.

———. *The Forgiveness of Sins*. London: William Hunt, 1891.

———. *For Kings*. London: William Hunt, 1887.

———. *Form or Heart?* London: Drummond's Tract Depot, 1900.

———. *The Garden Inclosed*. London: William Hunt, 1869.

———. *George Whitefield: A Lecture*. London: Seeleys, 1852.

———. *Go, and Do Thou Likewise*. London: William Hunt, 1882.

———. *A Good Heart*. London: William Hunt, 1887.

———. *A Guide to Churchmen about Baptism and Regeneration*. London: William Hunt, 1857.

———. *The Hand of the Lord! Being Thoughts on Cholera*. London: William Hunt, 1866.

———. *Have You a Priest?* London: William Hunt, 1871.

———. *Have You Charity?* London: William Hunt, 1864.

———. *Have You Peace?* London: William Hunt, 1854.

———. *Have You the Spirit?* London: William Hunt, 1854.

———. *He Whom Thou Lovest Is Sick*. Ipswich: William Hunt, 1859.

———. *A High Church Clergyman on the Ritualists*. London: Church Association, 1876.

———. *His Presence: Where Is It?* London: William Hunt, 1873.

———. *Hold Fast*. London: William Hunt, 1890.

———. *Holiness: Its Nature, Hindrances, Difficulties, and Roots*. Revised and enlarged edition. 1879. Reprint, Moscow, Idaho: Charles Nolan Publishers, 2001.

———. *The Holy Communion*. London: William Hunt, 1869.

———. *Home Truths: Being Miscellaneous Addresses and Tracts by the Rev. J. C. Ryle, B.A.* 8 vols. Ipswich: W. Hunt, 1852–1872.

———. *How Do You Do?* London: William Hunt, 1875.

———. *How Do You Worship?* London: William Hunt, 1868.

———. *How Readest Thou?* London: William Hunt, 1852.

———. *Hymns for the Church on Earth: Being Three Hundred Hymns and Spiritual Songs (for the Most Part Modern Date)*. Ipswich: William Hunt, 1860.

———. *Hymns for the Church on Earth: Containing Four Hundred Hymns (for the Most Part Modern Date)*. London: William Hunt, 1876.

———. *I Am a Churchman! And Why?* London: William Hunt, 1886.

———. *Idolatry*. London: William Hunt, 1851.

———. "Idolatry, a Predicted Sin of the Visible Church, with Its Abolition at Christ's Coming." In *Popish Darkness and Millennial Light: Being Lectures Delivered during Lent, 1851, at St. George's Bloomsbury*, 55–89. London: James Nisbet, 1851.

———. *If Any Man*. London: William Hunt, 1879.

———. *I Fear! A Caution for the Times*. London: William Hunt, 1877.

———. *I Have Somewhat to Say unto Thee*. London: William Hunt, 1845.

———. *I Hope!* London: William Hunt, 1887.

———. Introduction to *The Authoritative Inspiration of Holy Scripture as Distinct from the Inspiration of Its Human Authors*, by C. H. Waller, 9–46. London: William Hunt, 1887.

———. Introduction to *A Book of Remembrance; Being Recollections of the Late Colonel Holden of Nuttal Temple, Nottingham*, by F. M. W. C., ix–xvi. London: James Nisbet, 1873.

———. Introduction to *The Christian in Complete Armour; A Treatise of the Saints' War against the Devil*, by William Gurnall, xv–xliii. London: Blackie and Son, 1865.

———. Introduction to *Christ the True Altar, and Other Sermons, with the Charge, The Christian Ministry Not Sacerdotal but Evangelistic*, by Samuel Waldegrave, v–vii. London: William Hunt, 1875.

———. Introduction to *The Imperial Bible Dictionary*, edited by Patrick Fairbairn, xi–xxi. London: Blackie and Son, 1886.

———. "In What Manner Can Greater Unity of Action between the Council and the Branches of the Association Be Secured, in Order to Carry Out the Original Objects of the Association as a Centre of Union?" *The Church Association Monthly Intelligencer* 7 (1873): 108–11.

———. "The Importance of the Clear Enunciation of Dogma in Dispensing the Word, with Reference to Instability among

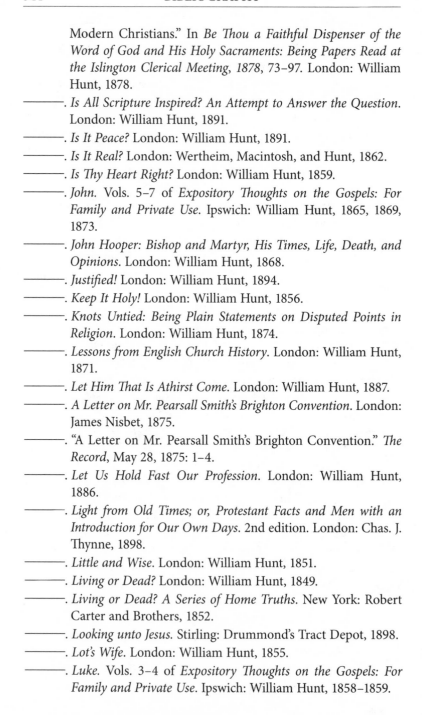

Modern Christians." In *Be Thou a Faithful Dispenser of the Word of God and His Holy Sacraments: Being Papers Read at the Islington Clerical Meeting, 1878*, 73–97. London: William Hunt, 1878.

———. *Is All Scripture Inspired? An Attempt to Answer the Question.* London: William Hunt, 1891.

———. *Is It Peace?* London: William Hunt, 1891.

———. *Is It Real?* London: Wertheim, Macintosh, and Hunt, 1862.

———. *Is Thy Heart Right?* London: William Hunt, 1859.

———. *John.* Vols. 5–7 of *Expository Thoughts on the Gospels: For Family and Private Use.* Ipswich: William Hunt, 1865, 1869, 1873.

———. *John Hooper: Bishop and Martyr, His Times, Life, Death, and Opinions.* London: William Hunt, 1868.

———. *Justified!* London: William Hunt, 1894.

———. *Keep It Holy!* London: William Hunt, 1856.

———. *Knots Untied: Being Plain Statements on Disputed Points in Religion.* London: William Hunt, 1874.

———. *Lessons from English Church History.* London: William Hunt, 1871.

———. *Let Him That Is Athirst Come.* London: William Hunt, 1887.

———. *A Letter on Mr. Pearsall Smith's Brighton Convention.* London: James Nisbet, 1875.

———. "A Letter on Mr. Pearsall Smith's Brighton Convention." *The Record*, May 28, 1875: 1–4.

———. *Let Us Hold Fast Our Profession.* London: William Hunt, 1886.

———. *Light from Old Times; or, Protestant Facts and Men with an Introduction for Our Own Days.* 2nd edition. London: Chas. J. Thynne, 1898.

———. *Little and Wise.* London: William Hunt, 1851.

———. *Living or Dead?* London: William Hunt, 1849.

———. *Living or Dead? A Series of Home Truths.* New York: Robert Carter and Brothers, 1852.

———. *Looking unto Jesus.* Stirling: Drummond's Tract Depot, 1898.

———. *Lot's Wife.* London: William Hunt, 1855.

———. *Luke.* Vols. 3–4 of *Expository Thoughts on the Gospels: For Family and Private Use.* Ipswich: William Hunt, 1858–1859.

————. *Many Shall Come*. London: William Hunt, 1885.

————. *Mark*. Vol. 2 of *Expository Thoughts on the Gospels: For Family and Private Use*. Ipswich: William Hunt, 1857.

————. *Matthew*. Vol. 1 of *Expository Thoughts on the Gospels: For Family and Private Use*. Ipswich: William Hunt, 1856.

————. "Memoir of Samuel Ward." In *Sermons and Treatises by Samuel Ward, B.D.*, v–xvi. Edinburgh: James Nichol, 1862.

————. *Merry and Happy*. London: Wertheim, Macintosh, and Hunt, 1863.

————. "A Minister's Parting Address to the Inhabitants of Exbury." In *Bishop J. C. Ryle's Autobiography: The Early Years*, 223–26. Edited by Andrew Atherstone. Edinburgh: Banner of Truth, 2016.

————. *More Prayer and Work: Being Thoughts on Missions*. London: William Hunt, 1872.

————. *The Morning without Clouds*. London: William Hunt, 1885.

————. *Neglect Not the Gift*. Weston-Super-Mare, U.K.: J. Whereat, 1853.

————. *Never Perish*. London: William Hunt, 1857.

————. *A New Birth*. London: William Hunt, 1892.

————. *None of His!* London: William Hunt, 1857.

————. "Notes on 1 Tim. iv. 15." In *The Church: Its Duties, Claims, Perils, and Privileges. Being the Substance of the Addresses and Sermons Delivered at the Fifth Combined Clerical Meeting at Weston-Super-Mare*, 150–55. Weston-Super-Mare, U.K.: J. Whereat, 1858.

————. "Notes on 2 Cor. ii.17." In *The Church: Its Duties, Claims, Perils, and Privileges. Being the Substance of the Addresses and Sermons Delivered at the Fifth Combined Clerical Meeting at Weston-Super-Mare*, 130–36. Weston-Super-Mare, U.K.: J. Whereat, 1858.

————. *Occupy Till I Come*. London: William Hunt, 1853.

————. *Old Paths: Being Plain Statements on Some of the Weightier Matters of Christianity*. London: William Hunt, 1877.

————. *One Blood: Being Thoughts on Acts xvii.26*. London: William Hunt, 1884.

————. *Only One Way*. London: William Hunt, 1850.

————. *The Opening Address at the Diocesan Conference*. London: William Hunt, 1889.

———. *The Oracles of God*. London: William Hunt, 1881.

———. *The Ornaments Rubric*. London: Church Association, n.d.

———. *Our Diocesan Conference: What Good Is It Likely to Do? And What Dangers Must It Try to Avoid?* London: William Hunt, 1879.

———. "Our Diocese, Our Church, Our Times." In *Charges and Addresses*, 185–202. Edinburgh: Banner of Truth, 1978.

———. *Our Gathering Together!* London: William Hunt, 1868.

———. *Our Home!* London: William Hunt, 1867.

———. *Our Position and Dangers*. London: William Hunt, 1885.

———. *The Outlook*. London: William Hunt, 1886.

———. "A Paper on Brotherhoods." In *The Official Report of the Church Congress Held at Hull*, 350–55. London: Bemrose and Sons, 1890.

———. "Paper on Christian Unity with Nonconformity." In *Authorized Report of the Church Congress Held at Southampton*, 354–60. London: Rivingtons, 1870.

———. *A Pastor's Address to His Flock at the Beginning of a New Year*. Ipswich: Hunt and Sons, 1846.

———. *Peace! Be Still!* London: William Hunt, 1853.

———. *Perilous Times!* London: William Hunt, 1886.

———. *The Position of the Laity*. London: William Hunt, 1886.

———. Preface to *Devout Thoughts by Deep Thinkers*, by Susan Coalbank, v–vii. London: James Nisbet, 1867.

———. Preface to *The Keepsake Scripture Text Book*. London: W. H. and L. Collingridge, 1870.

———. Preface to *Moses, or the Zulu? A Detailed Reply to the Objections Contained in Parts I and II of Bishop Colenso's Work*, by the Rev. W. Wickes, v–ix. London: Wertheim, Macintosh, and Hunt, 1863.

———. Preface to *Remember the Sabbath Day to Keep It Holy: A Catechism*. London: William Hunt, 1856.

———. Preface to *The Protestantism of the Prayer Book*, by Dyson Hague, ix–x. London: Church Association, 1893.

———. Preface to *The Sabbath*, by Andrew Thomson. London: James Nisbet, 1863.

———. Preface to *The Story of Madame Therese: The Cantiniere; or, The French Army in '92*, by Emile Erckmann, translated by

Pierre Alexander Chatrain, v–xii. London: William Hunt, 1869.

———. Preface to *Temper: A Treatise on Its Use and Abuse*, by a Staffordshire Curate, v–xii. London: Seeley, Jackson, and Halliday, 1865.

———. Preface to *Texts Misquoted and Misapplied*, by R. C. L. B., v–xiii. London: Hatchards, 1877.

———. Preface to *The Words of the Angels*, by Ewald Rudolf Stier, ix–xiv. London: Daldy, Isbister, 1887.

———. *The Present Crisis: Some Words about the Privy Council Judgment and Old Testament Criticism*. London: William Hunt, 1892.

———. *The Present Distress*. London: Chas. J. Thynne, 1898.

———. *The Priesthood of Christ*. London: Church Association, n.d.

———. *The Priest, the Puritan, and the Preacher*. New York: Robert Carter and Brothers, 1856.

———. *Practical Religion: Being Papers on the Daily Duties, Experiences, Dangers, and Privileges of Professing Christians*. London: William Hunt, 1879.

———. *Principles for Churchmen: A Manual of Positive Statements on Doubtful or Disputed Points*. London: William Hunt, 1884.

———. *Prove All Things: A Tract on Private Judgment*. Ipswich: Hunt and Son, 1851.

———. *Prove and Hold Fast: A Motto for 1884*. London: William Hunt, 1884.

———. *The Reading Which Is Blessed*. London: William Hunt, 1855.

———. *The Real Presence: What Is It?* London: William Hunt, 1869.

———. *Reasons for Opposing Ritualism*. London: Church Association, n.d.

———. *Regeneration*. London: William Hunt, 1850.

———. "Regeneration." In *Evangelical Principles: A Series of Doctrinal Papers Explanatory of the Positive Principles of Evangelical Churchmanship*, 124–46. London: William Hunt, 1875.

———. *Regeneration and Baptism*. London: Church Association, 1900.

———. *Regulations Respecting Honorary Canons*. Liverpool: Cathedral Church of St. Peter, 1880.

———. *Remember Lot*. London: William Hunt, 1849.

————. *Repentance; Its Nature and Necessity*. London: Seely, Jackson, and Halliday, 1858.

————. "The Revelation and Its Blessing." In *The Gifts of the Kingdom: Being Lectures Delivered During Lent, 1855, at St. George's Bloomsbury*, 1–37. London: John Farquhar, 1855.

————. *Rich and Poor*. London: William Hunt, 1853.

————. *The Rights and Duties of Lay Churchmen*. London: William Hunt, 1886.

————. *The Sacrament of the Lord's Supper: Its True Intention and Rightful Position in the Church of Christ*. London: William Hunt, 1866.

————. *Scattered and Gathered!* London: William Hunt, 1858.

————. *Seeking the Lord Early*. London: William Hunt, 1845.

————. *Seest Thou These Great Buildings?* London: William Hunt, 1889.

————. *A Self-Portrait: A Partial Autobiography*. Edited by Peter Toon. Postscript by Michael J. Smout. Swengel, Pa.: Reiner, 1975.

————. "Sermon on Matt. xvi. 18." In *The Church: Its Duties, Claims, Perils, and Privileges. Being the Substance of the Addresses and Sermons Delivered at the Fifth Combined Clerical Meeting at Weston-Super-Mare*, 74–98. Weston-Super-Mare, U.K.: J. Whereat, 1858.

————. *A Sermon on the Lord's Supper*. Manchester: John Heywood, 1887.

————. *A Sermon Preached before the Church Pastoral-Aid Society at Its Anniversary, in St. Dunstan's Church, Fleet Street, on Wednesday Evening, the 6th of May, 1868*. London: Church Pastoral Aid Society, 1868.

————. *A Sermon Preached to St. Bride's Church, Fleet Street, on Monday Evening, May 5th 1862, Before the Church Missionary Society*. London: T. C. Johns and Son, 1862.

————. *Sermons to Children*. New York: Protestant Episcopal Society for the Promotion of Evangelical Knowledge, 1856.

————. *Shall We Go?* London: William Hunt, 1878.

————. *Shall We Know One Another, and Other Papers*. London: Cassell, Petter, and Galpin, 1870.

————. *Shall We Surrender?* London: William Hunt, 1876.

————. *Shall You Be Saved?* London: William Hunt, 1852.

————. *Simplicity in Preaching*. London: William Hunt, 1882.

————. *A Sketch of the Life and Labors of George Whitefield.* New York: Anson D. F. Randolf, 1854.

————. *Soldiers and Trumpeters.* London: William Hunt, 1882.

————. *Special Hymns for Special Occasions.* London: William Hunt, 1872.

————. *The Spirit's Message to the Churches.* London: Partridge and Oakey, 1853.

————. *Spiritual Songs: Being One Hundred Hymns Not to Be Found in Many of the Hymn Books Commonly Used.* 10th ed., enlarged. Ipswich: William Hunt, 1858.

————. *Spiritual Songs: Being Twenty-Six Hymns Not to Be Found in the Hymn Books Most Commonly Used.* Ipswich: Hunt and Sons, 1849.

————. *Spiritual Songs for a Month: Being Sixty-Two Hymns, Not to Be Found in the Hymn Books Most Commonly Used.* 3rd ed., enlarged. Ipswich: Hunt and Sons, 1850.

————. *Stand Firm!* London: William Hunt, 1893.

————. *Startling Questions.* New York: Robert Carter and Brothers, 1853.

————. *St. Peter at Antioch.* London: William Hunt, 1856.

————. *Strike: But Hear!* London: William Hunt, 1868.

————. *Strive!* London: William Hunt, 1855.

————. *The Teaching of the Ritualists Not the Teaching of the Church of England.* London: Church Association, n.d.

————. *Tell Them!* London: William Hunt, 1866.

————. *The Thing as It Is: Being Questions and Answers about the Lord's Supper.* London: William Hunt, 1885.

————. *This Is for You.* London: William Hunt, 1890.

————. *This Is the Finger of God! Being Thoughts on the Cattle Plague.* London: William Hunt, 1866.

————. *Thoughts about a Mission.* London: William Hunt, 1890.

————. *Thoughts about Sunday.* London: William Hunt, 1893.

————. *Thoughts and Questions about Holiness.* London: Chas. J. Thynne, 1900.

————. *Thoughts for Parents.* London: William Hunt, 1886.

————. *Thoughts for the Times.* London: William Hunt, 1891.

————. *Thoughts for Thinkers.* Liverpool: J. A. Thompson, 1897.

————. *Thoughts on Immortality.* London: William Hunt, 1883.

———. *Thoughts on Sickness for Invalids and Their Friends.* London: William Hunt, 1884.

———. *Thoughts on the Prayer Book and on Church and Dissent.* London: William Hunt, 1887.

———. *Thoughts on the Supper of the Lord, for the Use of Present and Future Communicants.* London: William Hunt, 1883.

———. *Three Pictures! And Which Is Mine?* London: William Hunt, 1881.

———. *To Whom Shall We Go?* London: William Hunt, 1880.

———. *Train Up a Child in the Way He Should Go.* London: William Hunt, 1846.

———. *Tried by Its Fruits.* London: William Hunt, 1884.

———. *The True Priest.* Dublin: George Herbert, 1859.

———. *Twelve Reasons against the Distinctive Vestments.* London: Church Association, n.d.

———. *The Two Bears.* London: William Hunt, 1866.

———. *The Two Bears, and Other Sermons for Children.* London: William Hunt, 1869.

———. *Unbelief a Marvel.* London: William Hunt, 1880.

———. "The Unexpected Delay of the Kingdom of God." In *The Parables Prophetically Explained: Being Lectures Delivered during Lent, 1853, at St. George's Bloomsbury*, 1–25. London: John Farquhar Shaw, 1853.

———. *Unsearchable Riches.* London: William Hunt, 1879.

———. *The Upper Room: Being a Few Truths for the Times.* London: William Hunt, 1888.

———. *Watch.* London: William Hunt, 1851.

———. *Watchman, What of the Night?* London: William Hunt, 1894.

———. *We Must Unite! Being Thoughts on the Necessity of Forming a Well Organized Union of Evangelical Churchmen.* London: William Hunt, 1868.

———. *What Canst Thou Know?* Stirling: Drummond's Tract Depot, 1884.

———. *What Did He Choose?* London: William Hunt, 1886.

———. *What Do the Times Require?* London: Church Association, n.d.

———. *What Do the Times Require?* London: William Hunt, 1879.

———. *What Do We Owe the Reformation?* London: Church Association, n.d.

———. *What Good Will It Do? A Question about the Disestablishment of the Church of England, Examined and Answered.* 3rd ed. London: William Hunt, 1872.

———. *What Is Evangelical Religion?* London: William Hunt, 1894.

———. *What Is the Church?* London: William Hunt, 1852.

———. *What Is Truth?* London: William Hunt, 1887.

———. "What Is Wanted?" In *The Bishop, the Pastor, and the Preacher*, 11–59. Ipswich: William Hunt, 1854.

———. *What Is Wanted? The Opening Address at the Fourteenth Liverpool Diocesan Conference, November 5, 1895.* London: William Hunt, 1895.

———. *What Is Written about the Lord's Supper?* London: William Hunt, 1889.

———. *What Is Your Hope?* London: William Hunt, 1856.

———. *What Practical Course of Action Should Now Be Taken to Give Effect to the Various Judgments on Disputed Points of Ceremony in the Church?* London: Church Association, 1877.

———. *What Shall a Man Give in Exchange for His Soul?* London: Seely, Jackson, and Halliday, 1857.

———. *What Think Ye of Christ?* London: William Hunt, 1863.

———. *What Time Is It?* London: William Hunt, 1854.

———. *Wheat or Chaff?* London: William Hunt, 1851.

———. "Where Are We?" *The Churchman*, October 1879: 31–38.

———. *Where Are Your Sins?* London: William Hunt, 1858.

———. *Where Art Thou?* London: William Hunt, 1852.

———. *Where Does This Road Lead To? A Question about Ritualism.* London: William Hunt, 1879.

———. *Where Is the Good Way?* London: William Hunt, 1882.

———. *Which Class?* Stirling: Drummond's Tract Depot, 1900.

———. *Who Is the True Churchman? Or, the Thirty-Nine Articles Examined.* London: William Hunt, 1872.

———. *The Whole Family!* London: William Hunt, 1864.

———. *Whose Word Is This?* London: William Hunt, 1877.

———. *Why, and Why Not?* London: William Hunt, 1869.

———. *Why Were Our Reformers Burned?* London: Office of the Church Association, 1871.

———. *Without Christ!* London: William Hunt, 1865.

———. *A Word for Sunday.* London: William Hunt, 1880.

———. *A Word for the Irish Church.* London: William Hunt, 1868.

———. "The Work of the Holy Ghost." In *Things That Accompany Salvation: In Nineteen Sermons, Preached at St. Ann's Church, Manchester,* 120–43. London: James Nisbet, 1857.

———. *Work to Be Done!* London: William Hunt, 1866.

———. *Worldly Conformity: What It Is Not, and What It Is.* London: William Hunt, 1878.

———. *Yes or No! Is the Union of Church and State Worth Preserving?* London: Church Defense Institution, 1871.

———. *Your Election!* London: William Hunt, 1868.

———. *Your Soul!* London: William Hunt, 1857.

———. *Your Ways?* London: William Hunt, 1885.

Sargent, John. *A Memoir of the Rev. Henry Martyn, B.D.* 2nd ed. Boston: Perkins and Marvin, 1832.

Savile, Bourchier Wrey. *A Letter to the Rev. J. C. Ryle, B.A., On the Subject of His Recent Tract Entitled* "A Guide to Churchmen about Baptism and Regeneration." London: Judd and Glass, 1858.

Scott, Thomas. *The Force of Truth: An Authentic Narrative.* Brookfield, U.K.: Merriam and Company, 1816.

———, ed. *The Holy Bible: Containing the Old and New Testaments, According to the Authorized Version; with Explanatory Notes, Practical Observations, and Copious Marginal References.* Latest ed. New York: W. E. Dean, 1851.

———. *Remarks on the Refutation of Calvinism by George Tomline, D.D., F.R.S., Lord Bishop of Lincoln and Dean of St. Paul's London.* 2nd ed. London: A. Macintosh, 1817.

Simeon, Charles. *Horae Homileticae, or Discourses in the Form of Skeletons upon the Whole of Scripture.* London: Richard Watts, 1819.

Simpson, Johnson. *Edward Sunners: The Liverpool Cabmen's Missionary, His Life and Work.* Liverpool: Adam Holden, 1886.

Smith, Benjamin. *Methodism in Macclesfield.* London: Wesley Conference Office, 1875.

Smith, Hannah Whitall. *The Christian's Secret of a Happy Life.* London: E. F. Longley, 1876.

Smith, Robert Pearsall, ed. *Account of the Union Meeting for the Promotion of Scriptural Holiness Held at Oxford, August 29 to September 7, 1874.* London: Daldy, Isbister, 1874.

———. *Holiness through Faith: Light on the Way of Holiness.* Rev. ed. New York: Anson D. F. Randolf, 1875.

———. *Hymns of Consecration and Faith and Sacred Songs.* London: Morgan and Scott, 1875.

Society for Promoting Christian Knowledge. *The Official Year-Book of the Church of England.* London: Society for Promoting Christian Knowledge, 1880–1900.

Society for the Liberation of Religion from State Patronage and Control. *Canon Ryle on the Advantages of Disestablishment.* London: Society for the Liberation of Religion from State Patronage and Control, 187?.

———. *The Case for Disestablishment: A Handbook of Facts and Arguments in Support of the Claim for Religious Equality.* London: Society for the Liberation of Religion from State Patronage and Control, 1894.

———. *The Rev. Joseph Bardsley versus Canon Ryle: Extracts from Letters Addressed to the "Record" December 13th, 1875, in Reply to a Tract by Canon Ryle, Entitled, "Shall We Surrender?"* London: Society for the Liberation of Religion from State Patronage and Control, 1875.

Speck, Edward John. *Church Pastoral-Aid Society: A Sketch of Its Origin and Progress.* London: Seeley, Jackson, and Halliday, 1881.

Spurgeon, Charles Haddon. *Autobiography.* 2 vols. 1897–1900. Reprint, Edinburgh: Banner of Truth, 2005.

———. *Commenting and Commentaries.* London: Passmore and Alabaster, 1876.

———. "Even So, Father!" In *The New Park Street and Metropolitan Tabernacle Pulpit*, 7:369–76. Pasadena, Tex.: Pilgrim Publications, 1969.

———. *Lectures to My Students.* First Series. New York: Sheldon, 1875.

———. "A Mystery! Saints Sorrowing and Jesus Glad!" In vol. 10 of *The Metropolitan Tabernacle Pulpit*, 461–72. Pasadena, Tex.: Pilgrim Publications, 1969.

———. "A Political Dissenter." In *The Sword and the Trowel*, 106–9. London: Passmore and Alabaster, 1873.

Sterry, Wasey. *Annals of the King's College of Our Lady of Eton beside Windsor.* London: Methuen, 1898.

Steven, James. *Essays in Ecclesiastical Biography.* 2nd ed. 2 vols. London: Longman, Brown, Green, and Longmans, 1853.

Stock, Eugene. *The History of the Church Missionary Society: Its Environment, Its Men, and Its Work.* 3 vols. London: Church Missionary Society, 1899.

————. *My Recollections.* London: J. Nisbet, 1909.

Stowell, Hugh. "Address, by the Rev. Canon Stowell." In *The Church: Its Duties, Claims, Perils, and Privileges. Being the Substance of the Addresses and Sermons Delivered at the Fifth Combined Clerical Meeting at Weston-Super-Mare,* 17–42. Weston-Super-Mare, U.K.: J. Whereat, 1858.

————. *Tractarianism Tested by Holy Scripture and the Church of England in a Series of Sermons.* London: J. Hatchard and Son, 1845.

Straton, Norman D. J. *Why We Should Join the Protestant Churchmen's Alliance: Being an Address at a Conference of Churchmen in London, June 19th, 1889.* London: John Kensit, 1889.

Sumner, George Henry. *Life of Charles Richard Sumner, D.D. Bishop of Winchester.* London: John Murray, 1876.

Sumner, J. B. *Apostolical Preaching Considered in an Examination of St. Paul's Epistles.* 3rd ed. London: J. Hatchard and Son, 1820.

————. *A Practical Exposition of the Gospels of St. Matthew and St. Mark.* London: J. Hatchard and Son, 1831.

Tait, Archibald Campbell. *The Church of the Future.* New York: Macmillan, 1881.

Temple, Frederick, and William Dalrymple Maclagan. *The Archbishops on the Lawfulness of the Liturgical Use of Incense and the Carrying of Lights in Procession, Lambeth Palace, July 31, 1899.* London: Macmillan, 1899.

Thackeray, Francis St. John. *Memoir of Edward Craven Hawtrey D.D., Headmaster and Afterward Provost of Eton.* London: George Bell and Sons, 1896.

Thompson, Henry Lewis. *Christ Church.* London: F. E. Robinson, 1900.

Thompson, William. *Aids to Faith: A Series of Theological Essays by Several Writers Being a Reply to "Essays and Reviews."* London: John Murray, 1862.

Walker, Charles, ed. *The Ritual Reason Why*. London: J. T. Hayes, 1866.

Walker, Samuel A. *No! An Answer to Canon Ryle's Tract "Shall We Go?" Being Thoughts about Church Congresses, etc.* London: Elliot Stock, 1879.

Watson, Richard. *An Apology for the Bible*. London: J. Rider, 1799.

Weldon, G. W. *The Ridsdale Judgment: The Testimony It Affords to the Protestant Character of the Church of England*. London: Church Association, 1877.

Whately, Richard, ed. *Cautions for the Times*. London: John Parker and Sons, 1853.

————. *Christian Evidences*. London: J. W. Parker, 1838.

Wilberforce, Robert Isaac. *The Doctrine of the Holy Eucharist*. 3rd ed. London: John and Charles Mozley, 1854.

————. *The Doctrine of the Incarnation of Our Lord Jesus Christ: In Its Relation to Mankind and to the Church*. London: John Murray, 1848.

Wilberforce, William. *A Practical View of the Prevailing Religious System of Professed Christians in the Higher and Middle Classes in This Country Contrasted with Real Christianity*. 17th ed. London: T. Cadell, 1829.

Wilson, Daniel. *The Evidences of Christianity*. London: G. Wilson, 1830.

Windle, William, ed. *The Church and Home Metrical Psalter and Hymnal*. London: George Routledge and Son, 1870.

Secondary Works

Archibald, Malcolm. *Liverpool Gangs, Vice, and Packet Rats: 19th Century Crime and Punishment*. New York: Black and White Publishing, 2015.

Aristotle. *The Art of Rhetoric*. Translated by H. C. Lawson. London: Penguin Books, 1991.

Atherstone, Andrew, ed. *The Heart of Faith: Following Christ in the Church of England*. Cambridge: Lutterworth Press, 2008.

————. "J. C. Ryle's Evangelistic Strategy." *Churchman* 125 (2011): 215–27.

Balleine, G. R. *A History of the Evangelical Party in the Church of England*. London: Longmans, Green, 1908.

Bebbington, David. *The Dominance of Evangelicalism: The Age of Spurgeon and Moody*. Downers Grove, Ill.: InterVarsity, 2005.

———. "Edward Miall." In *Oxford Dictionary of National Biography*, 12–14. Edited by H. C. G. Matthew and Brian Harrison. Oxford: Oxford University Press, 2004.

———. *Evangelicalism in Modern Britain: A History from the 1730s to the 1980s*. Grand Rapids: Baker, 1989.

———. "Gladstone and the Baptists." *The Baptist Quarterly* 26 (1976): 224–39.

———. *Holiness in Nineteenth-Century England*. Carlisle, U.K.: Paternoster, 2000.

———. "J. C. Ryle." In *The Heart of Faith: Following Christ in the Church of England*. Edited by Andrew Atherstone, 101–10. Cambridge: Lutterworth Press, 2008.

———. "The Life of Baptist Noel: Its Setting and Significance." *The Baptist Quarterly* 24 (1972): 389–411.

———. *Victorian Nonconformity*. Rev. ed. Eugene, Ore.: Cascade Books, 2011.

———. *William Ewart Gladstone: Faith and Politics in Victorian Britain*. Grand Rapids: Eerdmans, 1993.

Beeke, Joel R. *Puritan Reformed Spirituality*. Grand Rapids: Reformation Heritage Books, 2004.

Benson, Louis F. *The English Hymn: Its Development and Use in Worship*. 1915. Reprint, Richmond, Va.: John Knox Press, 1962.

Bentley, Anne. "The Transformation of the Evangelical Party in the Church of England in the Latter Nineteenth Century." PhD diss., University of Durham, 1971.

Best, Geoffrey. "Evangelicals and the Established Church in the Early Nineteenth Century." *Journal of Theological Studies* 10 (1959): 63–78.

———. *Mid-Victorian Britain 1851–75*. London: Fontana Press, 1979.

Binns, L. E. *The Evangelical Movement in the Church of England*. London: Methuen, 1928.

———. *Religion in the Victorian Era*. 2nd ed. London: Lutterworth Press, 1946.

Boast, G. C. "Henry Melvill." In *Oxford Dictionary of National Biography*. Edited by H. C. G. Matthew and Brian Harrison, 764–65. Oxford: Oxford University Press, 2004.

The Book of Common Prayer. 350th anniversary ed. New York: Penguin Books, 2012.

Bowen, Desmond. *The Idea of the Victorian Church: A Study of the Church of England, 1833–1887*. Toronto: University of Toronto Press, 1968.

Bradley, Ian. *Abide with Me: The World of Victorian Hymns*. Chicago: GIA Publications, 1997.

———. *The Call to Seriousness: The Evangelical Impact on the Victorians*. Oxford: Lion Hudson, 2006.

Brent, Richard. "The Whigs and Protestant Dissent in the Decades of Reform: The Case of the Church Rates, 1833–1841." *English Historical Review* 102 (1987): 887–910.

Broadus, John A. *Lectures on the History of Preaching*. New York: A. C. Armstrong and Son, 1901.

Brock, M. G., and M. C. Curthoys, eds. *Nineteenth-Century Oxford, Part 1*. Vol. 6 of *The History of the University of Oxford*. Oxford: Oxford University Press, 2007.

Brown, Callum G. *The Death of Christian Britain: Understanding Secularization 1800–2000*. 2nd ed. London: Routledge, 2009.

Brown, Ralph. "The Evangelical Succession? Evangelical History and Denomination Identity." *Evangelical Quarterly* 68 (1996): 3–13.

Brown, Stewart J. *Thomas Chalmers and the Godly Commonwealth in Scotland*. Oxford: Oxford University Press, 1982.

Bruce, Steve. *God Is Dead: Secularization in the West*. Oxford: Blackwell Publishing, 2003.

Bullock, F. W. B. *The History of Ridley Hall, Cambridge*. Vol. 1. Cambridge: Cambridge University Press, 1941.

Burn, W. L. *The Age of Equipoise: A Study of the Mid-Victorian Generation*. New York: W. W. Norton, 1965.

Burns, Arthur. *The Diocesan Revival in the Church of England, c. 1800–1870*. Oxford: Oxford University Press, 1999.

Carpenter, S. C. *Church and People, 1789–1889: A History of the Church of England from William Wilberforce to "Lux Mundi."* London: Society for Promoting Christian Knowledge, 1933.

Carrick, John. *Evangelicals and the Oxford Movement*. London: Evangelical Press of Wales, 1984.

Carter, Grayson. *Anglican Evangelicals: Protestant Sessions from the Via Media, 1800–1850*. Oxford: Oxford University Press, 2001.

———. "Baptist Wriothesley Noel." In *Oxford Dictionary of National Biography*. Edited by H. C. G. Matthew and Brian Harrison, 969–70. Oxford: Oxford University Press, 2004.

Chadwick, Owen. *The Spirit of the Oxford Movement: Tractarian Essays*. Cambridge: Cambridge University Press, 1995.

———. *The Victorian Church*. 2 vols. London: SCM Press, 1987.

———. *Victorian Miniature*. Cambridge: Cambridge University Press, 1960.

Chapman, Alister. *Godly Ambition: John Stott and the Evangelical Movement*. Oxford: Oxford University Press, 2012.

Chavasse, Francis James. *Address Delivered at the Nineteenth Annual Meeting of the Liverpool Diocesan Conference*. Liverpool: Henstock and Foulkes, 1900.

Cicero. *De Inventione*. Translated by H. M. Hubbell. Vol. 2, Loeb Classical Library. Cambridge, Mass.: Harvard University Press, 1976.

———. *De Oratore*. Translated by E. W. Sutton. Vols. 3–4, Loeb Classical Library. Cambridge, Mass.: Harvard University Press, 1977.

Clark, G. Kitson. *The Making of Victorian England*. London: Routledge, 1962.

Clark, M. Guthrie. *John Charles Ryle 1816–1900: First Bishop of Liverpool*. London: Church Book Room Press, 1947.

Cocksworth, Christopher J. *Evangelical Eucharistic Thought in the Church of England*. Cambridge: Cambridge University Press, 1993.

Curthoys, Judith. *The Cardinal's College: Christ Church, Chapter and Verse*. London: Profile Books, 2012.

Dargan, Edwin Charles. *From the Close of the Reformation to the End of the Nineteenth Century 1572–1900*. Vol. 2 of *A History of Preaching*. New York: Hodder and Stoughton, 1912.

Davies, C. Stella. *A History of Macclesfield*. Manchester: Manchester University Press, 1961.

Davies, Horton. *Worship and Theology in England: From Watts and Wesley to Martineau, 1690–1900*. Combined ed. Grand Rapids: Eerdmans, 1996.

Dorsett, Lyle W. *A Passion for Souls: The Life of D. L. Moody*. Chicago: Moody Publishers, 1997.

Earwaker, J. P. *East Cheshire Past and Present: A History of the Hundred of Macclesfield, in the County of Palatine of Chester.* 2 vols. London: J. P. Earwaker, 1877, 1880.

Edwards, O. C., Jr. *A History of Preaching.* Nashville: Abingdon, 2004.

Ellison, Robert H., ed. *A New History of the Sermon: The Nineteenth Century.* Leiden: Brill, 2010.

———. *The Victorian Pulpit: Spoken and Written Sermons in Nineteenth-Century Britain.* London: Associated University Presses, 1998.

Ewing, John William. *Goodly Fellowship: A Centenary Tribute to the Life and Work of the World's Evangelical Alliance, 1846–1946.* London: Marshall, Morgan and Scott, 1946.

Farley, Ian D. "J.C. Ryle—Episcopal Evangelist: A Study in Late Victorian Evangelicalism." PhD diss., University of Durham, 1988.

———. *J. C. Ryle, First Bishop of Liverpool: A Study in Mission among the Masses.* Waynesboro, Ga.: Paternoster, 2000.

———. "Neither Open nor Conservative: J. C. Ryle, Radical Evangelical." *Anvil* 22 (2005): 199–210.

Finlayson, Geoffrey B. A. M. *The Seventh Earl of Shaftesbury 1801–1885.* Vancouver: Regent College Publishing, 2004.

Francis, Keith A., and William Gibson, eds. *The Oxford Handbook of the British Sermon 1689–1901.* Oxford: Oxford University Press, 2012.

Fulweiler, Howard W. "Tractarians and Philistines: The *Tracts for the Times* versus Victorian Middle-Class Values." *The Historical Magazine of the Protestant Episcopal Church* 31 (1962): 36–53.

Gilley, Sheridan, and Brian Stanley, eds. *World Christianities c. 1815–c. 1914.* Vol. 8 of *The Cambridge History of Christianity.* Cambridge: Cambridge University Press, 2006.

Gordon, James M. *Evangelical Spirituality.* Eugene, Ore.: Wipf and Stock, 2006.

Greenman, Jeffrey P. "Anglican Evangelicals on Personal and Social Ethics." *Anglican Theological Review* 94 (2012): 179–205.

Haig, Alan. *The Victorian Clergy.* London: Croom Helm, 1984.

Hardman, B. E. "The Evangelical Party in the Church of England, 1855–65." PhD diss., Cambridge University, 1963.

Hart, G. W. *Bishop J. C. Ryle: Man of Granite.* London: Falcon Booklets, 1963.

Haykin, Michael A. G., and Kenneth J. Steward, eds. *The Advent of Evangelicalism: Exploring Historical Continuities.* Nashville: B&H Academic, 2008.

Hennell, Michael. *Sons of the Prophets: Evangelical Leaders of the Victorian Church.* London: SPCK, 1979.

Hilton, Boyd. *The Age of Atonement: The Influence of Evangelicalism on Social and Economic Thought.* Oxford: Oxford University Press, 1991.

———. *A Mad, Bad, and Dangerous People? England 1783–1846.* Oxford: Oxford University Press, 2006.

Hindmarsh, Bruce D. *John Newton and the English Evangelical Tradition.* Grand Rapids: Eerdmans, 1996.

Hiscock, W. G. *A Christ Church Miscellany.* Oxford: Oxford University Press, 1946.

Hollis, Christopher. *Eton: A History.* London: Hollis and Carter, 1960.

Hopkins, Hugh Evan. *Charles Simeon of Cambridge.* Grand Rapids: Eerdmans, 1977.

Hoppen, K. Theodore. *The Mid-Victorian Generation 1846–1886.* Oxford: Clarendon Press, 1998.

Hylson-Smith, Kenneth. *Evangelicals in the Church of England: 1734–1984.* Edinburgh: T&T Clark, 1989.

Inglis, K. S. "Patterns of Religious Worship in 1851." *Journal of Ecclesiastical History* 2 (1960): 78–92.

Jacobs, Alan. *The Book of Common Prayer: A Biography.* Princeton, N.J.: Princeton University Press, 2013.

Jenkins, Roy. *Gladstone.* London: Papermac, 1996.

Jones, James. "Ryle for the Third Millennium." *Churchman* 114 (2000): 114–22.

Kapic, Kelly M., and Randall C. Gleason, eds. *The Devoted Life: An Introduction to the Puritan Classics.* Downers Grove, Ill.: InterVarsity, 2004.

Kent, John. *Holding the Fort: Studies in Victorian Revivalism.* London: Epworth Press, 1978.

Knockles, Peter B. *The Oxford Movement in Context: Anglican High Churchmanship 1760–1857.* Cambridge: Cambridge University Press, 1994.

Lancelot, J. B., and J. W. Tyrer. "A History of the Diocese: 1880–1930." *Liverpool Diocesan Review* 5 (1930): 239–64.

Larsen, Timothy. *Contested Christianity: The Political and Social Contexts of Victorian Theology*. Waco, Tex.: Baylor University Press, 2004.

———. *A People of One Book: The Bible and the Victorians*. Oxford: Oxford University Press, 2011.

———. "The Reforming Project of English Evangelical Dissenters." *Fides et History* 33 (2001): 109–19.

Liturgies of the Western Church. Selected and introduced by Bard Thompson. Philadelphia: Fortress Press, 1990.

Loane, Marcus L. *John Charles Ryle 1816–1900*. London: Hodder and Stoughton, 1983.

———. "John Charles Ryle 1816–1900." In *Makers of Our Heritage: A Study of Four Evangelical Leaders*, 20–56. London: Hodder and Stoughton, 1967.

———. *Oxford and the Evangelical Succession*. 3rd ed. Fearn, Scotland: Christian Focus, 2007.

Macilwee, Mick. *The Liverpool Underworld: Crime in the City 1750–1900*. Liverpool: Liverpool University Press, 2011.

Mackerness, E. D. *The Heeded Voices: Studies in the Literary Status of the Anglican Sermon, 1830–1900*. Cambridge: W. Heffer and Sons, 1959.

Marsh, P. T. *The Victorian Church in Decline: Archbishop Tait and the Church of England 1868–1882*. London: Routledge and Kegan Paul, 1969.

Matheson, George. *O Love That Wilt Not Let Me Go: Meditations, Prayers, and Poems*. Selected and introduced by Ian Bradley. London: Fount Paperbacks, 1990.

Meacham, Standish. *Lord Bishop: The Life of Samuel Wilberforce*. Cambridge, Mass.: Harvard University Press, 1970.

Moorman, J. R. H. *A History of the Church in England*. 3rd ed. Harrisburg, Pa.: Morehouse Publishing, 1980.

Moule, H. C. G. *The Evangelical School in the Church of England: Its Men and Its Work in the Nineteenth Century*. London: James Nisbet, 1901.

Muir, Ramsay. *A History of Liverpool*. 2nd ed. London: University Press of Liverpool, 1907.

Munden, Alan. *Bishop J. C. Ryle: Prince of Tract Writers*. Leominster, U.K.: Day One Publications, 2012.

———. "J. C. Ryle—The Prince of Tract Writers." *Churchman* 119 (2005): 7–13.

———. "The 'Prophetical Opinions of J. C. Ryle." *Churchman* 125 (2011): 251–62.

Murray, Iain H. *J. C. Ryle: Prepared to Stand Alone*. Edinburgh: Banner of Truth, 2016.

Neill, Stephen. *Anglicanism*. 3rd ed. London: Penguin Books, 1965.

Newby, John. "The Historical Relevance of the Writings of Bishop J. C. Ryle." MA thesis, University of South Africa, 1983.

———. "The Theology of John Charles Ryle." PhD diss., Potchefstroom University for Christian Higher Education, 1992.

Newman, John Henry. *Apologia Pro Vita Sua*. Edited by Ian Ker. London: Penguin Books, 2004.

Newsome, David. *The Parting of Friends: The Wilberforces and Henry Manning*. Grand Rapids: Eerdmans, 1966.

Nockles, Peter B. *The Oxford Movement in Context: Anglican High Churchmanship 1760–1857*. Cambridge: Cambridge University Press, 1994.

Noll, Mark. *The Rise of Evangelicalism: The Age of Edwards, Whitefield and the Wesleys*. Downers Grove, Ill.: InterVarsity, 2003.

Noll, Mark A., David W. Bebbington, and George A. Rawlyk, eds. *Evangelicalism: Comparative Study of Popular Protestantism in North America, the British Isles, and Beyond 1700–1990*. Oxford: Oxford University Press, 1994.

O'Day, Rosemary. *The Debate on the English Reformation*. London: Methuen, 1986.

Old, Hughes Oliphant. *The Modern Age*. Vol. 6 of *The Reading and Preaching of the Scriptures in the Worship of the Christian Church*. Grand Rapids: Eerdmans, 2007.

Ollard, S. L., ed. "John Charles Ryle." In *A Dictionary of English Church History*, 529. 2nd ed. rev. London: A. R. Mowbray, 1919.

Orr, J. Edwin. *The Light of the Nations: Evangelical Renewal and Advance in the Nineteenth Century*. Grand Rapids: Eerdmans, 1965.

———. *The Second Evangelical Awakening: An Account of the Second Worldwide Evangelical Revival Beginning in the Mid-Nineteenth Century*. Rev. ed. London: Lowe and Brydone, 1964.

Packer, J. I. *Faithfulness and Holiness: The Witness of J. C. Ryle*. Wheaton, Ill.: Crossway, 2002.

———. *A Quest for Godliness: The Puritan Vision of the Christian Life*. Wheaton, Ill.: Crossway, 1990.

Pattison, J. Harwood. *The History of Christian Preaching*. Philadelphia: American Baptist Publication Society, 1903.

Pickering, W. F. S. *Anglo-Catholicism: A Study in Religious Ambiguity*. London: SPCK, 1989.

Pickering, W. "The Religious Census of 1851—A Useless Experiment?" *British Journal of Sociology* 18 (1967): 382–407.

Pollock, John. *The Keswick Story: The Authorized History of the Keswick Convention*. London: Hodder and Stoughton, 1964.

Proby, W. H. B. *Annals of the "Low Church" Party in England: Down to the Death of Archbishop Tait*. 2 vols. London: J. T. Hayes, 1888.

Quintilian. *Institutio Oratoria*. 4 vols. Translated by H. E. Butler. Loeb Classical Library. Cambridge, Mass.: Harvard University Press, 1976–1980.

Rack, H. D. "Domestic Visitation: A Chapter in Early Nineteenth-Century Evangelism." *Journal of Ecclesiastical History* 24 (1973): 357–76.

Reardon, B. M. G. *Religious Thoughts in the Nineteenth Century*. Cambridge: Cambridge University Press, 1966.

Reynolds, J. S. *The Evangelicals at Oxford 1735–1871: A Record of an Unchronicled Movement with the Record Extended to 1905*. Oxford: Marcham Manor Press, 1975.

Richards, Noel J. "Disestablishment of the Anglican Church in England in the Late Nineteenth Century: Reasons for Failure." *Journal of Church and State* 12 (1970): 193–211.

Roberts, Vaughan. "J. C. Ryle: Evangelical Churchman." *Churchman* 128 (2014): 25–38.

Rogers, Bennett W. "Ryle and Evangelical Identity." *Foundations: An International Journal of Evangelical Theology* 70 (2016): 94–111.

Rogers, John Frederick. "Woe Is Unto Me: John Charles Ryle, Agonist of the Evangelicals." MA thesis, General Theological Seminary, 2008.

Rogerson, John. *Old Testament Criticism in the Nineteenth Century: England and Germany*. London: Fortress Press, 1985.

Rose, Jonathan. *The Intellectual Life of the British Working Classes.* 2nd ed. New Haven, Conn.: Yale University Press, 2010.

Roseman, Doreen. *Evangelicals and Culture.* 2nd ed. Eugene, Ore.: Pickwick Publications, 1992.

Russell, Eric. "Bishop J. C. Ryle." *Churchman* 113 (1999): 232–46.

———. *J. C. Ryle: That Man of Granite with the Heart of a Child.* Fearn, Scotland: Christian Focus, 2008.

Russell, George W. E. *A Short History of the Evangelical Movement.* London: A. R. Mowbray, 1915.

Schlossberg, Herbert. *Conflict and Crisis in the Religious Life of Late Victorian England.* New Brunswick, N.J.: Transaction Publishers, 2009.

Scotland, Nigel. *'Good and Proper Men': Lord Palmerston and the Bench of Bishops.* Cambridge: James Clark, 2000.

———. *John Bird Sumner: Evangelical Archbishop.* Leominster, U.K.: Gracewing Books, 1995.

Short, Kenneth Richard. "Baptist Wriothesley Noel." *The Baptist Quarterly* 20 (1963): 51–61.

Skedd, S. J. "Hannah More." In *Oxford Dictionary of National Biography.* Edited by H. C. G. Matthew and Brian Harrison, 39–46. Oxford: Oxford University Press, 2004.

Smith, Alan. *The Established Church and Popular Religion.* London: Longman Group, 1971.

Smith, Mark. *Aspects of the History and Sociology of Evangelicalism in Britain and Ireland.* Vol. 1 of *British Evangelical Identities Past and Present.* Eugene, Ore.: Wipf and Stock, 2009.

———. "David Simpson." In *Oxford Dictionary of National Biography.* Edited by H. C. G. Matthew and Brian Harrison, 683–84. Oxford: Oxford University Press, 2004.

Smith, Mark, and Stephen Taylor, eds. *Evangelicalism in the Church of England c. 1790–c. 1890: A Miscellany.* Woodbridge, U.K.: Boydell Press, 2004.

Somerveil, D. C. *English Thought in the Nineteenth Century.* 2nd ed. London: Methuen, 1929.

Spall, Richard Francis, Jr. "The Anti-Corn-Law League's Opposition to the English Church Establishment." *Journal of Church and State* 32 (1990): 97–123.

Stubenrauch, Joseph. "Silent Preachers in the Age of Ingenuity: Faith, Commerce, and Religious Tracts in Early Nineteenth-Century Britain." *Church History* 80 (2011): 547–74.

Sykes, Stephen, John Booty, and Jonathan Knight. *The Study of Anglicanism*. Rev. ed. London: SPCK, 2004.

Symondon, Anthony, ed. *The Victorian Crisis of Faith*. London: SPCK, 1970.

Thomas, W. H. Griffith. *The Work of the Ministry*. London: Hodder and Stoughton, 1911.

Thompson, D. M. "The 1851 Religious Census Problems and Possibilities." *Victorian Studies* 11 (1968): 263–80.

Thompson, Henry L. *Christ Church*. London: F. E. Robinson, 1900.

———. *Henry George Liddell: A Memoir*. New York: Henry Holt, 1899.

Timmins, T. C. B., ed. *Suffolk Returns from the Census of Religious Worship, 1851*. Suffolk, U.K.: St. Edmundsbury Press, 1997.

Tollemache, E. D. H. *The Tollemaches of Helmingham and Ham*. Ipswich, U.K.: W. S. Cowell Butter Market, 1949.

Toon, Peter. *Evangelical Theology 1833–1856: A Response to Tractarianism*. Atlanta: John Knox, 1979.

———. "J. C. Ryle and Comprehensiveness." *The Churchman* 89 (1975): 276–83.

Toon, Peter, and Michael Smout. *John Charles Ryle: Evangelical Bishop*. Swengel, Pa.: Reiner Publications, 1976.

———. *Spiritual Companions: An Introduction to the Spiritual Classics*. London: Marshall Pickering, 1990.

Turner, Frank M. *John Henry Newman: The Challenge to Evangelical Religion*. New Haven, Conn.: Yale University Press, 2002.

Walker, R. B. "Religious Changes in Cheshire, 1750–1850." *Journal of Ecclesiastical History* 17 (1966): 77–94.

———. "Religious Changes in Liverpool in the Nineteenth Century." *Journal of Ecclesiastical History* 19 (1968): 195–211.

Watts, Michael. *The Expansion of Evangelical Nonconformity*. Vol. 2 of *The Dissenters*. Oxford: Clarendon Press, 1995.

Webb, C. C. J. *Religious Thought in the Oxford Movement*. London: SPCK, 1928.

Wellings, Martin. *Evangelicals Embattled: Responses of Evangelicals in the Church of England to Ritualism, Darwinism, and Theological Liberalism 1890–1930*. Carlisle, U.K.: Paternoster, 2003.

———. "John Charles Ryle." In *Oxford Dictionary of National Biography*. Edited by H. C. G. Matthew and Brian Harrison, 486–88. Oxford: Oxford University Press, 2004.

Whisenant, James. "Anti-Ritualism and the Moderation of Evangelical Opinion in England in the Mid-1870s." *Anglican and Episcopal History* 70 (2001): 451–77.

Wilcox, Alastair. *The Church and the Slums: The Victorian Anglican Church and Its Mission to Liverpool's Poor*. Newcastle-upon-Tyne, U.K.: Cambridge Scholars Publishing, 2014.

Wilkinson, William Cleaver. *Modern Masters of Pulpit Discourses*. London: Funk and Wagnallis, 1905.

Wolffe, John. *The Expansion of Evangelicalism: The Age of Wilberforce, More, Chalmers and Finney*. Downers Grove, Ill.: InterVarsity, 2007.

Yates, Nigel. *Anglican Ritualism in Victorian Britain 1830–1910*. Oxford: Oxford University Press, 1999.

Index